HOW THEY LIVED

HOW THEY LIVED

*An Anthology of original accounts
written before 1485*

Compiled by

W. O. HASSALL

BASIL BLACKWELL
OXFORD

First published in 1962
Reprinted 1965

PRINTED IN GREAT BRITAIN
BY A. T. BROOME AND SON, 18 ST. CLEMENT'S, OXFORD
AND BOUND BY THE KEMP HALL BINDERY, OXFORD

CONTENTS

LIST OF PLATES

ACKNOWLEDGEMENTS

The author and publisher wish to thank the following for permission to publish copyright material:

Extracts in the text, which are shown under ' *Sources* ' in each section.

Illustrations, which are numbered consecutively throughout the plates, as follows:

The Trustees of the British Museum, 29, 34, 39, 40, 42, 47, 61, 62, 63, 64, 70, 77, 79, 80.

The President and Scholars of Corpus Christi College, Oxford, 1, 2, 3, 4, 5, 6, 7, 8, 12, 59, 71, 72.

The Master and Fellows of University College, Oxford, 38, 51.

The Warden and Fellows of New College, Oxford, 65, 73

Tue Warden and Fellows of All Souls College, Oxford, 50, 66.

The Master and Fellows of Corpus Christi College, Cambridge, 69.

The Bodleian Library, Oxford, 1, 2, 3, 4, 5, 6, 7, 8, 9, 10, 11, 13, 17, 18, 19, 20, 21, 22, 23, 24, 25, 26, 30, 35, 36, 37, 43, 44, 45, 46, 48, 49, 52, 53, 54, 58, 60, 76, 78.

The Earl of Leicester, 70, 79, 80.

Photographs as follows:

The University Press, Oxford, 1, 2, 3, 4, 5, 6, 7, 8, 9, 10, 17, 18, 19, 20, 21, 22, 23, 24, 25, 26, 30, 35, 36, 37, 38, 43, 44, 45, 46, 48, 49, 50, 51, 52, 53, 54, 59, 60, 65, 66, 67, 68, 71, 72, 76, 78.

The Courtauld Institute of Art, 29, 34, 39, 40, 42, 47, 61, 62, 63, 64, 70, 77, 79, 80.

The National Buildings Record, 27, 28, 32, 33, 41, 56, 73.

Lady Trenchard Cox, 14, 15, 55.

Mrs. M. Crossley, 16, 57.

Mrs. Ollard, 74, 75.

E. C. Legrice, Esq., 31.

FOREWORD

This book shows how people lived in England and Wales up to 1485 so far as a selection of passages from original writers allows. Translations from Latin or French are taken, so far as suitable ones are available, from existing published texts by English writers from King Alfred onwards, as this will enable any reader wishing to delve deeper to do so. Thanks are due to all the publishers mentioned in the notes on sources for allowing translations to be thus reprinted, and I hope that such kindness will be fitly rewarded by increased demands for their publications.

The arrangement of this book is by topics, so that anyone interested in any particular aspect of life will find related matter brought together. It is, however, necessary to consult the index, for there are many passages included which throw interesting sidelights on more than one aspect of life.

How They Lived is a companion to *They Saw It Happen* and to *Who's Who in History*, both of which were are arranged by date, and both of which contain notes on the leading chroniclers here quoted. Many important passages from early writers were printed in *They Saw It Happen*, and this fact makes necessary the inclusion of cross-references to them. *They Saw It Happen* and *Who's Who in History* are abbreviated to *T.S.I.H.* and *W.W.I.H.*

These extracts from medieval writings reflect most of the chief aspects of daily life. There are, however, some ideas, such as the nature of buildings, which can better be conveyed by photographs and plans of existing remains and commentaries thereon based on recent scholarship. Other ideas, such as styles of art, and the way that certain religious ideas were envisaged, are also unsuitable for inclusion in an anthology of the written word. The nature of the sources is such that it is much easier to find good extracts to illustrate some aspects of life than others. 'Courtesy books' and household ordinances and accounts are full of fascinating passages illustrative of domestic manners, especially among the upper classes and their servants. On the other hand vivid and brief accounts of very ordinary but important subjects such as the interior of a poor cottage are ones which there was less need ever to convey in words. The nature of the material inevitably must condition to a large extent the content of this collection and it is a fortunate chance that the acute observation and lively pen of Giraldus Cambrensis means that a reasonable proportion of the extracts included relate to Wales, a part of the kingdom from which one might have expected to derive fewer written reflections of daily life than one would wish.

Passages in this book are meant to illustrate how people lived. A reader, when for example prices are quoted, may be often conscious of contrasts with the modern world and at other times surprising similarities may strike him. I have not chosen any of the passages in order to illustrate such contrasts or to stress such similarities, nor have I pointed out in the notes changes after the medieval period. For most topics later periods are naturally richer in material than earlier centuries and I hope that people interested in particular aspects of life will be able to find here material on their chosen topics earlier than most of the material which they can readily find elsewhere. Particular attention is devoted to fundamental subjects which are generally neglected by historians —such as food and sleep.

Neither under *Women* nor under *Religious Life* is there any extract relating to nuns or to a prioress. No passage about a prioress can equal in observation and choice of phrase Chaucer's description in the *Prologue* to the *Canterbury Tales* but space here is devoted to extracts less well known and on other topics. If any reader of these lines has not read the *Prologue* he should read the whole of it as soon as possible. Little, however, need here be said about printed sources for further study. The best works on various periods are indicated in *They Saw It Happen*, and detailed books and articles on particular themes are indicated in the introductory notes which precede the various extracts included in this book. These works enable a start to be made by anyone who wants to go further along any of the avenues of study which the book suggests. There is however a great and little explored source which touches on every aspect of medieval life and which the written word does little to reveal. There are in existence many thousands of medieval pictures, each one opening a colourful window on the world and enabling us to see one facet of the past as if we could travel about in past centuries and see through the eyes of our ancestors. Some indications of these are found in the illustrations selected from the Holkham Bible and from other manuscripts, such as those of various centuries which contain calendars showing the ' Occupations of the Months '. I have published, while this book has been in the press, many thousands of these in the form of 35 mm. coloured filmstrips and separate slides, and indeed all the pictures in all the manuscripts reproduced in this book from the Bodleian Library, Oxford, and all the pictures in the Holkham Bible are available in this way. Those in the Holkham Bible are especially interesting as the original only passed from private hands into the British Museum recently, so that few of the many useful pictures in it have as yet been reproduced except in the facsimile edition published by the Dropmore Press with a commentary by myself. The existence of these transparencies was continually in mind when this book was written and many of the introductory paragraphs contain references to pictures in the Holkham Bible which provide vivid illustrations of the texts.

Thanks are due to the kindness of all owners and custodians of pictures listed on pp. iv–vi for allowing reproductions to be made and also to the owners of copyrights of photographs.

The illustrations in *How They Lived* break away from an unscholarly custom. All of them come from original medieval illustrations of English or Anglo-Norman origin. In a book which is not dealing with the continent of Europe and which is dealing with a period when local differences meant more than they do in a world of mass production it is obvious that they should. Yet a high proportion of the pictures chosen to illustrate most of the great books on medieval English life are drawn from French and Flemish originals. It would be invidious to name them, but they would include the names of the most celebrated medieval historians. It might seem odd to illustrate a book on modern Russia with photographs largely taken in America, but this bad habit has been accepted hitherto by uncritical publishers because it is much easier to find naturalistic and convincing pictures of fifteenth century life in Flemish and other foreign manuscripts than in ones of English production.

The reproduction of medieval illustrations is a difficult problem. Colour plates are seldom anything like true and medieval miniatures are often too complicated and too finely drawn to tell their story readily to untrained eyes, especially if, as is often the case, the reduction has been excessive. On the face of things a photograph seems always preferable to a line block, but this is not in fact wholly so, for sometimes a skilled draughtsman can reproduce faithfully the salient passages in a complicated original omitting the distractions of irrelevant detail. This book contains thirty-two pages of half-tone photographic reproductions and in them care has been taken to include only such examples of English draughtsmanship as are not too complicated, and considerable reduction in size has only been made in the drawings from a calendar on plate v, where the original is a large crude sketch capable of accepting such treatment. I am indebted to my daughter, Cory Hassall, for the line drawings in which she has given simple and faithfully rendered extracts from medieval originals without the misleading distortion and sweetening of the faces which are unfortunate commonplaces in many line-drawings. Some line-drawings in elementary books on English medieval life are derived at several removes from the original and are indeed hardly recognisable—when their sources can be traced at all.

The illustrations in *How They Lived* are supplemented by the end papers of *They Saw It Happen* and *Who's Who in History*. The former bring together in a convenient form a number of drawings scattered through the Holkham Bible illustrative of such themes as women at work, and the types of weapon and armour in simultaneous use among different social classes at a single date in the fourteenth century. The latter is an assemblage of portraits but gives, incidentally, a series of male and female costumes in order of date. Later medieval artists had more interest in topographical truth than is generally realised and apart from the drawing on plate xxiii of Winchester College (from a manuscript which contains a faithful representation of New College, Oxford, as well) the dust-jacket gives a vivid idea of medieval London with

London Bridge and White Tower, from a British Museum manuscript. The guiding thread of this book is, however, themes, and not famous places or great men, and in accord with this purpose, the pictures are selected to show characteristic classes of people, characteristic tools, and the costume is that suitable for particular functions, times, seasons and activities.

As this book deals with centuries which are unfamiliar except to historical specialists there is danger that the subject arrangement may blur the distinction between those centuries in the minds of readers who read the book independently from the two others in the trilogy, *They Saw it Happen* and *Who's Who in History*. To remedy this there are brief tables of dates, intended to draw attention to significant changes and events and to give character to the centuries and a framework of time to the book. Some are interesting and significant dates in their own right, but not readily available in one place. Its compilation brought home to me how much I should wish to know certain exact dates which may never be known—such as the invention of the pulley, of the wheelbarrow or of the spinning wheel.

DATES: IMPORTANT PEOPLE (*see W.W.I.H.*, i)

Cunobelinus, c. A.D. 15–42, King at Colchester.

Emperor Claudius conquers southern Britain, 43.

Boudicca burns London and poisons herself, 60.

Agricola reaches Clyde and Forth, 81.

Hadrian visits northern frontier and builds wall, 121–2.

Carausius rules independently, 286–7.

Magnus Maximus, proclaimed Emperor, takes army to Gaul, 383.

St. Ninian converts Picts and builds stone church, 397.

St. Patrick, apostle of Ireland, 389–461.

Arthur resists Saxons, 496.

St. Columba, founder of Iona, 521–97.

Gildas laments destruction of Britain by the Saxons, 539.

King Ethelbert of Kent receives St. Augustine, 597.

Penda of Mercia kills Edwin of Northumbria, 633.

St. Theodore of Tarsus, Archbishop of Canterbury, d. 690.

The Venerable Bede, Europe's greatest historian, 673–735.

King Offa of Mercia, builder of dyke, d. 796.

Alcuin of York, Europe's greatest scholar, adviser to Charlemagne, 735–804.

Alfred makes Watling St. the Danish boundary, 878.

Alfred builds ships with 60 oars or more, to beat the Danes, 897.

King Athelstan of Wessex, codifier of laws, 925–40.

St. Aethelwold, Bishop of Winchester, revives Benedictine monasteries, 963–84.

Emma married Ethelred, 1002, and then Cnut, 1017.

King Edward the Confessor, early user of a waxen seal, 1042–66.

Hereward the Wake resists William I, 1070–1.

St. Wulfstan, Bishop of Worcester, last Saxon bishop, 1062–95.

St. Stephen Harding, Abbot of Cîteaux, 1110–33.

Roger, Bishop of Salisbury, organizer of Exchequer, 1102–39.

William of Malmesbury finishes his *Chronicles*, 1125.

Hundred cartloads of lead leaves Newcastle for Clairvaux abbey roof, 1179.

Walter Map writes gossip about Angevin court, c. 1140–c. 1205.

DATES: TOWN AND COUNTRY

Claudius invades Britain, Roman roads started, 43 A.D.

Roman temple built at Colchester, 49.

Roman market place at St. Albans, 79.

First Saxon shore fort built at Reculver, Kent, soon after 210.

Plantation of vines permitted by Emperor Probus, 280.

Christianity the official religion, 323.

Saxons ruin villas and Roman towns decay, fifth century.

Finest jewellery in Europe in royal grave at Sutton Hoo, ?655.

Brixworth church, late 7th century.

Bells first mentioned, at Whitby, 680.

Wall paintings at Hexham mentioned, 7th century.

England leads Europe in art and letters, 7th–8th century.

Carved Northumbrian crosses, late 7th—early 8th century.

Danish raids, 789, 793, 794.

Danes first winter in England, 850.

Nottingham Bridge built, 920.

Market place planned by Abbot of St. Albans, 950.

A bell-tower shown in Benedictional of St. Aethelwold, c. 970.

Aelfric describes typical daily occupations, 1005.

Norman type castle mounds only at Dover, Clavering, Hereford, and Richard's castle, 1055–65.

Bayeaux ' Tapestry ' (230 ft. strip) depicts tools, clothes, ship-building, armour, 1066.

Derbyshire lead, Gloucestershire iron and 5,000 watermills mentioned in Domesday Book. Birmingham, has only 10 houses. Half England held by 170 French barons, 1086.

First Gild Merchant mentioned, at Burford, Oxon, 1088.

Normans build 1,000 churches and 22 cathedrals and abbeys with round stone arches, square towers and small windows, c. 1090.

Weavers' gilds in five towns mentioned in earliest Exchequer ' Pipe Roll ', 1130.

Detailed description of Exchequer, c. 1136.

Canterbury plumbing planned, 1153.

William Marshall, ideal knight, 1146–1219.

Gerald of Wales, reads in public at Oxford where the university is forming, 1186.

John seals Magna Carta, 1215.

Matthew Paris, monk, historian and illustrator, c. 1200–59.

Simon de Montfort summons townsmen to Parliament, 1265.

Henry Bracton, writer on law and custom, d. 1268.

Llywelyn ab Gruffyd, Welsh leader, slain, 1282

Roger Bacon, friar and scientist at Oxford, c. 1214–94.

William Wallace, Scottish hero, 1297–1305.

Edward I starts to reform law, 1275.

Thomas of Lancaster, baronial leader, 1310–22.

William of Oakham, at Oxford, 1318–24.

Robert de Bruce, 1274–1329.

Alabaster effigy of Edward II sets fashion, c. 1330.

Wat Tyler, peasant leader, murdered, 1381.

Wyclif's heresies condemned, 1382.

John of Gaunt, 1340–99.

Parliament choses Henry IV to reign, 1399.

Chaucer, Richard II, and perhaps Langland, die, 1400.

Owen Glendower holds a Welsh parliament, 1404.

Henry V victorious at Agincourt, 1415.

John Oldcastle burnt, 1417.

Whittington, Mayor of London, 1397–8, 1406–7, 1419–20.

Humphrey Duke of Gloucester, 1391–1447, renaissance prince.

Jack Cade rebels, 1450.

Sir John Fastolf, Agincourt veteran, 1378–1459.

John Paston, Norfolk gentleman, 1421–66.

Richard Nevill, Warwick the Kingmaker, ' Last of the Barons ', 1428–71.

Edward IV owns The Mary and John (900 ton ship), d. 1483.

Henry Tudor beats Richard III, 1485.

Anglo-Saxon Chronicle stops and historians all write in Latin, 1154.

Cologne merchants have gildhall in London, 1157.

Canterbury rebuilt in new style which pilgrims spread, 1174.

Stone bridge built at London, 1176–1209.

Purbeck marble shafts fashionable, 1190–1340.

Soap, glazed pottery and (a few) bricks made, 12th century.

Stone building encouraged in London to stop fires, 1189.

First recorded fulling mills, c. 1190.

First true reference to a windmill in England, 1191.

First Mayor of London, 1191.

Attempt to standardize measures 1197.

Exports: wool, hides, lead, tin, cheese and (already) coal, 1200.

Towns had gained 300 charters already, 1216.

Earliest dateable churchbell at Caversfield, Oxon, pre-1219.

The Papacy at the height of its power (Innocent III), 1198–1216.

Royal orders for armorial glass begin, 1240.

Early English pointed architecture, mid-13th century.

Stamford cloth known to merchants at Venice, 1265.

Coal already a nuisance in London, 1285.

First decorated ' ogee ' arches, 1291–2.

The ' Babylonish Captivity ' of the Popes at Avignon, 1309–76.

16,000 wool sacks and 27,000 fells exported, 1313.

St. Catherine's lighthouse, Isle of Wight, built, 1314.

Stern-rudder shown on seal of Poole, 1325.

First pictures of, and reference to, cannon, 1326–7.

Monumental brasses of civilians appear, 1350.

Quarter Sessions instituted, 1362.

The Great Schism of the Papacy, 1378–1417.

Winchester College founded, 1382.

Westminster Hall roof, 67½ ft. wide, a record span, 1390's.

Sheen (Carthusian priory), a late monastic foundation, 1414.

First paper made in England, 1450.

Turks take Constantinople, 1453.

First picture of three-masted ship, 1466.

First book printed in English, 1475.

Oxburgh Hall, Norfolk, with many big windows, built, 1482.

PLATE I

COUNTRY LIFE

1. March, pruning

2. June, mowing with scythe

3. July, reaping

4. August, threshing with flail

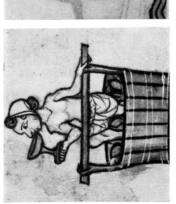

5. September, treading grapes

6. October, sowing

7. November, getting acorns for swine

8. December, slaughtering swine

9. Dairymaid (*cf. pp.* 8–9)

10. Harvest   11. Sheep shearing   12. Maytime

13. Bailiff and harvesting couple. Before 1300, national styles are indistinct
and this may come from the Low Countries

COUNTRYSIDE: FORESTS

Nowadays the word *forest* means a great wood. In the Middle Ages a *forest* was an area subject to special laws against trespassers and poachers, reserved for royal hunting. It was not necessarily wooded. There was much more woodland than now, but large areas of woodland were not necessarily *forest*, in the sense of being under forest law. Of course many large areas were both *forest* and woodland. Perhaps one eighth of England was 'forest', including a stretch of country from Stamford to Oxford, the New Forest, Sherwood Forest, much of Yorkshire, Cumberland and the West, and most of Essex. Early natural woodland did not include elms.

Further Reading: J. C. Cox, *Royal Forests of England*, 1905.

H. C. Darby, ' Domesday Woodland,' *Economic History Review*, 2nd series, vol. 3, 1950.

(1) *Source*: New Forest, 1087, William of Malmesbury, *Chronicle of the Kings of England*, transl. J. A. Giles, Bohn's Antiquarian Library, 1866, p. 306.

This is the place which William [the Conqueror] . . . . desolating the towns and destroying the churches for more than thirty miles, had appropriated for the nurture and refuge of wild beasts; a dreadful spectacle, indeed, that where before had existed human intercourse and the worship of God, there deer, and goats, and other animals of that kind, should now range unrestrained, and these not subjected to the general service of mankind. Hence it is truly asserted that, in this very forest, William [Rufus] his son, and his grandson Richard, son of Robert, Earl of Normandy, by the severe judgment of God, met their deaths, one by a wound in the breast by an arrow, the other by a wound in the neck, or as some say, from being suspended by the jaws on the branch of a tree, as his horse passed beneath it.

(2) Clearings, 1176–9.

Source: *Dialogus de Scaccario The Course of the Exchequer* (1176–9), ed. C. Johnson, Nelson 1950, p. 60.

Assarts (*essarta*) is the common name . . . when forests, woods, or thickets fit for feeding or covert are cut down. When they have been cut down and stubbed up, the soil is turned [by the

B

plough] and cultivated. But if woods are so severely cut that a man, standing on the half-buried stump of an oak or other tree, can see five other trees cut down round about him, that is regarded as ' waste ', which is short for ' wasted ' . . .

WOLVES

King Edgar exacted a yearly tribute of 300 wolves from a Welsh vassal.

In the early twelfth century wolves were rife round Byland, Yorks., but in the early thirteenth century they were so rare that John gave 15 s. reward for the destruction of three.

As late as 1284 royal orders were made for trapping them.

(1) *Source*: Penitential of Archbishop Ecgbert (735–766). B. Thorpe, *Ancient Laws and Institutes of England*, 1840, p. 381.

If a wolf rend any manner of cattle and thereafter it die, let no Christian taste thereof. If any man do this let him fast on bread and water for 4 weeks. If the beast live and afterwards be slain, then it can be freely eaten.

(2) *Source*: John Trevisa, Translation of Higden *Polychronicon* (1387).

There beeth schepe that bereth good wolle; there beeth many hertes and wylde bestes and fewe wolves; therefore the schepe beeth the more sikerliche [securely] without kepynge i-lefte in the folde.

FENS

In the tenth century the Abbots of Glastonbury were reclaiming their marshlands and the first Norman Abbot continued their policy, employing an expert, Girard *Fossarius* (the Dyker) thus trebling the value of Brent Marsh. In the same area the Abbeys of Muchelney and Athelney also dug ditches and planted osiers. Similar work was done in Lincolnshire by small peasants and by grandees like the Earl of Chester. See p. 65.

Further Reading: Sir W. Dugdale, *History of Imbanking and Drayning*, 2nd ed. 1772. H. C. Darby, *Draining of the Fens*, 1940.

(1) The Fens.

The following account of fenland activities omits turf-cutting and salt-pans, but in general it remained true for centuries and a similar account comes in Drayton's *Polyolbion* (1622).

Source: *Historiae Anglicanae Scriptores Varii*, ed. J. Sparke (1723) containing *Historiae Coenobii Burgensis*, p. 2. Translated in H. C. Darby, *The Medieval Fenland*, Cambridge, 1940, p. 21. (c. 1150)

From the flooding of the rivers, or from their overflow, the water, standing on unlevel ground, makes a deep marsh and so renders the land uninhabitable, save on some raised spots of ground, which I think that God set up for the special purpose that they should be the habitations of His servants who have chosen to live there. . . . *Burch* [Peterborough] is founded in the land of the Gyrvii, where the same marsh begins on its eastern side, to extend for sixty miles or more. This marsh, however, is very useful for men; for in it are found wood and twigs for fires, hay for the fodder of cattle, thatch for covering houses, and many other useful things. It is, moreover, productive of birds and fish. For there are various rivers, and very many waters and ponds abounding in fish. In all these things the district is most productive.

(2) Isle of Ely, late eleventh century.

Further Reading: E. O. Blake, ' The '*Historia Eliensis*' as a source for 12th century History,' *Bulletin John Rylands Library*, vol. 41, no. 2.

Source: Description given to William I by a French knight who had been captured by Hereward, *Liber Eliensis*, translated by J. W. Clark in *Cambridge*, 1893, p. 6.

In our Isle men are not troubling themselves about the siege; the ploughman has not taken his hand from the plough, nor has the hunter cast aside his arrow, nor does the fowler desist from beguiling birds. If you care to hear what I have heard and seen with my own eyes, I will reveal all to you. The Isle is within itself plenteously endowed; it is supplied with various kinds of herbage; and in richness of soil surpasses the rest of England. Most delightful for charming fields and pastures, it is also remarkable for beasts of chase; and is, in no ordinary way, fertile in flocks and herds. Its woods and vineyards are not worthy of equal praise; but it is begirt by great meres and fens as though by a strong wall. In this Isle there is an abundance of domestic cattle, and a multitude of wild animals; stags, roes, goats, and hares, are found in its groves and by these fens. Moreover, there is a fair sufficiency of otters, weasels, and polecats; which in hard winter are caught by traps, snares, or any other device. But what am I to say of the kinds of fishes and of fowls, both those that fly and those that swim? In the eddies at the sluices of these meres are netted innumerable eels, large water-wolves, with pickerels, perches, roaches, burbots [a fish full of prickles], and lampreys, which we call water-snakes. It is, indeed, said by many that sometimes salmon are taken there, together with the royal fish, the sturgeon. As for the birds that abide there and thereabouts, if you are not tired of listening to me, I will tell you about them, as I have told you about the rest. There you find geese, teal, coots, didappers [or dabchicks], water-crows, herons, and ducks, more than man can number, especially in winter or at moulting time. I have seen a hundred—nay, even three hundred —taken at once; sometimes by bird-lime, sometimes in nets or snares.

(3) Ramsey Abbey, a Fenland Island.

Source: Chronicon Abbatiae Ramesiensis, p. 8, translated H. C. Darby, *The Medieval Fenland*, Cambridge, 1940, p. 53. (twelfth century)

In length this island extends almost two miles; but in breadth not so much, being surrounded with alders, reeds, green canes, and bulrushes, which beautify it exceedingly; and before it became inhabited, it was full of all kinds of trees (especially wild ash), the size of which may be seen from the beams and rafters in the roof of the church. But now through the space of time the woods have for the most part disappeared, and the fertility of the turf is such that the land converted to tillage bears corn plentifully: nor is it less profitable otherwise, being full of fair gardens, rich pastures, shady groves, and rich meadows; which in the spring time look most beautiful.

FARM LABOURERS' WAGES

Wages and prices were both extremely low for money was more valuable than now.

(1) *Source*: undated tract on husbandry, printed with *Walter of Henley's Husbandry*, ed. Elizabeth Lamond, Longman Green, 1890, p. 69. (Late thirteenth century)

You can well have three acres weeded for a penny, and an acre of meadow mown for fourpence, and an acre of waste meadow for threepence-halfpenny, and an acre of meadow turned and raised for a penny-halfpenny, and an acre of waste for a penny farthing. And know that five men can well reap and bind two acres a day of each kind of corn, more or less. And where each takes twopence a day then you must give fivepence an acre, and when four take a penny-halfpenny a day and the fifth twopence, because he is binder, then you must give fourpence for the acre. And, because in many places they do not reap by the acre, one can know by the reapers and by the work done what they do, but keep the reapers by the band, that is to say, that five men or women, whichever you will, who are called half men, make a band, and twenty-five men make five bands, and twenty-five men can reap and bind ten acres a day working all day, and in ten days a hundred acres, and in twenty days two hundred acres by five score. And see then how many acres there are to reap throughout, and see if they agree with the days and pay them then, and if they account for more days than is right according to this reckoning, do not let them be paid, for it is their fault that they have not reaped the amount and have not worked so well as they ought.

(2) Farm wages.

Source: Statute of Labourers, 25 Edward III caps. 1–2 (translated as in edition of 1577). (1350)

1. First that the carters, ploughmen, dryvers of the plough, shepeheardes, swineheards, deies [dairy workers], and al other servants shal take liverie and wages, accustomed the said 20 yeare [of Edward III] or 4 yeares before, so that in the country, where wheate was wont to be given, they shall take for the bushel 10d. or wheate at the wil of the gever, til it be otherwise ordeyned. And they be allowed to serve by a whole yeare, or by other usual

termes, and not by the daye. And that none pay in the time of sarcling [weeding] or heymaking but 1d. the day. And a mower of medowes for the acre 5d. or by the daye 5d. And repers of corne in the first weeke of August 2d. and the seconde 3d. and so till the ende of Auguste, and lesse in the countrye where lesse was wont to be geven, without meate or drinke, or other curtesie to be demaunded, geven or taken. And that al workmen bring onely in their hands to the marchaunt townes their instrumentes, and there shalbe hyred in a common place and not privy.

2. Item that none take for the thrashing of a quarter of wheate or rye, over 2½d. and the quarter of barly, beanes, pease and otes 1½d. if so much were wont to be geven, and in the country, where it is used to repe by certaine sheves and to thrash by certain busheles, they shall take no more nor in other maner than was wont the said 20 yeare and before. And the same servaunts be sworne two times in the yeare before lordes, stewardes, bayliffes and constables of every towne, to hold and do this ordinaunce. And that none of them go out of the town, where he dwelleth in the winter to serve the sommer if he may have service in the same town, taking as before is said. Saving that the people of the counties of Stafforde, Lancaster and Derbie, and people of Craven, and of the Marches of Wales and Scotland, and other places, may come in time of Auguste, and labor in other counties and safely retourne, as they were wont to doe before this time. And that those whiche refuse to make such othe, or to perfourme that they be sworne to, or have taken upon them, shal be put in the stockes by the said Lordes, stewardes, bailiffes and constables of the townes, by three dayes or more, or sent to the next gaole, there to remaine til they wil iustifye themselves. And the stockes be made in every towne by suche occasion betwixte this and the feast of Penthecoste [Whitsun].

(3) Artisans' wages.

Source: Statute of Labourers 23 Edward III cap. 5 (translated as in edition of 1577). (1350)

5. Item that sadlers, skinners, whitetawyers [leatherworkers], cordwainers, tailors, smithes, carpenters, masons, tylers, shipwrightes, carters, and al other artificers and workemen, shall not

take for their labour and workemanship, above the same that was wont to be paid to such persons the said 20 yeare [of Edward III], and other common yeares next before, as afore is said, in the place where they shal happen to worke. And if any man take more, he shalbe committed to the next gaole in the maner as afore is said.

CLOSES AND OPEN FIELDS

In hilly or wooded districts there were small square fields (' closes ') but in open country, like most of the Midlands, there were great ' open fields '. In these, small strips, often of only half an acre each, lay in the various furlongs (=furrow-longs). A peasant might hold between about thirty and sixty of these, widely scattered. Details of such strips held by the Prior of Walsingham in 1456–7 at Holkham, Norfolk, are given in *TSIH*, i, 208–9. A very important date in the history of any district is that at which the common fields were ' enclosed ', the strips abolished, and the area divided up into modern rectangular fields. Often this did not happen until the eighteenth or nineteenth century. So far as the fields are concerned the date of the enclosure is the date when the landscape assumed a modern instead of a medieval appearance, with rectangular fields divided from each other by hedges.

Further Reading: H. L. Gray, *English Field Systems* (Harvard Historical Studies), 1915.
C. S. and C. S. Orwin, *Open Fields*, 1938.
E. Kerridge, ' Ridge and Furrow and Agrarian History,' *Economic History Review*, 2nd series vol. 4, 1951.

Source: Laws of Ine, (688–726) 40 and 42. B. Thorpe, *Ancient Laws and Institutes of England*, 1840, p. 55–6.

A 'ceorl's ' close [enclosed plot of land] ought to be fenced winter and summer. If it be unfenced, and his neighbour's cattle stray in through his own gap, he shall have nothing from the cattle: let him drive it out and bear the damage. . . .

If ' ceorls ' have a common meadow, or other partible land to fence, and some have fenced their part, some have not, and eat up their common corn or grass; let those go who own the gap, and compensate to the others, who have fenced their part, the damage which there may be done, and let them demand such justice on the cattle as it may be right. But if there be a beast which

breaks hedges and goes in everywhere, and he who owns it will
not or cannot restrain it; let him who finds it in his field take it
and slay it, and let the owner take its skin and flesh and forfeit
the rest.

CATTLE

Cattle were important not only for the dairy. Oxen were largely
used for drawing the plough. (See a comparison between oxen and
horses in *T.S.I.H.*,i, 128.) Oxen are often shown in scenes of the
Nativity. Our word *capital*, meaning savings, is derived from *cattle*.

Further Reading: J. Wilson; *Evolution of British Cattle and the Fashioning
of Breeds*, 1909; R. Lyddeker, *Ox and its kindred*, 1912.

Source: ordinance established by the English witan and the coun-
sellors of the 'Wealh' (Welsh) nation established among the 'Dun-
setas'. B. Thorpe, *Ancient Laws and Institutes of Englands*, 1840, p. 150.

If any one pursue the track of stolen cattle from one 'staeth'
[a station on the boundary river] to another, then let him commit
the tracing to the men of the country or show by some mark that
it is rightfully pursued. Let him then take to it who owns the land,
and have the inquiry to himself, and 9 days afterwards compensate
for the cattle, or deposit an 'underwed' [pledge] on that day,
which shall be worth half as much again as the cattle; and in 9
days from that time let him redeem the 'wed' [pledge] by lawful
payment. If it be said that the track is wrongfully pursued, then
must he who traces the cattle lead to the 'staeth', and there
himself one of six unchosen men, who are true, make oath that
he according to folk-right [customary law] makes lawful claim on
the land, as his cattle went thereup.

DAIRY

Thorold Rogers found from account rolls of 1259-1400 that
rennet was generally home-made though sometimes it was bought.
Sometimes registers of cheese-making were kept in detail. The largest
cheeses apparently weighed less than six to eight pounds. Butter
was made in pats or pressed into gallon tubs or jars. Dairy equipment
remained unchanged until modern mechanization and consisted of
pail, milk-pan, churn, cheese-press, cheese-shape, butter mould and

straining-cloths. Butter was used in sheep-dressing and cart grease, and was cheaper than other fats, of which there was a lack. After famines it rose 40 per cent, which was however less than rises in wages.

Further Reading: T. Davidson, ' Cattle-milking Charms and Amulets ', *Gwerin*,vol. 1, no. 4.

Source: tract on the Office of Seneschal, printed with *Walter of Henley's Husbandry*, ed. Elizabeth Lamond, Longman Green, 1890, pp. 117–119. A good dairymaid (late thirteenth century).

The dairymaid ought to be faithful and of good repute, and keep herself clean, and ought to know her business and all that belongs to it. She ought not to allow any underdairymaid or another to take or carry away milk, or butter, or cream, by which the cheese shall be less and the dairy impoverished. And she ought to know well how to make cheese and salt cheese, and she ought to save and keep the vessels of the dairy, that it need not be necessary to buy new ones every year. And she ought to know the day when she begins to make cheese and of what weight, and when she begins to make two cheeses a day, of how much and of what weight, and then the bailiff and the provost [reeve] ought to inspect the dairy often and the cheeses, when they increase and decrease in weight, and no harm be done in the dairy, nor any robbery by which the weight shall be lessened. And they ought to know and prove and see when the cows make a stone of cheese and butter, and when the ewes make a stone of the same, that they may be able the more surely to answer in the account. No cow shall be milked or suckled after michaelmas, and no ewe after the feast of our Lady. . . .

The dairymaid ought to help to winnow the corn when she can be present, and she ought to take care of the geese and hens and answer for the returns and keep and cover the fire, that no harm arise from lack of guard.

Note: an anonymous tract on Husbandry in the same volume contains a further discussion on the dairy. See Elizabeth Lamond, pp. 73–77.

THE SWINEHERD

Pigs were an important source of food for December, widely mentioned in the woodlands of Domesday Book and often illustrated in medieval Calendars. In London the pigs of St. Anthony's Hospital were allowed to scavenge. Sometimes children were bitten.

Further Reading: F. C. Sillar, *The Symbolic Pig*, 1961.

Source: tract on the Office of Seneschal, printed with *Walter of Henley's Husbandry*, ed. Elizabeth Lamond, Longman Green, 1890, pp. 113–115. (late thirteeenth century)

The swineherd ought to be on those manors where swine can be sustained and kept in the forest, or in woods, or waste, or in marshes, without sustenance from the grange; and if the swine can be kept with little sustenance from the grange during hard frost, then must a pigsty be made in a marsh or wood, where the swine may be night and day. And then when the sows have farrowed, let them be driven with the feeble swine to the manors and kept with leavings as long as the hard frost and the bad weather last, and then driven back to the others. And if there is no wood or marsh or waste where the swine may be sustained without being altogether kept on the grange, no swineherd or swine shall be on the manor, except only such as can be kept in August on the stubble and leavings of the grange, and when the corn is threshed for sale, and as soon as they are in good condition and well, let them be sold. For whoever will keep swine for a year from the cost of the grange alone, and count the cost and the allowance for the swine and swineherd, together with the damage they do yearly to the corn, he shall lose twice as much as he shall gain, and this will soon be seen by whoever keeps account.

CATS

The legend of Dick Whittington and his cat ignores the fact that patrons of ships would generally have had cats on their ships as otherwise they were liable for any damage done to goods on board by rats. A ship from Spain captured by pirates off Sandwich in 1228 contained 300 cat skins along with skins of kid, lamb, genet, hare and rabbit.

In 1467 the streets of Leicester were used as a receptacle for dead cats and other animals. Unlike larks, nightingales, parrots hounds, rabbits, squirrels and monkeys, cats do not seem to have been kept as pets, but Piers Plowman disliked the pitilessness of pedlars who like to catch them for their skins.

(1) *Source*: Trevisa, Translation of Bartholomew the Englishman, *Of the Nature of Things* (1398).

The catte is a beaste of uncerten heare [hair] and colour; for some catte is white, some rede, some blacke, some skewed [piebald] and speckled in the fete and in the face and in the eares. And he is . . . in youth swyfte, plyaunte, and mery, and lepeth and reseth [rusheth] on all thynge that is to-fore him; and is led by a strawe and playeth therwith. And is a right hevy beast in age, and ful slepy, and lieth slily in wait for myce . . . and when he taketh a mous he playeth therwith, and eateth him after play. . . . And he maketh a ruthefull noyse and gastfull when one proffereth to fyghte with another.

(2) The following extracts contain some typical early (and false) etymologies.

Source: T. H. White, *The Book of Beasts, being a translation from a Latin Bestiary made in the twelfth century*, Jonathan Cape, 1954, pp. 90–91.

She is called Mouser because she is fatal to mice. The vulgar call her Catus the Cat because she catches a thing while others say that it is because she lies in wait (*captat*) i.e. because she watches. So acutely does she glare that her eye penetrates the shades of darkness with a gleam of light. Hence from the Greek comes ' *catus* ', i.e. ' acute '.

Mus the Mouse, a puny animal, comes from a Greek word: although it may have become Latin, it really comes from that. Others say it is ' mice ' (*mures*) because they are generated from the dampness of the soil (*ex humore*). For '*humus*' is '*hu-Mus*', you see?

The liver of these creatures gets bigger at full moon, just as certain seashores rise and fall with the waning moon.

DOGS

Dogs of various kinds are often seen in medieval pictures of hunting and hounds chasing hares are common on Romano-British pottery. Sheep-dogs are sometimes shown with spiked collars, a protection from wolves. Beverley, Northampton, Coventry and Bristol had rules against dogs being loose in the streets.

Further Reading: G. R. Jesse, *Researches in the History of the British Dog*, 1866.

(1) *Source*: Gerald of Wales, *Itinerary of Archbishop Baldwin through Wales*, translated by Sir R. C. Hoare, 1806, i, 136–8 (late twelfth century).

A greyhound belonging to the aforesaid Owen (a twelfth century Welsh prince, murdered by his brother), large, beautiful and curiously spotted with a variety of colours, received seven wounds from arrows and lances, in the defence of his master, and on his part did much injury to the enemy and assassins. When his wounds were healed, he was sent to king Henry II by William Earl of Gloucester, in testimony of so great and extraordinary a deed. A dog, of all animals, is most attached to man, and most easily distinguishes him; sometimes when deprived of his master, he refuses to live, and in his master's defence is bold enough to brave death; ready therefore, to die, either with or for his master. . . . [Gerald then repeats accounts of dogs in classical authors] . . . I shall take this opportunity of mentioning what from experience and ocular testimony I have observed respecting the nature of dogs. A dog is in general sagacious, but particularly with respect to his master; for when he has for some time lost him in a crowd, he depends more upon his nose than upon his eyes; and, in endeavouring to find him, he first looks about, and then applies his nose, for greater certainty to his clothes, as if nature had placed all the powers of infallibility in that feature. The tongue of a dog possess a medicinal quality; the wolf's on the contrary, a poisonous: the dog heals his wounds by licking them, the wolf, by a similar practice, infects them; and the dog, if he has received a wound in his neck or head, or any part of his body where he cannot apply his tongue, ingeniously makes use of his hinder foot as a conveyance of the healing qualities to the parts affected.

(2) *Source*: T. H. White, *The Book of Beasts, being a translation from a Latin Bestiary made in the twelfth century*, Jonathan Cape, 1954, pp. 62, 66–67.

There are numerous breeds of dogs. Some track down the wild creatures of the woods to catch them. Others guard the flocks of sheep vigilantly against infestations of wolves. Other, the house-dogs, look after the palisade of their masters, lest it should be robbed in the night by thieves, and these will stand up for their owners to the death. They gladly dash out hunting with Master, and will even guard his body when dead, and not leave it. In sum, it is part of their nature that they cannot live without men. . . .

In certain ways, Priests are like watchdogs. They always drive away the wiles of the trespassing Devil with admonishments—and by doing the right thing—lest he should steal away the treasury of God, i.e. the souls of Christians.

The tongue of a dog cures a wound by licking it. This is because the wounds of sinners are cleansed, when they are laid bare in confession, by the penance imposed by the Priest. Also the tongue of a puppy cures the insides of men, because the inside secrets of the heart are often purified by the work and preaching of these learned men.

The dog is said to be very temperate in its diet, because that man only is truly on his guard who excels others in wisdom and studies. . . .

The fact that a dog returns to its vomit signifies that human beings, after a complete confession, often return incautiously to the crimes which they have perpetrated.

Because it leaves the true food in the river out of greed for the shadow, it symbolizes those silly people who often leave that which is peculiarly of the Law out of desire for some unknown thing. . . .

A GRUMBLING SHEPHERD, c.1350

England's wealth is symbolized by the Lord Chancellor's woolsack, the profits of wool paid for handsome churches and merchants houses in the towns of the Cotswolds and East Anglia and a contented clothier declares:

> ' I thank God and ever shall
> It was the sheep that payed for all '.

But the Second Wakefield Nativity Play opens with a declaration of discontent, put in the mouth of the ' first shepherd '.

The English language reflects the fact that the Saxon shepherd spoke of sheep and his Norman master spoke of mutton, for the first

Mobile hut for shepherd.   Fourteenth century.
(Egerton Genesis).

Sheepfold, c. 1340.   (Luttrell Psalter).

only knew the animal out of doors while the latter knew it on the table. Shepherds are perhaps more often found in medieval pictures than men of any other occupation except kings. They seem well clad. A shepherd's gild at Holbeach was dedicated to the Nativity. For the qualities of a shepherd, including kindness, see *T.S.I.H.*, i, 127–8. For wool and cloth see pp. 48, 51, 110 and 113.

Source: Second Wakefield Nativity Play, *Towneley Mysteries*. (c.1426)

Lord! what, these weathers are cold, and I am ill happed;
I am near hand-dold [numb], so long have I napped;
My legs bend and fold, my fingers are chapped.
It is not as I would, for I am all lapped
  In sorrow
In storms and tempest,
Now in the east, now in the west,
Woe is him that has never rest,
  Mid day nor morrow.
But we silly shepherds, that walk upon the moor,
In faith, we are near hands out of the door;
No wonder, as it stands, if we be poor,
For the tilth of our lands lies fallow as the floor,
We are so lamed,
So taxed and shamed.
We are made hand-tamed,
  With these gentlery-men. . . .
Thus they hold us under,
Thus they bring us in blunder,
It were a great wonder,
  And ever should we thrive. . . .
[He complains of those who make
 ' purveyance ', [requisitions] for the needs of the court.]
He must borrow my wain, my plough also,
Then I am full fain to grant or he go.
Thus live we in pain, anger, and woe,
  By night and day; . . .
I were better be hanged
  Than once say him nay.
It does me good, as I walk thus by mine own,
Of this world for to talk in manner of moan
To my sheep will I stalk and hearken anon
There abide on a balk, or sit on a stone. . . .

PLOUGHS

The process of bringing heavy clay-lands under cultivation began in Roman times, perhaps halted temporarily in late Roman times and during the Saxon invasions, grew in momentum after the eighth century and continued until about 1300.

Aelfric (1005) said that the ploughman's art was the most important one for he provided bread and ale and was better to stay with than the blacksmith. He describes in the ploughman's words the ploughman's hard life. (See *T.S.I.H.*, i, 26). There is a picture on p. 7 of a Saxon Ploughman in the Caedmon *Genesis*, and of an early fourteenth century one in the Holkham Bible Picture Book (reproduced at the end of *T.S.I.H.*). The latter differs from the famous picture in the Luttrell Psalter in being a disgruntled criminal, Cain, wearing, as in Piers Plowman, a ' lousy hat ', and accompanied, like Aelfric's ploughman and Cain in the *Towneley Mysteries*, by a boy. As the first ploughman, Cain is represented in medieval literature as a Type for Avarice, and is a bad tithe payer. He is very different from the good ploughman in Chaucer.

Further Reading: H. G. Richardson, ' Medieval Plough Team ', *History*, vol. 6, 1942; F. G. Payne, ' The Plough in Ancient Britain ', *Archaeological Journal*, vol. 104, 1947, p. 96 (discusses lengths of coulters in medieval pictures).

(1) The Plough (Saxon).

Source: Old English Riddle translated by W. S. Mackie in *The Exeter Book*, pt. ii, poems ix–xxxii, Early English Text Society, O.S. no. 194, 1934, for 1933, pp. 111–2.

My nose is pointed downwards; I crawl along
and dig in the ground. I go as I am guided
by the gray enemy of the forest, and by my lord,
who walks stooping, my guardian, at my tail,
pushes his way on the plain, lifts me and presses me on,
and sows in my track. Nose to ground, I move forwards,
having been brought from the wood, skilfully fastened together,
and carried on a wagon. I have many strange properties.
As I advance, on one side of me there is green,
while on the other my black track is clear.
Driven through my back there hangs under me
a well devised sharp weapon; another in my head,
firmly fixed and pointing forward, leans to the side,
so that I tear with my teeth, if from behind
he (that is, my lord) serves me well.

14. Hay harvest

15. Corn harvest

16. Slaughter

PLATE IV

FARMING

17. Shepherds at Bethlehem, with sheep, goats and dog with collar

The Plough. Eleventh century. (Caedmon MS.)

(2) Poor ploughman, fourteenth century.

The ploughing services to be rendered by serfs to their lords are frequently recorded in manorial *custumals* and in the *Hundred Rolls*. The backchat between Cain and his boy, whose duty is to goad the beasts as the wife does below, is a comic feature in Miracle plays. In fourteenth century pictures there is always a clear distinction between fashionable dress and the short tunics of the peasantry.

Source: *Piers Plowman's Crede* [giving a highly-coloured description of misery] (c.1377).

And as I went by the way weeping for sorrow
I saw a poor man by me on the plough hanging,
His coat was of clout that cary [coarse cloth] was called,
His hood was full of holes and his hair cut,
With his knobby shoes patched full thick.
His tongue peeped out as he the earth trod.
His hosen overhung his gaiters on every side
All beslobbered in mire as he the plough followed.
Two mittens so scanty made all of patches,
The fingers were worn and full of mud hung.
This fellow wallowed in the muck almost to the ankle,

C

Four heifers before him that weak had become,
You could count all their ribs so wretched they were.
His wife walked by him with a long goad
In a coat cut short, cut full high,
Wrapped in a winnowing sheet to cover her from the weather,
Barefoot on the bare ice that the blood followed.
And at the field end lay a little bowl
And on it lay a little child, wrapped in rags,
And two of two years old on another side.
And all they sang a song that was sad to hear,
They all cried a cry, a note full of care.
The poor man sighed sore and said ' Children be still '.

CORN

The speed of thrashing corn was much improved in the eleventh century by the adoption of a hinged flail such is often shown in medieval pictures of the Occupations of the Months. These remained in use until the appearance of thrashing machines in the nineteenth century and can still be seen in the Museum of Rural Life at Reading. For milling and bread see pp. 42–6 and 132–3

Further Reading: M. K. Bennett, *British Wheat Yield per Acre for Seven Centuries*, Economic History Supplement to the *Economic Journal*, 1937; J. Percival, *Wheat in Great Britain*, 1934.

Source: *Walter of Henley's Husbandry*, ed. Elizabeth Lamond, Longmans, 1890, p. 19. (late thirteenth century)

You know surely that an acre sown with wheat takes three ploughings, except lands which are sown yearly; and that, one with the other, each ploughing is worth sixpence, and harrowing a penny, and on the acre it is necessary to sow at least two bushels. Now two bushels at Michaelmas are worth at least twelvepence, and weeding a halfpenny, and reaping fivepence, and carrying in August a penny; the straw will pay for the threshing. At three times your sowing you ought to have six bushels, worth three shillings, and the cost amounts to three shillings and three halfpence, and the ground is yours and not reckoned.

Change your seed every year at Michaelmas, for seed grown on other ground will bring more profit than that which is grown on

Harrowing. c. 1330. (Holkham Bible).

your own. Will you see this? Plough two selions [arable strips or 'lands'] at the same time, and sow the one with seed which is bought and the other with corn which you have grown: in August you will see that I speak truly.

THE HAYWARD

Research has improved grass seed but pictures in Herbals show wild grass unchanged.

Source: tract on the Office of Seneschal, printed with *Walter of Henley's Husbandry*, ed. Elizabeth Lamond, 1890, p. 103. (late thirteenth century)

The hayward ought to be an active and sharp man, for he must, early and late, look after and go round and keep the woods, corn, and meadows and other things belonging to his office, and he ought to make attachments and approvements faithfully, and make delivery by pledge before the provost [reeve], and deliver them to the bailiff to be heard. And he ought to sow the lands, and be over the ploughers and harrowers at the time of each sowing. And he ought to make all the boon-tenants [tenants who should do unpaid tasks] and customary-tenants who are bound and accustomed to come, do so, to do the work they ought to do. And in haytime he ought to be over the mowers, the making, the carrying, and in August assemble the reapers and the boon-tenants, and the labourers and see that the corn be properly and cleanly gathered; and early and late watch so that nothing be stolen or eaten by beasts or spoilt. And he ought to tally with the provost all the seed, and boonwork, and customs, and labour, which ought to be done in the manor throughout the year, and what it amounts to the bailiff tallies and accounts for, and they ought to answer on the account for the rest.

VILLEINS

The circumstances of villeins were not all the same even on one manor at one date. This villein was a tenant of Westminster Abbey at Islip, Oxfordshire. Islip, the birthplace of Edward the Confessor, had been given by him to the Abbey and the Abbey still has the advowson. Many tenants had died of plague at Islip in 1348–9 and 1361–2 and the first outbreak led locally to the commutation of ' week work '. This was temporarily re-imposed but it was permanently commuted in 1386, five years after the Peasants' Revolt. After the plague of 1349 vacant land began to be leased, though the Abbot still hoped in 1391 that he would be able to restore such customary conditions of tenure as are here recorded.

The duties of boors or serfs in the eleventh century, manor court rolls referring to their successors absconding in 1351 after the Black Death and the story of the revolt in 1381 are printed in *T.S.I.H.*, i, 35–37, 258–9 and 165–180.

Source: *Custumal of the Manor of Islip*, edited with translation by Barbara F. Harvey, Oxfordshire Record Society, vol. 40, 1959, pp. 85 and 93. (1391)

William Cowpere holds in villeinage one messuage [a dwelling] and half-virgate of land [half the size of an average holding] lately held by Thomas Godhyne. This used to render 3s. a year

Weeding. Early fourteenth century. (Queen Mary's Psalter).

or 2½ works a week throughout the year, value of work ½d.; afterwards, when Nicholas was Abbot of Westminster [1362–86], it was conceded to the said William and to all holding by like tenure that each of them should pay 6s. a year for the commutation of the said works and, in addition, he shall do one day's ploughing with half a plough at the winter sowing without food, value of work 2d., and one day's ploughing with half a plough at the Lenten sowing with food provided by the lord, value of work 1d., and give one hen worth 1½d. at Christmas each year and 12 eggs worth ½d. at Easter. He used to pay ½d. a year at Whitsun for fencing for which he had a load of underwood, but this custom was to the lord's detriment, and so has ceased. He shall weed for 3 days, value of work ½d., mow for 3 days, value of work 4d., and carry hay for 3 days, value of work 1d. In autumn he shall do 3 boons [unpaid tasks] without food, value of work 2½d., and one boon with food at one meal provided by the lord, value of work 1½d. and one boon called the love boon for half a day without food or for the whole day with food at one meal provided by the lord, value of work 1½d. and he shall carry hay for one day and corn for one day, value of work 4d. He used to collect nuts for one day, value of work 1d., but, for the remission of this work, he and his peers shall mow all the second crop of hay in Le Mellehamme. He shall cut and carry wood for Christmas, value of work 1d. He used to do one day's carrying work each week with one horse and a sack, value of work 1½d., but this is remitted on account of the increase of the above-mentioned rent of 6s. He shall pay tallage [tax] and merchet [fine on child's marriage] with his peers and pay pannage, that is to say, for a pig a year or more old, 1d., for a pig of half a year, ½d., and for a pig three months old, ¼d.; and each customary tenant shall have free pannage for one full grown pig. If he threshes for one day he should have one truss of straw. If he mows for a whole day he should have one truss of grass. If he goes to the wood for a bundle of wood he should have a stick to carry it on. If he is reeve, or if he does the aforesaid works, he shall be quit of the aforesaid rent. He may collect dead wood if he wishes for his own use; the aforesaid hen and eggs are given in return for this. All the customary tenants below along with this customary shall have 3s. 4½d., and 1 quarter and 2 bushels of wheat for a custom called Mathshup [at Buckland, Gloucestershire, *Madschep* was a sheep given to the mowers]. In addition, the said customary tenants shall have 6d. a year for mowing a certain piece of meadow in addition to their customary obligation. He shall not give his daughters in marriage, or sell a horse or ox of his own breeding without the lord's permission. He shall give heriot, do three-weekly suit to the lord's court and render yearly etc. 6s. . . .

William Coupere holds 1 messuage and 9 acres of land formerly held by William Coupere his father. He shall plough, weed, mow and carry hay, reap, give tallage and merchet according to the entry under his name above. He shall stack hay for 1 day, value of work 2d., and corn for 1 day, value of work 2½d., give 1 cock and 4 hens at Martinmas and 9 eggs at Easter and render yearly 3s.

He also holds a certain parcel of demesne land [the lord's home farm] lying at Buryslade, rendering yearly etc.. 16d.

A GARDEN

A cottage garden, if like Piers Plowman's croft, would yield beans and peas, leeks, parsley, shallots, ' chiboles (small onions) and chervils (potherbs) and cherries, half red '.

Ornamental medieval gardens were small as they were confined by the walls of a castle. Such a garden is indicated by the old name for the ' Bloody Tower ' in the Tower of London, for it was called once the ' Garden Tower '. The lily and the rose symbolized Virginity and the Virgin as well as French royal family and the Houses of York and Lancaster.

This is an account by a Canterbury man of how Chaucer's pilgrims would have behaved at Canterbury in the inn, the Cathedral and the town.

Source: Supplementary Canterbury Tales, 1, *The Tale of Beryn*, ed. by F. J. Furnivall and W. G. Stone, Chaucer Soc., second series, vol. 17, p. 10. The Pardoner and the Miller make silly guesses at the meanings of stained-glass windows, and buy pilgrim badges; the knight and the squire change their clothes and cast a professional eye over the fortifications; and the Wife of Bath and the Prioress examine the garden of the ' Cheker-of-the Hope ' inn. (Fifteenth century)

The wyff of Bath was so wery, she had no will to walk;
She toke the Priores by the hond: ' madam! wol ye stalk
Pryvely into the garden, to se the herbis growe?
And aftir, with our hostis wyff, in hir parlour rowe [rest],
I woll gyve yewe the wyne, & yee shull me also;
For tyll wee go to soper [supper] wee have naught ellis to do.'
The Priores, as womman taught of gentil blood, & hend [courte-
        ous],
Assentid to hit counsell; and forth tho [then] gon they wend,
Passyng forth ful sofftly into the herbery;
For many a herbe grewe, for sew [soup] & surgery;
And al the Aleyis feir I-parid [adorned], I-raylid, & I-makid;
The sauge, & the Isope [hyssop], I-frethid [protected] & I-stakid;
And othir beddis by & by ful fressh I-dight:
For comers to the hoost, righte a sportful sight. . . .

MINERALS

Caesar mentions tin ore in Britain and mining was sufficiently developed for one gold-mine to have pit-head baths. Mining was much improved in the thirteenth century when some of the trenches cut into rocks in the Forest of Dean were 20 feet and more deep. The skill of the miners was such that they were recruited into the royal armies and their tunnels undermined Scottish and Gascon fortifications. As in Roman times, short iron pick-hammers were used. Shovels were made of oak.

Further Reading: H. R. Schubert, *History of the British Iron and Steel Industry*, Routledge and Kegan Paul, 1957; A. K. H. Jenkin, *Cornish Miner*, 1948.

(1) *Source*: John Trevisa, Translation of Higden, *Polychronicon* (1387).

The erthe of that lond is copious of metal ore and of salt welles; of quarers of marbel: of dyuers manere stones, of reed, of whyte; of nesche [soft], of hard; of chalk and of whyte lyme. There is also white cley and reed forto make of crokkes and stenes [pots] and other vessel, and brent tyle to hele [roof] with hous and cherches. . .

(2) Mendip lead miners.

The following laws are attributed to the reign of Edward IV but they are very possibly a later codification, perhaps under Mary Tudor, of ancient custom.

Further Reading: George Zarnecki, *English Romanesque Lead Sculpture*, Tiranti, 1957; J. W. Gough, *The Mines of Mendip*, Oxford, 1930.

Source: J. W. Gough, *Mendip Mining Laws and Forest Bounds*, Somerset Record Soc. vol. 45, 1931, pp. 3–5.

1.   First That if any man whatsoever hee bee that doth intend to venter his life to bee a workman in the mynedery Occupacion hee must first of al require Lycence of the Lord of the Soyle where hee doth purpose to worke or in his absence of his officer as Lead Reve or Bailye and the Lord nother his Bayliffe or officer can deny him.

2.   Item that after the first Lycence had the workmen shall never need to aske leave againe but to bee at his freewill to pitch within the said fforrest and to breake ground where and in what

place itt shall best like him to his behoofe and profitt using himselfe justie and trulie.

3. Item. That every man that doth begin his pitt or Groove
shall have his hacks throw two wayes after the Rake [i.e. in both
directions along the line of the vein of ore]; And note that hee
that doth throwe the hack must stand in his said Groove to the
girdle or wast And then noe man shall or may worke within the
Compasse of his said hacks throw.

4. Item. That when a workman hath landed any oare hee
may carry the same to clensing and blowing to what minedrie
hee shall please for the more speedy making of the same soe that
hee doe trulie pay the tenth thereof to the Lord of the soyle
where itt was landed.

5. Item that if any Lord or his officer have once given
Lycence to any man to build or sett upon any Hearth or washing
house to wash and cleanse and blow theire oare hee who hath soe
once leave shall for ever keepe itt sell itt or give itt to whome itt
shall please him soe that he doe trulie and justlie pay the Lott
Lead which is the tenth pound that shall bee blowne att the same
Hearth or Hearths And alsoe if hee doe keepe itt tenantable as the
Craft doth require.

6. Item That if any man of that occupacion doe pick or steale
any Lead or Lead oare to the value of 13½d. the Lord or his
officer may arrest all his Lead and oare house or hearths with all
his Grooves and workes and keepe them as a forfeit to his owne
use And shall take the person that soe hath offended and bring
him where his house or worke and all his tooles and Instruments
belonging to the same occupacion bee and put him into his
house or worke and set fire in all together about him and banish
him from that occupacion before all the Myneders for ever.

7. Item That if ever that person doe pick or steale there any
more hee shall bee tryed by the Comon Law, for this Custome and
law hath noe more to doe with him.

8. Item that every Lord of soyle or soyles ought to keepe two
Mynedrie Courts by the yeare and to sweare twelve man or more

of the same occupacion for the redresse of all misdemeanours and wrongs touching the Mynedries.

9. Item the Lord or Lords may make three manner of Arrests [That is to say] the first is for strife betweene man and man for theire workes under the earth. The second is for his owne dutye for Lead or oare wheresoever hee find itt within the said fforrest, The third is upon felons goods of the same occupacion wheresoever hee find itt within the same Hill.

10. Item That if any man by the meanes of this doubtfull and dangerous occupacion doe by misfortune take his death as by falling the earth upon him by drowning by stifleing with fire or otherwise as in times past many have bene The workmen of this occupacion are bound to fetch the body out of the earth and bring him to Christian buriall att theire owne proper Costs and Charges although hee bee threescore fathom under the earth as heretofore hath bene seene And the Coroner or any other officer att Jurye shall not have to doe with him nor them.

Note: There were four Lordships each with a central 'minery' for preparing and smelting the ore. Heaps of slag and nineteenth century ruins mark the sites. That of the Bishop of Bath and Wells was near that of Chewton in the hollow between Priddy Nine Barrows and Stock Hill. A few miles to the north is Harptree. 'West Minery' is at Charterhouse.

(3) London ironmongers shops, 1221.

Street names in old towns like the city of London show where once stood the booths of dealers in wood, fish, milk, meat, bread, poultry, skins, mercery, drapery or shoes. John Stow, writing in Elizabeth's reign about old London, found many references to ironmongers dwelling in Ironmonger Lane off Cheapside near the Mercers' Chapel in the reign of Edward I. He did not quote the following detailed description of shops there although he read the manuscript book in which it comes. These shops lay in the parish of St. Mary Colechurch near the birthplace of St. Thomas Becket, whose sister had given a rent in the parish to the Nuns of Clerkenwell.

Further Reading: H. R. Ellis Davidson, 'Weland the Smith', *Folklore*, vol. 69, Sept. 1958.

Source: translated from W. O. Hassall, *Cartulary of St. Mary Clerkenwell*, Camden third series, vol. 71, p. 140 (grant by Matthew Blund).

The first smith.   Eleventh century drawing.
(Caedmon MS.)

Eight shops built of stone in the Ironmongery on the north of my main house reaching from my wooden shops on the west to my ninth shop on the east. The first and most westerly has an upper chamber and measures in frontage along the king's highway 9' 2" and in depth 12' 10" and on the inner side 8' 3". The *solar* [upper room] above measures the same. The second shop and *solar* have 6' 10" frontage, 15' 4½" depth. The *solar* on top measures the same. The third shop has 6' 11" frontage and 15' 9" depth with *solar* above measuring the same. The fourth shop has 7' 4½" frontage and 17' 7½" depth with *solar* measuring the same only. The fifth shop has 7' 2½" frontage and 18' 9" depth with *solar* ditto. The sixth shop 17' 6½" in frontage and 7' 4½" depth with *solar* ditto. The seventh shop 7' 2½" frontage and 16' 2¾" depth with solar *ditto*.

(4) Nails.

Seven tons of Roman nails were unearthed at Inchtuthil in 1961. In 1390 stores at Calais included 494,900 nails of various kinds, but Salzman finds that there was no uniformity in the use of the numerous technical sounding names for different varieties. ' For lack of a nail a shoe was lost, for lack of a shoe a horse was lost, for lack of a horse a rider was lost, for lack of a rider a battle was lost—and all for the lack of a horseshoe nail.'

Source: Exchequer list of nails bought for York Castle in 1327, printed by L. F. Salzman, *Building in England down to* 1540, *a documentary history*, Clarendon Press, 1952, chapter on Ironwork and Nails, p. 304.

> 220 braggenayl, at 15d. the hundred
> [the great hundred, i.e. six score].
> 100 knopnayl, at 6d.
> 3,260 doublenail, at 4d.
> 1,200 greater spyking, at 4d.
> 5,200 spyking, at 3d.
> 3,250 thaknail, at 3d.
> 1,800 lednail, at 2d.
> 300 grapnayl, at 2d.
> 7,760 stotnayl, at 2d.
> 1,100 smaller stotnayl, 1½d.
> 300 tyngilnayl, at 1d.
> 18,600 brodd', at 1d.

GOLD

Gold was produced in Ireland from perhaps as early as 2000 B.C. It also occurs in Wales, the Britons had gold coins before the Roman Conquest and British gold was regarded by Tacitus as one of the rewards of conquest. Jewelry found at Faversham and elsewhere in Kent and in the burial ship at Sutton Hoo testify to the skill of early goldsmiths working for Anglo-Saxon courts. The London goldsmiths obtained a royal charter in 1327, and Edward III succeeded, unlike Henry III, in establishing a gold coinage, like the florins and ducats of Florence and Venice. In the fifteenth century Portugal secured the golddust of West Africa and in the sixteenth century Spain obtained much gold from the New World.

Further Reading: W. Chaffers, *Gilda Aurifabrorum*, 1899; C. H. V. Sutherland, *Gold, Its Beauty, Power and Allure*, 1959

(1) *Source*: U. T. Holmes, Jr., *Daily Living in the Twelfth Century, based on the Observations of Alexander Neckam*, Madison, The University of Wisconsin Press, 1952, p. 142. For Alexander Neckam, see *W.W.I.H.*, i, 112–3 (late twelfth century).

The goldsmith should have a furnace with a hole at the top so that the smoke can get out by all exits. One hand should operate the bellows with a light pressure and the greatest diligence, so that the air inside the bellows, being pressed through the tubes, may blow up the coals and that the constant spread of it may feed the fire. Let there be an anvil of extreme hardness on which iron and gold may be softened and may take the required form. They can be stretched and pulled with the tongs and the hammer. There should be a hammer also for making gold leaf, as well as sheets of silver, tin, brass, iron, or copper. The goldsmith must have a very sharp chisel by which he can engrave in amber, diamond . . . . or marble, or jacinth, emerald, sapphire, or pearl, and form many figures. He should have a hardness stone for testing metals, and one for comparing steel with iron. He must also have a rabbit's-foot for smoothing, polishing, and wiping the surface of gold and silver, and the small particles of metal should be collected in a leather apron. He must have small boxes, flasks, and containers, of pottery, and a toothed saw and a gold file, as well as gold and silver wire, by which broken objects can be mended or properly constructed. The goldsmith should be skilled in feathery work as well as in bas-relief, in fusing as well as in hammering. His apprentice must have a waxed or painted table, or one covered with clay, for portraying little flowers and drawing in various ways. That he may do this conveniently let him have litharge and chalk. He must know how to distinguish solid gold from brass and copper, that he may not purchase brass for gold. . . .

(2) This list of goods shows what burglars found in a London shop. The burglars were able to read and claimed ' benefit of clergy ' exempting them from a normal secular trial.

Source: London, Letter-Book F, translated by H. T. Riley, *Memorials of London*, 1868, p. 470. (1382)

2 silver girdles, with red *corses* in silk [silk braid], value 46s.; one other small silver chain, 5s.; one girdle of red silk, with a *bokele*, and studded with silver gilt, 16s.; one silver chalice, with paten, 38s.; 2 sets of phials of silver, their *swages* (necks) gilt, 20s.; one osculatory [pax-bread] of silver gilt, 20s.; two mazer cups, bound with silver gilt, 33s. 4d.; 6 silver spoons, 14s.; 2 gold rings, with two *dynamaundes*, 15 £; one gold ring with a *balaye* [a pale rose kind of ruby inclining to orange], 26s. 8d.; 3 strings of pearls, 70s.; 6 gold necklaces, 100s.; and other goods and chattels,

such as formails [buckles or clasps] and rings of silver gilt, broken
silver, girdles set with silver, buckles and pendants for girdles,
and *paternosters*, of silver and pearls, to the value of 40 £; which
goods and chattels the same Walter atte Watre and Nicholas
Somersete, on the Wednesday next after the Feast of the Assump-
tion of the Blessed Virgin Mary, in the year aforesaid, feloniously
stole by night at the corner of Fridaystrete in Westchepe, in the
Parish of St. Matthew, in the Ward of Farndone Within, in
London, and then and there feloniously broke into the shop of
him, John Frensshe, etc. . . . .

MENDIP SILVER

Abbot Nicholas Litlyngton of Westminster left over 120 pieces of
silver plate. This is one of a number of ' strikes ' of ore reported in
the Mendips in the early fourteenth century.

Further Reading: Charles Oman, *English Church Plate, 597–1830*,
Oxford University Press, 1957.

Source: A letter from a landreeve to the Bishop of Bath and Wells,
translated from Ancient Correspondence in the Public Record Office
by L. F. Salzman, *English Industries of the Middle Ages*, Clarendon Press,
1923, p. 65.

Know, my lord, that your workmen have found a splendid
mine of lead on the Mendips to the east of Priddy, and one that
can be opened up with no trouble, being only five or six feet
below the ground. And since these workmen are so often
thieves, craftily separating the silver from the lead, stealthily
taking it away, and when they have collected a quantity fleeing
like thieves and deserting their work, as has frequently happened
in times past, therefore your bailiffs are causing the ore to be
carried to your court at Wookey where there is a furnace built at
which the workmen smelt the ore under supervision of certain
persons appointed by your steward. And as the steward, bailiffs,
and workmen consider that there is a great deal of silver in the
lead, on account of its whiteness and sonority [ringing sound],
they beg that you will send them as soon as possible a good and
faithful workman upon whom they can rely. I have seen the first

piece of lead smelted there, of great size and weight, which when it is struck rings almost like silver, wherefore I agree with the others that if it is faithfully worked the business should prove of immense value to yourself and to the neighbourhood, and if a reliable workman is obtained I think that it would be expedient to smelt the ore where it is dug, on account of the labour of carrying so heavy a material such a distance. The ore is like grains of sand.

COINAGE

Coins were struck before the Roman conquest. Roman coins were not struck in Britain until the late third century when the principal mint was at London. In the seventh century there was a mint for gold coins at Canterbury and there Offa had made the first silver pennies, the characteristic coin of medieval England. Howel Dda was the only Welsh prince to issue coins. Shillings were used in reckoning, but were not coined before the fifteenth century. Edward III issued gold as well as silver coins in 1344, and from 1346 the ratio between gold and silver remained unchanged until South American silver flooded the market.

Further Reading: G. C. Brooke, *English Coins from the Seventh Century to the Present Day*, 1932; Sir John Craig, *The Mint*, 1953.

(1) *Source*: The Laws of King Aethelstan (succeeded 924), I, 14. B. Thorpe, *Ancient Laws and Institutes of England*, 1840, p. 88.

We ordain . . . that there be one money over all the king's dominion, and that no man mint except within port. And if the moneyer [maker of coin] be guilty, let the hand be struck off with which he wrought that offence, and be set up on the money-smithy; but if it be an accusation, and he is willing to clear himself; then let him go to the hot-iron, and clear the hand therewith with which he is charged that fraud to have wrought. And if at the ordeal he should be guilty, let the like be done as is here before ordained.

In Canterbury 7 moneyers—4 the king's and 2 the bishop's and 1 the abbot's.

At Rochester 3—2 the king's and 1 the bishop's.

At London 8.

At Winchester 6.
At Lewes 2.
At Hastings 1.
Another at Chichester.
At Hampton 2.
At Wareham 2.
At Exeter 2.
At Shaftesbury 2.
Else, at the other burgs 1.

(2) *Source*: The Laws of Ethelred (986–1016), IV, 5. *Id.* p. 128.

. . . And any moneyers who work in woods or operate in similar places, are to be liable to the death penalty, unless the king should wish to show mercy.

(3) *Source*: Treatise on the New Money, Late thirteenth century, translated in C. Johnson, *The De Moneta of Nicholas Oresme and English Mint Documents*, Nelson, 1956, pp. 89–91.

. . . there are in the London Mint two persons concerned with keeping the king's dies; one on behalf of the king, whose duty it is to buy the iron and steel, and to have the finished plates conveyed from the smith to the hands of the engraver of the dies, and to deliver the dies engraved duly prepared for use as often as money has to be struck and coined, and to see that the moneyers strike the blanks in view of the public; and another on behalf of John de Botetourt, who is married to the daughter and heir of Thomas FitzOtho, who has the hereditary duty of cutting the king's dies used throughout England, and receives for the engraving and fashioning of every dozen dies, seven shillings. It is also his duty to deface the worn-out dies so that they may not be used again, and to keep in his hands all the old dies to the use of his master, and for his fee. But because an indenture is made between these two keepers, both of the new dies and of the old and worn-out ones, and both of their deliveries and their restitutions, and because it is their affair to answer to the Barons of the King's Exchequer and to their Warden how many pounds have been coined with each worn-out die at London, Canterbury, St. Edmund's, Durham and elsewhere, when coining has been going

18. March, pruning

19. June, weeding

20. July, mowing with scythe

21. August, reaping

22. September, threshing

23. October, sowing

24. Harry the Hayward

25. November, butcher

26. Peter the Pinder who
impounds stray stock

PLATE VI

MINERALS

27. Lead miner with hammer
    (*cf.p.* 24)

28. Iron miner with pick,
    candle and hod (*cf. p.* 27)

on all over England by the aforesaid indenture and by a tally made between the smith, the engraver and themselves; it is expedient and well worth while that the Warden of any mint, as often as he sends to London for dies and receives new dies from the keepers and restores the old ones, should enrol the day of the receipt of the new dies and the restitution of the old and the sum of money struck with them, to the best of his recollection. . . When the Master of the Mint has brought the pence, coined, blanched and made ready, to the place of trial, e.g. the Mint, he must put them all at once on the counter which is covered with canvas. Then, when the pence have been well turned over and thoroughly mixed by the hands of the Master of the Mint and the Changer, let the Changer take a handful in the middle of the heap, moving round nine or ten times in one direction or another, until he has taken six pounds. He must then distribute these two or three times into four heaps, so that they are well mixed. Then he must weigh out, from these well mixed pence, three pounds . . . correct to a grain . . . one pound to the Warden to count, another to the Master of the Mint, the third to any company or to himself, and they shall count diligently . . . [Payment of shearers and moneyers and Methods of assaying follow.]

(4) Cash.

Money was kept in chests (see p. 116), or in purses. Part of a very handsome early English purse has been found at Sutton Hoo. Chaucer's Summoner spoke of a man whose soul was in the purse. Chaucer here speaks of his own as being his ' lady dear '. Spare money was invested by buying land or articles of gold or silver. Some deposited it for safe keeping in a religious place like the Temple.

Source: The Compleint of Chaucer to his Empty Purse. (late fourteenth century)

> To you, my purse, and to non other wight
> Compleyne I, for ye be my lade dere!
> I am so sory, now that ye be light;
> For certes, but ye make me hevy chere,
> Me were as leef be leyd up-on my bere;
> For whiche un-to your mercy thus I crye:
> Beth hevy ageyn, or elles mot I dye!

D

Now voucheth sauf this day, or hit be night,
That I of you the blissful soun may here,
Or see your colour lyk the sonne bright,
That of yellownesse hadde never pere.
Ye be my lyf, ye be my hertes stere,
Quene of comfort and of good companye:
Beth hevy ageyn, or elles mot I dye!

(5) Usury.

Source: Penitential of Archbishop Ecgbert (735–766). B. Thorpe, *Ancient Laws and Institutes of England*, 1840, p. 373.

It is forbidden to all believers to lend money or goods for any unjust interest. That is to say no demand is to be made for a return of more than what was originally lent; but anyone who makes a loan of money or goods to another must do it for love and out of necessity, just as he would wish that it were done to himself. If any one do this out of wicked avarice, the sacred books prescribe for him a fast of 3 years, 1 year with bread and water and 2 according as his confessor prescribes for him. . . .

If a bishop or an abbot or a priest or any minister of God whatsoever makes a loan of money for interest which is unjust and does not remember that which the Saviour says through the Psalmist David that those enjoy His kingdom who do not lend their money for usury [*Psalm* 15.5]; if any violate this law he is not worthy to receive the Eucharist, before he has amended, as is written above, that is to say through a fast of 3 years.

(6) Credit.

A distinction is necessary between debts incurred through thrift-lessness and the raising of loans to pay for profitable and useful undertakings. Here is the story of Bury St. Edmunds in 1172–80.

Further Reading: M. Postan, ' Credit in Medieval Trade ', *The Economic History Review*, 1928.

Source: *The Chronicle of Jocelin of Brakelond concerning the Acts of Samson Abbot of the Monastery of St. Edmund*, translated by H. E. Butler, Nelson 1951, pp. 1–3.

. . . Abbot Hugh was grown old and his eyes waxed somewhat dim. Pious he was and kindly, a strict monk and good, but in the business of this world neither good nor wise. For he trusted those about him overmuch and gave them too much credence, relying always on the wisdom of others rather than his own. Discipline and religion and all things pertaining to the Rule were zealously observed within the cloister; but outside all things were badly handled, and every man did, not what he ought, but what he would, since his lord was simple and growing old. The townships of the Abbot and all the hundreds were given out to farm; the woods were destroyed, the houses of the manors threatened to fall in ruin, and day by day all things went from bad to worse. The Abbot found but one remedy and one consolation—to borrow money, that thus at least he might be able to maintain the honour of his house. No Easter nor Michaelmas came round during the eight years before his death but that one or two hundred pounds were added to his debt; the bonds were continually renewed, and the interest as it grew was turned into capital. This infirmity spread from the head to the members—from the superior to the subjects. And so it came about that each obedientiary [departmental bursar] had his own seal and bound himself in debt to Jews and Christians as he pleased. Often silken copes and flasks of gold and other ornaments of the church were placed in pawn without the knowledge of the Convent. I saw a bond given to William Fitz Isabel for one thousand and forty pounds, and have never known the why or the wherefore. I saw another bond given Isaac the son of Rabbi Joce for four hundred pounds, but I know not why; and yet a third to Benedict the Jew of Norwich for eight hundred and fourscore; and the cause of this last debt was as follows: our chamber was fallen in ruin, and the Sacrist, willy-nilly, undertook to restore it, and secretly borrowed forty marks at interest from Benedict the Jew and gave him a bond sealed with the seal that used to hang from the feretory [box of relics] of St. Edmund, and with which the instruments of the guilds and fraternities used to be sealed: it was broken up afterwards, at the bidding of the Convent, but all too late. Now when this debt had increased to one hundred pounds, the Jew came with letters from our Lord the King concerning the Sacrist's debt, and at last that which had been hidden from the Abbot and the Convent was revealed. . . . The same Jew also held a number of bonds for smaller debts and one that was of fourteen years' standing, so that the total debt due to him amounted to twelve hundred pounds not counting the accumulated interest. . .

(7) Jews.

The medieval church regarded loans of money for interest as sinful and Christians were forbidden to be usurers. The Norman kings protected Jews settled in London and other authorised towns and many wealthy Christians fell deeply into their debt. Christians and Jews were enemies of each other's deeply cherished beliefs and the crusading spirit found a cruel expression at the coronation of Richard I in a massacre of the London Jewry, although Jews were the property of the King. Similar atrocities at Lynn, Norwich, Bury St. Edmunds and Lincoln culminated in a massacre at York in 1190 when the poet, Rabbi Yom Tob said suicide was better than apostasy. In the thirteenth century merchants from Cahors, the ' Caorsins ', took to lending money and the Jews were expelled from England in 1290.

Further Reading: Cecil Roth, *The Challenge to Jewish History* (The Jewish Hist. Soc. of England, University College, London), 1936–7.

Source: William of Newburgh, translated in G. G. Coulton, *Medieval Panorama, the English Scene from Conquest to Reformation*, Cambridge University Press, 1938, pp. 362–3 (1190).

[The Jews of York fled to the Royal Castle where an elder advised them to kill themselves rather than fall into the hands of their persecutors]. Then, at the will of this most crazy elder, lest their foes should enrich themselves with the spoils, their precious garments were burned under the eyes of all, while the much-prized vessels, and whatsoever else could not be consumed with fire, were rendered worthless. . . . This done, they set fire to the roof: yet this, with its too solid materials, burned but slowly. While this horrible business was in progress, the elder prepared for sacrifice in rebuke to those also who had separated themselves for love of their own lives. So, when that man, grown old in evil days, directed that those who had more constancy of mind should slay their own wives and children, then that most renowned Joce cut with his keenest knife the throat of his own beloved wife Anna, nor did he spare his own children also. When the other men in turn had done thus, that most unhappy elder slaughtered Joce, as being more honourable than the rest. Soon all were slain, together with their master in error, and the tower began to burn within . . . . [Survivors begged for baptism and were promised their lives by the mob.] No sooner had they come forth than, although they constantly demanded baptism, these butchers most cruelly slew them. I myself would unhesitatingly affirm concerning these whom that beastly cruelty thus sacrificed, that if there was no falsity in their petition for holy baptism, then they were in no wise defrauded thereof; in their own blood were they baptized. But, whether it were falsely or truly that they sought the sacred font, we cannot excuse that execrable cruelty of their butchers. Beyond all doubt these men's first crime is that, without any orderly power, they presumed to shed man's blood like water. The second was, that their rage was rather in envy and malice than in righteous zeal; their third, that they grudged the Jews the Christian grace which these implored; and the fourth, that with a lie they betrayed these poor wretches . . . The whole city was indeed horrible and foul to behold, with so many miserable bodies that lay unburied all around the castle.

FAIRS

Merchants from distant lands brought rare commodities to sell at Fairs. These lasted longer than markets but were held less often. Only one fair, Aspall (Suffolk), is mentioned in Domesday Book, but fairs became important annual gatherings of merchants and customers and a profitable source of income to their owners in the thirteenth century. Famous ones were held at Winchester, granted to the Bishop by Rufus and much extended in 1233 when the powerful Peter des Roches owned it, as bishop, Weyhill (near Andover), which Piers Plowman mentions, Smithfield (Bartholomew Fair), St. Ives (Hunts., the property of Ramsey Abbey), Yarmouth (herrings), Abingdon (cattle), Boston, Stamford, Northampton, St. Edmunds and elsewhere. In the fifteenth century Stourbridge (Cambridge) overtook all others. It lasted three weeks in September and specialized in ironmongery, cloth, wool, leather and books. Booths were set up, those for particular trades being grouped together as the shops were in medieval towns. Trade rivalry could arouse hostility to particular fairs and lead to efforts to get them suppressed.

Piepowder Courts gave a chance for travellers from a distance to settle disputes without long delays. The word is derived from *pede pulverizato* or *pied poudre'* meaning ' dusty foot '. Fairs were worth much to their owners.

Further Reading: W. A. Bewes, *Romance of the Law Merchant*: *some account of the Commerce and Fairs of the Middle Ages*, 1923; W. Addison, *English Fairs and Markets*, 1953 (bibliography).

Source: Abridged English translation of rolls of piepowder court, town court, court of the fairs, and great tourn. *Caernarvon Court Rolls*, 1361–1402, ed. by G. P. Jones, Hugh Owen, 1951. Caernarvonshire Historical Society, Record Series, vol. 1.

Piepowder Court held at Caernarvon from Michaelmas 35 Edward III to Michaelmas following [29th September 1361 to 29th September 1362].

Stephen le Glouere amerced [fined] 3d. for withholding 21s. 11d. due, as he recognised to William de Haunton. An action for trespass between Dafydd ab Ieuan Wyne, plaintiff, and John Sperowe, defendant. . . . The following were amerced for failing to be present at an enquiry on behalf of the Prince [of Wales] into divers trespasses committed in the street near Simon de Farley's house during the time of market and while the court was sitting: John Stel [2d.], Stuagh [2d.], Ken' ap Goue [2d.], Einion Boledan [2d.] [and others named]. . . .

John Sparowe amerced 6d. and Gwyn ab Adda 12d. for disturbing the peace with drawn swords in the time of session.

Ken' ap Hostiler amerced 3d. for a trespass against Ranulph Champeneys. Kenrys Tew amerced 3d. for withholding a kerchief value 18d. belonging to Roger le Flechewer. . . .

MARKETS

Many markets originally sprang up through people meeting on Sundays at church. The Saxons forbade Sunday markets without success in 906, 925, 1008 and 1014. In 1275 the Bishop of Salisbury himself had Sunday markets at Warminster and Ramsbury, the Tynemouth Priory had one at Tynemouth and Battle Abbey had one which continued to be held on Sunday until the reign of Elizabeth. There was a great attempt, in part successful, to suppress them in the thirteenth century. To prevent sale of stolen goods Saxon kings wanted to confine trading to market towns (called ports) and there was a market place at Canterbury as early as the eighth century. In the thirteenth century there were 3,000 grants of rights to hold markets and larger towns had special markets for each commodity as street names like ' Cornmarket ' recall.

Further Reading: W. J. Passingham, *London Markets, their Origin and History*, 1935; *Report on Fairs and Markets* (Parliamentary Papers, vol. 37), 1889; J. L. Cate, ' The Church and Market Reform in England during the Reign of Henry III ', *Medieval and Historical Essays in Honor of J. W. Thompson*, 1938.

(1) Market Competition, 1201.

Source: *The Chronicle of Jocelin of Brakelond concerning the Acts of Samson Abbot of the Monastery of St. Edmund*, translated by H. E. Butler, Nelson, 1951, p. 132–4.

. . . the monks of Ely set up a market at Lakenheath, having the King's assent and a charter to that effect. At first we dealt peaceably with our friends and neighbours, and after sending letters to the Lord Bishop of Ely, we sent messengers to the Chapter of Ely, asking them to desist from their enterprise, and adding that, for the sake of peace and for the preservation of our mutual love, we would, in all friendship, pay them fifteen marks, which was the sum given by them to secure the King's charter. I will say no more than this; they refused to desist, and threatening words were bandied to and fro *and Roman spears menaced the spears of Rome* (Horace, *Epistles* I, i, 100). But we secured a writ of recognition to decide whether that market had been set up to our prejudice and to the detriment of the market of St. Edmund. And oath being taken, it was declared that it was done to our detriment. [The King decided against Ely]. . . The Provost of the Hundred therefore, coming thither on the market day with freemen to bear him witness, publicly on the King's behalf forbade the market, showing the letters both of the King and the Sheriff; but being received with insult and injury, he retired, having accomplished nothing. The Abbot postponed the matter for a time, being then in London; but after consulting wise men on the matter, he ordered his bailiffs to take men of St. Edmund with horses and arms and to remove the market and carry off in chains such buyers and sellers as they could find. Now about midnight some six hundred well-armed men set out for Lakenheath. But since scouts gave warning of their approach, all those who were at the market ran this way and that, so that not one of them was to be found . . . they overthrew the forked poles of the meat-market and the planks of the stalls in the market, and carried them off, and leading with them all the cattle, ' all sheep and oxen, yea, and the beasts of the field ', they proceeded towards Icklingham . . . the Bishop of Ely, an eloquent and fluent speaker, complained in person concerning this affair to the Justiciar and magnates of England, saying that an act of unprecedented arrogance had been committed on the land of St. Ethelreda in time of peace; and many others were stirred to indignation against the Abbot by his words.

SHOPS

H. M. Colvin remarks that many Oxford shops were less than 8 ft. wide while in Burford High Street in the fifteenth century some were 17½ ft. long, 7 ft. broad and 7 ft. high. Froissart describes how, when attacked, the Constable of France once was saved by falling through the half-opened hatch of a baker's shop. Surviving fifteenth century shops in Butchers' Row, Shrewsbury displayed their meat on similar hinged flaps. The Shrewsbury shops have timber frames with a projecting top floor, unlike the stone houses below. Gables faced the street.

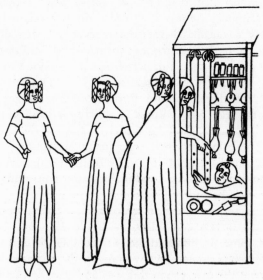

Women visiting a shop which displays belts, knives and purses. (Story of Dinah). Fourteenth Century. (Egerton Genesis).

Further Reading: H. E. Salter, Medieval Oxford, 1936. Maps of localized trades in Bruges, Paris and London in George Unwin, The Gilds and Companies of London, Methuen, 1908, pp. 31–4.

Source: ' London Lickpenny ', formerly attributed to John Lydgate, Minor Poems of Lydgate (? d. 1451), ed. J. O. Halliwell, 1840.

> Then to the Chepe I began me drawne,
> Where mutch people I saw for to stande;
> One ofred me velvet, sylke and lawne,
> An other he taketh me by the hande,
> ' Here is Parys thred, the fynest in the land ';
> I never was used to such thyngs indede,
> And wantyng mony I myght not spede.
> Then went I forth by London stone,
> Throughout all Canwyke street;
> Drapers mutch cloth me offred anone . . .
> Then I hyed me into Est-Chepe;
> One cryes rybbes of befe, and many a pye;
> Pewter pottes they clattered on a heape;
> There was harpe, fyfe, and mynstrelsye . . .
> The taverner took mee by the sleve,
> ' Sir,' sayth he, ' wyll you our wyne assay? '

(2) A retailer's stock at York, 1446.

Source: Translated from Testamenta Eboracensia, A selection of Wills form the Registry at York, vol. 3, Surtees Soc. vol. 45 for 1864, pp. 101–5. The original is half in Latin and half in English.

[Various lengths at various prices] Braban cloth. [Do.] Chaumpan cloth. [Do.] Laune....[Do.] Fustian. 4 ells bokeram, 16d....3 dozen Rede ledyr [leather] 9s. 2½ dozen Quysshyn-cloth, 6s. 3d....1 reme White pauper, spendable, 12d. 1 reme Spendable pauper, blak [parcel paper], 8d. 4 London coffyrs 2s. 8d. 1 Book of paper, 8d. 6 Glassez, 4d. 2 Pulder [powder] boxes, 2d. 11 Ynk hornes, 11d. 1 blak skyn, 1d. 1 Rone [deer] skyn, 1d. Spectacles, 20d. 1 dozen Gloves, cheverall [kid]. 2s. 4d. 2 Cordwaner skynse 4d....2 Barbour myrors, 2d. ½ lb. Red threde, 2d. 2 London pursez, 8d. Old Tyssuz, 6d. Threde gyrdils, 3d. Rede pursez, 3d. Barne powches, 11d. 4 Purses, rede, 3d. 2 pare Gloves, 3d. 1 Pautener [purse or scrip] of yhalowe ledir,

1d....Poyntels [writing instuments], 4d. 3 dozen Tyn chapes, 6d. Hertes of jete, 4d. Laton rynges and ulyettes [eyelets], 6d.... 3 Chapletes, 12d., 5 Rede caps, 2s. 6d., 8 Bonet caps, 2s....3 Mens bonettes, 3s., 1 dozen Single preste caps, 4d. 2 Powches, 4d. 6 Bonetes, 18d....1 little Coffre of Flanders, 2d., 12 Painted papers, 4s. 1 Tuell of twill, 10d....Canvas pokez [bags], 6d.... 12 Horns, 22d....1 Spiceplate, 3d....5 pair Knives of bone, 2s. 5 pare Doncaster knyfes, 2s. 11d. 12 pare Doncaster knyfes, 12s....1 London girdle, 2d. 14 Images, 7d....1 Woman cap, 6d. 1 Standyng cap for a boy, 1½d....6 Pursez, half peny ware, 2d. 7 Rede Gyrdyls, 3d. 3 Black gyrdyls, 4d....6 dozen Myrours, hapeny ware, 9d. 6 Comes [combs], 1½d. 8 dozen Rasyns [razors?] of Cologne, at 2s. 6d. the dozen 20s. 4 lb. Clowes [cloves], 9s. 4d....1 barell Grene Gynger weight 2 dozen and 7 lbs, 31s. 8 Pottes for Grene Gynger, 8d. 4 Pottes for Grene Gynger, 4d. Poder gynger 2 lb, 2s. & dozen and 11 lb. Pepper, at 7s. the dozen, 55s. 6d....4 lb. Suger, 4s....2 lb. Cynamonn, 2s. 4d.......1 dozen Dornyk [Tournai] pawteners [purses or scrips], 10s. 8d. 3 dozen Felt hattes, 21s.... [More purses and gloves]....Frengez, 2s. 7 Truloff [true-love] pursez, 9½d. 8 Swan weng pursez, 3s....9 pare Ledir glovez for women, 18d.... 10 pare Women Gloves, furred, 2s. 6d....3 Otter-skyns, 20d. 2 gros of Neweyere gyfts, 2s. Silke rybbans, 7 oz. at 14d. an oz., 8s. 2d. Tyssuz, 8½ oz. at 2s. 4d. an oz., 19s. 10d....3 dozen Hertes of laton, 6d....1 dozen Trewlufe pursez, 18d....2 full boxes, 2d. (etc.)

WATER MILLS

In the ancient world corn was ground in hand querns by women or slaves. From the time of Hesiod this grinding toil caused misery and fatigue. Hand querns were used in Western Ireland in the twentieth century. There were a few watermills in Roman Britain. In the middle of the third century the high king of Ireland abducted a Pictish princess. His jealous queen condemned her to grind meal daily to an impossible amount; so the king sent to Britain ' for an artificer who could construct a mill '. The Saxons built so many mills that Domesday Book records about five thousand mills in England. These had horizontal axles and were called ' undershot wheels '. In the fourteenth century ' overshot ' wheels began to appear. Nine examples are known from the second to the fourteenth centuries of water power being applied to ironworks. Millers were regarded with jealousy. Chaucer's miller was annoyed by the vivid but discreditable story of life in a mill told in *The Reves Tale*.

Further Reading: E. C. Curwen, ' Early Water Mills ', *Antiquity*, no. 71, 1944; R. Bennett and J. Elton, *History of Corn Milling*, 4 vols., 1898.

Eel traps and water-mill. c. 1340. (Luttrell Psalter).

(1) Mill-stones, 1330–1.

An important purchase of five foreign millstones meant special journeys over the Chilterns to London whence they were sent up the Thames by water to Henley. They cost £3 3s. 4d. each. The position of Cuxham and the adjoining market town of Watlington was favoured as compared with other places along the ' spring-line ' at the foot of the Chilterns because there alone was the water of sufficient force to work mills. There is still a mill-house at Cuxham.

Source: Translated from the Cuxham, Oxon, Manorial Accounts, 1330–1, Merton College, Oxford, by J. E. Thorold Rogers, *History of Agriculture and Prices in England*, vol. 1, 1259–1400, Clarendon Press, 1866. The Cuxham accounts are some of the finest in existence and are being edited for the Oxfordshire Record Society.

Argentum dei, i.e. the luck or bargain penny, 1d.

Five gallons of wine bought for the same, ' pro beveria ', 2s. 1d.

Loading in a ship at London, 5s.

Wharfage, 7½d.

Murage [tax for repair of city walls], 10d.

Carriage, London to Henley, 11s. 2d.

Murage at Mayden-church [Maidenhead], 10d.

Journey of bailiff, servant, and horse, to and from London, 3s. 0¼d., the journey taking three days.

Expenses on another occasion for four days in seeing to the carriage of the stones, 4s.

Expenses of three men for three days at Henley boring the stones, and the expenses of two carters carrying two stones to Cuxham, 3s. 9d. Iron bought, 2½d.

Steel bought for ' biles ' to bore the stones, 9d.

Smith for making the biles and sharpening them again and again, 2s.

Two hoops bought for carrying two stones to Oxford, 6d.

WINDMILLS

The earliest genuine reference to a European windmill occurs about 1180 in Normandy and the earliest picture is in the ' Windmill Psalter ', written at Canterbury about 1270. Windmills are mentioned in Persia in the seventh, and again in the tenth century, but the construction of Eastern windmills is different from, and less efficient than, Western mills. Within a century of their introduction windmills became a common means of providing power. They were sometimes built on city walls.

The importance of grinding corn in a fortified place, for unground corn lasts longer than meal, encouraged the development of windmills. They were too, a device for breaking the monopoly of watermills. In the Holkham Bible a windmill is one of the symbols of worldly wealth in the scene of the Temptation of Christ.

It is a postmill in which the whole mill revolves to face the wind on a wooden stand. Later mills were immobile and had a cap at the top which alone revolved. These appear in the fifteenth century.

Windmill, c. 1330. (Holkham Bible).

Further Reading: Rex Wailes, *Windmills in England,* 1948; J. Salmon, ' The Windmill in English Medieval Art ', *Journal of the British Archaeological Association,* 3rd Series, vol. 6, 1941.

Source: The Chronicle of Jocelin of Brakelond concerning the Acts of Samson Abbot of the Monastery of St. Edmund, translated by H. E. Butler, Nelson and Sons, 1951, pp. 59–60. (1191)

Herbert the Dean set up a windmill on Haberdun; and when the Abbot heard this, he grew so hot with anger that he would scarcely eat or speak a single word. On the morrow, after hearing mass, he ordered the sacrist to send carpenters thither without delay, pull everything down, and place the timber under safe custody. Hearing this, the Dean came and said that he had the right to do this on his free fief, and free benefit of the wind ought not to be denied to any man; he said also that he wished to grind his own corn there and not the corn of others, lest perchance he might be thought to do this to the detriment of neighbouring mills. To this the Abbot, still angry, made answer, ' I thank you as I should thank you if you had cut off both my feet. By God's face, I will never eat bread till that building be thrown down. You are an old man, and you ought to know that neither the King nor his Justiciar can change or set up anything within the liberties of this town without the assent of the Abbot and the Convent. Why have you then presumed to do such a thing? Nor is this thing done without detriment to my mills, as you assert. For the burgesses will throng to your mill and grind their corn there to their heart's content, nor should I have the lawful right to punish them, since they are free men. I would not even allow the Cellarer's mill, which was built of late, to stand, had it not been built before I was Abbot. Go away,' he said, ' go away; before you reach your house, you shall hear what will be done with your mill.' But the Dean, shrinking in fear from the face of the Abbot, by the advice of his son Master Stephen, anticipated the servants of the Abbot and caused the mill which he had built to be pulled down by his own servants without delay, so that, when the servants of the Sacrist came, they found nothing left to demolish.

A HORSE-MILL

A woman might own a mill but it might not always be a great source of profit.

Source: *The Book of Margery Kempe, A modern version by W. Butler-Bowdon*, Jonathan Cape 1939, pp. 28–9. (1436)

Yet she left not the world altogether, for she now bethought herself of a new housewifery. She had a horse-mill. She got herself two good horses and a man to grind men's corn, and thus she trusted to get her living. This enterprise lasted not long, for in a short time after, on Corpus Christi Eve, befell this marvel. This man, being in good health of body, and his two horses sturdy and gentle, had pulled well in the mill beforetime, and now he took one of these horses and put him in the mill as he had done before, and this horse would draw no draught in the mill for anything the man might do. The man was sorry and essayed with all his wits how he should make this horse pull. Sometimes he led him by the head, sometimes he beat him, sometimes he cherished him and all availed not, for he would rather go backwards than forward. Then this man set a sharp pair of spurs on his heels and rode on the horse's back to make him pull, and it was never the better. When the man saw it would work in no way, he set up this horse again in the stable, and gave him corn, and he ate well and freshly. And later he took the other horse and put him in the mill, and like his fellow did, so did he, for he would not draw for anything the man might do. Then the man forsook his service and would no longer remain with the aforesaid creature. Anon, it was noised about the town of [Lynn] that neither man nor beast would serve the said creature.

Then some said she was accursed; some said God took open vengeance on her; some said one thing and some said another. Some wise men, whose minds were more grounded in the love of Our Lord, said it was the high mercy of Our Lord Jesus Christ that called her from the pride and vanity of the wretched world.

DRINKINGS OF THE BRISTOL CRAFT GILDS

At Bodmin there were about 40 religious gilds. Wymondham had 10 gilds, Lynn had 75 and there were 909 gilds in Norfolk. Gilds at Thame and Abingdon kept local roads repaired.

Source: *The Great Red Book of Bristol, pt. 1*, ed. by E. W. W. Veale, Bristol Record Society, vol. 4, 1933, pp. 125–6.

Memorandum that the xx^{ti} day of May [1450] . . . William Canynges Mayre of the town of Bristow . . . with alle the notable and worthi persones beyng assembled in the Commune Councell House of the seide town the day and yere aboue said havyn ordeyned establed and graunted that the drinkynges on Seynt Iones nyght and Seint Petres nyght from this tyme forward shall vtterly be lefte a monge persones of Craftes goynge tho nyghtes be fore the seide Mayre Sheref and notable persones and her successoures And that the Mayre for the tyme beyng shall ordeyne at his dispence wyne to be disposed to the seyde craftes to ther halles a seynt Iones day vnder the forme that folweth. And the Sheref for the tyme beyng on seynt Petres day in lyke wyse Alwey purveyed, that the seyde persones of Craftes shall send their own seruantis and ther own pottes for the seide wyne which ordinance and establyshment the seide Mayre Sheref and notable persones comaunded me Iohn Ioce her commune Clerke in ther boke of recorde to enacte which is this

In primis to the Weuers		Hopers	iij gal.
	x galons'		
Item to the Toukers	x gals.		
Item Dyers	v gal.	Barbours and Wexmakers	
			iiij gal.
Item Taylours	viij gal.	Coruesers	viij gal.
Item Skynners	iiij gal.	Tanners	iiij gal.
Item Bouchers	vj gal.	Whitawers	iiij gal.
Item Bakers	v gal.	Bowyers and Flechers	ij gal.
Item Bruers	v gal.	Wyredrawers	iij galons
Smithes Ferrours Cotillers			
Lokyers and Cardemakers		Shermon'	v galons
	iiij gals.		

Masons   iij gal.
Tylers   iij gal.
Carpenters   iij gal.

Note: Coruesers are shoemakers, waxmakers are chandlers and whitawyers are dressers of white leather with alum, salt and other mixtures.

The first process to which cloth is submitted after leaving the loom is fulling or ' towking ', to clean, thicken, and scour it. Trampling in a trough was superceded by a fulling mill. Thereafter the cloth was dried, stretched on tenters.

LONDON CRAFTS, 1422

Source: A list of the names of all the crafts exercised in London from of old, and still continuing in this ninth year of King Henry V, and here set down in case it may in any wise profit the hall and Company of Brewers (1922). G. Unwin, *The Gilds and Companies of London*, Methuen 1908, pp. 370–371 translating document reproduced from Brewers' Records on p. 167.

Weaving. Fourteenth century.
(Egerton Genesis).

Mercers, Grocers, Drapers, Fishmongers, Goldsmiths, Vintners, Skinners, Tailors, Saddlers, Ironmongers, Girdlers, Cordwainers [a worker in cordovan or cordwain, a hoemaker],

PLATE VII

BUSINESS

29. 'Merours also large and brode and ffor the syght, wonder gode.' Woman's shop. The customer, with pointed stick and purse, sees his lady's face in the mirror. Combs, curlers, cosmetics, and glazed windows (*cf. p.* 40)

30. Grist for the mill (*cf. p.* 43)

PLATE VIII

CRAFTSMEN

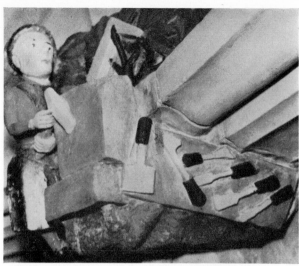

31. Tools of mason building Babel (*cf. p.* 49)

32. Noah the shipwright

Haberdashers, Cutlers, Armourers, Weavers (wool), Weavers (linen), Fullers, Dyers, Plasterers, Carpenters, Pewterers, Plumbers, Joiners, Founders, Leathersellers, Bakers, Shearmen, Lorimers [makers of horse-furniture], Waxchandlers, Tallowchandlers, Tanners, Curriers [dressers of tanned leather], Pouchmakers, Bowyers, Fletchers, Horners, Spurriers [makers of spurs], Hatters, Cofferers, Pointmakers, Wiremakers, Cardmakers [makers of combs for carding or combing wool or flax], Pinners, Whittawyers (see p. 48), Leather-dyers, Stainers, Hostillers [inn-keepers], Cooks, Piemakers, Bellmakers, Corsours [horse-dealers], Chariotmakers, Broochmakers, Jewellers, Paternosters [makers of rosaries], Turners, Bookbinders, Writers of Texts, Stationers, Poulters, Clockmakers, Chapemakers [makers of metal plates for the points of scabbards, etc.], Sheders [combers], Malemakers [trunk makers], Tablemakers, Lockyers, Fourbours [polishers], Burlesters [cloth dressers?] Lateners [workers in brass], Potters, Stuffers, Fruiterers, Cheesemongers, Stringers, Basketmakers, Barbers, Brewers, Butchers , Tapicers [tapestry makers], Broderers, Painters, Salters, Brasiers [brass workers], Smiths, Hurers [hatters], Woodmongers, Writers of Courtletters, Limners [artists], Leches [doctors], Ferrours [ironworkers], Coppersmiths, Upholders [upholsterers], Galochemakers, Carvers, Glassiers, Felmongers [dealers in skins], Woolmen, Cornmongers, Blacksmiths, Ropers, Lanternmakers, Haymongers, Bottlemakers, Marblers, Netmakers, Potmakers, Glovers, Hosiers, Orglemakers [organ makers], Soapmakers.

TOOLS

The simpler tools are unchanged since Roman times as exhibits from Silchester at Reading University show.

Further Reading: Lynn White, ' Technology and Invention in the Middle Ages ', *Speculum*, vol. 15; V. G. Childe, *Story of Tools* (Story of Science Series), 1944.

Source: Duties of a Reeve (eleventh century). Skeat's translation from W. Cunningham, *The Growth of English Industry and Commerce*, Cambridge University Press, 1915, I, 575.

He should provide many tools for the homestead, and get many implements for the buildings:

E

An axe, adze, bill, awl, plane, saw, climbe-iron [? spoke-shave], tie-hook [? vice or hook], auger, mattock, prise [lever], share, coulter; and also a goad-iron, scythe, sickle, weed-hook, spade, shovel, woad-dibble, barrow, besom, beetle, rake, fork, ladder, horse-comb and shears, fire-tongs, weighing-scales, and many spinning-implements, [such as]: flax-threads, spindle, reel, yarn-winder, stoddle [an unknown weaving tool], weaver's beams, press, comb, carding-tool, weft, woof, wool-comb, roller, slay [?], winder with bent handle, shuttle, seam-pegs [to hold things for sewing], shears, needle, slick-stone.

And if he has skilled workmen, he should provide them with tools. As for the mill-wright, shoe-maker, plumber, and other artisans, each work itself shews what is necessary for each; there is no man that can enumerate all the tools that one ought to have.

One ought to have coverings for wains, ploughing-gear, harrowing-tackle, and many things that I cannot now name; as well as a measure, an awl, and a flail for the threshing-floor, and many implements besides; as, a caldron, leaden vessel, kettle, ladle, pan, crock, fire-dog, dishes, bowls with handles, tubs, buckets, a churn, cheese-vat, bags, baskets, crates, bushels, sieves, seed-basket, wire-sieve, hair-sieve, winnowing fans, troughs, ashwood-pails, hives, honey-bins, beer-barrels, bathing-tub, bowls, butts, dishes, vessels, cups, strainers, candle-sticks, salt-cellar, spoon-case, pepper-horn, chest, money-box, yeast-box, seats [?], foot-stools, chairs, basins, lamp, lantern, leathern bottles, box for resin [or soap?], comb, iron bin, rack for fodder, fire-guard, meal-ark, oil-flask, oven-rake, dung-shovel.

It is toilsome to recount all that he who holds this office ought to think of; he ought never to neglect anything that may prove useful, not even a mouse-trap, nor even, what is less, a peg for a hasp. Many things are needful for a faithful reeve of a household and for a temperate guardian of men.

DISTAFFS

The Holkham Bible is typical in showing Eve spinning while Adam delves. Spindle whorls, commonly found on early inhabited sites, and, later, spinning wheels, could not keep pace with the demand by weavers for spun wool. So universal was spinning that the female side of a family is called ' the distaff ' side, and in medieval pictures women are often shown with a distaff, sometimes used as a weapon— as suggested in the incidental allusion here and the drawing on p. 110.

Further Reading: R. Petterson, ' Spinning and Weaving ', in C. Singer, E. J. Holmyard, A. R. Hall and T. I. Williams, *A History of Technology*, vol. 2, Clarendon Press 1956, pp. 191–220.

(1) Late twelfth century.

Source: *The Chronicle of Jocelin of Brakelond concerning the Acts of Samson Abbot of the Monastery of St. Edmund*, translated by H. E. Butler, Nelson 1951, pp. 99–100.

Many wondered at the changes in ancient customs that were made by order of the Abbot or with his permission. From the time when the town of St. Edmund received the name and liberty of a borough, men used at the beginning of August to give the Cellarer one penny for each house towards the cutting of our corn, which due was called ' repselver '. And before the town received its liberty, all of them used to reap as though they had been serfs: only the dwellings of knights, chaplains, and servants of the court were exempt from such a due. But in process of time the Cellarer spared some of the richer men of the town, demanding nought of them; wherefore the other burgesses seeing this said openly that no man, who had a messuage of his own, should pay that penny, but only those who hired houses that belonged to others. And afterwards they all in common demanded this liberty, speaking to the Lord Abbot on the matter and offering him a yearly payment in lieu of this exaction. And noting how the Cellarer went through the town to collect the repselver without any regard to his dignity, and how he caused security for payment to be taken in the houses of the poor, sometimes three-legged stools, sometimes doors and sometimes other utensils, and how old women came out with their distaffs, threatening and abusing the Cellarer and his men, the Abbot ordered that twenty shillings should be given to the Cellarer every year

at the next portmanmoot before August, this sum to be paid
through the town reeve by burgesses who assigned a revenue for
the payment of this due. This was done and confirmed by our
charter.

(2) Late fourteenth century.

Source: Chaucer, *The Wife of Bath's Prologue*.

> Deceite, weping, spinning god hath give
> To women kindely, whyl they may live;

SKINS USED FOR BOATS

Coracles are still used by those fishing for salmon. They are boats
made of skins stretched on wooden frames and can be seen in Gloucester Museum. Similar boats, called curraghs, went to sea. Caesar
describes their construction in his *Civil War* and used them in Spain
in 49 B.C. In the sixth century St. Brendan used one, stocked with
food for forty days, and butter to dress the skins.

Further Reading: James Hornell, *British Coracles and Irish Curraghs*,
London 1938.

Source: Gerald the Welshman, *Description of Wales*, translated by
Sir R. C. Hoare, 1806, pp. 332–2. (1188)

The boats which they employ in fishing or in crossing the
rivers are made of twigs, not oblong nor pointed, but almost
round, or rather triangular, covered both within and without with
raw hides. When a salmon thrown into one of these boats strikes
it hard with his tail, he often oversets it, and endangers both the
vessel and its navigator. The fishermen, according to the custom
of the country, in going to and from the rivers, carry these boats
on their shoulders; on which occasion that famous dealer in
fables, Bledherc, who lived a little before our time, thus
mysteriously said: ' There is amongst us a people who, when they
go out in search of prey, carry their horses on their backs to the
place of plunder; in order to catch their prey, they leap upon their
horses, and when it is taken carry their horses home again upon
their shoulders.

LEATHER POUCHES

A leather pouch or budget has given its name to the bag in which the Chancellor of the Exchequer keeps his papers. Such budgets, used in balancing pairs, were used for carrying water in days when piped supplies were rare, and such water budgets are sometimes represented on Coats of Arms. Pictures of bagpipes, played by the shepherds at Bethlehem, are common and occur in the Holkham Bible where other uses of leather bags are also illustrated in bellows, both for use on a domestic fire and at a smithy. The answer to the following Saxon riddle is ' bellows '. For leatherworkers see *T.S.I.H.*, i, 29.

Source: Old English Riddle translated by W. S. Mackie in *The Exeter Book*, pt. ii, poems ix–xxxii, Early English Text Society, O.S. no. 194, 1934 for 1933, pp. 127–8.

I saw a creature. Behind it was its belly,
hugely distended. It was served by an attendant.
a man of great strength. . .
It never dies when it must give
What is inside it to the other, but this is restored again
in its bosom, its breath is revived.
It creates a son and is its own father.

PURBECK MARBLE

Source: Extract from contract (now lost) for Beauchamp Chapel, Warwick, W. Dugdale, *The Antiquities of Warwickshire*, 1656, p. 355.

. . . John Bourde of Corff Castle in the County of Dorset Marbler 16 Maii, 35 H[enry] 6 [1457] doth covenant to make a Tombe of Marble, to be set on the said Earles grave; the said Tombe to be made well, cleane, and sufficiently, of a good and fine Marble, as well coloured as may be had in England . . . [Measurements given]. And in and about the same Tombe to make xiv. principall housings [for ' xiv. Images embossed, of Lords and Ladyes in divers vestures, called Weepers ' contracted for by William Austen, Citizen and Founder of London], and under every principall housing a goodly quarter for a Scutcheon of copper and gilt to be set in. . . The said Marbler shall pullish and clense the said Tombe in Workmanlike sort: And for all the

said Marble, carriage and work, he shall have in sterling money
xlv li.

The said Marbler covenanteth to provide, of good and well
coloured Marble, so many stones as will pave the Chapell where
the Tombe standeth, every stone containing in thicknesse two
inches, and in convenient bredth, and to bring the same to
Warwick and lay in: And for the stuff, workmanship, and carriage
of every hundred of those stones, he shall have xl s. which in the
totall comes to iv li. xiii s. iv. d.

GLASS

The Romans made window glass, Bede mentions it at Wearmouth
(674) and a Norman Castle at Ascot Doilly (Oxon.) had a pale green
glass.   But glass was rare and as late as the sixteenth century was
moved from house to house.

Further Reading: Writings by P. Nelson, C. Woodforde, J. D. Le
Couteur, B. Rackham (on Canterbury) and J. A. Knowles (on York).

Source: Chaucer, *The Book of the Duchesse*.

And, sooth to seyn [say], my chambre was
Ful wel depeynted, and with glas
Were al the windowes wel y-glased,
Ful clere, and nat an hole y-crased,
That to beholde hit was gret joye.
For hoolly al the storie of Troye
Was in the glasing y-wroght thus,
Of Ector and king Priamus,
Of Achilles and Lamedon,
Of Medea and of Jason,
Of Paris, Eleyne [Helen of Troy] and Lavyne.
And alle the walles with colours fyne
Were peynted, bothe text and glose,
Of al the Romaunce of the Rose.
My windowes weren shet echon,
And through the glas the sunne shon
Upon my bed with brighte bemes,
With many glade gilden stremes. . . .

TILES

At Holbeach there was a gild of Tilers. The most famous man called after this occupation was the leader of the Peasants' Revolt in 1381. Tilehurst near Reading was so called by the twelfth century. Many churches contain examples of ornamental floor tiles.

Further Reading: G. E. C. Knapp, ' Flemish Medieval Paving Tiles in Hampshire ', *Hants. Field Club and Archaeological Society*, vol. 20, is one of many regional studies.

Source: *Legend of Good Women*, ii, Thisbe.

'At Babiloine whylom fil it thus
The whiche toun the queen Semiramus
Leet dichen al about, and walles make
Ful hye, of harde tyles wel y-bake.'

WOODWORK

A woodworker in 1005 knew his importance as a builder of houses, ships and chests (*W.W.I.H.*, i, 31), his craft came, by the fourteenth century, to excel that of France when carpenters were the captains of an industry which was patron of lesser arts and crafts. In the *Miller's Tale* Chaucer makes the reeve, who was a carpenter, resent a story which reflected on his craft, and the carpenters were so proud of the part played by Biblical carpenters that Noah and St. Joseph at work with their adzes were portrayed on the walls of Carpenters' Hall in London. Hammer-beam roofs, especially in fifteenth-century East Anglian churches, are their chief monuments. The earliest important example to survive is the roof of chestnut made for Richard II in Westminster Hall with its 67 ft. span. For Hugh Herland, who made this marvel, see *W.W.I.H.*, i, 205.

Fine examples of chests, the main article of wooden furniture except tables, three-legged stools and the chairs of the great, are chests at Westminster Abbey and the Public Record Office.

Further Reading: J. H. Harvey, ' The King's Chief Carpenters ', *Journal of the British Archaeological Association*, 3rd ser. vol. 11, 1948. E. B. Jupp and W. W. Pocock, *An Historical Account of the Worshipful Company of Carpenters*, 1887.

(1) *Source*: Good Carpenter but bad monk, 704, Bede, *Ecclesiastical History*, translated by J. A. Giles, 1881, p. 261.

I knew a brother myself, would to God I had not known him, whose name I could mention if it were necessary, and who resided in a noble monastery, but lived himself ignobly. He was frequently reproved by the brethren and elders of the place, and admonished to adopt a more regular life; and though he would not give ear to them, he was long patiently borne with by them, on account of his usefulness in temporal works, for he was an excellent carpenter; he was much addicted to drunkenness, and other pleasures of a lawless life, and more used to stop in his workhouse day and night, than to go to church to sing and pray, and hear the word of life with the brethren. For which reason it happened to him according to the saying, that he who will not willingly and humbly enter the gate of the church, will certainly be damned, and enter the gate of hell whether he will or no. For he falling sick, and being reduced to extremity, called the brethren, and with much lamentation, and like one damned, began to tell them, that he saw hell open, and Satan at the bottom thereof; as also Caiaphas, with the others that slew our Lord, by him delivered up to avenging flames. ' In whose neighbourhood,' said he, ' I see a place of eternal perdition provided for me, miserable wretch.' The brothers, hearing these words, began seriously to exhort him, that he should repent even then whilst he was in the flesh. He answered in despair, ' I have no time now to change my course of life, when I have myself seen my judgment passed.'

Whilst uttering these words, he died without having received the viaticum [the eucharist given to persons in danger of death], and his body was buried in the remotest parts of the monastery, nor did any one dare either to say masses or sing psalms, or even to pray for him. How far has our Lord divided the light from darkness! . . . This happened lately in the province of the Bernicians, and being reported abroad far and near, inclined many to do penance for their sins without delay, which we hope may also be the result of this our narrative.

(2) *The Debate of the Carpenter's Tools* is an imaginary discussion. Some tools say the master is drunk, others say how they will work for him. The tools numbered twenty-seven and were ship axe, belte (a kind of axe), twybylle (mortising axe), wymbylle (gimlet), compass, groping iron (concave chisel), saw, whetstone, adze, chisel,

line and chalk (for marking), pricking knife (pencil), ' persore ', ' skan-
tillon' (gauge), crow, rule, plane, broad axe, ' twyvete ', ' polyff '
(awl), ' wyndas ', rule stone, gouge, cable rope, square and ' draught
nayle ' (punch).

Source: Bodleian Library, MS. Ashmole 61 fol. 23 seq.; quoted in
C. F. Innocent, *Building Construction* (Cambridge Technical Series),
1916, pp. 95–102; printed, W. Hazlitt, *Early Popular Poetry of England*,
1780–90; the tools are discussed in the light of records, by L. F.
Salzman, *Building in England down to* 1540, *a documentary history*, Clarendon Press, 1952, pp. 340–6.

The shype ax seyd unto the wryght:
Mete and drynke I schall the plyght,
Clene hose and clene schone [shoes],
Gete them wer as euer thou kane . . . .
Wherefore, seyd the belte,
With grete strokes I schalle hym pelte;
My mayster schall full welle thene,
Both to clothe [and] fede his men.
Ye, ye, seyd the twybylle,
Thou spekes euer ageyne skylle . . . .
Yis, yis, seyd the wymbylle,
I ame als rounde as a thymbyll;
My maysters werke I wylle remembyre,
I schall crepe fast into the tymbyre,
And help my mayster within a stounde [hour]
To store his cofere with xx pounde. . . .
Than seyd the whetstone:
Thoff my mayster thryft be gone,
I schall hym helps within this yere
To gete hym xx merke clere;
Hys axes schall I make fulle scharpe,
That thei may lyghtly do ther werke;
To make my master a ryche man
I schall asey, If that I canne. . .

TOWNS: ROMAN TOWNS

Parts of Roman walls survive, as at London, Colchester, York, Lincoln and Chester. At Leicester, Colchester, Lincoln, Chichester, Gloucester and Chester lines of main roads from the gates, and crossing each other at right angles, have survived through medieval into modern times, though the Roman street plans are generally blurred and dislocation has often been caused by the building of a great Cathedral or Norman castle. The desertion of Silchester near Reading meant a local change in the patterns of roads, but London, Winchester, Canterbury, Cirencester, Leicester and Lincoln remain at nodal points in the network of long through-roads designed by the Romans.

(1) St. Albans, excavations, 900. Roman bricks are a conspicuous element in the monastery church, now the Cathedral of St. Albans.

Source: Accounts of acts of Ealdred and Eadmar the eighth and ninth abbots of St. Albans. *Chronica Monasterii S. Albani, Gesta Abbatum Monasterii Sancti Albani*, ed. H. T. Riley, Rolls Series, 1867, vol. 1, pp. 24–28, translated.

He [Ealdred] made as level as possible the dykes and cellars of the city for they were frequented as refuges by criminals from the surrounding woods. He segregated any unbroken bricks or stones which were found suitable for building and kept them for the fabric of the church. For he intended, if resources allowed, to build a new church and destroy the old one. So he dug deep to find stone structures. . . .

In the time of Abbot Eadmar while the excavators were exploring the walls at a low level, they turned up in the middle of the ancient city the foundations of a great palace. While they were amazed at its size they found in a hollow in a wall, like a cupboard, an unknown volume with other lesser books and rolls. It had hardly suffered at all from the long lapse of time. The script and language were too ancient to be understood, but it was beautiful and clearly written, with golden initials and titles. It had oak boards and silk ties which largely retained their original strength and beauty. After long and wide research they found a decrepit old priest, a man of learning called Unwona. He was skilled in scripts and languages and he could easily construe the book. He also explained the other manuscripts found in the same cupboard. It was the script which used to be written when

Werlamnescestra [Verulamium] was inhabited. The language was ancient British with some Latin. . . .

In the first book he found the History of St. Alban, the Proto-martyr of the English, such as is recited every day in the church . . . but in the other books he found the invocations and rites of the heathen citizens of Warlamcestra. From these he learnt that they especially worshipped Phoebus, the god of the sun . . . and in the second place Mercury, called in English *Woden*, after whom the fourth day of the week is named. . . .

The books containing devilish matter were thrown away and burnt, and only the one containing the History of St. Alban was kept. It was placed lovingly in the treasury. . . . When a Latin translation had been written out, the original manuscript fell into dust.

When this Abbot dug deeper in the remains of Verulamium to find stones, bricks and columns needed for building the church intended for St. Alban the Martyr, the diggers found in the foundations of the ancient buildings and in underground cellars well made pots and amphorae and also glass vases containing the ashes of the dead.

(2) Caerleon visited, 1188.

Further Reading: G. Webster, *The Roman Army: an Illustrated Study*, Grosvenor Museum 1956.

Source: *Gerald the Welshman, Description of Wales*, translated by Sir R. C. Hoare, 1806, ii, 102–4.

Passing from thence [Usk] through Caerleon, and leaving far on our left hand the castle of Monmouth, and the noble forest of Dean, situated on the other side of the Wye and on this side the Severn, and which amply supplies Gloucester with iron and venison, we spent the night at Newport, having crossed the river Usk three times. Caerleon means the city of Legions, Caer, in the British language, signifying a city or camp, for there the Roman legions, sent into this island, were accustomed to winter, and from this circumstance it was styled the city of legions. This city was of undoubted antiquity, and handsomely built of masonry, with courses of bricks, by the Romans. Many vestiges of its former splendour may yet be seen; immense palaces, formerly ornamented with gilded roofs, in imitation of Roman magnificence, inasmuch as they were first raised by the Roman princes, and embellished with splendid buildings; a tower of prodigious size, remarkable hot baths, relics of temples, and theatres, all inclosed within fine walls, parts of which remain standing. You will find on all sides, both within and without the circuit of the walls, subterraneous buildings, aqueducts, underground passages; and what I think worthy of notice, stoves contrived with wonderful art, to transmit the heat insensibly through narrow tubes passing up the side walls.

Julius and Aaron, after suffering martyrdom, were buried in this city, and had each a church dedicated to him. After Albanus and Amphibalus, they were esteemed the chief protomartyrs of Britain Major. In ancient times there were three fine churches in this city: one dedicated to Julius the martyr, graced with a choir of nuns; another to Aaron, his associate, and ennobled with an order of canons; and the third distinguished as the metropolitan of Wales. Amphibalus, the instructor of Albanus in the true faith, was born in this place. This city is well situated on the river Usk, navigable to the sea, and adorned with woods and meadows. The Roman ambassadors here received their audience at the court of the great king Arthur; and here also, the archbishop Dubricius ceded his honours to David of Menevia, the metropolitan see being translated from this place to Menevia, according to the prophecy of Merlin Ambrosius. . . .

MEDIEVAL TOWNS

Compared with modern towns the size of medieval towns was minute. Of the million or million and a half inhabitants of England at the Norman Conquest perhaps twenty thousand lived in London; but only York, Norwich and Lincoln had a thousand houses and Oxford and Thetford were the only other towns approaching that number. But this does not mean that they were unimportant and the political importance of London in times of crisis was very great.

By the end of the thirteenth century there were nearly two hundred cities and boroughs in England. Of these about half had the king as their lord, while the others had lesser lords.

Further Reading: the histories of individual towns are as distinct as the histories of separate countries. Histories and records of many towns have been printed, but the full titles cannot be given here. Such are the records of London, Beverley, Cambridge, Chester, Colchester, Coventry, Gloucester, Henley, Liverpool, Leicester, Northampton, Norwich, Nottingham, Reading, Southampton, Winchester and York. The town sections of county histories are important.

James Tait, *The Medieval English Borough*, Manchester University Press 1936. (Difficult).

James Tait, ' The Study of Early Municipal History of England ', *Proceedings of the British Academy*, 1922, vol. 10.

(1) Inflammable wooden houses, 619.

Source: Bede, *Ecclesiastical History*, translated by J. A. Giles, 1881, p. 80.

. . . it happened once that the city of Canterbury, being by carelessness set on fire, was in danger of being consumed by the spreading conflagration; water was thrown over the fire in vain; a considerable part of the city was already destroyed, and the fierce flame advancing towards the bishop, when he, confiding in the Divine assistance, where human failed, ordered himself to be carried towards the raging fire, that was spreading on every side. The church of the Four Crowned Martyrs was in the place where the fire raged most. The bishop being carried thither by his servants, the sick man averted the danger by prayer, which a number of strong men had not been able to perform by much labour. Immediately, the wind, which blowing from the south had spread the conflagration throughout the city, turning to the north, prevented the destruction of those places that had lain in its way, and then ceasing entirely, the flames were abundantly extinguished. And thus the man of God, whose mind was inflamed with the fire of Divine charity, and who was wont to drive away the powers of the air by his frequent prayers, from doing harm to himself, or his people, was deservedly allowed to prevail over the worldly winds and flames, and to obtain that they should not injure him or his.

Note: Canterbury was of great political importance in early Saxon times as capital of Kent, the most prominent and civilized of the kingdoms into which England was divided, until the conversion of Northumbria. It was for this reason that archbishops ruled from Canterbury and York and not from London.

(2) Stone town houses, 1189.

Source: Henry Fitzailwine's Assize of Buildings; *Liber Albus the White Book of the City of London compiled in* A.D. 1419 *by John Carpenter and Richard Whittington*, translated by H. T. Riley, Richard Griffin, 1891, pp. 284–285.

It should be remarked, that in ancient times the greater part of the City was built of wood, and the houses were covered with straw, stubble, and the like.

Hence it happened, that when a single house had caught fire, the greater part of the City was destroyed through such conflagration; a thing that took place in the first year of the reign of King Stephen, when, by reason of a fire that broke out at London Bridge, the church of Saint Paul was burnt; from which spot the conflagration extended, destroying houses and buildings, as far as the church of Saint Clement Danes.

After this, many of the citizens, to the best of their ability, to avoid such a peril, built stone houses upon their foundations, covered with thick tiles, and so protected against the fury of the flames; whence it has often been the case that, when a fire has broken out in the City, and has destroyed many buildings, upon reaching such houses, it has been unable to do further mischief, and has been there extinguished; so that, through such a house as this the houses of the neighbours have been saved from being burnt.

Hence it is, that in the aforesaid Ordinance, called the 'Assize ', it was provided and ordained, in order that the citizens might be encouraged to build with stone, that every one who should have a stone-wall upon his own land sixteen feet in height, might possess the same as freely and meritoriously as in manner already stated; it always being the duty, that is to say, of such man's neighbour, to receive upon his own land the water falling from the house built upon such wall, and at his own cost to carry off the same; and if he shall wish to build near the wall, he is bound to make his own gutter under the eaves of the said house for receiving the water therefrom. And this, to the end that such house may remain secure and protected against the violence of fire when it comes, and so, through it, many a house may be saved and preserved unharmed by the violence of the flames.

(3) English towns, 1192.

Source: The Jew's advice to the Christian French boy, in Richard of Devizes; *Chronicles of the Crusades*, Bohn's *Antiquarian Library*, 1865, pp. 49–51.

When you have entered England, if you should come to London, you will quickly pass through it, as that city greatly displeases me. Every race of men, out of every nation which is under heaven, resort thither in great numbers; every nation has introduced into that city its vices and bad manners . . . there, in proportion as any man has exceeded in wickedness, so much is he the better . . . avoid . . . the dice, the theatre and the tavern. You will find more braggadacios there than in all France, while the number of flatterers is infinite. Stage-players, buffoons, . . . musical girls, druggists, lustful persons, fortune-tellers, extortioners, nightly strollers, magicians, mimics, common beggars, tatterdemalions—this whole crew has filled every house. . . .

. . . if you should land near Canterbury, you will have to lose your way, if even you should but pass through it. It is an assemblage of the vilest, entirely devoted to their—I know not whom, but who has been lately canonized, and had been the archbishop of Canterbury [Becket], as everywhere they die in open day in the streets for want of bread and employment. Rochester and Chichester are mere villages, and they possess nothing for which they should be called cities, but the sees of their bishops. Oxford scarcely, I will not say satisfies, but sustains, its clerks. Exeter supports men and beasts with the same grain. Bath is placed, or rather buried, in the lowest parts of the valleys, in a very dense atmosphere and sulphury vapour, as it were at the gates of hell. Nor will you select your habitation in the northern cities, Worcester, Chester, Hereford, on account of the desperate Welshmen. York abounds in Scots, vile and faithless men, or rather rascals. The town of Ely is always putrefied by the surrounding marshes. In Durham, Norwich, or Lincoln, there are very few of your disposition among the powerful; you will never hear any one speak French. At Bristol, there is nobody who is not, or has not been a soapmaker, and every Frenchman esteems soapmakers as he does nightmen. After the cities, every market, village, or town, has but rude and rustic inhabitants. Moreover, at all times account the Cornish people for such as you know our Flemish are accounted in France . . . in every place there are some good, but much fewer in them all than in Winchester alone. This is in those parts the Jerusalem of the Jews, in it they alone enjoy perpetual peace. . . . There is but one fault, and that alone in which they customarily indulge too much. With the exception of the learned and the Jews, the Winchester people tell lies like watchmen. . . . For in no place under heaven so many false rumours are fabricated so easily as there; otherwise they are true in everything.

(4) Town walls.

Source: Statute of Winchester, 13 Edward I, cap. 4 (translated as in 1577 edition).

And for the more suretie of the countrey, the king hath commanded that in greate townes beinge walled, the gates shalbe closed from the sonne resting until the sonne rysing, and that no man do lodge in suburbes, nor in any place out of the towne from 9 of the clocke untill daye, without hys hoste will answere for him, and the bailiffes of townes every weke, or the leaste every 15 daie, shal make inquiry of all persons beynge lodged in the suburbes or places of the towns. And if thei do find any that have lodged or receyved any straungers or suspicious persons, gaynste the peace, the bailiffes shall doe ryghte therein. And the kynge commaundeth that from hensforth all townes be kept as it hath ben used in times passed, that is to witte from the feast of Ascension unto Mighelmas in every citie 6 men shall kepe at every gate, in every boroughe 12 men, every towne 6 or 4 accordinge to the numbre of inhabitauntes of the towne, and shal watch the town al night from the son resting unto the son rising. And if any straunger do passe by them, he shalbe arrested unto morning. And if no suspicion be found, he shal goe quite, and if they finde cause of suspicion, they shal forthewith deliver him to the shiriffe, and the shiriffe may receive him without damage, and shal kepe him saufly until he be acquited in due maner. And if thei will not obey the arrest, they shall levie hue and crie with al the towne and the towns nere, and so from town to town, until that they be taken and delivered to the shiriff, as before is said, and for the arrestments of such straungers none shalbe punished.

33. Fuller's tools and cloth (*cf. p.* 48)

34. Monumental
masons and
patroness

PLATE X

35. Earliest road map of Great Britain, c. 1360. Wales and Severn portion. It is meant
to be seen with the east at the top (*cf. p.* 70)

TRANSPORT

(1) Rivers

Rivers had provided means of access for Saxon and Danish raiders. In time of peace they were important highways and were ranked one of England's greatest assets. The Romans made artificial links between the Witham and both the Trent at Torksey and the Nene. In the eleventh century the course of the Thames was improved to Oxford, and in 1121 Henry I recut the Foss Dyke.

Trading wealth made possible fine parish churches in towns by rivers, like Newark on Trent, and Hull, Partington and Beverley on Trent, all monuments of fourteenth century 'Decorated' taste.

Source: Sir John Fortescue, ' These be the Comodytes of Englond ', written in or before 1451, Thomas (Fortescue) Lord Clermont, *The Works of Sir John Fortescue, Knight, Chief Justice of England and Lord Chancellor to King Henry the Sixth*, London, privately printed 1869, vol. 1, p. 549.

Ffyrst Englond hath three Ryverse with in hym selffe comynge owte of the See in to the myddes of the londe, whereby the shyppes of all maner charge, of all maner natyons, may convey and seylle to in the greteste cytes of the lond, both ebbe and flodde with all manner marchandyes.

1.   The fyrst Ryver ys callyd Humber, that comyth to Yorke and so forth uppe into the contrey.

2.   The second Ryver ys called Temys, whych comyth uppe to London and so forth into the contrey.

3.   The thyrde Ryver us callyd Saverne which comyth to Brystowe and so forth into the contrey.

(2) Embanking and conservancy.

In Roman times drainage and land reclamation had been achieved at Romney Marsh and before the Norman Conquest great banks were constructed to keep back the tidal waters of the Wash. This work continued in the twelfth and thirteenth centuries. Fifteenth century Priors of Canterbury made great reclamations of Kent marshlands.

Further Reading: See p. 2.

(3) *Source*: Thames Conservancy, 1419, *Liber Albus the White Book of the City of London compiled in* A.D. 1419 *by John Carpenter and Richard Whittington*, translated by H. T. Riley, Richard Griffin 1861, pp. 498–501.

F

[A long list of official documents indicates the kind of orders made:]

That no Ship or Boat shall anchor at night, or moor, between sunset and sunrise, except at Queen-Hythe and Byllynggesgate; nor shall at night remain upon the bankside of Suthewerk, under pain of loss of vessel and imprisonment of body. . . . That Ships and Boats which come by Thames with victuals, shall lie one day in peace without selling aught. . . .

Writ for Enquiry as to Stakes and Piles driven into the bed of the water of Thames.

Writ commanding that the waters in which Salmons are taken, shall be under prohibition from the Feast of the Nativity of the Blessed May [8 September] until the Feast of Saint Martin [11 November]

Ordinance for cleansing the Hythe [landing place] of Dounegate [Dowgate]

Writ commanding that no one shall bathe in the water near the Tower Foss, or in the Thames near the Tower.

Commission appointed by the Mayor, to take certain Prisage [requisition] of Ships and Boats, for repair of Queen-Hythe

Commission for cleansing the Hythe of Est Watergate

That no one shall throw dung, rubbish, gravel, or other refuse into the Thames, Flete, or Fosses of the City. . . .

Ordinance that all Boats which go to Graveshende shall be laden at the Wharf of Seynt Botulf

That no dung shall be placed upon the said Quay

Ordinance that no one shall throw into the Thames rushes, straw, rubbish, or filth

Item, that every Boat laden with rushes, hay, or straw, shall take due care as to such refuse at its departure

Item, that every Alderman shall enquire at his Wardmote whether any person does the contrary hereof

Item, that twelve carts, each with two horses, shall be provided to carry away the filth.

Item, if any person shall be held in suspicion of having acted against this Ordinance, and shall not be willing to acquit himself by his oath, he shall incur the penalty. . . .

That no Boatman, shall take between London and Westminster more than two pence, or three pence at most, for the hire of the whole of his Boat

Commission for the levying of twelve pence from every Boat with rushes, for the Cleansing of the place where it is unloaded. . . .

Commission for the Cleansing of the Fosses of Flete [river] . . . .

That no Purpresture [encroachment] or Nuisance, by Quays or by Buildings, shall be made upon the water of Thames. . . .

Writ of his lordship King Richard, as to not throwing dung into the Thames, under penalty of forty pounds. . . .

Of the Conservancy of the Thames, and of the Liberties hereof as exhibited before his lordship the King.

(4) Weirs in the River Severn, 1252.

Magna Carta forbade obstructions to rivers caused by fishermen's weirs. In the same way in 1356 objection was made to a new Medway bridge at Rochester because it hindered barges of Kentish stone coming up for Westminster Abbey.

Source: The Index Library, *Inquisitions Post Mortem for Gloucestershire*, vol. iv (Gloucestershire Records, part 8 for 1903), British Record Society 1903. The earliest of these inquisitions relating to Gloucestershire is dated 1236. Most relate to the lands, tenants and heirs of dead tenants of the Crown. They were made in pursuance of writs. Four score survive for the reign of Henry III.

Inquisition taken before A. de Husted, sheriff of Gloucester, and Sir Matthew de Bysil, constable of Gloucester, 36 Henry III, to ascertain who after the first coronation of the King raised, removed, and enclosed the weirs in the water of the Severne to the damage of the King, otherwise than before his said coronation were wont to be made and enclosed, and who fished in the said water with nets and ' Kydells ' [weirs made of fagots] to take fresh salmon contrary to the King's prohibition, by the oath of Thomas de Templo [and others], who say that:

The Countess of Kent has a weir at Elmoure in the water of the Severne, enclosed to the damage of the King, otherwise than before his coronation, and removed upon the King's land.

And Sir William de Valencia has a weir at Eppen', enclosed as above, for which cause it was wont to be taken into the King's hand in the time of Robert de Pundelarge.

There are no fishers with nets or ' Kydells ' in the said water to take fresh salmon contrary to the King's prohibition.

Note: A charter from Richard I to the City of London granted that all kidels should be removed from the Thames.

(5) River transport,

Water transport was of great importance and gave importance to the inland ' ports ' of Cambridge, Henley, Norwich, York, and Worcester and to maritime harbours at the mouths of rivers like Lynn, Bristol and London, and in 1276 the king ordered the widening of the Avon for ships going between Bristol and Bath. Goods for the royal manor of Woodstock and for Merton College, Oxford, were landed at Henley and taken by road for the last stage of the journey. This letter shows purchases in London for the Stonors, whose house three miles from Henley is still, after 650 years, occupied by the same family, for when this letter was written they were already long established. The Borough records show that John Baker was well known in the public life of Henley. Some London merchants had interests at Henley whence grain was brought for London.

Further Reading: E. A. Pratt, *History of Inland Transport in England*, 1912.

Source: Letter from H. Unton to Sir William Stonor, 1482, *Stonor Papers*, Camden Society, 1919, vol. 2, p. 146.

Syr, as for wyne I have sent you by John Somer, to be deliveret to John Baker, a[t] Henley, 2 hogges hedes of Claret wyne, a hogges hed of red wyne, a hogges hede of white wyne. And as for spices I spake to Maister Russh; . . . thai loke for a galey comys nowe in, as he sais, and then he will by be gret [wholesale], and then ye shall have with him as moche as he will: bot he will lay down now no money for noon. And as for candell, we can have non such as ye send fore, as Taylboys can tell your Maistership. And as for fyssh, I can none by withoute money. And rysshes and sope I have send you by John Somers barge, the which wilbe at Henley opon Sonday or Monday at the forthest.

ANCIENT ROADS

Medieval travellers inherited from the past the roads which the Romans had constructed and the ancient trackways which the Romans had inherited from earlier times as dictated by the lie of the land and by what lay beneath the top soil. ' Kyng Belin ' was a legendary British ruler. The ' Laws of Edward the Confessor ' ordain peace on the Four Roadways of England.

Further Reading: I. D. Margary, *Roman Roads in Britain*, 2 vols., 1955, 1957.

F. M. Stenton, ' Road System of Medieval England ', *Economic History Review*, vol. 7, 1936.

(1) *Source*: a metrical chronicle of England written by Robert of Gloucester, who was alive about 1260–1300. His chronicle, edited by W. Aldis Wright is printed in the Rolls Series, but this extract is quoted by W. Dugdale, *The Antiquities of Warwickshire*, 1656, p. 6.

Faire weyes many on ther ben in Englonde;
But four most of all ther ben I understonde,
That thurgh an old Kyng were made ere this,
As men schal in this boke aftir here telle I wis.
Fram the South into the North takith Ermingestrete.
Fram the East into the West goeth Ikeneld strete.
Fram Southest to Northwest, that is sum del grete.
Fram Dover into Chestre goth Watlyngstrete.
The ferth of thise is most of alle that tilleth fram Toteneys.
Fram the one end of Cornwaile anone to Canteneys.

Fram the Southwest to Northest into Englondes ende
Fosse men callith thilke wey that by mony town doth wende.
Thise foure weyes on this londe Kyng Belin the wise
Made and ordeyned hem with gret Fraunchise;

ROADS

Under the Saxon kings the repair of bridges was an obligation laid upon every free tenant of land. When manor court rolls begin in the second half of the thirteenth century there are frequent references to roads being damaged by the neglect of neighbouring ditches or by people using them as quarries, but these are indications of a will to keep them passable rather than evidence of their evil condition. From time to time the Close Rolls or the Patent Rolls record royal orders for the repair of this or that important road. Medieval highways are thought to have carried some 1000 tons a year. In 1332 the journey between Oxford and Newcastle took 9 or 10 days.

Further Reading: *Public Works in Medieval Law* (Selden Soc.), 2 vols., 1915. *The Map of Great Britain circa* A.D. 1360 known as the Gough Map, facsimile with introduction by E. J. S. Parsons and Sir F. Stenton. Bodleian Library and Royal Geographical Society, 1958.

(1) *Source*: Statute of Winchester, 13 Edward I, cap 5 (translated as in 1577 edition).

And further it is commaunded, that highe waies ledyng from one market towne to an other shalbe from henceforth inlarged, where as bushes, woodes, or dykes be, so that there be neither dyke, tree, nor bushe, wherby any trespaser may escape within 200 fote of eache syde the way, so that this statute shall not extende unto ashes nor unto great trees, for that it shalbe understanden clerely out of this. And if by the defaulte of the lord, that wil not avoyde the dyke, underwoode or bushes in the maner aforesayde, any robberies bedone therein, the lorde shalbe aunswerable for the felony. And if murder be done, the lorde shall make a fine at the kings pleasure. And if the lord be not able to fell the underwoodes, the countrey shal aide him therin. And the king willeth that in his demean landes and woods within his foreste and without, the wayes shalbe enlarged [as before is sayd]. And yf percase a parke be taken from the hyghe waye, it is requisite that the lord shall sette his parke the space of 200 foote from the highe wayes, as before ys sayde, or that he make suche a wall, dyke or hedge, that the evill doers maie not passe ne retourne for to doe evill.

(2) Crossroads at Dunstable, early twelfth century.

Highway robbery was common in the Middle Ages except under such very strong rule as that of William I. Popular tradition even made a heroic legend about Robin Hood (see *W.W.I.H.*, i, p. 118). The effort by Henry I described below was followed by the terrible disorder under Stephen.

Source: College of Arms MS. translated from W. Dugdale, *Monasticon Anglicanum, A History of the Abbies and other Monasteries, Hospitals, Frieries and Cathedral and Collegiate Churches*, vol. 6, pt. 1, 1830, pp. 239–240.

The Lord Henry [I], King of England, son of William the Conqueror had in demesne [in hand] the vills of Houghton and Kenesworth. The country round Houghton where the two royal thoroughfares of Watling Street and Ickneld intersect, is so wooded in every direction and so full of robbers that a law abiding person can scarcely get through without losing his life, his limb, or his goods. The king wanted to remedy this evil so he ordered the whole district to be cleared and then built a royal palace there which he called Kingsbury. This place covers nine acres. He wanted to establish a settlement there too, so he had a proclamation made in every part of the kingdom declaring that anybody who migrated thither might have land at 12d. an acre a year. Immigrants and their heirs would have the same freedoms and privileges throughout the kingdom as the city of London or any other English borough had ever had. Thus the area was built up by such people across and along the two highways. A robber who used to operate there was called Dunning and so the town was called Dunningstable.

The king kept the town of Dunstable as a free borough in his own hands for 17½ years and its burgesses were free throughout England throughout his reign as explained; and they never had to go outside the town of Dunningstable to answer the justices in eyre or other royal officials, but such judges and officials always made a diversion and came to Dunstable . . . and he established a market twice a week and a three day fair . . . and gallows. . . At last the king built a church in honour of St. Peter at the end of the town and built a monastery, and, as he had long intended, established there a prior and canons regular [Augustinians, such as his queen had established at Aldgate, London]. He gave them . . the borough with the market and the fair.

QUICKSANDS, 1188

Medieval pictures of the loss of Pharoah's host in crossing the Red Sea were relevant to life.

The story of the loss of King John's baggage in the Wash is famous. Here is a parallel from the west coast.

Source: *Gerald the Welshman, Description of Wales*, translated by Sir R. C. Hoare, 1806, ii, 156–7.

Continuing our journey, not far from Margam, where the alternate vicissitudes of a sandy shore and the tide commence, we forded over the river Avon, having been considerably delayed by the ebbing of the sea; and under the guidance of Morgan, eldest son of Caradoc, proceeded along the sea-shore towards the river Neth [Neath], which, on account of its quicksands, is the most dangerous and inaccessible river in South Wales. A pack-horse belonging to the author, which had proceeded by the lower way near the sea, although in the midst of many others, was the only one which sunk down into the abyss, but he was at last, with great difficulty, extricated, and not without some damage done to the baggage and books. Yet, although we had Morgan, the prince of that country, as our conductor, we did not reach the river without great peril, and some severe falls; for the alarm occasioned by this unusual kind of road, made us hasten our steps over the quicksands, in opposition to the advice of our guide, and fear quickened our pace; whereas, through these difficult passages, as we then learned, the mode of proceeding should be with moderate speed. But as the fords of the river experience a change by every monthly tide, and cannot be found after violent rains and floods, we did not attempt the former, but passed the river in a boat, leaving the monastery of Neth [Neath] on our right hand, approaching again to the district of St. David's, and leaving the diocese of Landaf [which we had entered at Abergavenny] behind us.

PILGRIMS

At Ludlow those who had made pilgrimages founded a Palmer's gild.

Further Reading: T. Borenius, *Mediaeval Pilgrims' Badges*, Privately Printed, 1930. See also p. 83.

Source: Canons enacted under King Edgar (956–975). B. Thorpe, *Ancient Laws and Institutes of England*, 1840, pp. 411–2.

It is a deep penitence, that a layman lay aside his weapons and travel barefoot, and nowhere pass a second night, and fast, and watch much, and pray fervently, by day and by night, and voluntarily suffer fatigue, and be so squalid, that iron come not on hair, nor on nail.

Nor that he come into a warm bath, nor into a soft bed, nor taste flesh, nor anything from which drunkenness may come, nor that he come within a church; but yet diligently seek holy places, and declare his sins, and implore intercession, and kiss no one, but be ever fervently repenting his sins.

Roughly he fares who thus constantly criminates himself, if he never relax, till he make full 'bot' [amends]; because no man in the world is so very criminal, that he may not make atonement to God, let him undertake it fervently.

BRIDGES

The replacement of fords and ferries by bridges was regarded as a work of piety, and the Roman's word for a priest, pontifex, meant 'bridge-builder'. In Saxon times the duty of contributing to their repair was laid upon everyone. More medieval bridges survive in the remoter parts of Wales than on busier routes. Of ancient bridges Monnow Bridge at Monmouth and Warkworth Bridge, Northumberland, retain fortified towers such as once were common. Houses on bridges occur at High Bridge, Lincoln, as well as one on Elvet Bridge, Durham. Examples of chapels on bridges are Rotherham, Yorks. Bradford on Avon, Wilts, St. Ives, Hunts, and Wakefield, Yorks. The church at Henley stands at the end of the bridge and the churchwardens were identical with the bridgewardens and some endowments were common to the bridge and the church. Parts of long bridges survive at Wakefield, Chester, Durham (Framwellgate and Elvet), Hereford, Bideford, Llangollen, Dumfries, Huntingdon, St. Ives, Norwich (Bishop's Bridge), Potter's Heigham and Tewkesbury. Surviving bridges with single arches are more common. The longest is that over the moat at Norwich Castle. Bridges occur on seals of Stirling, Barnstaple, Bideford, Bridgewater, Cambridge and Grampound. Local gilds helped to build bridges at Abingdon and Stratford-on-Avon.

Further Reading: W. J. and S. R. Watson, *Bridges in History and Legend*, 1937. E. Jervoise, *Ancient Bridges of England*, 4 vols., 1930–6.

Source: Olaf the Stout breaks through London Bridge, 1009, *The Saga of St. Olaf* (King Olaf), quoted by R. R. Sellman, *The Vikings*, Methuen's Outlines, 1959 reprint, p. 64.

Olaf had large hurdles made of withies and soft wood, so cut as to make a wicker-house, and thus covered his ships, so that the hurdles reached out over their sides; he had posts put beneath them so high that it was easy to fight beneath them, and the covering was proof against stones thrown down on it. When the host was ready they rowed up the river; as they came near the bridges they were shot at, and such large stones thrown down on them that neither their helmets nor shields could withstand them; and the ships themselves were greatly damaged, and many retreated. But Olaf and the Northmen with him rowed up under the bridges, and tied ropes round the supporting posts and rowed their ships down stream as hard as they could. The posts were dragged along the bottom until they were loosened from under the bridges. As an armed host stood thickly on the bridges, and there was a great weight of stones and weapons upon them, and the posts beneath were broken, the bridges fell with many of the men into the river; the others fled into the city, or into Southwark. After this they attacked Southwark, and captured it. [Tooley St., Southwark, commemorates the name of St. Olaf.]

HORSES

The horse, as a beast of burden, had rivals in the ox and the ass, but was of tremendous importance as a means of personal transport. Like motor cars in the twentieth century different types at different prices served different purposes and indicated the status of the owner. There is a vivid description of the horses on show in Norman Smithfield (see *T.S.I.H.*, i, 95–6). The stables at the Tabard, Chaucer says ' weren wide ' and the characters of the pilgrims were partly distinguished by their mounts: the Knight's ' horse were gode, but he was nat gay '. The squire ' wel coude he sitte on hors, and faire ryde '. When the monk rode ' men mighte his brydel here ginglen in a whistling wind as clere, and eek as loude as dooth the chapel-belle.' The merchant sat ' hye on horse '. The clerk of Oxenford had a horse, but lean ' as is a rake '. The man of law ' rood hoomly in a medlee cote '. The shipman ' rood up-on a rouncy, as he couth '. The wife of Bath ' Up-on an amblere esily she sat. . . . And on hir feet a paire of spores sharpe '. The plowman ' In a tabard he rood upon a mere '. The reve ' sat up-on a ful good stot, that was al pomely [dappled] grey, and highte Scot.'

Further Reading: M. Holzheimer, 'Evolution of the Domestic Horse,' *Antiquity*, no. 34, 1938.

Source: Chaucer, *The Persones Tale*.

Also the sinne of aornement or of apparaille is in thinges that apertenen to rydinge, as in manye delicat horses that been holden for delyt, that been so faire, fatte, and costlewe; and also to many a vicious knave that is sustened by cause of hem; in to curious harneys, as in sadeles, in crouperes, peytrels [breast pieces], and brydles covered with precious clothing and riche, barres and plates of gold and of silver. For which God seith by Zakarie the prophete, 'I wol confounde the ryderes of swiche horses'. This folk taken litel reward of the rydinge of Goddes sone of hevene, and of his harneys whan he rood up-on the asse, and he hadde noon other harneys but the povre clothes of hise disciples.

HORSEMEN

The heavily armed mounted Normans defeated the Saxon infantry in 1066 as shown in the Bayeux Tapestry. William the Conqueror distributed the lands of the conquered in return for military service by warriors thus equipped at their own cost. Bishops, abbots and some 180 lay barons had thus to produce a force which probably exceeded 6,000 knights. Such knights, armed with lances, with a sword hanging from their belts and carrying each an axe or mace on his saddle, rode strong war-horses. R. C. Smail remarks that in the fourteenth century a trained war-horse might cost £100, ten times as much as the horses of less fully equipped sergeants, but that knights so mounted and wearing the most elaborate armour did not exceed a few hundred in England.

Further Reading: H. M. Chew, *The English Ecclesiastical Tenants-in-Chief and Knight Service*, Oxford, 1932. J. E. Morris, 'Mounted Infantry in Medieval Warfare', *Transactions Royal Historical Society*, 3rd series, vol. 8, 1914. E. H. Fellowes, *Knights of the Garter*, 1348–1939, 1939; F. W. Cornish, *Chivalry*, Social England Series, 1901.

Source: Letter from Roger de Marlowe, Rector of Harwell, Berks, to a monk of Hayles, Gloucs. Rosalind M. T. Hill, 'A Berkshire Letter-Book ', *Berkshire Archaeological Journal*, vol. 41, 1937, pp. 18–19.

To the religious man and his beloved friend Sir J . . . de H . . . monk of the Abbey of Hayles, R. de Marlowe chaplain of H. sends greeting in Him Who is the true safety and Saviour of the world. As I should like to hear good news of your health and safety I am writing to you, as my particular friend, eagerly desiring you to send me by the bearer news of yourself and the brethren and my friends in the neighbourhood. Also, since having lost some of my horses I am hardly able to go about, and there is at present a fair at Winchcombe near you, where as I have often heard, many horses are to be found, I earnestly beg you to look about and get some of your people to give their advice and help to the bearer and Sir Thomas de Sandford, canon, and also to assist them yourself, so that I may be provided with some suitable horse there, costing not more than four or five marks. May you fare well, as I would fare well. Greet your brethren and companions from me.

HORSESHOES, HARNESS AND SPURS

The development of iron horseshoes and improved harness in the tenth century is said to have given the horse for the first time the pulling power of ten slaves. This increased the value of horses compared with slaves. (The military value of horsemen compared with infantrymen had been increased by the development of stirrups by the Barbarians five centuries before, in the last days of the Roman Empire.) Fifty thousand horse-shoes were forged at St. Briavels for the crusade of Richard I.

Rules for the London lorimers (makers of horse bits) forbade nightwork, regulated half holidays and forbade refurbishing second-hand bits.

Details of harness can be seen in many illuminated manuscript illustrations.

Further Reading: R. W. Murray, ' Old English Horseshoes ', *Journal of the British Archaeological Association*, 3rd series, vols. 1–2), 1937. C. de L. Lacy, *History of the Spur*, 1911; E. M. Jope, ' The tinning of iron spurs, a continuous practice from the tenth to the seventeenth century ', *Oxoniensia*, vol. 21.

(1) *Source*: U. T. Holmes, Jr., *Daily Living in the Twelfth Century, based on the Observations of Alexander Neckam*, Madison, The University of Wisconsin Press 1952, pp. 20–1. For Alexander Neckam see *W.W.I.H.*, i, 112–3.

Let the horse's back be covered with a canvas, afterwards with a sweat pad or cloth; next let a saddle be properly placed with the fringes of the sweat cloth hanging over the crupper. The stirrups should hang well. The saddle has a front bow or pommel and a cantle. . . . Folded clothing may be well placed in a saddlebag behind the cantle. A breast strap and the trappings for the use of someone riding should not be forgotten: halter and headstall, bit covered with bloody foam, reins, girths, buckles, cushion, padding . . . which I intentionally pass over. An attendant should carry a currycomb. . . .

Let one who is about to ride have a *chape* with sleeves, of which the hood will not mind the weather, and let him have boots, and spurs that he may prevent the horse from stumbling, jolting, turning, rearing, resisting, and make him *bien amblant*, ' possessed of a good gait ', and easily manageable. Shoes should be well fastened with iron nails.

(2) *Source*: ' The Order, and Manner of Creating Knights of the Bath ', College of Arms MS., W. Dugdale, *The Antiquities of Warwickshire*, 1656, p. 533.

. . . the Horse must be accoutred, as followeth: The Saddle having a cover of black-leather, the bow of the Saddle being of white wood quartered. The Stirrop-leathers black; the Stirrops gilt; The Paitrell of black lether gilt, with a Cross patè, gilt hanging before the breast of the Horse, but without any Crooper: The Bridle black, with long notched Raines, after the Spanish fashion, and a Cross patè on the front.

CARTS

It has generally been supposed that cross-country loads were more often carried by packhorses than on carts and that communications almost ceased in the bad weather of winter and spring when ways were foul. It is therefore surprising to find that in 1439–40 1,637 carters paid dues at Bargate, Southampton compared with only 17 packhorses and fewest carts went through in the summer. It has been supposed that this might be due to the heavy demand for carts for agricultural purposes in the summer. This is confirmed by an observant resident at Southampton in the early nineteenth century, Miss Jane Austen. In *Mansfield Park* Miss Crawford is amazed to find that in seeking a cart to transport her harp ' I had been asking the most unreasonable, most impossible thing in the world '. Edmund explains: ' You could

A Cart.   c. 1340.   (Luttrell Psalter).

Fantasy of monkey driving cart.   c. 1340.   (Luttrell Psalter).

not be expected to have thought of the subject before; but when you *do* think of it, you must see the importance of getting in the grass.'

Further Reading: J. F. Willard, ' The Use of Carts in the fourteenth Century ', *History*, vol. 17, no. 67, 1932. M. N. Boyer, ' Medieval Suspended Carriages ', *Speculum*, vol. 34, no. 3.

(1) *Source*: Letter to Bishop of Chichester from his agent, second quarter thirteenth century, translated in Mary Bateson, *Mediaeval England* 1066–1350, T. Fisher Unwin, 1903, p. 251.

Can you send your long cart to Aldingburn? so that on it I can send your venison up to London, with other garnison, and cloth for the poor, as much as you like, for I bought 300 yards at Winchester fair; I can't send your small carts because the time of sowing is at hand.

(2) *Source*: from Chaucer, *The Freres Tale*.

They saugh a cart, that charged was with hey,
Which that a carter droof [drove] forth in his wey.
Deep was the wey, for which the carte stood.
The carter smoot, and cryde, as he were wood,
' Hayt, Brok! hayt, Scot! what spare ye for the stones?
The feend,' quod he, ' yow fecche body and bones,
As ferforthly as ever were ye foled!
So muche wo as I have with yow tholed [suffered]!
The devel have al, bothe hors and cart and hey!' . . .
This carter thakketh his hors upon the croupe,
And they bigonne drawen and to-stoupe;
' Heyt, now! quod he, ' ther Jesu Crist yow blesse,
And al his handwerk, bothe more and lesse!
That was wel twight [drawn quickly], myn owene lyard [grey]
      boy!
Now is my cart out of the slow, pardee! '

(3) *Source*: Tolls and other payments made by carters passing
Bargate, Southampton, on 30 September, 1439. *The Brokage Book of
Southampton from* 1439–40, ed. by Barbara D. M. Bunyard, vol. 1,
Publications of the Southampton Record Society, 1941, pp. 3–5 (Latin).

From John Ymine carting towards Salisbury with 1 pipe of oil of
      William Warwyke custom 4d. Brokage with pontage
      [bridge toll] 2½d.   Sum 6½d.
From William Browter carting towards Romsey with 1 tun of oil
      of John Bocher' custom 16 d. Brokage with pontage 2d.
                                                      Sum 18d.
From John Haywarde carting towards London with 9 balets
      [half bales] of woad [blue dye] of Gregor' Catan' custom paid
      at sea. Brokage with pontage 9d.   Sum 9d.
From Wat' Man' for 4 quarters of malt custom 2d.   Sum 2d.
From John Stokker' coming in with cloth, for pontage 1d. and
      going out towards London with 9 balets of woad of Angell'
      de Neg' custom paid at sea, Brokage with pontage 9d.
                                                      Sum 10d.
From John Hoker coming in with cloth for pontage 1d. and going
      out towards Coventry with 1 tun of oil of Roger Costantyne,
      custom free, for pontage 1d.   Sum 2d.

From John Chawyn' carting towards Salisbury with 1 pipe of oil of Symon Poy custom 4d. and 3 balets of woad of Henry Twengow, merchant of Frome, custom 3d. brokage with pontage 4d.   Sum 11d.

From Henry Chawyn' carting towards Salisbury with 4 balets of woad of Simon Poy custom 2d. and with 1 balet of woad of John Soper custom ½d. and 1 barrel of sayme [lard] of John Gorweser' custom 2d. Brokage with pontage 3d. Sum 7½d.

From Nicholas Gode coming in with cloth, for pontage 1d. and going out towards London with 8 bales of almonds of Gregor' Catan, custom paid at sea, for pontage 1d.   Sum 2d.

From William Rabayne carting towards London with 4 bales of almonds and 1 bale of paper of Gregor' Catan paid at sea. Brokage with pontage 6d.   Sum 6d,
                                     Sum 6/2.

From John Stondrirowte carting towards Romsey with 6 balets of woad and 1 bale of alum [for dyeing] of John Bocher' custom 8d. Brokage with pontage 2d.   Sum 10d.

From Robert Gyssch' and Yngram Twynham carting towards London with 8 bales of almonds and 8 balets of woad of Angell' de Neg' custom paid at sea for pontage 2d.   Sum 2d

From William Heckele carting towards Coventry with 2 tuns of oil of Thomas Raskell' and William Per', custom free. Brokage with pontage 18d.   Sum 18d.

From John Skarlet coming in with wool, for pontage 1d. and going out towards London with 9 balets of woad of Gregor' Catan' custom paid at sea. Brokage 9d.   Sum 10d.

From John Blower' coming in with wool for pontage 1d. and going out towards Whitchurch with 1 pipe load of iron and 4 barrels of [Fuller's] earth for his own use, custom free, for pontage 1d.   Sum 2d.

From John Corborow coming in with wool for pontage 1d. and going out empty.   Sum 1d.

36. Shoeing.   French smiths still hold the leg thus (*cf. p.* 76)

37. Carriage folk (*for carts see p.* 78)

38. Horse with saddle, fur saddle cloth and two girths. Food found
by horse in answer to prayer (Life of St. Cuthbert)

39. Packhorses

40. Packhorses

41. Pedlar with pack

SHIPS

(1) Viking ships.

A well built Saxon ship found at Sutton Hoo was 89 feet long and 15 feet amidships. Iron nails were used. It had no keel or sail, showing thus an important point wherein the boats of the Saxon invaders were inferior to those of the Vikings.

The fjords of Norway, with land on both sides of a calm stretch of water, encouraged shipbuilding and the islands off the coast encouraged sailors to venture out into the open sea. Square-sailed ships with oars as well as sails, and hulls made of overlapping planks (' clinker built ') became treasured possessions for trade or piracy. Some, designed for war, were long and narrow and others (' knarrs ') were of tubby shape to accommodate heavy cargoes. Leaders were buried in ships over which mounds were erected. One of the most famous ships thus discovered is the Gokstad ship from near Oslo. In such a ship the warriors used to hang their shields, to the number of thirty or forty, or even (in the late tenth century) sixty-four, over the gunwales. The prow bore a dragon-head.

Further Reading: A. W. Brøgger and Haakon Shetelig, *The Viking Ships: their Ancestry and Evolution*, Edward Stanford 1951.

Source: *Alfred's addition to his Anglo-Saxon version of Orosius*, translated by B. Thorpe, Bohn's Antiquarian Library, 1873, p. 249.

Ohthere told his lord King Aelfred, that he dwelt north-most of all the Northmen. He said that he dwelt in the land to the northward, along the West-Sea; he said, however, that that land is very long north from thence, but it is all waste, except in a few places, where the Finns here and there dwell, for hunting in the winter, and in the summer for fishing in that sea. He said that he was desirous to try, once on a time, how far that country extended due north, or whether any one lived to the north of the waste. He then went due north along the country, leaving all the way the waste land on the right, and the wide sea on the left, for three days: he was as far north as the whale-hunters go at the farthest. Then he proceeded in his course due north, as far as he could sail within another three days; then the land there inclined due east, or the sea into the land, he knew not which, but he knew that he there waited for a west wind, or a little north, and sailed thence eastward along that land as far as he could sail in four days; then he had to wait for a due north wind, because the land there

G

inclined due south, or the sea in on that land, he knew not
which; he then sailed thence along the coast due south, as far
as he could sail in five days. There lay a great river up in that
land; they then turned up in that river, because they durst not
sail on by that river, on account of hostility, because all that
country was inhabited on the other side of that river; he had not
before met with any land that was inhabited since he came from
his own home; but all the way he had waste land on his right,
except fishermen, fowlers, and hunters, all of whom were Finns,
and he had constantly a wide sea to the left. The Beormas had
well cultivated their country, but they did not dare to enter it;
and the Terfinna land was all waste, except where hunters, fishers,
or fowlers had taken up their quarters.

The Beormas told him many particulars both of their own
land, and of the other lands lying around them; but he knew not
what was true, because he did not see it himself; it seemed to him
that the Finns and the Beormas spoke nearly one language. He
went thither chiefly, in addition to seeing the country, on account
of the walrusses, because they have very noble bones in their
teeth, some of those teeth they brought to the king: and their
hides are good for ship-ropes. This whale is much less than other
whales, it being not longer than seven ells; but in his own
country is the best whale-hunting, there they are eight-and-
forty ells long, and most of them fifty ells long; of these he said
that he and five others had killed sixty in two days. He was a
very wealthy man in those possessions in which their wealth
consists, that is in wild deer. He had at the time he came to the
king, six hundred unsold tame deer. These deer they call reindeer,
of which there were six decoy rein-deer, which are very valuable
amongst the Finns, because they catch the wild rein-deer with
them.

He was one of the first men in that country, yet he had not
more than twenty horned cattle, and twenty sheep, and twenty
swine, and the little that he ploughed he ploughed with horses.
But their wealth consists for the most part in the rent paid them
by the Finns. That rent is in skins or animals, and birds' feathers,
and whalebone, and in ship-ropes made of whales' hides, and of
seals'. Every one pays according to his birth; the best-born, it is

said, pay the skins of fifteen martens, and five rein-deer's, and one bear's-skin, ten ambers of feathers, a bear's or other's skin kyrtle, and two ship-ropes, each sixty ells long, made either of whale-hide or of seal's.

He said that the Northmen's land was very long and very narrow; all that one man could either pasture or plough lies by the sea, though it is in some parts very rocky; and to the east are wild mountains, parallel to the cultivated land. . . .

(2) The one-masted ship, *c.* 1400.

Viking ships had bows and sterns of the same shape. The stern was modified when a straight stern post on which to hang a rudder was invented. An exceptionally early rudder is shown on the font of about 1180 in Winchester Cathedral, perhaps the second earliest European example is on a seal of Elbing, Germany, of 1242. Previously large oars were used as side-rudders. Bowsprits were invented about the same time as true rudders and stern-posts. In the Mediterranean ships had hulls like Roman ships with two masts, but they developed lateen, ' fore-and-aft ' sails for an enlarged foremast. The Shipmen's gild of Holy Trinity Hall, founded in 1369, still survives.

Further Reading: H. H. Brindley, ' Seals illustrating the Evolution of the Sailing Ship ', in National Maritime Museum, *Impressions and Casts of Seals, Coins, Tokens, Medals and other Objects of Art exhibited in the Seal Room*, 1938; and ' Medieval Ships in painted Glass and Seals' C. Johnson ' The London Galleys ', *Mariner's Mirror*, vols. 1–3, 1915–7. *Antiquaries, Journal*, vol. 7, 1927.

Source: ' Men may leve all gamys ', a poem describing a voyage by pilgrims to St. James of Compostella in a fifteenth century MS. at Trinity College, Cambridge, translated (with technical discussion) by Romola and R. C. Anderson, *The Sailing-ship, Six Thousand Years of History*, G. G. Harrap 1926, pp. 94–5.

Men that sail to St. James may say farewell to all pleasures, for many people suffer when they set sail. For when they have put to sea from Sandwich or Winchelsea or Bristol, or wherever it happens to be, their hearts begin to fail.

Soon the master orders his seamen to hurry up and take their places round the mast for setting sail. Then they cry ' Yo ho, hoist! What ho, mate, you are standing too close, your comrade has not room to haul.' Thus they begin to talk.

A boy or two climb up at once and lie across the yard; the

rest cry ' Yo ho, tally [haul]! ' and pull with all their might.
'Get the boat stowed, boatswain, for our pilgrims to occupy
ihemselves with it, for some of them will very likely be coughing
and groaning before it is midnight.'

' Haul the bowline. Now veer the sheet. Cook, make our
food ready at once. Our pilgrims have no desire to eat. I pray
God to give them rest. Go to the helm. What ho. No closer.
Steward fellow, a pot of beer.' ' You shall have, sir, with good
cheer, all of the best directly.'

' Yo ho, truss! Haul in the brails. You are not hauling; s.'
God, you are shirking. Oh, see how well our good ship sai'by
And that is how they talk. ' Haul in the wartack [an extra rope].l
' It shall be done.' ' Steward, lay the table at once and put bread
and salt on it, and don't take too long about it.'

Then some one comes and says: ' Be merry, you will have a
storm or a squall.' ' Be quiet. You never can. You are a sorry
meddler.' Meanwhile the pilgrims lie with their bowls close
beside them and shout for hot Malvoisie wine to restore their
health.

And some ask for a salted toast, because they cannot eat either
boiled or roast meat. A man could just as well pay for their keep
for two days as for one. Some laid their books on their knees and
read till they could see no longer. 'Alas, my head will split in
three,' so says another, ' I am certain of it.'

Then our owner comes like a lord and speaks many royal
words and goes to the high table to see everything is well.
Presently he calls a carpenter and tells him to bring his gear to
make cabins here and there and many small compartments.

'A sack of straw would be very good there, for some of them
will have to sleep in their cloaks.' ' I would as soon be in the
wood without meat or drink; for when we go to bed the pump
will be close to the head of our bed, and a man who smells its
stink is as good as dead.'

(3) A royal ship, 1338.

After the death of King Robert Bruce in November 1337 Lord
James Douglas embarked the following spring from Montrose for
Sluys in Flanders hoping to hear of an expedition to Jerusalem which
he might join in order to carry out Bruce's wish by taking his heart for

burial in the Holy Sepulchre. After twelve days off Sluys he heard of
a war against the Saracen King of Granada. This he joined.

Source: J. Froissart, *Chronique*, vol. 1 chapter 21, translated extract.

He stayed at Sluys for twelve days and he would not land but
spent the whole time on board. He kept an honourable table all
the while, with trumpets and nakers [drums], just as if he was the
King of Scotland. He had in his company a knight-banneret and
seven of the best knights in the kingdom of Scotland too, not to
speak of his other retainers. All his plate was gold and silver,
with pots, basins, porringers, goblets, bottles, barrels, etc. He
had too twenty-six young and gentle squires, of the best in
Scotland, to wait upon him. You must know that anybody who
wanted to see him, provided he was of sufficient rank, was
entertained with two kinds of wine and two kinds of spice.

SAILORS

On big ships the mariners had meat three times a week. For their
evening meal there was bread with cheese, onions, sardines or some
other fish. Fines and ducking enforced some order. Sometimes
sailors had shares in the cargo. A ship would have to be sold rather
than that their wages should remain unpaid. There was a gild of
ferry-shippers at Dover (1312).

Further Reading: L. F. Salzman, *English Trade in the Middle Ages*,
Clarendon Press, 1931, pp. 226–279 (distribution by sea). Kingsford,
' West Country Piracy ' in *Prejudice and Promise in xvth Century England*.

Source: *The Black Book of the Admiralty*, ed. Sir T. Twiss, vol. 1,
Rolls Series 1871, p. 105. (This passage relates to 1337–51).

A mayster hyreth his maryners, and ought to kepe them
pesably, and offre to be theyr juge, and yf any say that his felow
lyeth, having brede and drynke at the table, ought to pay four
pence; and yf any belyeth the mayster, to pay eight pence; and yf
the mayster smyte any of the maryners, the maryner ought to
abyde the fyrste buffet be it with fyst, or flat with his hande, but
yf he smyte any more he may defend him; and if a maryner smyte
the mayster to pay five shillings or to lese his fyst. The jugement
is suche.

DANGER AT SEA, THIRTEENTH CENTURY

Storms were a greater peril than the hostile sailors of rival ports. There is an account of the loss of the White Ship (1120) in *T.S.I.H.*, i, 63–64. St. Nicholas, patron saint of Seafarers, was a popular subject for decorators of English churches (e.g. Kidlington, Oxon, and North Moreton, Berks, and York Minster).

Further Reading: Select Pleas in the Court of Admiralty, Selden Society, ed. R. G. Marsden, vols. 6 and 11 (from 1892 and 1897); P. Studer, *The Oak Book of Southampton*, Southampton Record Society, 1910–11.

Source: Vale Royal Cartulary, translated from W. Dugdale, *Monasticon Anglicanum, A History of the Abbies and other Monasteries, Hospitals, Frieries and Cathedral and Collegiate Churches*, vol. 6, pt. 1, 1830, p. 704.

. . . once when he [Edward I, as prince, after a crusading expedition] was on his way back to England and had reached the coast and had been received on board ship in a fitting manner he was sailing to England with a great company. Storms suddenly arose at sea so that imminent destruction threatened the whole structure of the vessel. The sailors could do no more and gave up all hope of rescue, so in terror they prayed loudly to God and the passengers decided each to vow to God whatsoever the Holy Spirit should prompt. All did this devoutly but still the storms did not abate but went on increasing in force. In the face of death everybody on board with one accord begged the prince with tears, as he had not made a vow with the others, to deign to make a vow pleasing to the Lord that he might speedily rescue them from their present peril.

The prince yielded and humbly promised to God and to the Virgin that if the Lord would save him and his and theirs and bring them unharmed to shore, he would then forthwith found a monastery of white monks of the order of the Cistercians in their honour within England. He would endow it so richly that it could support one hundred monks for ever. God's strength in saving his people was at once revealed for hardly had the most Christian prince stopped speaking when the storm was quite dispersed and there was calm. Everyone was amazed at the change. The ship was miraculously brought to land though broken and torn in many places and with many perilous leaks, thanks to the Virgin Mary in whose honour the prince had made his vow. This was done without human aid. All saw this and were amazed with joy and were filled with happy devotion towards the glorious Virgin who had not allowed them to perish. In the same hour a marvel took place which should not be passed over in silence. When all had taken their gear out of the ship the prince remained on board last of all. When the boat was empty and he had disembarked the ship fell in two parts, in the twinkling of an eye. Thus it was shown that the ship was kept whole while the good man was in her. . . .

A STOWAWAY FROM GRIMSBY, 1074

This is how Turgot, an Angle hostage in Lincoln Castle for the behaviour of Lindsey, reached the court of Olaf, King of Norway. He was subsequently the chaplain and biographer of St. Margaret, the Saxon Queen of Scotland. Trade with Norway, important in Norman times, became in later centuries, less important, relatively, than trade in the south.

Source: Simeon of Durham, translated by Rev. J. Stevenson in *The Church Historians of England*, vol. 3, pt. 2, Seeleys, 1855 p. 560.

Obtaining by money a mitigation of his imprisonment, he at great risk privily made his escape to the Norwegians, who were then loading a merchant vessel at Grimsby for Norway. In this vessel also certain ambassadors, whom king William was sending to Norway, had procured a passage; and now when the ship in full sail was out of sight of land, lo! the king's run-away hostage emerging from the hold of the vessel in which the Norwegians had concealed him, astounded the ambassadors and their companions. For when a diligent search had been everywhere made, the king's inspectors had examined this very vessel, but the cunning of the concealers baffled the observation of the searchers. The ambassadors then insisted that they should lower the sails, and should somehow or other take back the ship with the king's fugitive to England. This the Norwegians sharply resisted, as a voyage so well begun would carry the vessel forward prosperously. Such a quarrel of the parties ensued that they betook themselves to arms on both sides; but since the force of numbers was with the Norwegians, the insolence of the ambassadors was soon repressed, and the nearer they approached the land the more submissive did they become. When they arrived there, the young refugee by his modest and discreet behaviour rendered himself agreeable to the nobles and the gentry.

HARBOURS

When ships were smaller, smaller harbours were of use than in modern times, and trade was more widely distributed. The port of London should be added to the following list. The north west coast is omitted.

(1) *Source*: Sir John Fortescue, ' These be the Comodytes of Englond ', written in or before 1451, Thomas (Fortescue) Lord Clermont, *The Works of Sir John Fortescue, Knight, Chief Justice of England and Lord Chancellor to King Henry the Sixth*, London, privately printed 1869, vol. I, pp. 549–550.

. . . Englond ys induyd and honouryd with many goode harbouers, and goode roodys, and goode covertts; that ys to undyrstand from the New Castell upe unto the Ryver Saverne.

The fyrste ys Tynmouth havyn, the seconde ys Hartylpole havyn, the third Wythby havyn, the 4th Scarborough, the 5th Ffleynborough, the 6th Humbur, the 7th Lynne, the 8th Deepes [Deeping on the Welland, Lincs.], the 9th Eley, the 10th Yearmouth, the 11th Kyrkeley Roode [Kirkly near Lowestoft], the 12th Downenych havyn, the 13th Orforde havyn, the 14th Orwell havyn, the 15th Thanet over Temys Mouth, the 16th Sanwych havyn, the 17th Downys, the 18th Dover, the 19th Lewys, the 20th Camber [a castle, now inland, between Winchelsea and Rye], the 21st Wynchelse, the 22nd Rye, the 23rd Appolder [Appledore on the Rother, Kent], the 24th Pevensey, the 25th Borne, the 26th Seforde, the 27th Deende [?West Deane, on the Cuckmere, near Seaford, Sussex], the 28th Havent.

Here folowyth the goode havyns within the Ille of Whyght. Fyrst, the whych ys the 29th havyn of Englond, that is to wet Porttsmouth, the 30th Gosporte, the 31st Portchester, the 32nd Hamelle [Hamble] Ryce, the 33rd Hamelle the Hoole, and all the holle Ryver up to [South] Hampton the whyche is the 34th havyn, the 35th ys Leymyngton, the 36th Polle havyn, the 37th

Weymothe, the 38th Exmoth, the 39th Dertmouthe, the 40th Plymouthe, the 41st Ffowe, the 42nd Falmouth, the 43rd Bryge Watter, the 44th the hole ryver of Saverne. And there be many other goode havyns that I have not named, and there be many other goode havyns in the cost of Walys, as Tynby the whych ys the 45th haven of Englond, the 46th Mylforde, the 47th Cayrdefe [Cardiff], and many oon moo. The 48th Bristowe.

(2) Silt in Yarmouth harbour, 14th century.

The drifting of sand southwards along the East coast has continually caused trouble to harbours. This is well reflected in the formal language of a charter of Richard II to Yarmouth. (The contents of all royal charters are readily discoverable thanks to the publication of the *Calendar of Charter Rolls* in the Public Record Office by Her Majesty's Stationery Office.) In 1230 and 1250 royal aid was given to help get Hythe and Dunwich harbours reopened. King John made sea walls at Portsmouth and early in the thirteenth century Bristol spent £5,000 on a new harbour.

Source: Rev. C. Parkin, *An Essay towards a Topographical History of the County of Norfolk*, vol. 11 (in continuation of F. Blomefield's *History*), 1810, pp. 264–5.

Richard by the grace of God, King of England and France, and Lord of Ireland, to all to whom these present letters shall come greeting. Know ye, that whereas Lord John, formerly King of England, our progenitor, by his letters patent, had granted to the bailiffs and commonalty of our town of Great Yarmouth, the same town with the haven thereof, to be holden to them and their successors, in fee farm, paying thence to the same our progenitor and his successors fifty and five pounds by the year; and afterwards, because the said town was so straitened, by the casting out of the gravel and soil of the sea, that ships and boats could not arrive at the town aforesaid, as formerly they used, very many of the commons of the town aforesaid had withdrawn their abiding out of the same, whereby the same town was on the point of destruction. By reason of which, Lord Edward, formerly King of England, our grandfather, by advice of his council, considering the loss aforesaid, granted to the same bailiffs and commonalty . . . a certain place called Kirkley Road. . . And so it is that hitherto from day to day that haven has become so narrow and much worse and dangerous than it was formerly, so that ships and boats cannot have their course and application to the town aforesaid, as they have been wont, nay more frequently have been in danger, whereby many of the commons aforesaid have pulled down and sold their houses, and withdrawn themselves out of the said town, whence the same town is at the point of ruin. And the aforesaid commonalty cannot support, as they say, the charges of our farm aforesaid, and the repairs of the wall of the same town, and the tenths and fifteenths, when they shall happen, which amount to £100 at every grant of a whole tenth and a fifteenth.

We . . . have granted . . . that they may make a certain new haven, near the said town, within their liberty there, in a certain place called the Horse-Ferry, containing 100 perches in length, and 10 perches in breadth, for an aid of the same town, and the whole country adjacent. . . . Witness myself at Westminster, the 14th day of May, in the 16th year of our reign [1393].

LIGHTS AT SEA

The Virgin, often poetically called the Star of the Sea, was thought of as a lantern shining for voyagers on the sea of evil. A lighthouse occurs in the Holkham Bible Picture Book of the storm on the lake. The Bayeux tapestry shows a lantern on the ship of William the Conqueror and Wace says that it carried one. The ship of Richard I rallied his fleet ' as a hen gathers her chicks ', and that of Henry III had lanterns.

As in Roman times there were lights at the entrances of Dover and Calais harbours; and lights were maintained at the entrance of Yarmouth (1261). Between 1314 and 1328 an octagonal lighthouse 35 feet high was built at St. Catherine's, Isle of Wight; and in 1427 a hermit built Ravenspur lighthouse.

The earliest representation of an admiral's lantern known to the National Maritime Museum is on the seal of Sir William Hylton, Admiral of the Humber towards Scotland, in the reign of Richard II. It is at a staff in the stern.

Further Reading: Sir Mortimer Wheeler's account of Roman lighthouses at Dover, *Archaeological Journal*, vol. 86 (for 1929), 1930, pp. 29–46, Account of three successive lighthouses at St. Catherine's point, *Proceedings Isle of Wight Natural History and Archaeological Society*, iv, 1951, pp. 199–204.

Source: The Black Book of the Admiralty, ed. Sir T. Twiss, vol. 1, Rolls Series 1871, pp. 13–19 (perhaps 1338).

Christ calming the storm. c. 1330. (Holkham Bible). Note moveable rudder and lighthouse.

And because that the admirall is governor of the marriners and ought to rule them and uphold them in all their laws and customs, and defend them from all injuries against all persons, and if neede be to sue for their wages and cause them to bee paid the same, hee shall have and take out of each pound paid for the wages of the marriners four pence, for which four pence the admirall shall in the night tyme, all the while that the ffleet is at sea, carry at the topp of his mast two lanthornes, to the end that all the masters of the ffleet may know and perceive by the light and the admiralls course what course thay shall steer. . . And because that every one shall follow the admirall, the admirall ought to carry a light, unles it be for certaine necessary causes otherwise ordered by the king, his lieutenant, or by the admirall.

Item, if the king is in his own person in the fleete, then there ought to bee in his shipp three great lanthornes at the two parts of the mast head of the shipp wherein hee is, to the end hee may be knowne to be admirall. And if hee hath an under-admirall (or rear-admirall), hee may lett each of them carry one lanthorne and no more at the topp of his mast for seeing and knowing the ffleete, and to the end that the shipps of the ffleet may not be separated for want of light. And if it happen that the admirall be lieutenant for the king upon the sea, then hee shall carry his lanthornes as the kings lieutenant.

Item, the under-admirall of the west [first mentioned 1338], ought by his office to carry two lanthornes in manner as above said, from the fforland of Thanet towards all the coasts of south and west, and the under-admirall of the north ought to carry in those parts but one lanthorne.

Item, in the same manner the under-admiral of the north ought by his office to carry two lanthornes from the said fforeland towards all the parts of the north and east, and then the under admiral of the west shall carry but one lanthorne.

CARGOES ENTERING PORT OF SOUTHAMPTON, 11 OCTOBER, 1469

The *Oak Book* shows that there was a public crane at Southampton harbour, as there was at Antwerp in the fifteenth century. Ones at Trier (erected 1413) and Danzig (erected 1443, of record size) still survive.

Source: *The Port Books or Local Customs Accounts of Southampton in the Reign of Edward IV*, ed. by D. B. Quinn, vol. 1, 1469–71, Publications of the Southampton Record Society no. 37, 1937, pp. 2–3.

. . . John Jamys, burgess, 2 barrels soap, 1 barrel green ginger, 2 C. [hundred] linen cloth. . . . .

Vyncent Tehy, burgess, 1 sack hemp, 1 cwt, frying-pans, 3 C. stockfish, 3 full cauldrons, 2 barrels soap. . .

John Aport, citizen of Nova Sarum, 3 sacks hemp; 9 cwt., £6. . .

6 barrels cork. . .

2 barrels green ginger; 80 lb., £2. . .

Goslyn of Wynchester. 1½ sacks hemp; 4½ cwt., £3. . .

1 barrel oil; 30 gall. . . .

1 bale madder [red dye] . . .

Henre Tayler, 1 barrel oil; 22 gall. . . .

2 barrels salmon . . .

1 C. stockfish . . .

6 firkins salt eels, £1/6/8 . . .

1 barrel soap, 16/8 . . .

Edmond Gradclyfe, 1 bale hemp; 300 lb., £2/5/0 . . .

1 bale madder . . .

2 barrels soap, £1/13/4 . . .

2 full cauldrons, 6/8 . . .

Clement Glose, 8 balets woad . . .

John Tardyffe, ½ barrel lathnails, £1/6/8 . . .

SEA-WATCHES ON THE KENTISH COAST

From the time of the late Roman ' Counts of the Saxon shore ' to the modern coastguard there have appeared various organizations for watching the approaches to England by sea. In the details here given provision is made to prevent any unexpected French counter attacks during the Hundred Years' War. The ' hobilers ' employed were men in quilted doublets, lightly mounted. Some of the tenants at medieval Holkham on the Norfolk coast were bound to do service of ' Ward-sea '.

Source: Translated from Latin text in T. Philipott, *Villare Cantianum or Kent Surveyed*, Lynn 1776, pp. 4–7.

Ward assessed by Lord William de Clinton, the Earl of Huntingdon, John de Cobham and Thomas de Aldon, in the county of Kent, upon the coast of the sea in the eleventh year of the reign of Edward III.

At Yenlade in Hoo.

Men at arms	*Hobilers in the same watch*
Prior of Rochester 8—	
Philip de Pimpe 2	Roger de Escheker
Thomas Malmains 2	John Atford
John de Fremingham 2	Robert Viane
Stephen de Dalham 2	Henry Lomes
Thomas Warran 2	Robert le Fane
John Gifford 2	Michael Somers of Higham
Henry de Gresford 1	John Mortimer of Clives

Total in this ward 13 men at arms and 7 hobilers.

Night watches on the coast of the sea by men of towns of various Hundreds as was customary in the old days.

Hundred of Hoo 9 men to watch at Yenlade, viz. from Hoo Hundred 2, from Malling 1, from Shamed 5 from Dertford 1.

Watches of Shepeia.

They should be had at Feversham by 33 men, whereof 25 are from Milton and Merden, 2 from Bocton 5 from Feversham. [Then follow particulars of numbers of men at Dengenesse, Swale, Greistone, Elmes, Broadhul, Sebroke and Dangate and particulars of men at arms and hobilers for the wards of Shepey, Fordmer, Werden, Mosehole, Ryde, Greston, Tenet, Sandwich with St. Margaret at Dale, Walmer, and Denge Mersh.]

And that each of these men at arms have with him a good archer on the sea coast. And that signals be made with pitchpot on top, and not of mere twigs, to show better and last longer.

WOMEN

The good influence of St. Margaret on the Scottish court, the escape of Queen Matilda from Oxford in 1142, the marriage of Eleanor of Provence in 1236, the merciful character of Queen Philippa of Hainault and the troubles of Queen Margaret of Anjou in 1463 are all described by eye-witnesses in *T.S.I.H.*, vol. 1. Far greater than the honour given to the foremost lady in the land was the increasing devotion for the Heavenly Queen. The cult of the Virgin cannot have failed to be reflected in an increasing respect for women. Anti-feminist morals were drawn from the facts that Eve was created later than Adam, that she succumbed to temptation first, and that the woman Salome and not the wild beasts of the wilderness caused the death of John the Baptist. A common belief often reflected in art, suggested that the serpent adopted a female face the better to tempt Eve. The wife of Bath's last husband vexed her by reading similar stories.

Further Reading: A. R. Myers, ' The Household of Queen Margaret of Anjou, 1452–3 ', *Bulletin of John Rylands Library*, vol. 40, nos. 1 and 2.

Source: Report on prospective bride for Edward III made for his father by Bishop Stapeldon, founder of Exeter College, translated, G. G. Coulton, *Medieval Panorama, The English Scene from Conquest to Reformation*, Cambridge University Press, 1938, p. 644 (chapter on Marriage and Divorce), from *Register Stapeldon*, 169 (A.D. 1319).

Inspection and Description of the Daughter of the Count of Hainault, Philippa by name.

The lady whom we saw has not uncomely hair, betwixt blue-black and brown. Her head is clean-shaped; her forehead high and broad, and standing somewhat forward. Her face narrows between the eyes, and the lower part of her face is still more narrow and slender than her forehead. Her eyes are blackish-brown and deep. Her nose is fairly smooth and even, save that it is somewhat broad at the tip and also flattened, and yet it is no snub-nose. Her nostrils are also broad, her mouth fairly wide. Her lips somewhat full, and especially the lower lip. Her teeth which have fallen and grown again are white enough, but the rest are not so white. The lower teeth project a little beyond the upper; yet this is but little seen. Her ears and chin are comely enough. Her neck, shoulders, and all her body are well set and unmaimed; and nought is amiss so far as a man may see. More-over, she is brown of skin all over, and much like her father; and in all things she is pleasant enough, as it seems to us. And the damsel will be of the age of nine years on St. John's day next to come, as her mother saith. She is neither too tall nor too short for such an age; she is of fair carriage, and well taught in all that becometh her rank, and highly esteemed and well beloved of her father and mother and of all her meinie, in so far as we could inquire and learn the truth.

PUNISHMENTS FOR FEMALE BOLDNESS, 878

It was difficult to enforce the rule that priests should never marry. St. Cuthbert disliked women, and stories of his dislike seemed more edifying than they do to modern feminists. At Coldingham there were both monks and nuns. The former grew lax and the latter ' devoted themselves to the sewing of robes of the finest workmanship, in which they either adorned themselves like brides, thereby endangering their own estate of life and profession or they gave them to men who were strangers, for the purpose of thereby securing their friendship '. St. Cuthbert, on becoming bishop, separated the monks and nuns com-pletely and built a separate church for the nuns. Thereafter no women were to enter the monks' church. He thrashed a handmaid of Tostig's countess, Judith, who approached his shrine on her behalf and even prevented the construction of a Lady Chapel near it by miracles wrought after his death.

Source: Simeon of Durham, translated by Rev. J. Stevenson in *The Church Historians of England*, vol. 3, pt. 2, Seeleys, 1855, p. 658.

This custom is so diligently observed, even unto the present day, that it is unlawful for women to set foot even within the cemeteries of those churches in which his body obtained a temporary resting-place, unless, indeed, compelled to do so by the approach of an enemy or the dread of fire.

There have been women, however, who in their boldness have ventured to infringe these decrees; but the punishment which has speedily overtaken them, gave proof of the magnitude of their crime. One of these, named Sungeova, the wife of the son of Bevo, who was named Gamel, as she was one night returning home from an entertainment, was continually complaining to her husband that there was no clean piece of road to be found, in consequence of the deep puddles with which it was everywhere studded. So at last they determined that they would go through the churchyard (that is, of Durham), and that they would afterwards make an atonement for this sin by almsgiving. As they were going on together, she was seized with some kind of indefinite horror, and cried out that she was gradually losing her senses. Her husband chid her, and urged her to come on, and not to be afraid; but as soon as she set foot outside the hedge which surrounds the cemetery of the church, she immediately fell down; and being carried home, she that very night ended her life.

. . . A certain rich man—who afterwards resided amongst us in this church, wearing the dress of a monk—had a wife; and she, having heard many persons talk of the beauty of the ornaments of the church was inflamed, woman-like, with the desire of seeing these novelties. Unable to bridle her impetuous desires, for the power of her husband elevated her above her neighbours, she walked through the cemetery of the church. [She was punished by going mad, biting out her own tongue, and cutting her own throat.]

A DEVOUT WOMAN, EARLY FIFTEENTH CENTURY

A suspected Lollard is threatened with a cartful of thorns and a barrel with which to be burnt.

Margery Kempe was in trouble as a suspected Lollard at Leicester as related in *T.S.I.H.*, i. Here she is in trouble again at Canterbury.

Source: W. Butler-Bowdon, *The Book of Margery Kempe*, Oxford University Press, 1954, pp. 54–5.

On a time, as this creature was at Canterbury in the church amongst the monks, she was greatly despised and reproved because she wept so fast, both by the monks and priests, and by secular men, nearly all day both forenoon and afternoon also, so much indeed that her husband went away from her as if he had not known her, and left her alone amongst them, choose how she might. Further comfort had she none of him that day.

So an old monk, who had been Treasurer with the Queen whilst he was in secular clothing, a rich man, and greatly dreaded by many people, took her by the hand, saying unto her:

' What canst thou say of God? '

' Sir,' she said, ' I will both speak of Him, and hear of Him,' repeating to the monk a story of Scripture.

' The monk said: ' I would thou wert enclosed in a house of stone, so that, there, no man should speak with thee.'

'Ah! Sir,' she said, ' ye should maintain God's servants. Ye are the first that hold against them. Our Lord amend you.'

Then a young monk said to her: ' Either thou hast the Holy Ghost, or else thou hast the devil within thee, for what thou speakest to us here is Holy Writ, and that hast thou not of thyself.'

Then said this creature: ' I pray you, sir, give me leave to tell you a tale.'

Then the people said to the monk: ' Let her say what she will.'

[Her story is of a man who was glad when people mocked him as he had been accustomed to pay people to humiliate him. Thus she too is glad at being despised.]

Then she went out of the monastery, they following and crying upon her: ' Thou shalt be burnt, false Lollard. Here is a cartful of thorns ready for thee, and a tun to burn thee with.'

[Eventually two fair young men befriend her and take her to her inn, where she found her husband.]

H

BETROTHING A WOMAN

Source: Laws of King Edmund (940–946), B. Thorpe, *Ancient Laws and Institutes of England*, 1840, p. 108.

1. If a man desire to betroth a maiden or a woman, and it so be agreeable to her and her friends, then is it right that the bridegroom, according to the law of God, and according to the customs of the world, first promise, and give a ' wed ' [pledge] to those who are her ' foresprecas ', that he desire her, in such wise that he will keep her, according to God's law, as a husband shall his wife: and let his friends guarantee that.

2. After that, it is to be known to whom the ' foster-lean ' [expense of having a child reared] belongs: let the bridegroom give a ' wed ' [pledge] for this; and let his friends guarantee it.

3. Then, after that, let the bridegroom declare what he will grant her, in case she choose his will [accept him as her lord], and what he will grant her, if she live longer than he.

4. If it be so agreed, then is it right that she be entitled to half the property, and to all, if they have children in common, except she again choose a husband.

5. Let him confirm all that which he has promised with a ' wed ' [pledge]; and let his friends guarantee that.

6. If they then are agreed in every thing, then let the kinsmen take it in hand, and betroth their kinswoman to wife, and to a righteous life, to him who desired her, and let him take possession of the ' born ' [surety] who has control of the ' wed ' [pledge].

7. But if a man desire to lead her out of the land, into another thane's land, then it will be advisable for her that her friends have an agreement that no wrong shall be done to her; and if she commit a fault, that they may be nearest in the ' bot ' (compensation), if she have not whereof she can make ' the bot '.

8. At the nuptials, there shall be a mass-priest by law; who shall with God's blessing bind their union to all prosperity.

9. Well is it also to be looked to, that it be known, that they, through kinship, be not too nearly allied; lest that be afterwards divided, which before was wrongly joined.

MARRIAGE

The Church courts and not those of the king dealt with all questions of marriage. No female tenant might marry without the permission of her feudal lord so that land held of him should not pass to a husband who was the lord's enemy. If a military tenant's heir was under twenty-one or if his heiress was under fourteen when the father died the lord obtained the right to decide who the young person should marry. The lord could make a profit of selling the right to marry an heir or heiress, but he was bound not to arrange a marriage with a person of a lower class.

Further Reading: C. Moor, ' The Medieval Marriage Market ', *Genealogists Magazine*, vol. 12.

Source: Constitutions of Richard de Marisco, Bishop of Durham, at the Council of Durham 1220; D. Wilkins, *Concilia Magnae Britanniae et Hiberniae*, 1737, vol. 1, p. 581.

Further we enjoin that marriages be decently celebrated, with reverence, not with laughter and ribaldry, not in taverns or at public drinkings and feastings. Let no man place a ring made of rushes or of any worthless or precious material on the hand of a woman in jest that he may more easily gain her favours lest in thinking to jest the bond of marriage be tied. Henceforth let no pledge of contracting marriage be given save in the presence of a priest and of three or four respectable persons summoned for the purpose. . . .

HUSBAND AND WIFE

Source: Penitential of Archbishop Ecgbert (735–766). B. Thorpe, *Ancient Laws and Institutes of England*, 1840, p. 371.

Holy books teach what every faithful man should do when first he leads his lawful wife home; that is, according to the teaching of the books, to keep their chastity for the space of three days and three nights and on the third day to be present at Mass and both to take the Eucharist and then to keep his marriage before God and the world as is needful for them. And all wives should keep their chastity for 49 days and nights before Easter and all through Easter week, and always on the night of the Lord's day, and Wednesday and Friday. And every religious woman should keep her chastity for 3 months before childbirth and for 60 nights and days after, whether the child be male or female.

WIVES

In Anglo-Saxon England Lady Stenton finds that women were ' more nearly the equal companions of their hubands and brothers ' than in any generation before ours. The military basis of Norman society shattered this equality.

Further Reading: Doris Mary Stenton, *The English Woman in History*, Allen and Unwin, 1957.

Source: ' The Wise Man and his Son ' in *The Babees' Book Medieval Manners for the Young done into modern English from Dr. Furnivall's Texts*, by Edith Rickert, Chatto and Windus, 1923, pp. 45–6 (mid fifteenth century).

And son, if ye would have a wife, take her not for her money, but inquire wisely of all her life, and give good heed that she be meek, courteous and prudent, even though she be poor; and such an one will do you more good service in time of need, than a richer.

And if your wife be meek and good, and serve you well and pleasantly, look ye be not so mad as to charge her too grievously, but rule her with a fair hand and easy, and cherish her for her good deeds. For a thing unskilfully overdone makes needless grief to grow, and it is better to have a meal's meat of homely fare with peace and quiet, than an hundred dishes with grudging and much care. And therefore learn this well that if you want a wife to your ease, take her never the more for the riches she may have, though she might endow you with lands.

And ye shall not displease your wife, nor call her by no villainous names, for it is a shame to you to miscall a woman; and in so doing, ye are not wise, but if ye defame your own wife, no wonder that another should do so! Soft and fair will tame alike hart and hind, buck and doe.

On the other hand, be not too busy to fight and chide, if thy wife come to you at any time with complaint of man or child; and be not avenged till you know the truth, for you might make a stir in the dark, and afterwards it should rue you both.

WIVES OF PRIESTS

The Struggle of the Church to enforce the celibacy of the clergy was long and difficult, and the appearance of married clergymen after the Reformation might be regarded less as a revolution than a revival.

Further Reading: C. N. L. Brooke, ' Gregorian Reform in Action: Clerical Marriage in England; 1050–1200 ', *Cambridge Historical Journal*, vol. 12, no. 1. W. A. C. Sandford, ' Medieval Clerical Celibacy in England ', *Genealogists Magazine*, vol. 12.

Source: A vision of the dead, 1093. Simeon of Durham, translated by Rev. J. Stevenson in *The Church Historians of England*, vol. 3, pt. 2, Seeleys 1855.

[Boso, a knight of the Bishop of Durham, was ill. After three days of unconsciousness he recovered, having seen many visions. When he became stronger he undressed and took some rods in his hands to the prior weeping. After confessing his sins and receiving ' healing for the wounds inflicted by them through the medium of stripes ' he described how a guide had led him through places both terrible and pleasant. Most of the monks of Durham were in the latter.

A longer account of the other world is given in the celebrated Vision of the Monk of Eynsham. Both accounts are much earlier than Dante's *Divine Comedy*.]

So he led me to where I could observe all the inhabitants of this province assembled in a field of immense extent; they were mounted on very fat horses, and (according to their usual custom) were carrying long spears; and as they tilted with these the one against the other, the shivering of the lances occasioned a considerable noise, and the riders swelled with pride. Hereupon my guide asked me if I knew who these persons were; and my reply was, that I recognised first one, then another; and, lastly, that I could distinguish every single individual of their number. Whereupon he added, 'All these persons are on the very verge of destruction '; and immediately as he spoke the words, the whole multitude vanished away like smoke from before my eyes. . . . Casting my eyes over the field once more, I saw it covered, for some miles, with a large body of women; and while I was in astonishment at their number, my guide informed me that they were the wives of priests. He spoke thus: ' These wretched women, and those persons also who were consecrated for sacrificing to God, but who, unworthy, have become enchained in the pleasures of the flesh, are awaiting the eternal sentence of condemnation, and the severe punishment of the fires of hell.'

WIDOWS

Magna Carta protected widows from forcible remarriage and in enjoying this freedom they had a privileged position in feudal society.

(1) *Source*: (Saxon) Institutes of Polity, Civil and Ecclesiastical. B. Thorpe, *Ancient Laws and Institutes of England*, 1840, p. 431.

It is right that widows earnestly follow the example of Anna, who was in the temple day and night, zealously serving; she fasted very often, and was devoted to prayers, and with groaning mind called to Christ, and distributed alms, oft and frequently, and ever propitiated God, as much as she was able, by word and deed, and has now for reward heavenly mirth. So should a good widow obey her Lord.

(2) *Source*: *The Book of Vices and Virtues, a Fourteenth century English translation of Somme le Roi of Lorens d'Orleans*, ed. by W. Nelson Francis, Early English Text Society, 1942, pp. 250–1.

Thre thinges longen to the estate of widowhode. The first is to hide hire and be priveliche dwellyng in hire place and nought for to folewe suspecious felawschep, and ther-of have we ensaumple of Iudith, that was widowe and was wonder fair and comeliche, wher-of men reden in holy writt that sche hilde [held] hire in hire chaumbre y-schut with hire maidenes; wherefore seynt Poule undertaketh thes yonge wommen widowes that were idel and besy to go alday hider and thider and iangelode [chatter] and speke to moche, but thei shulde schut hem wuth-ynne houses and entende and be besy to do goode dedes, as seynt Poule techeth. The secunde thing is to entende to bidde God goode praiers, and goodliche to be at chirche in devocion and in teeres weping, as men redeth in the gospel of seynt Luke that thilke good widowe that higt Anne yede [went] nevere out of the temple and served God bothe nygt and day in biddynges and wepynge and fastynge. The thridde [third] thing is scharpe metes and drynkes. For as seynt Poule seith, ' The womman that is widowe and ledeth hire lif in delite is ded in synne.' For, as seynt Bernard seith, chastite is loste in delices, rigt as he that is under the water is loste, for he may nougt drawe his breth. Non may have his heued [head] ne his herte longe in the delite of this world that hym ne behoueth to lese [lose] his breth, that is the grace of the Holy Gost, wher-bi the soule lyueth in God. To suche staate belongeth also meke clothes, that is no grete arraye ne riche robes ne queynte, as bi the ensaumple of Iudith, that lefte hire riche robes and noble atire whan hire lord was ded and toke clothinge of widowhode, meke and symple, that was more token-yng of wepyng and sorwe than of ioye or of veyne glorie; and for sche toke chastite and wolde kepe it al hire lif, sche dide vpon hire flesche the hayre, and faste euery day but the hiye holi daies, and yet sche was wonder fair and yong and wise and riche, but goodnesse of herte and loue to be chaste made hire do this. Thus schulde thei lyve that wolde kepe chastite in that estate.

BAPTISM

As Baptism was regarded as a sacrament without which no child might attain Heaven pictures of the Baptism of Christ, scenes from the life of St. John the Baptist and handsome fonts are important monu-ments of medieval art. The history of the Baptist is to be seen in the Chapter House, Westminster, Catfield and Elsing (Norfolk) and Wiston (Suffolk) and in glass at Battlefield (Salop), St. Mary's Newington (Middlesex) and Wateringbury (Kent).

For St. John Baptist's day see p. 175.

Further Reading: A. C. Fryer, ' On Fonts and Representations of Baptism and the Holy Eucharist ', *Archaeological Journal*, vol. 60, 1903. A. C. Fryer, ' On Fonts with representations of the Seven Sacra-ments ', *Archaeological Journal*, vol. 59, 1902; vol. 87, 1930; vol. 90, 1933. See also below, p. 317.

Source: *English Fragments from Latin Medieval Service-Books* (ed. H. Littlehales, Early English Text Society, extra series vol. 90 (1903), p. 5. (Fourteenth century).

N[ame]. I cristene the in the name of the fader, and of the sone, and of the holy gost. Godfaderis and godmoderis, I charge yow, and the fader and the moder, that this child be kept this

seven yere fro water, fro feer, fro hors fot, fro hondes toth; and
that he ligge not be the fader and be the moder unto tyme he
conne sey ' ligge outter '' [lie further away], and that he be con-
fermyd of a byschop that next cometh to contre be seven myle
behalve [around], and that he be taught his beleve, that is for to
sey, Pater noster, Ave Maria, and Credo; And that ye wasche
your hondes er ye goon owt of chirche, in peyne of fastyng 40
fridayes.

A CHILD'S NURSE

Source: Translated from Bartholomew the Englishman. *On the Properties of Things*, Book 6 chapter 9. (Thirteenth century)

A rocking cradle by mother's bed. Early fourteenth century.
(Queen Mary's Psalter).

. . . A nurse rejoices with a boy when it rejoices and weeps
with him when he weeps, just like a mother. She picks him up
when he falls, gives the little one milk when he cries, kisses him
as he lies, holds him tight and gathers him up when he sprawls,
washes and cleans the little one when he makes a mess of himself,
feeds him with a finger when he pushes, teaches the boy to talk
and babbles at him in his ignorance, and almost breaks his tongue
to teach him to talk more easily. She gives him medicine when
proper and nurses him through sickness. She takes him and lifts
him up when he howls, now in her hands, now on her shoulders

and now on her knees. She chews up his food first and by chewing it makes it ready for the toothless boy so that he can swallow better, and thus she eases his hunger. When the boy is asleep she soothes him with whistlings and lullabies. She binds up his limbs with splints and rags while they are young and corrects them so that the little one does not contract any ugly bandiness. She cherishes the little one's flesh with bath and ointments.

BOYS

Source: Translated from Bartholomew the Englishman, *On the Properties of Things*, Book 6 chapter 5. (Thirteenth century)

. . . Boys are soft of flesh and pliable of body, agile and light in motion, teachable in mind, carefree and thoughtless, and in the whole conduct of their life only value frivolities. They fear no peril greater than a rap with the stick. They value an apple more than gold, and while they are young no shame prompts them to hide their nakedness. . . . Their anger is quickly aroused and calmed, and because their bodies are tender they are easily hurt. They do not like work. . . They have great appetites and are readily disposed to various maladies through overeating. Their voices and faces distinguish them from adults. . . . Many little boys have bad habits. . . . They care nothing about the future at all and love games and vanities. They refuse to attend to what is profitable and useful. They value trifles as if they were important and regard important matters as if they were trifles or nothing at all. They like what is bad for them. They make more fuss about the loss of an apple or of a pear than of an inheritance. They have no memory for past kindness. They clamour and snatch greedily at everything they see. They like the talk and ideas of boys like themselves and shun the company of the old. They do not keep a secret but repeat tactlessly everything they see or hear. They suddenly laugh, they suddenly cry, they make a ceaseless noise and endless chatter. They hardly shut up for sleep. As soon as they have been washed they make themselves filthily dirty. They make violent resistance when their mothers wash or comb them. They only think of their own stomachs . . . and are scarcely out of bed before they demand food.

GIRLS

Source: Translated from Bartholomew the Englishman, *On the Properties of Things*, Book 6 chapter 6. (Thirteenth century).

. . . As Aristotle says a girl's hair is generally wavier and softer than a man's and her neck longer. Usually the female complexion is fairer and the face more cheerful, gentle, calm and amiable. From the shoulders to the navel the body is narrower, but from thence to the knees and feet it is wider. The ends of all the limbs are more subtle and less stiff. The voice is gentle, the flow of speech ready and ample, the gait has shorter and more constricted steps, the spirit is cheeky and easily annoyed, full of hate, mercy and jealousy, impatient of sustained effort, easily led, sly, bitter and determined to get its whims instantly. . . .

BREAKING WINDOWS

Source: Excommunication by the Bishop of London of tradesmen and naughty boys who desecrate St. Paul's Cathedral, 1385, translated from Wilkins' *Concilia*, iii, 194, by Edith Rickert, *Chaucer's World*, Oxford University Press, 1948, pp. 48–9.

. . . Certain [boys], also, good for nothing in their insolence and idleness, instigated by evil minds and busying themselves rather in doing harm than good, throw and shoot stones, arrows, and different kinds of missiles at the rooks, pigeons, and other birds nesting in the walls and porches of the church and perching [there]. Also they play ball inside and outside the church and engage in other destructive games there, breaking and greatly damaging the glass windows and the stone images of the church, which, having been made with the greatest skill, are a pleasure to the eyes of all beholders, adorning the fabric and adding to its refinement. This they do not without great offense to God and our church and to the prejudice and injury of us as well as to the grave peril of their souls.

THE YOUNG SQUIRE

' Courtesy,' the good manners of the aristocracy, was inculcated in books of etiquette and permeates medieval romances like the one quoted below. It was thought to have begun at the Annunciation and the Visitation. Chaucer's description of the squire carving before his father at the table and Lydgate's poetical address to the dear child standing at table were written several generations after this passage. Intermediate between the two is the picture in the Holkham Bible Picture Book in which Christ is shown waiting on his parents.

Further Reading: G. R. Owst, *Literature and Pulpit in Medieval England*, pp. 460–8 (upbringing of children).

Chaucer's Squire. Fourteeth century.
(Ellesmere Chaucer).

Source: *The Romance of Blonde of Oxford and Jehan of Dammartin by Philippe de Reimes a Trouvère of the thirteenth century*, ed. by M. Le Roux de Lincy, Camden Society, 1858, p. vii. This romance provides an intimate picture of baronial manners in the latter half of the thirteenth century. Jean de Dammartin has been taken into the household by the Earl of Oxford and has been appointed by the Countess to wait upon their only child, Blonde, aged eighteen. The girl's French

was like that of Chaucer's prioress, for she spoke it not quite as well
as if she were born at Pontoise. Jean became a general favourite
with the family and servants. The tables were laid, all sat down
according to rank and Jean stood before Blonde and carved for her.
(Later in the poem he forgets to carve through love).

After the meal, they wash their hands, and then go to divert
themselves, according as each pleases, either in the forests or on
the rivers [in hunting or hawking], or in amusements of other
kinds. Jean goes to which he likes, and when he returns he often
goes to play in the Countess's chambers with the ladies, who kept
him occupied in teaching them French. And he does and says
courteously whatever they please to ask him, as one who was
ready at anything. Of chamber pastimes he knew enough, chess,
tables, and dice, with which he entertained his lady; he often
said to her ' check ' and ' mate '. He taught her many a game, and
instructed her in better French than she spoke when he came.
Thus she became much attached to him; for he laboured diligently
to do whatever he thought would please her.

A LOST BALL, 1337

Source: London, Coroner, *Calendar of the Coroners Rolls*, p. 191,
quoted with a series of other mishaps in childhood by Edith Rickert,
Chaucer's World, Oxford University Press, 1948, p. 99.

On Tuesday in Pentecost week John, son of William atte
Noke, chandler, got out of a window in the rent of John de
Wynton, plumber, to recover a ball lost in a gutter at play. He
slipped and fell, and so injured himself that he died on the Satur-
day following, of the fall.

APPRENTICES

Gilds protected the working conditions of their members and the
quality of their products by controlling the admission and training of
apprentices long before 1383 when the first act of Parliament noticed
the system. The Holkham Bible shows a dyer instructing his apprentice
(*T.S.I.H.*, i, back endpaper). In the original the apprentice is an

idealised drawing of the child Christ, so a more suitable figure of a boy from another page has been reproduced instead. The usual period for apprenticeship was seven years.

Source: Chaucer, *The Cook's Tale*.

A Prentis whylom [once] dwelled in our citee,
And of a craft of vitaillers was he;
Gaillard [lively] he was as goldfinch in the shawe [wood],
Broun as a berie, a propre short felawe,
With lokkes blake, y-kempt [coombed] ful fetisly [trimly],
Dauncen he coude so wel and jolily,
That he was cleped Perkin Revelour,
He was as ful of love and paramour
As is the hyve ful of hony swete;
Wel was the wenche with him mighte mete.
At every brydale wolde he singe and hoppe,
He loved bet [better] the tavern than the shoppe.
For when ther any ryding [pageant] was in Chepe,
Out of the shoppe thider wolde he lepe.
Til that he hadde al the sighte y-seyn,
And daunced wel, he wolde nat come ageyn.
And gadered him a meinee [gang] of his sort
To hoppe and singe, and maken swich [such] disport.
And ther they setten steven [fixed a date] for to mete
To pleyen at the dys in swich a strete.
For in the toune was ther no prentys,
That fairer coude caste a paire of dys
Than Perkin coude . . .
This joly prentis with his maister bood [lived]
Til he were ny out of his prentishood
Al were he snibbed [chidden] bothe erly and late,
And somtyme lad with revel to Newgate;
But atte laste his maister him bithoghte,
Up-on a day, when he his paper soghte,
Of a proverbe that seith this same word,
' Wel bet is roten appel out of hord
Than that it rotie al the remenaunt.'
[He releases the boy from his service so that he shall not demoral-
ize his servants.]

A HANDMAID

Housewives believed in discipline. In the *Monk's Prologue*, Chaucer makes the innkeeper say of his wife

> ' By goodes bones! whan I bete my knaves,
> She bringth me forth the grete clobbed staves,
> And cryeth, ' slee the dogges everichoon,
> And brek hem, bothe bak and every boon.'

This woman was, however, very assertive of her position in church, chiding her husband ' I wold have thy knyf, And thou shalt have my distaf and go spinne' '.

(1) *Source*: Translated from Bartholomew the Englishman, *On the Properties of Things*, Book 6, chapter 11. (Thirteenth century)

A mistress beats her maid with a distaff. Fourteenth century.
(Egerton Genesis).

A handmaid is the servant deputed to obey the wife. She must do the more laborious and dishonourable duties. She feeds on the coarser food, wears the rougher clothing, and is oppressed by the yoke of servitude. . . . If the handmaid is of servile origin she may not marry according to her wishes. . . .

. . . Fear keeps servile persons and handmaids down and in their place. Kindly affection sometimes raises them up to arrogant pride. . . . It is written that he who nourishes his slave delicately, will find him insolent.

(2) *Source*: Canons enacted under King Edgar (956–975). B. Thorpe, *Ancient Laws and Institutes of England,* 1840, p. 406.

If a woman give her maid a whipping with evil malice and if death is caused by the whipping and the maid be innocent, the mistress is to fast for 7 years. If, however, the maid was at fault, the mistress should fast [cf. p. 308] for 3 years and should do penance for her sins.

SERVANTS

(1) *Source*: Statute of Labourers 23 Edward III, cap. 1–2 (translated as in edition of 1577). (1349).

1. . . . . Because a great part of the people, and especially of workemen and servantes late died in pestilence, many seeing the necessity of maisters, a great scarceity of servauntes, wil not serve unlesse they may receive excessive wages, and some rather willing to beg in idlenesse, then by labour to get their living: we considering the grevous discommoditie, which of the lacke especially of the ploughmen and such labourers may hereafter come, have thereupon be deliberation and treatie with the prelates and the nobles and wisemen assisting us, of whose mutual counsaile it is ordained, that every man or woman of our realme of England, of what condition he be, free or bound, able in bodie, and within the age of 40 yeares, not living in marchandise, nor exercising any craft, nor having of his owne, wherof he may live, nor proper land, about whose tillage he may himselfe occupie and not serving any other, if he in convenient service (his estate considered) be required to serve, he shalbe bounden to serve him which so shal him require. And take onely the wages, livery, meede or salary, which were accustomed to be geeven, in the places where hee oweth to serve, the 20 yeare of our raign of England, or 5 or 6 other common yeares nexte before. Provided alwaies, that the Lordes be preferred before other in their bond-

men or their land-tenantes, so in their service to be reteined. So that neverthelesse the said Lords shall receive no more than be necessary for them. And if any such man or woman, being so required to serve, wil not the same doe, that proved by 2 true men before the shiriffe or the bayliffes, of our soveraigne lord the king, or the constables of the towne where the same shall happen to be done, he shal anone be taken by them or any of them, and committed to the nexte gaole, there to remain under streit keping, til he find suretie to serve in the forme aforesaid.

2.   Item if any reaper, mower, or other workeman or servant, of what estate or condition that he be, reteined in any mans service, do depart from the said service without reasonable cause or lycense, before the terms agreed, he shal have paine of imprisonment. And that none under the same pain presume to receive or to retaine any such in his service. . . .

AN UNTRAINED SERVANT, c. 1460

Source: ' The duties of a Panter or Butler ' in John Russell's ' Book of Nurture '; *The Babees Book Medieval Manners for the Young done into modern English from Dr. Furnivall's Texts* by Edith Rickert, Chatto and Windus, 1923, pp. 56–8.

I will that ye eschew forever the ' simple conditions ' of a person that is not taught.

Do not claw your head or your back as if you were after a flea, or stroke your hair as if you sought a louse.

Be not glum, nor twinkle with your eyes, nor be heavy of cheer; and keep your eyes from winking and watering.

Do not pick your nose or let it drop clear pearls, or sniff, or blow it too hard, lest your lord hear.

Twist not your neck askew like a jackdaw; wring not your hands with picking or trifling or shrugging, as if ye would saw wood; nor puff up your chest, nor pick your ears, nor be slow of hearing.

Retch not, nor spit too far, nor laugh or speak too loud. Beware of making faces and scorning; and be no liar with your mouth.   Nor yet lick your lips or drivel.

Do not have the habit of squirting or spouting with your mouth, or gape or yawn or pout. And do not lick a dish with tongue to get out dust.

Be not rash or reckless—that is not worth a clout.

Do not sigh with your breast, or cough, or breathe hard in the presence of your sovereign, or hiccough, or belch, or groan never the more. Do not trample with your feet, or straddle your legs, or scratch your body—there is no sense in showing off. Good son, do not pick your teeth, or grind, or gnash them, or with puffing and blowing cast foul breath upon your lord. . . .

SOAP AND FULLER'S EARTH

The fat of Cotswold sheep was the basis of a soap industry at Bristol by the twelfth century which appeared in the thirteenth century at Coventry and London—where the name Soper Lane first occurs in the 41st year of Henry III. In the early thirteenth century the *Ancren Riwle* alludes to pedlars bringing soap (and needles) to three anchoresses, with whom they could talk through a stuff shutter in their hermitage window. Soda, and wood ash (which Bristol could get from the forest of Dean) were necessary raw materials. Cheap, black, sandy soap was used for scouring, soap was used to lubricate mills, but fine toilet soap was scented with herbs in private stillrooms, and as it was soft was kept in wooden bowls. Laundresses sometimes used fuller's earth, white clay, or a strong alkaline solution, made from ash, called lye. In 1376 the city of London forbade fullers to use urine as a detergent in preparing cloth.

Further Reading: C. Ross, ' The Household Accounts of Elizabeth Berkeley, Countess of Warwick, 1420–1 ', *Transactions Bristol and Gloucs. Archaeological Society*, vol. 70, 1951.

Source: Royal writ to protect the cloth industry, 1326, H. T. Riley, *Memorials of London and London Life, 1276–1419*, pp. 150–1.

. . . we do therefore desire that none of the thistles that in English are called ' *taseles* ' [teasels used for carding cloth], and no fullers' earth, shall be carried out of the same kingdom and lands [of England]: We do command you, strictly enjoining, that in the same our city you do cause proclamation publicly to be made, and in our behalf strict prohibition to be made, that any merchant, foreigner or native, or other person, shall carry or

I

send such manner of thistles or such fullers' earth out of the same our realm and lands, on pain of heavy forfeiture to us; or that any one sell, or cause to be sold, such thistles or fullers' earth to the merchants aforesaid, or other persons, to carry the same out of our said realm and lands. Nor are you in any way to allow such thistles or earth to be taken or sent out of the city [of London] aforesaid to any foreign parts.

LAUNDRY

As soap was largely home made when sufficient mutton fat had accumulated, it was customary to allow the dirty washing to mount up and to do a large quantity at a time. This might often be before one of the great feasts of the church. Yet London, Bristol and Coventry soapers flourished and by the fourteenth century ' soap-sellers and their sons for silver have been made knights '.

Early in the reign of Stephen a survey of the household shows that there was doubt about the establishment of the laundress, but under John, Florence, the royal laundress, was regularly established and is found receiving periodical payments of 18d. for shoes.

At Sandwich the Common Sergeant had to take especial care to prevent washerwomen rinsing clothes and tubs in the public stream. In 1120 the women washing in the brook at Reading made such a disturbance with their battle-dores, beating the washing, that it disturbed the burghers in the new Guildhall. They were not to use the wells at Leicester or the stews (public hot baths) at Southwark. The Holkham Bible Picture Book contains a picture of the Virgin with a battledore doing the washing for the Christ child in a stream and various prints show the same theme. A four-legged stool keeps the clothes off the dirty ground. Washerwomen's legs became very muddy. *The Merry Wives of Windsor* concerns Falstaff's misadventures in a washing basket.

Source: *Household of Edward IV*, *the Black Book and the Ordinance of* 1478, ed. A. R. Myers, Manchester University 1958, pp. 195–7.

Offyce of Lauendrye, ij yoman wherof one moste specially shall fet or receyue be taile, safly to kepe and tenderly to wasshe and preserue diligentlye the stuf for the kinges proper persone of the warderobis of beddes and robez, ewery, and of alle other offices in houshold that minister such naprye or lynyn clothe for the kynges use, and truly to delyuer such stuf agayne to euerye office be tale as he receyuyd or by mark and that any straungeors

set none handes upon hit. That other yoman shall with a grome
or page fet and reciue of thofficers of ewry all sortes of napry,
table clothis, long towellies, short napkyns, and other soylyd
lynyn cloth be tailles and mark; and of alle other offices the
kynges stuf soylyd, as alle the surplices of syngers of chapelle
and awbis [albs] and amices soylyd from the vestery the neck
towelles of pantry . . . and all that is the kinges stuf, and truly to
delyuer hit agayne upon payne of making good therfor or the
leste pece therof. This yoman shall fet the gret spicery asmuch
white sope, gray, and blak, as can be thought reasonable. . . .
Also they haue . . . for the grete basons, for vatis and asshis
bougght for the use of householde, yf hit nede; but the custom is
that they shall haue asshis clothes of the spicerye to fet asshis in
theym from euery man's chamber and kychins within the corte
. . . if there be a quene in householde, than there be women
lauenders. . . .

CHESTS

Treasure was kept in chests. So too were clothes and books, in the
absence of more specialized kinds of furniture. The earliest chests
were dug out of the trunk of a tree, generally oak, but examples of elm
occur and Cleveley and Swaffham Bulbeck churches contain examples
made of cypress and cedar. The oldest are perhaps those at Wimborne
and West Grinstead but ones of greater length and weight are at Curd-
worth and Shustoke in Warwickshire and at West Hanningfield,
Essex. In the thirteenth century chests came to be carpentered and
were strengthened and ornamented with iron scrolls and in the fourteenth century they had carved panels with Gothic architectural tracery.
Such chests have survived in greater numbers in parish churches than
in private houses.

Further Reading: F. Roe, *Ancient Coffers and Cupboards*, 1902.

Source: extract from inventory from Warwick, 1464, J. Charles
Cox, *English Church Fittings Furniture and Accessories* (1923), p. 279.

It. in the lowe house under the vestry ii old ire [iron] bound
coofres.

It. in the vestrye i gret olde arke to put in vestryments.

It. in the Sextry above the Vestrye i olde arke . . . i old coofre
ire bonde having a long lok of the olde fasion and i large new

Burgling chest in royal bedroom.
Thirteenth century.
(Life of Edward the Confessor).

coofre having iii loks called the tresory cofre, and contayne
almaries [cupboards].

It. in the inner hous i newe hie almarie with ii dores to kepe
in the evidence [muniments] of the Churche, and i gret olde arke
and certayne old Almaries.

It. in the house afore the Chapter hous i old ire bond cofre
having hie feet and rings of iron in the endes thereof to heve it
bye. And therein lieth certain bokes belonging to the Chapter.

A LUXURIOUS BEDROOM

Here is a room very different from the bedroom of Chaucer's
Miller of Trumpington in the *Reves Tale* where the scene of a low
comedy is a room containing five adults in three beds, plus a baby in a
cradle. Even in that room the miller's wife thought one of two clerks
from Cambridge was wearing a white *volupeer* (night cap).

Further Reading: R. W. Symonds, 'Domestic Comfort in the
Medieval Home: an Illusion Dispelled', *Connoisseur*, March 1951.

Source: Chaucer, *The Book of the Duchesse*.

If he wol make me slepe a lyte [little]
Of downe of pure dowves whyte
I will give him a fether-bed,
Rayed [striped] with golde, and tight wel cled
In fyn blak satin doutremere [imported],
And many a pilow, and every bere [pillow-case]
Of clothe of Reynes, to slepe softe;
Him thar not nede to turnen ofte.
And I wol give him al that falles
To a chambre; and al his halles
I wol do peynte with pure golde,
And tapite hem ful many folde
Of oo sute [uniform pattern] . . .

READING IN BED

Chaucer's Clerk of Oxenford preferred to ' have at his beddes
heed twenty bokes, clad in blak or reed, of Aristotle and his philosphye,
than robes riche, or fithele (fiddle), or gay sautrye '. The less learned
when they could read liked something lighter.

Source: Chaucer, *The Book of the Duchesse*.

So whan I saw I might not slepe,
Til now late, this other night,
Upon my bedde I sat upright,
And bad oon reche me a book,
A romaunce, and he hit me took
To rede and dryve the night away;
For me thoghte it better play
Then playen either at chesse or tables.
And in this boke were writen fables
That clerkes hadde, in old tyme,
And other poets, put in ryme
To rede. . . .

BEDROOM HANGINGS, 1386

Adela, daughter of William I, had bed hangings like the Bayeux Tapestry, but considered finer. Henry III ordered drapery to be painted above the head of his bed at Guildford (1259).

Source: Essex Record Office, F. G. Emmison's translation of Arnald Monteny's inventory, 1386, in F. W. Steer, ' Smaller Houses and their Furnishings in the Seventeenth and Eighteenth Centuries ', *Journal of the British Archaeological Association*, 3rd series, vols. 20–21, 1958, p. 155 (with farm stock, buttery, kitchen and napery stuff).

. . . one great chamber striped in white and red of worsted, that is to say, 1 coverlet, 1 tester, 1 bed-ceiling, 3 curtains, 6 hangings of 5 yards in length and 2 yards and a half in width, 2 tapestries for forms, each of 4 yards in length and 6 cushions; also one other red chamber, that is to say 1 coverlet, one tester [head-piece] with a half-ceiling, 3 curtains, 4 hangings, each hanging of 5 yards in length and 2 yards and a half in width and 1 tapestry for 1 form of five yards in length; also 1 other room striped in red and white worsted, that is to say, 1 coverlet, 1 tester with a half-ceiling and 3 curtains; also 1 tester of white worsted; also 1 coverlet and 1 tester of green powdered with birds; also 1 mattress of large size; also 1 other mattress of half size of green; also 1 pair of blankets of 4 ells of length and 3 of width; also 1 other pair of middle size; also 1 other pair of sheets of 3 webs, each of 4 yards in length; also 1 sheet of the same, the cloth for the head of 2 webs, and in length 3 yards; also 1 pair of sheets of 2 webs and of 3 yards and ¾ in length and 1 other pair of sheets of 2 webs and a half and in length, 3 yards and ¾; also 1 other pair of sheets of 3 webs and 4 yards in length and 1 sheet for the head of 2 webs and 3 yards in length; also 1 other pair of sheets of 2 webs and 1 other pair of sheets of 3 webs; also of canvases, 2, of which 1 is large size and the other half size; also 1 covering of pure miniver of 26 timbers [40 skins is 1 timber] and 38 skins and 1 fur of martens of 60 skins and 1 fur of squirrel of 5 timbers and 15 skins and 1 covering of conies. . . .

GROOMS OF THE ROYAL CHAMBER, c. 1471-2

Further Reading: G. S. Thompson, *Two Centuries of Family History*, 1930.

Source: *The Household of Edward IV, the Black Book and the Ordinance of* 1478, ed. A. R. Myers, Manchester University Press 1959, pp. 120-1.

Gromes of Chambyr, x. Thereof one is grome porter that berith wood, straw, russhes for the kinges chambre, making the kinges litters of his bed and to fylle the paylettes. And he fettith nyghtly, after the seasons of the yere, torchys, tortays [tall candles], candylles of wax, morters [lamps]; and he settith up the sises [tall candles] in the kinges chaumbre with out ony wast or giftes or taking of fees, but that the jentylman ussher assigne hit in the kinges honour with profit, and dayly recordith that he settith truly in the countynghouse by tayle, so that his good dealing may be knowe. And if he lese eny thing hereof, than to awnswere therefore and to make hit good as the juges of the countynghouse woll award. He takith a dayly peny alowed in the byll of the hall, and for his reward and clothing with the household lyke to the gromez of chaumbyr and wardrobes aforesayd, besydes his waching, clothing and othyr; but he takith no part, nor none of thes gromez nor pages of chambre, of ony gyft that shall be made to the household. And he etith dayly out of the kinges chambre, to be nyghe the ussher's comaundmentes or callinges, taking in opyn dayes ij loues, ij messes of grete mete, 1 gallon ale for all day; he is permitted to haue into this court a seraunt to help hym bere such necessarijs. And dayly iiij other of thes gromes, called wayters, to make fyres, to set trestyls and bourdes, with yomen of chambre, and to helpe dresse the beddes of sylke and arras uppon the ussher's apoyntment, and to geve the yoman water after dyner and souper, and to help hang the chambre and to kepe hem clene from dogges and other unclennes. Thes gromes also ete with out the grete chambre pryuatly, as theyre course goith about dayly in opyn dayes, taking iiij loues, iij messe of kychyn of grete mete, ij gallons ale; the remnaunt of all thes gromyz dyne and soupe in the hall with yomen of houshold. Another of thes gromes is called ' of the armory for the kinges person '; another callid ' grome surgeon '; another

' grome pulter [poulterer] '; and another as the chambrelayne
woll apoynt. Euery grome quarterly as the countynghouse
rewardithe, xl d. and clothing with the household or ellez vj s.
viij d., besidez there waching clothing of the warderober; and
besidez the grete reward yeven from the kinges priuy cofers to
the gromes and pages of his chambre. Also ij gromes of chambre
be suffred to haue in to this court j honest seruant, and they haue
lyuerey for theyre horse assigned in the contrey by the herbiger
[harbinger who purveys in advance]; and also the kinges chambrelayn to assigne for the ij garderobes and the kinges chambre, for
the male [pack] and stoole [commode] and other stuf nedefull,
to the some of xij or xvj sompters, whereof the thesaurere of
household berith no charge but for horsmete, shoyng, kepers'
wages, and other clothing. Thes gromez of chaumbre, one of
them fettyth nygtly bred, j lofe, a gallon ale, for the kinges bed-
making, with a torter of the grome porter of chambre.

ROYAL BEDCLOTHES, c. 1471-2

In medieval pictures of bedrooms people in bed are generally
shown naked though Froissart mentions a nobleman's nightshirt.
Women when sick sometimes wore turbans, as does St. Peter's mother-
in-law as pictured in her bedroom in the Holkham Bible Picture Book.
The yeoman and groom here mentioned were supplied with rushes and
litter for their own pallets.

Source: *Household of Edward IV*, *the Black Book and the Ordinance of*
478; ed. A. R. Myers, Manchester University Press, 1959, p. 119.

. . . And this yoman, or this grome berith up nyghtly stuf for
the kinges bed and bideth there till hit be made; and in the
mornynge they fett hit down to their office [of warderobe of
beddes] ageyn saufly and clenly, that no stranger shall touche hit.
In wynter or somer, and hit nede, the berer upp of this stufe shall
haue a torche before of the grome porter, borne by the grome or
page of warderobe or chambre: and if this office require more
largesse of wood or coole, then to haue comaundement therefor
by the countynhouse. . . . The officers of this office serue the king
for all thing that longeth to his body day and nygt in tym of pees;
they bringyth hit upp and fett hit down, and brusshe hit, and

clense hit, and saufly keepe hit; and the stoole [commode] is here
kept. . . . Also in this office gromes, ij . . . Thes ij gromez haue
into court on honest childe. Also in this office, a page, keping
and atending in this office, to see in all maner lyuerez, to kepe,
trusse, and bere the harneys and stuf, to wayte upon the caryagez.
They should be sumewhat understanding with nedyll worke. . . .

CANTERBURY DORMITORY, LATE TWELFTH CENTURY

Further Reading: J. Armitage Robinson, 'The Early Community
at Christ Church, Canterbury', *Journal of Theological Studies*, vol. 27,
1926, pp. 225–40.

Source: *The Monastic Constitutions of Lanfranc*, Nelson, 1951, p. 144.

. . . he [a brother] goes to the dormitory and there rests in
absolute silence and quiet, so that neither by sound of voice nor
by movement of any object does anyone make a noise nor do
anything that may be heard by his neighbour or may in any way
be a nuisance to his brethren. Let him place his habit tidily
before his bed so that he may find it to hand in the morning, and
similarly let him put his footwear at the foot of his bed. If anything is done or shifted or placed untidily or awkwardly, the
watchman, that is, the monk who remains awake in the dormitory
and goes round often in the night to see if there be anything
needing correction, shall tell of it in the morning at chapter in
the presence of all, and satisfaction shall be made. Therefore we
must take care that nothing be done at night that will be shameful
to hear in the morning. . . .

When day has dawned he should rise straightway when the
signal is heard and take his night shoes and go to the church, and
there say the *Miserere* at the desks until *Deus in adjutorium* is said.
After Prime the seven penitential psalms are straightway said
with the litany and prostration—that is, we prostrate ourselves
after the seven psalms. After the litany and the collects that
follow he goes forthwith to the dormitory and then taking his
book, descends into the cloister, and there sits and studies in his
book, each in his appointed place, until the signal known as the

' shoe-signal ' is heard. Then, shod and carrying knife and comb, he descends again to the cloister, and putting the books on the seat goes to the washing-place, and having washed his hands stands again by his book and combs his hair. Then, book in hand, he goes in order to church for Terce. . . .

EARLY TO BED, FOURTEENTH CENTURY

The original author of this treatise, Lorens d'Orleans, was a thirteenth century Dominican friar.

Source: *The Book of Vices and Virtues, a Fourteenth Century English translation of the Somme le Roi of Lorens d'Orleans*, ed. by W. Nelson Francis, Early English Text Society, O.S. 217, 1942, p. 49.

And wite [know] wel, as a man synneth to ete bifor tyme, rigt so synneth a man to ete over late or soupe. And therfore thes men and wommen that loven so wel to wake longe and spende that tyme in ydelnesse and gon late to bedde and ariseth late aday, they synneth in many maneres. First in that thei wasteth tyme and turneth up-so-doun, for of the nygt thei maketh day. Suche folk God curseth bi the prophete, for on the day men schulde do good, and on the nygt serve God, thanke hym, and praie to hym; for who-so goth to bedde whan he scholde arise, he most slepe whan he scholde praye and heere his servise and thanke God, and thus he leseth al the tyme, bothe, nygt and day. And after, in suche wakynges me [one] doth moche harme, as to pleye at the chesse or at the tables, at the hasard, at the queke [chequers], and othere synful games with the dees; and many sweren and speken wikkede wordes of lecherie and othere vices, and therwith cometh reere-soperes [late suppers] and ofte drynkynges, and thus wasteth wrecches the tyme and his witt and spendeth his good wikkidly and wraththeth God and schent [ruins] his body and lest [loses] his soule.

BEDS

The association of beds with birth, marriage and death meant that they were often pictured in manuscripts in such scenes as the Birth of the Virgin, David and the Shunamite Woman, and the Death of Edward the Confessor. A Virgil at Holkham shows a fine early fifteenth century bed, like the treasured beds mentioned in the wills of the rich. The Three Kings, on their way to Bethlehem, are sometimes shown sleeping all in one bed, and it was quite customary to have several beds in one room. A noble moving from manor to manor might take his beds (like his window glass) with him.

A low wooden Viking bedstead survives from the ' Gokstad ship '. A pole or perch for hanging up clothes is shown in the Holkham Bible picture Book in the scene of the Nativity of St. John the Baptist.

There is a bedroom fire-place in the thirteenth century Salt Tower in the Tower of London. Chaucer's clerk of Oxenford had books by his bed and one tripped over books on the floor of Bishop Ricard de Bury (see *W.W.I.H.*, i, p. 168).

Source: U. T. Holmes, Jr., *Daily Living in the Twelfth Century, based on the Observations of Alexander Neckam*, Madison, The University of Wisconsin Press 1952, p. 82–3. For Alexander Neckam see *W.W.I.H.*, i, 112–3.

In the bedchamber let a curtain go around the walls decently, or a scenic canopy, for the avoiding of flies and spiders. . . . A tapestry should hang appropriately. Near the bed let there be placed a chair to which a stool may be added, and a bench nearby the bed. On the bed itself should be placed a feather mattress to which a bolster is attached. A quilted pad of striped cloth should cover this on which a cushion for the head can be placed. Then sheets of muslin, ordinary cotton, or at least pure linen, should be laid. Next a coverlet of green cloth or of coarse wool, of which the fur lining is badger, cat, beaver, or sable, should be put—all this if there is lacking purple or down. A perch should be nearby on which can rest a hawk. . . . From another pole let there hang clothing . . . and let there be also a chambermaid whose face may charm and render tranquil the chamber, who, when she finds time to do so may knit or unknit silk thread, or make knots of orphryes [gold lace], or may sew linen garments and woollen clothes, or may mend. Let her have gloves with the finger tips removed; she should have a leather case protecting the finger from needle pricks, which is vulgarly called a ' thimble '. She must have scissors and a spool of thread and various sizes of needles—small and thin for embroidery, others not so thick for feather stitching, moderately fine ones for ordinary sewing, bigger ones for the knitting of a cloak, still larger ones for threading laces.

MAKING THE BED, AND SLEEP, c. 1460

Source: ' The Office of a Chamberlain ' in John Russell's ' Book of Nurture ';*The Babees' Book Medieval Manners for the Young done into Modern English from Dr. Furnivall's Texts* by Edith Rickert, Chatto and Windus, 1923, pp. 65–67.

Then return in hast to your lord's chamber, strip the clothes off the bed and cast them aside, and beat the feather-bed, but not so as to waste any feathers, and see that the blankets and sheets be clean. When you have made the bed mannerly, cover it with a coverlet, spread out the bench-covers, and cushions, set up the head-sheet and pillow, and remove the basin. See that carpets be laid round the bed, and dress the windows and the cupboard with carpets [tapestries] and cushions. See there be a good fire conveyed into the chamber, with plenty of wood and fuel to make it up. . . .

If your lord take a nap after his meal to digest his stomach, have ready kerchief and comb, pillow and head-sheet; yet be not far from him—take heed what I say—for much sleep is not good in the middle of the day, and have ready water and towel so that he may wash after his sleep.

When he has supped and goes to his chamber, spread forth your foot-sheet, as I have already shown you, take off his gown or whatever garment by the license of his estate [sumptuary laws] he wears, and lay it up in such place as ye know best. Put a mantle on his back to keep his body from cold, set him on the foot-sheet, made ready as I have directed, and pull off his shoes, socks and hosen, and throw these last over your shoulder, or hold them on your arm. Comb his hair, but first kneel down, and put on his kerchief and night-cap . . . in seemly fashion. Have the bed, head-sheet and pillow ready; and when he is in bed, there to sleep safe and sound, draw the curtains round about the bed, set there his night-light with wax or [lofty] Paris-candle, and see that there is enough to last the night, drive out the dog and the cat, giving them a clout, take no leave of your lord, but bow low to him and retire, and thus shall ye have thanks and reward whensoever it fall.

PRINCELY MANNER, c. 1475

The importance attached to ' courtesy ' is clear in medieval romances and was a great civilizing influence. One of the most important tracts for teaching manners was *The Babees' Book*, written for young princes about 1475, and very likely for those very two princes, Edward V and Richard Duke of York, who were murdered in the Tower. The influence of such training is reflected in Chaucer's descriptions of the Prioress and of the Squire.

Source: Edith Rickert, *The Babees' Book Medieval Manners for the Young done into Modern English from Dr. Furnivall's Texts*, Chatto and Windus, 1908, p. 3ff.

When you enter your lord's place, say ' Good speed ', and with humble cheer greet all who are there present. Do not rush in rudely, but enter with head up and at an easy pace, and kneel on one knee only to your lord or sovereign, whichever he be.

If any speak to you at your coming, look straight at them with a steady eye, and give good ear to their words while they be speaking; and see to it with all your might that ye jangle [chatter] not, nor let your eyes wander about the house, but pay heed to what is said, with blithe visage and diligent spirit. When ye answer, ye shall be ready with what ye shall say, and speak ' things fructuous ', and give your reasons smoothly in words that are gentle but compendious, for many words are right tedious to the wise man who listens; therefore eschew them with diligence.

Take no seat, but be ready to stand until you are bidden to sit down. Keep your hands and feet at rest; do not claw your flesh or lean against a post, in the presence of your lord, or handle anything belonging to the house.

Make obeisance to your lord alway when you answer; otherwise, stand as still as a stone, unless he speak.

Look with one accord that if ye see any person better than yourself come in, ye go backwards anon and given him place, and in nowise turn your face from him, as far forth as you may.

If you see your lord drinking, keep silence, without loud laughter, chattering, whispering, joking or other insolence.

If he command you to sit in his presence, fulfill his wish at once, and strive not with another about your seat.

When you are set down, tell no dishonest tale; eschew also, with all your might, to be scornful; and let your cheer be humble, blithe, and merry, not chiding as if ye were ready for a fight.

If you perceive that your better is pleased to commend you, rise up anon and thank him heartily.

If you see your lord and lady speaking of household matters, leave them alone, for that is courtesy, and interfere not with their doing; but be ready, without feigning, to do your lord service, and so shall you get a good name.

Also, to fetch him drink, to hold the light when it is time, and to do whatsoever ought to be done, look ye be ready; for so shall ye full soon get a gentle name in nurture. And if you should ask a boon of God, you can desire no better thing than to be well-mannered.

If your lord is pleased to offer you his own cup to drink, rise when you take it, and receive it goodly with both your hands, and when you have done, proffer it to no man else, but render it again to him that brought it, for in nowise should it be used commonly—so wise men teach us.

Now must I tell you shortly what you shall do at noon when your lord goes to his meat. Be ready to fetch him clear water, and some of you hold the towel for him until he has done, and leave not until he be set down, and ye have heard grace said. Stand before him until he bids you sit, and be always ready to serve him with clean hands.

When ye be set, keep your own knife clean and sharp, that so ye may carve honestly your own meat.

Let courtesy and silence dwell with you, and tell no foul tales to another.

Cut your bread with your knife and break it not. Lay a clean trencher before you, and when your pottage is brought, take your spoon and eat quietly; and do not leave your spoon in the dish, I pray you.

Look ye be not caught leaning on the table, and keep clear of soiling the cloth.

Do not hang your head over your dish, or in any wise drink with full mouth.

Keep from picking your nose, your teeth, your nails at meal-time—so we are taught.

Advise you against taking so muckle meat into your mouth but that ye may right well answer when men speak to you.

When ye shall drink, wipe your mouth clean with a cloth, and your hands also, so that you shall not in any way soil the cup, for then shall none of your companions be loth to drink with you.

Likewise, do not touch the salt in the salt-cellar with any meat; but lay salt honestly on your trencher, for that is courtesy.

Do not carry your knife to your mouth with food, or hold the meat with your hands in any wise; and also if divers goodmeats are brought to you, look that with all courtesy ye assay of each; and if your dish be taken away with its meat and another brought, courtesy demands that ye shall let it go and not ask for it back again.

And if strangers be set at table with you, and savoury meat be brought or sent to you, make them good cheer with part of it, for certainly it is not polite when others be present at meat with you, to keep all that is brought you, and like churls vouchsafe nothing to others.

Do not cut your meat like field-men who have such an appetite that they reck not in what wise, where or when or how ungoodly they hack at their meat; but, sweet children, have always your delight in courtesy and in gentleness, and eschew boisterousness with all your might.

When cheese is brought, have a clean trencher, on which with a clean knife ye may cut it; and in your feeding look ye appear goodly, and keep your tongue from jangling, for so indeed shall ye deserve a name for gentleness and good governance, and always advance yourself in virtue.

When the end of the meal is come, clean your knives, and look you put them up where they ought to be, and keep your seat until you have washed, for so wills honesty.

When ye have done, look then that ye rise up without laughter or joking or boisterous word, and go to your lord's table, and there stand, and pass not from him until grace be said and brought to an end. . . .

CLEAN AND UNCLEAN FOOD

Source: Confessional of Archbishop Ecgbert (735–766). B. Thorpe, *Ancient Laws and Institutes of England*, 1840, pp. 358–360.

You may eat fish although it has been found dead because it is not of our nature. Horse flesh is allowed, although many people will not eat it. Birds and other creatures found strangled in nets are not to be eaten; even if a hawk pecked them if they are found dead they are not to be eaten for in the Acts of the Apostles it is commanded to keep yourselves from fornication and from things strangled and from blood and from idolatry. You may eat a hare and it is good against dysentery and diarrhoea if sodden in water. And mixed with pepper its liver is good for mouth-ache.

If bees kill a man let them be killed at once before they reach the honey, at any rate so that they do not stay there through the night; and let the honey which they have made be eaten. If a young pig fall into liquor and is taken out alive, let the liquor be sprinkled with holy water and fumigated with incense and let the liquor be taken; if it is dead and the liquor cannot be given let it be poured out. If any one touch any food with impure hands, or if a dog, or a cat, or a mouse touch it or any unclean animal, [Archbishop] Theodore has said that it comes to no harm. But if a mouse or a weasel fall into much liquor and die there let it be sprinkled with holy water and taken. No harm comes if any from necessity eat an unclean animal. A sick man may take food at any hour whatsoever and whenever he wish. . . .

If pigs eat any dead flesh or taste any human blood we do not think that they need be cast out; but it is not lawful to eat them until they are clean. If a hen drink human blood, it is lawful to eat it after 3 months; but on this point we have not ancient authority. If anyone eat anything with blood in half cooked food, if consciously, he is to fast 7 days, if unconciously, for 3 days or to sing the Psalter. If anyone unconsciously drinks his own blood in his saliva, there is no peril. If anyone eat anything from that of which a dog or a mouse has eaten or which a weasel had defiled, if consciously, he is to sing 100 psalms, if unconsciously, 50 psalms. If anyone gives to another liquor in which a mouse or a weasel has been drowned, if he is a layman, let him fast 3 days; if he is a monk, let him sing 100 psalms. If he knew it not at first but knew it later, let him sing the Psalter.

FOOD FOR THE COURT, c. 1471-2

Source: The Household of Edward IV, the Black Book and the Ordinance of 1478, ed. A. R. Myers, Manchester University Press 1959, p. 140.

Cooking, 1066. (Bayeux Tapestry).

Clerke of Markette . . . the clerk ridith in the contries before the kinges commyng to warn the peple to bake, to brewe, and to make redy othyr vytayle and stuff in to theire logginges. Also in euery goode market town, as hit shall seme hit most expedyent, he may charge xij the saddest [most serious] men of dwellers to preyse [value] the greynys [corn] and to sesse the prises [forced deliveries] of bred, wyne, ale, mannes mete, and horsmete, and othyr stuf, by theyre othis, for the king and his household.

K

ONE DAY'S ORDINARY MEALS

Source: The Household Book of Dame Alice de Bryene of Acton Hall, Suffolk, Sept. 1412–*Sept.* 1413, translated by Miss M. K. Dale, edited by V. B. Redstone, Suffolk Institute of Archaeology and Natural History, 1931, p. 40.

The baking: one qr. wheat, whence came 234 white, and 30 black, loaves.

The brewing: 2 qr. barley-malt, whence came 112 gall. ale.

Meals: Breakfast 12, dinner 26, supper 20. Sum 58.

Thurs., 16 Feb. [Guests] The lady Waldegrave with a son, maidservant, squire, 3 grooms and 2 boys, 2 carpenters making a plough, 2 carters of the manor, the whole day, 2 friars of Sudbury with one of their household. Thomas Barbour with one of his household, John Baketon, one repast.

PANTRY—62 white, and 8 black, loaves, whereof newly-baked 20 white, and 6 black, loaves; wine from supply; ale from stock.

KITCHEN—one quarter of bacon, one swan, 3 capons, one heron.

PURCHASES—veal 19 d., one young pig 5d.

PROVENDER—hay from stock for 16 horses; fodder for the same, 2 bush. oats.

Sum of purchases, 2s.

CORN DEALERS, 1419

Further Reading: N. S. B. Gras, *Evolution of the English Corn Market,* 1915.

Source: Liber Albus, the White Book of the City of London compiled in A.D. 1419 *by John Carpenter and Richard Whittington,* translated by H. T. Riley, Richard Griffin 1861, p. 229.

Also, as to corn-dealers who bring corn unto the City for sale that no one shall sell by show or by sample. But they shall come to certain places in the City established with their carts laden, and with their horses having the loads upon them, without selling anything, and without getting rid of anything, until they reach the established places; that is to say, within the Gate of Neugate, before the Friars Minors there, and at Graschirche; and this, without putting anything into house or into hiding-place, whether the same arrive by night or by day. And that no corn shall be sold upon the hour of Prime rung at Saint Paul's, under penalty of forfeiting such corn. And that all vessels, scouts, and boats, of whatever kind they may be, that bring corn to sell, as well at Billyngesgate as elsewhere on the Thames, shall remain upon common sale after they have arrived, without selling anything in gross for one whole day; that so the common people may buy for their sustenance what they shall need; and this under heavy forfeiture.

And whereas some buyers and brokers of corn do buy corn in the City of country folks who bring it to the City to sell, and give, on the bargain being made, a penny or halfpenny by way of earnest; and tell the peasants to take the corn to their house, and that there they shall receive their pay. And when they come there and think to have their payment directly, the buyer says that his wife at his house has gone out, and has taken the key of the room, so that he cannot get at his money; but that the other must go away, and come again soon and receive his pay. And when he comes back a second time, then the buyer is not to be found; or else, if he is found, he feigns something else, by reason whereof the poor men cannot have their pay. And sometimes, while the poor men are waiting for their pay, which was agreed upon, they are told to wait until such a day as the buyer shall choose to name, or else to take off a part of the price; which if they will not do, they may take their corn and carry it away; a thing which they cannot do, because it is wetted, and in another state than it was in when they sold it. And by such evil delays on part of the buyer, the poor men lose half of their pay in expenses before they are fully settled with. It is provided, that the person towards whom such knavishness shall be committed, shall make complaint unto the Mayor; and if he shall be able to make proof, and convict the buyer before the Mayor of the wrong so done to him, the buyer shall pay the vendor double the value, and full damages as well, in case the Mayor shall see that the value aforesaid does not suffice

for the damage which he has received; and nevertheless, let him
also be heavily amerced [fined] unto the King, if he have the
means. And if he have not the means of paying the penalty
aforesaid, or of finding the amercement, then he shall be put in
the pillory, and remain there one hour in the day at least, a
Serjeant of the City standing by the side of the pillory with good
hue and cry as to the reason why he is so punished.

MANORIAL BAKING OVENS

In many villages the peasants had to bake at the lord's oven as well
as having their corn ground at his mill. At Leicester the Earl kept
these rights until the late fourteenth century. For mills see pp. 42–6. In
some hamlets it was customary as late as the nineteenth century to take
food to be baked in the local baker's oven, but in Yorkshire there was
a strong tradition established of making bread at home. Sometimes the
oven was let to an individual or the village as a whole and sometimes
in court rolls fines are inflicted on those who did not bake at the oven;
for it is quite possible to bake good bread without an oven using an
iron pot as is still done sometimes in western Ireland. A baking oven
was made warm by a faggot, placed right inside. In the Holkham Bible
Picture Book there is a picture of a typical baking oven. Bakers were
as unpopular for cheating as millers.

Further Reading: Cases at Mamecestre, Tatenhill and Kettering in
Select Pleas in Manorial Courts, ed. F. W. Maitland, Selden Soc., vol. 2.

Source: *The Court Baron*, Ed. F. W. Maitland, Selden Soc., vol. 4, p.
73 (a typical case with no particular date or place).

It fell out that on Monday next after S. Andrew that M. wife
of the hayward and E. wife of a neighbour were baking at an
oven, to wit that of N., and a dispute arose between them about
the loss of a loaf taken from the oven, and the said old crones
took to their fists and each other's hair and raised the hue; and
their husbands hearing this ran up and made a great rout. . . .

BREAD

Source: Thomas Waleys, Moralitates, c. 1326–42. Translated from extract in Beryl Smalley, *English Friars and Antiquity in the Early Fourteenth Century*, Blackwell 1960, p. 309.

I heard that a bishop wanted a fishpond to be on one of his manors in England. Many peasants were summoned for the job and the bishop ordered them to be given daily good wheaten bread so that they should work with more strength and greater will. Within three or four days the work began to slacken. The bishop noticed and asked one why he was getting slower than at the start. He replied that he had no bread and so could not work. The bishop said he had told his steward to give them wheaten bread daily. The peasant replied ' That is not bread for the likes of us. I don't call it bread. Let us have bean bread and then we shall be able to work '. And so it was, once the wheaten bread was taken away from them.

THE PERFECT PANTRY, c. 1460

Source: ' The Duties of a Panter or Butler ' in John Russell's ' Book of Nurture '; *The Babees' Book Medieval Manners for the Young done into modern English from Dr. Furnivall's Texts* by Edith Rickert, Chatto and Windus, 1923, pp. 50–51.

. . . In the pantry, you must always keep three sharp knives, one to chop the loaves, another to pare them, and a third sharp and keen, to smooth and square the trenchers with.

Always cut your lord's bread, and see that it be new; and all other bread at the table one day old ere you cut it, all household bread three days old, and trencher bread four days old.

Look that your salt be fine, white, fair, and dry; and have your salt-plane of ivory, two inches wide and three long; and see to it that the lid of the salt-cellar touch not the salt.

Good son, look that your napery be sweet and clean, and that your table-cloth, towel, and napkin be folded neatly, your table-knives brightly polished and your spoon fair washed—ye wot well what I mean.

BUTCHERS' MEAT

A fitting punishment for a London butcher who sold bad meat was to burn it in front of his nose as he stood in the pillory unable to move his head. By a proclamation of 1378 London butchers had to close and sell no meat after candles were lighted.

Medieval pictures show tables laid with knives but not forks. Meat-hooks were used in the kitchen and Piers Gaveston, a by-word of wanton luxury, had some silver forks, but they were 'for eating pears,' while the kitchen meat-hooks, though in fact forks, had the prongs bent forwards at right-angles to the handle. Citizens carried long knives called baselards. They could be used as weapons and William Walworth killed Wat Tyler with one but their normal use was at table. The King-maker's largesse gave callers as much meat as they could carry away on such a dagger, and this they used to carry away to eat in the taverns. (See *T.S.I.H.*, i, 213) The London and Guildhall Museums have base-lards.

Shops. c. 1340. (Luttrell Psalter).

Further Reading: F. J. W. Harding, 'The Company of Butchers and Fleshers of Durham', *Trans. Archit. and Archaeol. Soc. Durham and Northumberland*, vol. 11, pts. 1–2. Joseph Daw, *Early History of Butchers*, 1869.

Source: *The first ledger book of High Wycombe*, ed. R. W. Greaves, Bucks. Record Society, vol. 11 for 1947, 1956, p. 6.

(Wycombe, on the road from London to Worcester, differed from other places in the Chilterns in having a stream sufficiently strong to drive a number of mills. This made it one of the sources of supply for London's bread. Local consumers are here seen protecting their interests against purchase of meat by outsiders.)

It was ordained [1313] and enacted that the butchers of the said town, all and severally, should take the skins and hides with the heads of the animals and cattle, which have been killed in their houses, into market on the stalls in which it is customary for them to be sold. Similarly they are to be taken and shown there, to be seen by all, and to be publicly exposed by the vendors in good faith. Provided, however, that after they have been so shown, seen, and publicly exposed by the vendors as aforesaid, if there are not to be found any suitable traders of the aforesaid town, that then it shall be permissible for the same butchers to take the aforesaid skins and hides out of the township, and carry them away and sell them to foreign merchants freely as they will. And all the butchers present, namely William le casiere, Benedict le casiere, Richard le casyere, Gilbert le casiere, John le casiere, Edward de Haveryngdon [a lost medieval village at West Wycombe], John Geky, Roger Robilard, Stephen le Woode, Robert le Knave, John the son of John, Andrew and Michael le portere, for themselves, have agreed and promised to keep this ordinance and statute, but they have asked that the community should, as a matter of grace, make the concession that at the showing of the aforesaid hides and skins, foreign merchants might come and buy along with the merchants of the aforesaid town. And because their petition would work to the prejudice of the liberty of the aforesaid town it was not granted to them. And therefore it is enjoined and commanded to the aforesaid bailiffs that they watch carefully for such defaults, and faithfully present them to the mayor and township with a view to their being punished.

TECHNICALITIES OF CARVING

The elaborate rituals of feasts of the nobility were enshrined, as was that of hunting, in a special language.

Source: *Booke of Kerving*, Wynken de Worde, 1508, fol. 1 b.

The termes of a Kerver be as here followeth:

Breke that dere—lesche that braune—rere that goose—lyste that swanne—sauce that capon—spoyle that hen—frusche that checkyn—unbrace that mallarde [duck]—unlace that conye —dismembre that heron—display that crayn—disfigure that pecocke—unjoynt that bytture [bittern]—untache that curlewe —alaye that fesande [pheasant]—wynge that partyche [partridge] —wyng that quayle—myne that plover—thye that pygion— border that pastry—thye that woodcock—thye all smale byrdes —tymbre that fyere—tyere that egge—chynne that samon— strynge that lamprye—splat that pyke—sauce that plaice—sauce that tenche—splaye that breme—syde that haddok—tuske that barbell—culpon that troute—syne that cheven [chub]—trassene that ele—trance that sturgion—under trance that porpose— tayme that crabbe—barbe that lopster. Here endethe the goodly termes of Kervinge.

SEA FISHERIES

Fish was a very important article in medieval diet and regulations against eating meat in Lent and the natural scarcity of meat in winter made it a necessity. The Fishmongers accordingly became one of the most important groups of tradesmen in London.

The most famous fishmonger was William Walworth, who, when Mayor of London in 1381, slew Wat Tyler (see *W.W.I.H.*, i). Fish is still sold at the traditional market in London, Billingsgate. Yorkshire fishermen were among the gilds which produced the *Towneley Mysteries*.

In the fifteenth century the Hanseatic League of North German Towns closed the Norwegian fisheries to England and cod fishers had to go as far afield as Iceland. Such voyages stimulated improvements in ocean going vessels.

Further Reading: A. M. Samuel, *The Herring: its effect on the History of Britain*, 1928; J. T. Jenkins, *The Herring and the Herring Fisheries*, 1928.

Source: *The First Register of Norwich Cathedral Priory*, ed., H. W. Saunders, Norfolk Record Soc., vol. 11, 1939, pp. 31–3. (110)

[The following account of the important seasonal herring fishery at Yarmouth must not be misunderstood as meaning that there was no settlement at Yarmouth before 1101. Domesday Book shows that as early as the reign of Edward the Confessor (d. 1066) the king had a town there which contained 70 burgesses.]

Grilling fish.   c. 1330.   (Holkham Bible).

There was at that time, however, on the beach at Yarmouth, a certain tiny Chapel built in which divine services were only celebrated during the season of the herring fishery, for there were not there more than four or five small houses [huts] provided for the reception of fishermen. The aforesaid Bishop [Herbert Losinga] besought King Henry [I] for a licence to build on the same sands a church. The desired licence being asked for and secured, he built a church there, placing therein a Chaplain to celebrate divine service always; and he provided the necessary equipment from his own possessions.

And after a time, those coming from the . . . ports turned out the said chaplain by force of arms, thinking to force their will on the same church [in order to have one under their own control.] Hearing which, the aforesaid Bishop directed letters to the king concerning the injury done to him by the men of the harbour in these parts. The king was at that time in Normandy and, having heard the aforesaid, directed letters to Roger Bigot guardian of Norfolk. The latter, desiring to carry out the command of the king directed to him, got together men of the country in order that he might restore to the said Bishop the church of Yarmouth and, if necessary, drive out with force the port men therefrom.

The port men resisted with force of arms and in the conflict which followed certain were killed by the sword and the remainder put to flight. And the Bishop restored anew to the possession of the said church, then gave . . . to his monks of Norwich the aforementioned church of Yarmouth. . . . .

SHELL FISH, 1375

Oyster shells are often found on Roman sites. Professor Thorold Rogers found that in the late thirteenth and fourteenth centuries oysters were reckoned by the hundred at Thorney in Sussex and by the bushel at Sharpness in Kent. They cost $\frac{1}{2}$d. a hundred, or about 7 d. a bushel while mussels cost 5 d. a bushel. A Saxon riddle about an oyster shows they were eaten alive.

Source: The Black Book of the Admiralty, ed. Sir T. Twiss, vol. 1, Rolls Series, 1871, pp. 157–8.

Item, lett inquiry be made of all those who dredge oysters or muscles out of season, [that is to say] from the beginning of the month of May till the day of the exaltation of the Crosse, commonly called Holyroode Day [14 September].

Item lett inquiry be made about all those whoe take brood or fry of oysters or musles in any season of the yeare to the destruction of the waters where oysters or musles are.

SALMON

Source: Statute 13 Edward I cap. 46 (translated as in 1577 edition).

It is provided, that the waters of Humbre, Owse, Trent, Dove, Aire, Derewent, Wherfe, Niddiore, Swale, Tese, Tyn, Eden, and al other waters [wherin salmons be taken] shalbe in defence for taking salmons from the Nativitie of our Lady unto saint Martines daie. And likewise that yong Salmons shall not be taken nor destroied by nets, nor by other ingins at mylle poles [pools], from the myddes of Apryll unto the Nativitie of saint John Baptiste. And in places where as freshe waters be, there shall be assigned overseers of this statute, whiche shal offtentimes see and enquire of the offenders, and for the fyrste trespasse they shalbe punished by burnynge of their nettes and ingins: And for the seconde tyme, they shal have imprysonment for a quarter of a yere. And for the thirde trespas they shal be imprisoned a whole yere. And as their trespasse increaseth, so shall the punishment.

FISHPOND AT BURY, LATE TWELFTH CENTURY

The importance of fresh water fish for food meant that monasteries had fishponds. The Latin word for a fishpond, *vivarium*, can be easily misread as the word for a vineyard, *vinarium*, and though England had its vineyards many ' vineyards ' mentioned in local histories were really fishponds.

Source: *The Chronicle of Brakelond concerning the Acts of Samson Abbot of the Monastery of St. Edmund*, translated by H. E. Butler, Nelson 1951, p. 131.

There is also another strain of evil-doing which, God willing, the Abbot will wash out with tears of penitence, that one transgression should not blacken such a multitude of good deeds. He raised the level of the fish-pond of Babwell by the new mill to such a height, that owing to the holding up of the waters, there is no man rich or poor, having lands by the waterside, from the Towngate to Eastgate, but has lost his garden and orchards.

The Cellarer's pasture on the other side of the bank is destroyed, the arable land of neighbours is spoilt. The Cellarer's meadow is ruined, the Infirmarer's orchard is drowned owing to the overflow of water, and all the neighbours complain of it. Once the Cellarer spoke to him in full Chapter concerning the greatness of the loss, but the Abbot at once angrily replied that he was not going to lose his fish-pond for the sake of our meadow.

POACHING FISH

Many were caught poaching with ' angleroddes ' or other ' engines ' like nest and eel traps, but the tenants of Eynsham Abbey paid a rent to be allowed to fish. In *Piers Ploughman* it is said that to the poor ' cold flesh and cold fish is to them like baked venison; on Fridays and fasting-days, a farthing's worth of mussels or so many cockles were a feast.'

Source: *The Court Baron*, Ed. F. W. Maitland, Selden Soc. vol. 4, p. 55 (a typical case with no particular date or place).

Sir, for God's sake do not take it ill of me if I tell the truth, how I went the other evening along the bank of this pond and looked at the fish which were playing in the water, so beautiful and so bright, and for the great desire I had for a tench I laid me down on the bank and just with my hands quite simply, and without any other device, I caught that tench and carried it off; and now I will tell thee the cause of my covetousness and my desire. My dear wife had lain abed a right full month, as my neighbours who are here know, and she could never eat or drink anything to her liking, and for the great desire she had to eat a tench I went to the bank of the pond to take just one tench; and that never other fish from the pond did I take.

FRESHWATER FISH

Before nineteenth and twentieth century industry polluted the rivers, freshwater fish were a really important part of the food supply.

The Fish House at Meare, with two living rooms over a store, was built between 1322 and 1335 for the chief fisherman of the Abbot of Glastonbury.

Further Reading: J. W. Kempster, *Our Rivers*, 1948 (bibliography).

Source: John Trevisa, Translation of Higden, *Polychronicon* (1398).

The lond is noble, copious, and riche of nobil welles and of nobil ryveres with plenté of fische; there is grete plenté of small fische, of samon, and of elys. So that cherles in som place fedith sowes with fische.

GAME AND POULTRY

In 1366 the Mayor of London told the mistery of poulterers that birds were not to be plucked in the streets. In 1444 his successor said they caused ' grete and noyous and grevous hurt ' through keeping ' swannes gees herons-ewes and other pultrie whereof the ordure and standyng of hem is of grete stenche and so evel savour that it causeth grete and parlous inffectyng of the people and long hath done.'

King John's requirements from the sheriff of Hampshire for Christmas, 1206, at Windsor Castle, included 1,500 chickens and 5,000 eggs.

(1) *Source*: ' The Squire of Low Degree ', *Early English Romances*, *Romances of Love*, done into modern English by Edith Rickert, Chatto and Windus 1908, p. 159. (The inclusion of stork in this ideal menu is unusual.)

Now when the squire had parted from his gentle lady, he went to his chamber and arrayed him in scarlet-red with a broad-barred girdle, a chaplet on his hair and a horn about his neck; and thus he went forth to do his office in the hall, among the lords of high and low degree.

With a white rod in his hand, he went to kneel before the king, and served him right royally with dainty meats, partridge, plover and peacock, and birds baked in bread, teal, duck and drake, cock, curlew and crane, pheasant, stork, snipe, and fresh venison of buck and doe, and many other dainties fit to set before a king.

And when the squire had so done, he served to and fro in the hall, honoured and loved by men of every degree. The king beheld him in his fair raiment, and thought him the comeliest man that he had seen in the world ever. . . .

(2) *Source*: *Liber Albus the White Book of the City of London compiled in* A.D. 1419 *by John Carpenter and Richard Whittington,* translated by H. T. Riley, Richard Griffin 1861, p. 401.

(Regulations about the times and places and manner of selling poultry are followed by maximum prices).

Catching rabbits, a novelty in early fourteenth century England. (Queen Mary's Psalter).

The best cygnet shall be sold for four pence; . . . the best goose, for six pence; the best capon, for six pence; the best hen, for six pence; the best pullet, for two pence; the best rabbit, with the skin for four pence; and without the skin, for three pence; —and no foreigner shall sell any rabbit without the skin;—the best river mallard [wild duck] for three pence; the best dunghill mallard [tame duck], for two pence halfpenny; the best teal, for two pence; the best snipe, for one penny; four larks, for one penny; the best woodcock, for three pence; the best pheasant, for twelve pence; the best curlew, for six pence; a dozen thrushes, for six pence; a dozen finches, for one penny; the best heron, for sixteen pence; the best bittern, for eighteen pence; the best brewe [possibly bald coot], for eighteen pence; the best egret, for eighteen pence; twelve pigeons, for eight pence.

(3) *Source*: A fifteenth century cookery book from the library of Sir Edward Coke (Holkham MS. 671, foll. 41 v.–45) printed by Mrs. A. Napier, 1882 (privately), pp. 60–66, and, unknown to her, by the early printer Pynson.

To sley a swan and al maner of foulle and to dight them, tak a swan and cutt hym in the roof of the mouthe toward the brayn of the hed and lett hym bled to dethe. Then kep the blod to colour with the chaudron [entrails] and knyt the nek and let hym dye. Then skald hym, drawe hym, rost hym and serve hym with chaudron.

A fessand roste

A fessand let hym blod in the mouthe to the dethe, then pull hym dry and cut of the hed and the nek and the leggs from the body. Parboille hym and lard hym. Then put the kneys in the vent and raise his leggs and his wings as it were a henne and no sauce but salt.

A pertuche rost

A pertuche tak a fedir and put it in to his hed and let hym dye and pull hym dry and draw hym and rost hym as ye wold raise the leggs and wings of an henne and mynce hym, sauce hym with wyne poudur of ginger and salt and warme it on the fyere and serve it.

Quayle rost

A quayle tak and sley hym and rost hym as a pertuche and raise his leggs and his wings as a hene and no sauce but salt and serve it.

[Then follow instructions for roasting ' crayne, heron, bittur, egret, curlew, brew [? bald coot], cony, rabettes, sarcelle [a kind of teal], plover, snyt, wodcock, kyd and venyson '.]

(3) *Source*: Ordinance of the Cooks and Pastelers, or Piebakers, 1378, H. T. Riley, *Memorials of London and London Life, 1276–1419*, p. 426.

The best roast pig, for 8d. Best roast goose, 7d. Best roast capon, 6d. Best roast hen, 4d. Best roast pullet, 2½d. Best roast rabbit, 4d. Beast rost river mallard, 4½d. [wild duck]. Best roast dunghill mallard, 3½d. [tame duck]. Best roast teal, 2½d. Best roast snipe, 1½d. Five roast larks, 1½d. Best roast woodcock, 2½d. Best roast pheasant, 13d. Best roast curlew, 6½d. Three roast thrushes, 2d. Ten roast finches, 1d. Best roast heron, 18d. Best roast bittern, 20d. Three roast pigeons, 2½d. Ten eggs, penny. For the paste, fire, and trouble upon a capon [provided by customer], 1½d. For the paste, fire and trouble upon a goose, 2d. The best capon baked in a pastry, 8d. The best hen baked in a pastry, 5d. The best lamb, roasted, 7d.

FRUIT

Apples were sold by the quarter at very varying prices. Pears were much dearer and averaged as much as 2s. 1d. a quarter. Cider was quite common and sometimes given to labourers instead of beer. It varied between ½d. and 1d. a gallon. Perry is only quoted once, at Cuxham in 1276. This parish adjoined Pyrton in Oxfordshire, a place-name which alludes to the growth of pears, as do Woodperry and Waterperry in the same county.

The churchwardens' accounts of St. Andrew for 1457–8 record 6d. received ' of Margaret Hubbard, London, the fruiteer for standynge at the churche dore '.

(1) *Source*: *Household of Edward IV*, *the Black Book and the Ordinance of* 1478, ed. A. R. Myers, Manchester University 1959, pp. 188–190 (c. 1471–2).

Picking Fruit.   c. 1340.   (Luttrell Psalter).

Office of Confeccionary hath in hym a sergeaunt to serue the king. He resceyuyth of the office of the grete spycery all such stuf by indenture, all maner spyces to make confeccions, card-qwyns [quince pulp preserves], plaates [dishes], sedes, and all other spycerez nedefull; dates, figges, raisons greate and smale, for the kinges mouth and for his household in Lente season;

wardens [warden pears], perys, apples, quincez, cheryez [cherries]; and all other fruytez after the seasons longing to this office. He resceuithe the spyce plates both of the countinghouse and iewelhouse, according to the rychesse after the dayis of astate, by indenture for the kinges voyders, whan the ussher of chambre comyth therefore; all the plates of peautyr by the purueyaunce of the sergeaunt squyloure [scullion], and indentures thereof betwext countinghouse and hym, by controlment of all weyghtes and numbyr; by the deleueraynce of the seyd chief clerk and his deputes, cofers, gardevyaundez [meat safes], towells of raynes [Rennes], of work [ornamented towelles] and hangers and other necessarijs, panys, basyns, and ladylles that he maketh his confecions dayly. . . . O[one] grome in this office, to help make the confeccions. . . and to bere the fruyte and in tyme of yere to kepe hit in hourd . . . Thez officers make prouysyons in seasons of the yere, according for fruytez to be had in the kinges gardynez without prisez [requisitions]; as cheryez, perez, apples, nuttes, greete and smalle for somer season; and lenton wardens [pears], quinces, and other, and also of presentes geuyn to the king; they be purueyours of blaundrels [special white apples] pepyns, and all other fruytez. . .

SALT, 1065

In Roman times salt was produced at brine-pits in Cheshire and Worcestershire and in pans by the sea in Essex, Lincolnshire and elsewhere. A Saxon salter explained that his line was essential for good meals as it gave a relish, as well as being necessary for preserving dairy produce and other food (*T.S.I.H.*, i, p. 29). Salt was conveyed to every household and routes by which it travelled are remembered in the names Salt Way, Salt Street, Salters Way and Salter's Corner in the Oxfordshire parishes of Shipton on Cherwell, Stratton Audley, Swalcliffe, Banbury, South Weston, Swinbrook and Widford and in the name of Salford itself. Bampton had salt rights at Droitwich and the salt came along the Salt Way in Worcestershire to the county boundary at Four Shire Stone and thence through Chipping Norton. Until recent years salt in a big vessel was the only condiment on many poor tables in western Ireland and ornamental ' salts ' often boat-shaped, were a feature of fine banquets marking the social barriers between those placed above and those below them. The London Salters formed

L

a Fraternity of Corpus Christi, a guild of Brethren and Sisters at All Hallows, Bread Street, and in 1378 sent three members to the city's Court of Common Council. They dealt not only in salted foods but in flax, hemp, logwood, cochineal, potashes and other chemicals, like a modern druggist and oilman. Their motto, *Sal sapit omnia* means ' Salt savours everything '.

Further Reading: Joan Varley, ' Salt-making in Mediaeval Middlewich ', *A Middlewich Chartulary*, 1941, Chetham Society New Series, Vol. 105, pp. 35–49. A. R. Bridbury, *England and the Salt-Trade in the Later Middle Ages*, Oxford 1955.

Source: *The Domesday Survey of Cheshire*, ed. J. Tait, 1916, Chetham Society, New Series, vol. 75, pp. 217–225.

In king Edward's time there was . . . a Wich [Nantwich] in which there was a brinepit for making salt, and there were 8 salthouses, so divided between the king and earl Eadwine that of all the issues and renders of the salthouses the king had 2 thirds and the earl a third. But besides these the said earl had a salthouse of his own which belonged to his manor Acatone [Acton by Nantwich]. From this salthouse the earl had sufficient salt for his house throughout the year. If however any was sold from that source, the king had 2 pence of the toll and the earl the third penny.

In the same Wich a number of the men of the country had salthouses, from which there was the following custom. From the Ascension of our Lord to the Feast of St. Martin anyone having a salthouse might carry home [free of toll] his own salt; but if he sold any of it either there or elsewhere in the county of Cheshire, he paid toll to the king and earl. After the Feast of St. Martin anyone who carried salt thence, whether his own or purchased, paid toll, the above-mentioned salthouse belonging to the earl excepted, as having its own custom.

The aforesaid 8 salthouses of the king and earl on the Friday in each week in which they were employed in boiling salt rendered 16 boilings, of which 15 made a horseload of salt. Other men's salthouses did not give these boilings on Fridays between the Ascension of our Lord and the Feast of St. Martin; but from the Feast of St. Martin to the Ascension of our Lord they all gave the boiling custom like the salthouses of the king and earl.

All these salthouses, both those that were and those that were not in demesne [i.e. held by the king or earl], were surrounded on one side by a certain stream [The Weaver] and on the other by a certain ditch. Anyone incurring a forfeiture within this boundary was allowed to make amends by a fine of 2 shillings or 30 boilings of salt, homicide excepted and theft where the thief was adjudged to die. These offences, if committed here, were amended for as in the rest of the shire.

If a man went from the aforesaid precinct of the salthouses to any part of the county without having paid his toll and was convicted thereof, he had to come back and pay it and to make amends there by a fine of 40 shillings, if he were a free man, 4 shillings, if he were not free. But if he went to some other county, leaving his toll unpaid, he had to pay the fine in the place where it was demanded . . . .

In Mildestvic [Middlewich, now Northwich] Hundred there was another Wich [Middlewich] shared between the king and the earl. There were no demesne salthouses there, however, but the same laws and customs were in force there as have been mentioned under the previous Wich. . . . Now the earl [of Chester] holds it for himself and it is let at farm for 25 shillings and 2 cartloads of salt. . . .

Whoever carried away purchased salt in a cart from these two Wiches, paid 4 pence in toll if he had 4 oxen or more in his cart; if 2 oxen, he paid 2 pence, provided there were 2 horseloads of salt.

A man from any other hundred paid 2 pence for a horseload. But a man from the same hundred paid only a halfpenny for a horseload. Anyone who so loaded his cart that the axle broke within a league of either Wich paid 2 shillings to the king's officer or the earl's, if he could be undertaken within a league. Similarly he who so loaded a horse as to break its back paid 2 shillings. . . . Men on foot from another hundred buying salt there paid 2 pence for 8 men's loads; men of the same hundred paid a penny for 8 loads. . . .

Note. Camden's *Britannia* describes the process used at Nantwich and Habington's *Survey of Worcestershire* (Worc. Historical Society, vol. 2, pp. 296–7) describes a similar process at Droitwich.

SCANTY FARE FOR A HUSBANDMAN, FOURTEENTH CENTURY

Poor people in lean years fared ill though their hardships, unlike battles and crimes, are not recorded in detail. Nineteenth century hardships were more fully recorded and described than those of the fourteenth century thanks to the work of philanthropists and Royal Commissions. For the earlier period one must turn to the often quoted words of a poet of the time.

Source: *Piers Plowman*.

' I have no penny,' quoth Piers, ' Pullets for to buy
Nor neither geese nor piglets, but two green [new] cheeses,
A few curds and cream and an oaten cake
And two loaves of beans and bran to bake for my little ones.
And besides I say by my soul I have no salt bacon,
Nor no little eggs, by Christ, collops for to make.
But I have parsley and leeks and many cabbages,
And besides a cow and a calf and a cart mare
To draw afield my dung the while the drought lasteth.
And by this livelihood we must live till lammas time [August].
And by that I hope to have harvest in my croft.
And then may I prepare the dinner as I dearly like.
All the poor people those peascods fatten.
Beans and baked apples they brought in their laps.
Shalots and chervils and ripe cherries many
And proffered pears these present. . .
Then poor folk for fear fed hunger eagerly
With great leeks and peas. . .
By then it came near harvest. New corn came to market.
Then were folk glad and fed hunger with the best,
With good ale as Glutton taught and got hunger to sleep.
And when wasters wouldn't work but wander about
Nor no beggar eat bread that beans within were
But two sorts of fine white or else of clean wheat
Nor no halfpenny ale in nowise drink,
But of the best and the brownest that in town is to sell,
Labourers that have no land to live on, only their hands,
Deigned not to dine each day on herbs not fresh gathered,

Have no penny-ale given them, nor no piece of bacon,
But if it be fresh flesh or fish, fried or baked,
And that warm or hot to avoid chilling their bellies.

FRATERNITY OF GROCERS FOUNDED, 1345

Religious ' fraternities ', meeting for social as well as devotional purposes, frequently grew up. Some of these, like the grocers, later developed in London into City Companies.

Source: J. A. Kingdom, *Facsimile, Transcript and Translation of Grocers' Records*, 1345–1463, 1883–6, Company of Grocers, p. 8, retranslated in G. Unwin, *Gilds and Companies of London*, Antiquary's Books, 1908, pp. 103–4.

Mem. That all the brethren of the fraternity dined the first time together at the house of the Abbot of Bury on the 12th June, 1345, at which dinner each paid 12 pence, and the whole was expended and 23 pence beside by the Warden. At which dinner we had a surcoat to be made of one livery, for which each paid his proportion. The same day after dinner ended, it was decreed by common consent to take and hire a priest at the Nativity of St. John next, to come to chant and pray for the members of the said company and for all Christians, and to maintain the said priest each one of the fraternity consented to give a penny a week, which amounts to 4s. 4d. to pay now for the year.

Mem. The priest commenced to sing July 3rd, and to receive each week 15d. It was agreed that none should be of the fraternity if he were not of good condition and of their mistery, that is to say a pepperer of Soper Lane, or a canvasser of the Ropery, or a spicer of Cheap, or other man of their mistery wherever he might dwell.

A WELL-LAID TABLE, c. 1460

Source: ' The duties of a Panter or Butler ' in John Russell's ' Book of Nurture '; *The Babees' Book Medieval Manners for the Young done into modern English from Dr. Furnivall's Texts* by Edith Rickert, Chatto and Windus, 1923, pp. 52–6.

My son, it is now the time of day to lay the table. First, wipe it with a cloth ere it be spread, then lay on it a cloth called a *cowche*. You take one end and your mate the other, and draw it straight; and lay a second cloth with its fold on the outer edge of the table. Lift the upper part and let it hang even. And then lay the third cloth with its fold on the inner edge, making a *state* half a foot wide, with the top. Cover your ewery-cupboard [for jugs] with a diapered-towel, and put a towel round your neck, for that is courtesy, and put one end of it mannerly over your left arm; and on the same arm place your lord's napkin, and on it lay eight loaves of bread, with three or four trencher-loaves. Take one end of the towel in your left hand, as the manner is, together with the salt-cellar—look you do this—and take the other end of the towel in your right hand with the spoons and knives.

Set the salt on your lord's right hand, and to the left of your salt, one or two trencher, and to the left again, your knife by itself and plain to see, and the white rolls, and beside them a spoon upon a fair folded napkin. Cover your spoon, napkin, trencher and knife, so that they cannot be seen; and at the other end of the table place a salt with two trenchers. . . .

When your sovereign's table is dressed in this array, place salts on all the other tables, and lay trenchers and cups; and then set your cupboard with gay silver and silver-gilt, and your ewery board with basins and ewers, and hot and cold water, each to temper the other. Look that you have ever enough napkins, spoons and cups for your lord's table; also, for your own dignity, that your pots of ale and wine be as clean as possible, and beware ever of flies and motes, for your own sake.

With lowly courtesy, make the surnape with a cloth under a double of fair napery; fold the two ends of the towel to the outer edge of the cloth, and so hold the three ends together; then fold them all so there is a pleat at about a foot's distance, and lay it fair and smooth for your lord to wash after meat, if he will at the right side of the table, you must guide it along, and the marshal must slip it further—the right side up of all those cloths. . . .

MANY COURSES

Service and entertainment at table. Early fourteenth century.
(Queen Mary's Psalter).

Source: *The Autobiography of Giraldus Cambrensis*, ed. and translated by H. E. Butler, Jonathan Cape, p. 71 (1179).

And as he sat there at the high table with the Prior [of Canterbury] and the seniors, he noted two things, the multitude of the dishes and the excessive superfluity of signs which the monks [forbidden to speak] made to one another. For there was the Prior giving so many dishes to the serving monks, and they in their turn bearing these as gifts to the lower tables; and there were those, to whom these gifts were brought, offering their thanks, and all of them gesticulating with fingers, hands and arms, and whistling one to another in lieu of speaking, all extravagating in a manner more free and frivolous than was seemly; so that Giraldus seemed to be seated at a stage-play or among actors and jesters. It would therefore be more consonant with good order and decency to speak modestly in human speech than with signs and whistlings thus jocosely to indulge in dumb garrulity. And as to the dishes and the number thereof, what shall I say, save that I have oft heard Giraldus himself declare that sixteen very costly dishes or even more were placed upon the table in order, not to say contrary to all order. Finally, potherbs were brought to every table but were little tasted. For you might see so many kinds of fish, roast and boiled, stuffed and fried, so many dishes contrived with eggs and pepper by dexterous cooks, so many flavourings and condiments, compounded with like dexterity to tickle gluttony and awaken appetite. Moreover you might see in the midst of such abundance ' wine and strong drink', metheglin [see p. 157] and claret, must, mead and mulberry juice, and all that can intoxicate, beverages so choice that beer, such as is made at its best in England and above all in Kent, found no place among them. There beer among other drinks is as potherbs are among made dishes. Such extreme superfluity and extravagance might you behold both in food and drink, as might not only beget loathing in him that partook thereof, but weariness even in him that beheld it.

ONE MEAL A DAY

Henry of Huntingdon says that Hardecanute had four meals a day ' when in our times through avarice, or as they pretend through disgust, the great set but one meal a day before their dependents.'

Source: William of Malmesbury, *Chronicle of the Kings of England*, transl. J. A. Giles, Bohn's Antiquarian Library, 1866, p. 441 (1119).

Robert, Earl of Mellent, possessed such mighty influence in England, as to change by his single example the long established modes of dress and of diet. Finally, the custom of one meal a day, is observed in the palaces of all the nobility through his means; which he, adopting from Alexius, Emperor of Constantinople, on the score of his health, spread, as I have observed, among the rest by his authority. He is blamed, as having done, and taught others to do this, more through want of liberality, than any fear of surfeit, or indigestion; but undeservedly: since no one, it is said, was more lavish in entertainments to others, or more moderate in himself. In law, he was the supporter of justice; in war, the ensurer of victory: urging his lord the king to enforce the rigour of the statutes; himself not only following the existing, but proposing new ones: free from treachery himself towards the king [Henry I], he was the avenger of it in others.

KITCHENS

The possession of a kitchen was a condition which enabled a Saxon to attain the rank of thegn.

Much medieval cooking was done out of doors in the way shown in the Bayeux Tapestry. Sometimes it seems that even important people had detached shacks built for their cooking, for in 1232 a gale blew down the royal kitchen at Oxford. Even imposing and large kitchens of stone or brick, great pyramidal structures with smoke creeping up the walls to a central opening in the roof, were separate from the halls. Such survive at Stanton Harcourt, Oxon, and Glastonbury, and a twelfth century example has been excavated at Clarendon Palace, Wilts. Norman London boasted a public cookshop open at all hours and suitable for all classes (*T.S.I.H.*, i, 94–5). Many recipes survive.

The London Museum has a mould for pastry made in the figure of St. Catherine. Ships and Castles were made among other elaborate confectionery shapes. The London Museum has, in addition to serving knives and spoons, fleshhooks with prongs at right-angles to the handles. In illustrated pictures of devils they often wield these as implements of torture.

Those who attracted 'Lickpenny' (p. 41) by crying out 'pies for sale' were forbidden to sell warmed up meat.

Source: U. T. Holmes, Jr., *Daily Living in the Twelfth Century, based on the Observations of Alexander Neckam*, Madison, The University of Wisconsin Press 1952, p. 93–4. For Alexander Neckam see *W.W.I.H.*, i, 112–3.

In a kitchen there should be a small table on which cabbage may be minced, and also lentils, peas, shelled beans, beans in the pod, millet, onions, and other vegetables of the kind that can be cut up. There should also be pots, tripods, a mortar, a hatchet, a pestle, a stirring stick, a hook, a cauldron, a bronze vessel, a small pan, a baking pan, a meathook, a griddle, small pitchers, a trencher, a bowl, a platter, a pickling vat, and knives for cleaning fish. In a *vivarium* [aquarium] let fish be kept, in which they can be caught by net, fork, spear, or light hook, or with a basket. The chief cook should have a cupboard in the kitchen where he may store many aromatic spices, and bread flour sifted through a sieve—and used also for feeding small fish—may be hidden away there. Let there be also a cleaning place where the entrails and feathers of ducks and other domestic fowl can be removed and the birds cleaned. Likewise there should be a large spoon for removing foam and skimming. Also there should be hot water for scalding fowl.

Have a pepper mill and a hand [flour?] mill. Small fish for cooking should be put into a pickling mixture, that is, water mixed with salt. . . . To be sure, pickling is not for all fish, for these are of different kinds. . . . There should be also a *garde-robe* pit through which the filth of the kitchen may be evacuated. In the pantry let there be shaggy towels, tablecloth, and an ordinary hand towel which shall hang from a pole to avoid mice. Knives should be kept in the pantry, an engraved saucedish, a saltcellar, a cheese container, a candelabra, a lantern, a candlestick, and baskets. In the cellar or storeroom should be casks, tuns, wine-skins, cups, cup cases, spoons, ewers, basins, baskets, pure wine, cider, beer, unfermented wine, mixed wine, claret, nectar, mead, ... pear wine, red wine, wine from Auvergne, clove-spiced wine for gluttons whose thirst is unquenchable.

COOKING POTS

Medieval Pottery has only been studied seriously in recent years. Compared with medieval metalwork it is very rough and though this appeals to modern taste it cannot be compared for finish to that of Greece or even to the mass-produced imported Samian ware of Roman Britain.

From this craft the surnames Potter and Crocker are derived. Apart from the use of flint for tools and weapons the use of clay for pottery, known in Neolithic times, is the earliest important example of a mineral applied to human needs. There were also bronze cauldrons and saucepans called skillets, often with three legs.

Further Reading: Recent articles on Saxon pottery by J. N. L. Myres, on medieval pottery by E. M. Jope and on Scottish medieval pottery by S. Cruden.

B. Rackham and H. Read, *English Pottery; its development from Early Times to the end of the 18tn Century*, 1924.

Source: *De gestis Herwardi Saxonis*, transcribed by S. H. Miller and translated by Rev. W. D. Sweeting, in Appendix to *Fenland Notes and Queries*, vol. 3, Peterborough 1895 (from twelfth century MS. at Peterborough).

[Hereward leaves the beleagured Isle of Ely to discover the plans of William I]. . . . And at last he set out taking with him his mare called in English Swallow, a creature always lean and ugly in appearance, whose speed we have described before, and how ready she was to undergo fatigue. As he went out he changed his dress, cut his hair and beard, and put on a dirty coat: and, meeting a potter, he took his pots, and assuming the character of a potter made his way to the King's court at Brandon. . . . Next morning Hereward took up his pots and departed [from the house of a widow, where a witch lodged, where he had spent the night], and roaming all about the King's court kept crying out, in potter's fashion, in English, ' Pots! pots! good pots and jars! first class earthenware!' Meanwhile he was taken by some servants into the King's kitchen, so that they might buy some pots. . . . [Someone says that the ' potter ' looks like Hereward. The ' potter ' says he hates Hereward]. . . . ' For he carried off a cow of mine, and four sheep, and everything I had except my pots and beast, whereby hitherto I have supported myself and my two sons.' But now the King's dinner was to be got ready, and Hereward went back to the kitchen. After dinner the servants and cooks, and the kitchen-boys with them, offered him wine and strong drink to make him drunk, and made great fun of him. At last mellowed with wine, they wanted to shave his head and pull out the hairs of his beard, and to blindfold him and so make him break his own pots which they put all about the ground for the purpose. As he was disinclined to submit to their jests, one man drew near and gave him a severe blow. But he returned the blow under the ear to such effect that he fell to the ground as it were dead. His companions seeing this, all rose against Hereward with three-pronged forks and pitchforks, so he seized a brand from the hearth and defended himself against them all, killing one man and wounding many more. [Hereward is arrested but escapes.]

COOKS

Chaucer's Cook was skilled at many processes and no doubt he could make sure that his turnspits saw that his roast was done to a turn (a phrase which still recalls the once general method of roasting in front of a fire). The *Knightes Tale* alludes to the perils of this trade, ' The cook y-scalded, for al his longe ladel '; but in the Prologue of the Cook of London it appears that 'many a pilgrim' cursed him 'For in thy shoppe is many a flye loos'. His excellent 'blankmanger' was for the public and not for a private household. The company of Canterbury pilgrims also included 'a gentil Maunciple . . . wyse in bying of vitaille'.

Source: Establishment of the Royal Household, c. 1136, translated in *Dialogus de Scaccario The Course of the Exchequer and Constitutio Domus Regis*, ed. C. Johnson, Nelson, 1950, p. 131 (after the Clerk of the Spence or Bread and Wine in the Steward's department, and the Pantry with bakers and the waferer).

A Cook.   Fifteenth century.
(Ellesmere Chaucer).

Cooks: The Cook of the upper kitchen shall eat in the house, and have three halfpence for his man. The *Usher* of the same kitchen, the customary diet and three halfpence for his man. The *Scullion* shall eat in the house and have three halfpence for his man, and have a sumpter-horse with his livery. The *Sumpterman* of the same kitchen, the like. The *Serjeant of the Kitchen*, the customary diet only. *The Cook of the King's personal servants and of the Dispensers*, the like. [Ralf de Marchia, who was cook, died before the King's death.] He shall eat in the house and have three halfpence a day for his man. *Great Kitchen*: Owen Polcheard has the customary diet and three halfpence a day for his man. Two

Cooks, each the customary diet and three halfpence a day for his man. *Serjeants* of the same Kitchen: The customary diet and three halfpence for his man. *Roaster*: The like. *Scullion*: The like, and a sumpter-horse besides with its livery. *Carter of the Great Kitchen*: Double diet, and the due livery for his horse.

Carter of the Larder: The like.

The Serjeant who received the Venison: Shall eat indoors, and have three halfpence for his man.

DRINK: MEAD

When 'waste' lands with wild flowers and woods were more widespread and when sugar was a costly foreign luxury bees and honey were important. The word mead is the Teutonic name for a drink made by fermenting honey and water. This drink was known also to the ancient Greeks and Romans. The word 'metheglin' is of Welsh origin, and means a spiced or medicated drink. Medieval illustrations of Virgil's *Georgics* show beehives and beekepers, sometimes veiled, beating gongs to make bees settle. For an eleventh century bee-keeper see *T.S.I.H.*, i, 36.

Source: Old English riddle in *The Exeter Book*, pt. ii, poems ix–xxxii, Early English Text Society, O.S. No. 194, 1934 for 1933, p. 119.

Bees, c. 1340. (Luttrell Psalter).

I am of value to men, found far and wide,
brought from the woods and the fortress-like hills,
from the valleys and the downs. In the day-time wings

carried me in the air, and bore me skilfully
under the shelter of a roof. Afterwards men
washed me in a tub. Now I am a binder
and a scourger, and soon become a thrower;
sometimes I cast an old fellow right to the ground.
Soon he discovers, he who grapples with me
and fights against my mighty assault,
that he must hit the ground with his back,
if he has not already desisted from his folly.
Robbed of his strength, loud in speech,
deprived of his might, he has no control over his mind,
his feet, or his hands. . . . Discover what I am called
who thus bind men upon earth
till they are dazed by my blows in the light of day.

DRUNKENNESS

Source: Penitential of Archbishop Theodore (d. 690), 26. B.
Thorpe, *Ancient Laws and Institutes of England*, 1840, p. 291.

. . . If a bishop, priest or deacon or anyone in holy orders has
a fault in the habit of drunkenness, he is to stop or to be deposed.
If a priest or deacon vomits through drunkenness he is to do
penance for 40 days with bread and water; a subdeacon 30 days;
a clerk 20; a layman 15. If a monk vomits through drunkenness
he is to do penance 30 days. If through drunkenness or greed
a bishop should vomit up the eucharist he is to do penance for 90
days; a priest for 70; a deacon and a monk for 60; a clerk 40; a
layman 30. If the cause is illness each should do 7 days; some a
psalter, some the psalter twice. If he casts forth the sacrifice into
the fire or into a river, he should sing 100 psalms. If dogs devour
it he should do penance for 100 days if it is with his knowledge;
otherwise 40 days. If a faithful layman makes another drunk
through wickedness, let him do penance 40 days. If any priest,
deacon, monk, subdeacon, clerk or layman vomits through
illness he is blameless. If anyone has been abstinent for a long
time and was not accustomed to drink and eat much, or if through
festivity at Christmas or at Easter or for the commemoration of

any of the Saints he has been sick, if on such an occasion he has not taken more than was ordained by his elders, he is guiltless. If priests become drunk through ignorance they are to do penance on bread and water for 7 days. If it is through negligence, 15 days. If through wantonness, they should do penance 40 days; deacons and monks 4 weeks; subdeacons 3; clerks 2; and laymen 1 week. If anyone compels a man to get drunk through kindness he is to do penance 20 days. If he did it for spite he is to be adjudged as a homicide. If any priest, or deacon, or clerk, drinks so much that he cannot sing the psalms but stumbles in his speech, let him do penance on bread and water for 12 days and purge his sin. If anybody feels an excessive swelling of his belly and pain through over-eating, that is to say to the point of vomiting without being ill, let him do penance for 7 days with bread and water. If any become drunk on wine or ale against the command of the Lord Saviour and His Apostles [drunkenness is defined as a change of mood, lack of control over the tongue, rolling eyes, giddiness of head, swelling of belly and consequent ache], a layman should do penance with bread for 1 week; a clerk for 2 weeks; a subdeacon for 15 days; a deacon and a monk for 3 weeks; a priest for 4; and a bishop for 5. If any clerk through gluttony takes food before the canonical hour and without the necessity of illness he is to have no dinner and to do penance for 2 days on bread and water.

DRINKING VESSELS

Metal vessels for the great have supplemented pottery ones since the Bronze age. Turning of wood probably made treen vessels available since about the time of the introduction of the potter's wheel. Such have been found at pre-Roman Glastonbury and in the Holkham Bible Noah has an inverted treen drinking bowl in his hand. Glass vessels were a rare luxury in Saxon England and were mostly imported though they may have been made in the seventh century at Faversham, Kent, and men came to teach the art at Wearmouth in 675. Glass from Rainham, Essex, in the British Museum imitates horn (cf. p. 256–7) in shape. Horns, like round-bottomed beakers, bottles and cups assume the presence of servants for they will not stand upright. In the fourteenth and fifteenth century cups were sometimes given personal names, for fine specimens were treated with the kind of affection given in the Romances to the sword of a Roland or an Arthur. Joan Evans cites *Christmas* and *Benison* and a mazer (or bowl) called *Crumpledud*. For chalices see p. 321.

Further Reading: D. B. Harden, ' Glass Vessels in Britain, A.D. 400–1100 ', in *Dark Age Britain*, Methuen 1956.

W. St. John Hope, ' On the English Mediaeval Drinking Vessels called Mazers,' *Archaeologia*, vol. 50, 1887, p. 129 articles by N. M. Penzer on famous cups at Oriel College, Oxford, and Lynn, *Connoisseur* 1946, vols. 117–8.

(1) *Source*: Fourteenth and fifteenth century inscriptions on jugs and mazers quoted by Joan Evans, *English Art*, 1307–1461, 1949, pp. 89–90.

Goddis grace be in this place amen. Stond uttir from
the fyre and lat ou lust [who likes] come here.

He that wyl not spare when he may be
schal not spend when he wold.
Deme the best in every dowt [doubt]
til the trowthe be tryed out.

Ho so ys lengyst alyue
Tak this cope withowtyn stryfe.

In the name of the trinite
fille the kup and drink to me.

Hold yowre tung and sey the best
And let yowre neghboure sitte in rest
Hoe so lyustth god to plese
Let hys neybore lyue in ese

(2). Chaucer, *The Wife of Bath's Prologue*.
For wel ye knowe, a lord in his household,
He hath nat every vessel al of gold:
Somme been of tree, and doon hir lord servyse.

42. Knight disarming, buttoned undervest

43. Early English headdresses

44. Norman mid-wife with bed and cradle (*cf. p.* 104)

45. New Year feast (*cf. p.* 151)

46. Horn and treen

47. High and Low tables

INNS AND TAVERNS

Quite small places might have inns in Roman times, as the story of Bethlehem shows. In Saxon times and later, monasteries and private houses would give hospitality to a traveller, but in places where these were so numerous as to be burdensome public inns arose. On the road from London about the time of the Conquest the Bishop of Worcester was well known at Wycombe where he dedicated the church and was miraculously saved when the old inn collapsed. Eighteen miles west on the same road the Abbot of Abingdon was freed by Henry I from having to entertain his servants at Wheatley and the Knights Templars obtained later a similar exemption there, alternative accommodation having presumably been provided. In the twelfth century Walter Map refers to places of refreshment. Fine medieval inns are the Angel at Grantham, the old White Hart at Newark and the Golden Cross at Oxford.

Chaucer has left a vivid portrait of the host of the Tabard in South-wark in the Prologue of the *Canterbury Tales*. His wife was less amiable (see p. 110).

Further Reading: W. A. Pantin and E. C. Rouse, ' The Golden Cross ', *Oxoniensia*, vol. 20.

(1) *Source*: *The Book of Margery Kempe, A modern version by W. Butler-Bowden*, Jonathan Cape 1939, p. 28. (1436)

Then for pure covetousness, and to maintain her pride, she began to brew, and was one of the greatest brewers in the town of [Lynn] for three years or four, till she lost much money, for she had never been used thereto. For, though she had ever such good servants, cunning in brewing, yet it would never succeed with them. For when the ale was as fair standing under barm as any man might see, suddenly the barm would fall down, so that all the ale was lost, one brewing after another, so that her servants were ashamed and would not dwell with her.

Then this creature thought how God had punished her afore-time—and she could not take heed—and now again, by the loss of her goods. Then she left and brewed no more.

Then she asked her husband's mercy because she would not follow his counsel aforetime, and she said that her pride and sin were the cause of her punishing, and that she would amend and that she had trespassed with good will.

M

(2) A manual on ' How to speak and write good French ', written at the end of the fourteenth century contains conversations showing ' How a man who is going far out of his own country, riding or walking, should behave himself and talk upon the way '. The servant goes ahead to book a room and hopes ' that there are no fleas, nor bugs, nor other vermin '. The host says ' No, sir, please God, for I make bold that you shall be well and comfortably lodged here—save that there is a great peck of rats and mice. The conversation below is from another chapter of the same book and is between two travellers who have just shared a bed.

Source: J. J. Jusserand, *English Wayfaring Life in the Middle Ages*, translated from the French by Lucy Toulmin Smith, Ernest Benn, fourth ed. (sixteenth impression), 1950, p. 63.

William, undress and wash your legs, and then dry them with a cloth, and rub them well for love of the fleas, that they may not leap on your legs, for there is a peck of them lying in the dust under the rushes. . . . Hi! the fleas bite me so! and do me great harm, for I have scratched my shoulders till the blood flows.

A GOOD CELLAR, c. 1460

Source: ' The Duties of a Panter or Butler ' in John Russell's ' Book of Nurture '; *The Babees' Book Medieval Manners for the Young done into modern English from Dr. Furnivall's Texts* by Edith Rickert, Chatto and Windus, 1923, p. 51–2.

Look ye have two wine-augers, a greater and a less, some gutters of boxwood that fit them, also a gimlet to pierce with, a tap and a bung, ready to stop the flow when it is time. So when you broach a pipe, good son, do after my teaching: pierce or bore with an auger or gimlet, slanting upward, four fingers' breadth from the lower rim, so as not to cause the lees to rise—I warn you especially. . . .

Take good heed to the wines, red, white, and sweet; look to them every night with a candle, to see that they neither ferment nor leak. Never forget to wash the heads of the pipes with cold water ever night; and always carry a gimlet, adze and linen clouts, large and small. If the wine ferment, ye shall know by its singing, so keep at hand a pipe of *couleur de rose* (a red malmsey wine) that has been spent in drinking and add to the fermentation the dregs of this, and it shall be amended. . . .

[Then follows a list of sweet wines.]

TAVERNS: MEASURES, 1419

Wine stocks in London taverns in December 1416, were, east of Walbrook, 154 tuns of red and white wine and 587 butts of sweet, and west of Walbrook, 124 tuns and 113 butts.

Source: Liber Albus, the White Book of the City of London compiled in A.D. 1419 *by John Carpenter and Richard Whittington,* translated by H. T. Riley, Richard Griffin 1861, p. 233.

Vinepress. c. 1330. (Holkham Bible).

And that the gallon of wine shall be sold at three pence, and not dearer. And that the gallon of ale shall be made for three farthings, and another gallon for one penny, and not dearer. And if any shall be found dearer, it shall be forfeited unto the use of the Sheriff.

And that no brewster or taverner shall sell from henceforth by any measures but by the gallon, pottle, and quart; and that these shall be sealed with the seal of the Alderman. And if any one shall be found selling by measure not sealed, she shall be amerced [fined], the first time, in the sum of forty pence, and the measure be burnt or broken. The second time, she shall be amerced to the amount of twenty shillings. And whereas it often happens, that gallons, pottles, and quarts are partly broken, and some of them, having been marked while they were green [being made of turned wood], after being used for a long time, through dryness shrink, and thereby become not so good as they ought to be—it is provided, that every taverner and brewster shall carry such gallons, pottles, and quarts unto the house of his or her Alderman four times in the year, that the same may be examined if sufficient in all respects; and for such labour and usage, and for the marks when made at first, two pence shall be given for the gallon, for the pottle one penny, and for the quart one halfpenny. And the same thing shall be done as to the gallon of taverners of wine, the bushel, and the half bushel. For one bushel so marked one penny shall be given, and for half a bushel one halfpenny. And if any one shall be found, who on summons to do this shall not come or send, or shall not do in manner aforesaid, such person shall be amerced by the Alderman in the sum of two shillings.

TAVERNS: CLOSING TIME

Ethelred inflicted penalties for disorder in an ale-house and William of Newburgh describes a Yorkshire peasant who went into an ale-house and saw devils seated on every customer's cup. These temporarily flew away when customary prayers were said. Taverns had to shut when curfew sounded and might not open until Sunday Mass. Regulation was needed, for one of the few drawbacks of Norman London, according to one admirer, was the ' immoderate drinking of fools '.

Further Reading: J. Bickersdyke (C. H. Cook), *The Curiosities of Ale and Beer*, 1886.

Source: *Liber Albus, the White Book of the City of London compiled in* A.D. 1419 *by John Carpenter and Richard Whittington*, translated by H. T. Riley, Richard Griffin 1861, pp. 240–1 (1419).

And whereas such [disreputable] persons going about by night do commonly have their resort and hold their common meetings in taverns more than elsewhere, and do there seek shelter, and lie in wait and watch their time to do ill—it is forbidden that any person shall keep a tavern for wine or for ale open after the hour of curfew aforesaid; but they shall keep their taverns closed after such hour. Nor shall they have persons therein, sleeping or sitting up; nor shall any one receive persons into his house from out of a common tavern, by night or by day, except those for whom he shall be willing to be answerable unto the peace of the King.

And if it shall be found that any taverner does otherwise, he shall be put on his surety, the first time by the hanap [a two-handled drinking cup often of silver] of the tavern, or by some other good pledge therein found; and he shall be amerced [fined] in the sum of half a mark; and the third time, in ten shillings. The fourth time he shall pay the whole penalty double, that is to say, twenty shillings. And the fifth time, he shall forswear such trade in the City for ever. And if any taverner shall receive any bad character, knowing that he has been a transgressor, he shall have the imprisonment that is provided for all receivers of felons.

HOLY DAYS

(1) *Source*: Canons enacted under King Edgar (956–975). B. Thorpe, *Ancient Laws and Institutes of England*, 1840, p. 397.

And we enjoin, that on feast-days heathen songs and devil's games be abstained from.

And we enjoin, that Sunday trading, and folk-moots, be abstained from.

And we enjoin, that unbecoming garments, and foolish dis-courses, and ignominious shavings be abstained from. . . .

And we enjoin, that on feast-days, and lawful fast-days, there be no strife, among men, to any excess.

And we enjoin, that on feast-days and fast-days, oaths and ordeals be foregone. . . .

And we enjoin, that every one, at the church wakes, be very sober, and earnestly pray, and suffer there be no drinking, nor any vanity.

(2) *Source*: Laws of King Ethelred (978–1016), V, 13–19. B. Thorpe, *Ancient Laws and Institutes of England*, 1840, p. 131.

Let Sunday's festival be rightly kept, as is thereto becoming; and let marketings and folk-motes be carefully abstained from on that holy day.

And let all St. Mary's feast-tides be strictly honoured; first with fasting, and afterwards with feasting: and at the celebration of every apostle, let there be fasting and feasting; except that on the festival of St. Philip and St. James [Mayday] we enjoin no fast, on account of the Easter festival.

Else, let other festivals and fasts be strictly observed, so as those observed them who best observed them. . . .

And to fast every Friday, unless it be a festival.

And ordeals and oaths are forbidden on festival-days, and on the regular Emberdays, and from Adventum Domini till the octaves of Epiphany; and from Septuagesima till 15 days after Easter.

And at those holy tides, let there be, as is right, to all Christian men general peace and concord; and let every strife be appeased.

HARVESTING ON A HOLY DAY, JULY 1297, 1303 or 1308

Even when St. Richard was Bishop of Chichester, the Bishop of Chichester's villeins had to do carrying services on Sunday. Bishop Grosseteste thought domestic staff should seldom or never have holidays.

Source: a complaint from Roger de Marlowe, rector of Harwell, presumably to the Archdeacon of Berkshire. Rosalind M. T. Hill, 'A Berkshire Letter-Book ', *Berkshire Archaeological Journal*, vol. 41, 1937, p. 23.

To the reverend and prudent man, etc. It is my duty to tell your discretion that last Sunday, the morrow of S. Margaret's day, H... C..., the Bishop of Winchester's harvester in Harwell, summoned or caused to be summoned all the tenants of the said Bishop in the said vill, ordering them to come to the park of the said Bishop immediately after nine o'clock to cart hay. For this purpose, while we were at breakfast he called them up to work by blowing a certain great horn through the whole village, as he is wont to do on working days. And this seemed to me unbearable, so I immediately sent Sir Thomas my colleague, chaplain of the parish, to prevent such work upon that day, but they would not listen to him or desist from their work. So I warned them three or four times to stop and afterwards threatened them with excommunication if they went on, but I laboured in vain, for the said H... answered me mockingly that he was going to cart the hay whether I liked it or not, nor would he cease work, or permit others to cease, for my threats or warnings. I therefore, being somewhat disturbed, summoned them generally and afterwards had them summoned separately to appear before you in your chapter held on Wednesday the vigil of S. James's day, to hear and receive the sentence which your discretion should declare according to justice. Wherefore I beg your discretion to give them a suitable sentence, punishing them so that others may not be tempted by the lightness of their sentence to follow their example, and let the harvester receive punishment for habitually working on holy days and encouraging others to do the same. He is a powerful man. Farewell and good wishes.

BUILDING WORKERS' HOLIDAYS: SOME WITH PAY, 1328

Work stopped on the great festivals of the church. It was customary on royal works for alternate feast days to be paid. The Statute of Labourers of 1360 said that no wages were to be taken on festivals. The loss of holidays caused by the Reformation did not therefore mean the loss of paid holidays.

Further Reading: D. Knoop, G. P. Jones and D. Hamer, *The Two Earliest Masonic MSS.*, Manchester University Press, 1938.

Source: Exchequer document printed by L. F. Salzman, *Building in England down to* 1540 *a documentary history*, Oxford, 1952, p. 66.

Note that on the Friday next following the 24th day of February was the feast of St. Matthias the Apostle, for which day the workmen seek and claim to have their wages by a custom of old standing, as they say; which custom is as follows: namely, that when any workmen, of whatever rank or craft they be, have been engaged on the King's works continuously for a fortnight or

Building. Thirteenth century. (Trinity College, Dublin, St. Alban).

three weeks, a month or more, and two or more feast days happen to occur within such time, exclusive of Sundays, the King always has one feast day, beginning with the first, and the workmen the other; so that the workmen shall receive from the King for every alternate feast day their wages full and complete, although they do not work on it, just as they would for a working day. And because the King has the day of the Purification of the Blessed Mary for the first feast day the workmen claim this feast day as the second; and payment was made to them of their wages for that day.

MORNING

Source: *Regularis Concordia Anglicae Nationis Monachorum Sanctimonialiumque*, translated by Dom Thomas Symons, Medieval Classics, T. Nelson and Sons, 1953, pp. 15–16 (c. 970).

When the bell is rung the brethren shall go and put on their day shoes: none but the ministers should presume to do this before the bell is heard. Nor fail to do so then without permission, lest the merit of obedience be sadly dimmed by his rashness and presumption. Next the entire *schola* [choir school] with their master and the abbot shall wash their faces as is customary, intent on the psalms as they do so. As for the seniors, let each one separately, according as God suggests to his heart by His divine inspiration, silently and with the whole bent of his mind apply himself to his duty, sanctifying his acts of obedience, as he should everything, with holy prayers, chanting the canonical hours, or the seven Penitential psalms or any other spiritual prayer apt for driving away the temptation of the devil; and so, having washed, let them proceed to the church. As the children enter the church the sacrist shall ring the first bell; and when they have said the *Trina oratio* [a prayer in honour of the Trinity] in the same way as the seniors have done, all shall take their places and the bell shall be rung for them to begin Tierce.

MEANING OF MATINS

The Church appointed eight special ' Hours ' in each 24 hour period as fixed times for services. The Augustinian Canons of Bridlington recited Prime at dawn, Terce at 9 a.m., Sext at noon, None at 3 p.m., Vespers at sundown, Compline at 9 p.m., Vigils (later called Matins) at midnight, and Matins (later called Lauds) at break of day. Thus they seem to have said Matins and Prime together.

Source: Robert of Bridlington, *The Bridlington Dialogue, An Exposition of the Rule of St. Augustine for the Life of the Clergy, Given through a Dialogue between Master and Disciple*, Translated and Edited by a Religious of C.S.M.V., A. R. Mowbray and Co., 1960 (mid-twelfth century).

To the antiquity of Matins the prophet David is once more the witness when he says, *O God, my God, early do I watch unto Thee*, and again, *Early in the morning will I think of Thee*. But the reason for praying at daybreak is to celebrate Christ's resurrection. For in the early morning Christ, rising from death and saving His people, condemned the devil and his satellites to everlasting chains. It was assuredly at the first ray of dawn that the Lord rose from Hades, when the light began to rise for the faithful which had set for sinners when he died. By the Morning Office is recalled also the baptism of the People of Israel, which typified our own. Exodus narrates that this took place in the morning watch, when the children of Israel crossed the Red Sea, after their enemies had been destroyed by the power of God. And, lastly, we believe that the hope of the future general resurrection, when all men, just and unjust, will awake, arising from this temporal death as from the stupor of sleep, will come at that time too.

SATURDAY

Source: *Regularis Concordia Anglicae Nationis Monachorum Sancti-monialium* translated by Dom Thomas Symonds, Medieval Classics, T. Nelson and Sons, 1953, p. 22. (c. 970).

On Saturdays the brethren shall wash their feet, for which purpose each shall have a suitable basin. Having washed their feet, those who need to shall wash their shoes also. Then the prior shall strike the little bell and all shall assemble with thanksgiving to draw their measure of drink. . . .

FEBRUARY

The illustrated calendars which precede many Books of Hours show pictures of the occupations suitable for the different months and the signs of the Zodiac for the different times of year.

Further Reading:

Source: Translated from *Bartholomew the Englishman, On the Properties of Things*, Book 9, chapter 9. (Thirteenth century).

February . . . is a very rainy month and watery because vapours have risen and are let down again as showers. So then the Sun is said to be in Aquarius because of the flooding of the waters. February is painted as an old man warming his feet at the fire because in that season the cold is at its greatest intensity because of the sun being distant for a long time.

LENTEN FARE

(1) *Source*: A fifteenth century cookery book from the library of Sir Edward Coke (Holkham MS. 671, fol. 26 v.–27), printed by Mrs. A. Napier, 1882 (privately), p. 37, and, unknown to her, by the early printer Pynson.

To rost eggs in Lent tak and blowe out the mete at the end of the eggs and wesche [wash] the shellis with warm water. Then tak thik mylk of almonds and set it to the fyere till it be at the boilling. Then put it in a canvas and let the water ryn out and kep all that levythe in the clothe and gadur it togedure in a dische. Put yt to whit sugure and colour the tone half with saffron and put ther in a litill newe berme and poudered gingyver and canelle [cinnamon] and put four of the whit in the egg shell and in the mydst put in of the yallow to be the yolk and fill it up with whit. Then set it in the fyere to rost. And to 40 eggs take a lb. of almond and a quarter gyngyver and canelle [cinnamon].

(2) *Source*: *id.*, foll. 27 v.–28 and pp. 38–9.

To make braun rialle in Lent tak sownds [the swimming bladder] of stokfische dry and do them in water 3 dais and chaunge the water every day. Tak them up and lay them upon a bord and scrape them clene with the bak of your knyf and wesche them and sethe them in water. Then tak them up and sethe them in freche fische brothe. And put to eles for to amend the brothe. Then tak blanchid almondes ground and draw them with the sam brothe hote and ye wille ye may mak ther of al maner of braun as ye did of flesche. Also tak egg and brek a hole in the gret ende and put one the mete and wesche them and dry them and set them in salt upright and luk it be sessounded. Then put in som of the whit braun and som of the same braun cold and colour it with saffron and put it in pepyns as gret as an egge and fille them up. And when they be cold pulle of the shellis and set them in salt and piche it with clowes [cloves] 4 or 8 above and fill up the crown with blanche pouder and serve then furthe insted of eggs. And in the same maner do with poudur or ginger and chaunge the colour and cutt it in gret peces and serve it furthe as ye do braun.

(3) *Source*: *id.*, foll. 28–28v. and pp. 39–40.

To mak a Breteyne in Lent take braun that is mad in Lent. Put therto pouder of pepper, pouder of clowes and canelle a goodelle [good deal] of sanders [a herb]. Then tak blanched almondes diced in a part of wyne and a part of venyger and put it togeder in a pot. And when it is boilid put it into another vesselle and when it is cold lesche [slice] it and serve it as ye did braun rialle. [In flesh time calves feet were used for Breteyn.]

(4) Pastries in the shape of hats.

Source: *id*., foll. 33v. and pp. 47–8.

To mak hattes in Lent mak a paist of purid flour knodene [kneaded] with mylk of almondes. Then tak saffron, eles, base or molet and the lever of the fishe soden and ground. Put therto a litille fritur, pouder of saffron and salt and mak the bater of purid floure and almond mylk.

EASTER

The great annual feast celebrating the Resurrection has a name which, according to Bede, is derived from *Eostre*, the Anglo-Saxon goddess of spring to whom *Eostur-monath* (April) was dedicated. Easter is the first Sunday after the full moon following the vernal equinox and the date has been the subject of many disputes, including an important one between Celtic Christians and those converted by Augustine's mission from Rome (see *W.W.I.H.*, i, p. 21). Since 1900 many have tried to get the date altered again in favour of a fixed one early in April. At Easter churches and altars were arrayed as finely as possible and in token of joy, light and purity white vestments were worn. In medieval France the year was reckoned as starting at Easter and it is the greatest Christian festival. On it captives and slaves were often freed and many were baptised. Christ rising from the tomb holding the cross as a triumphal banner is a common theme in miniatures and alabaster carvings. In the Holkham Bible the cross is green; for, as a modern Dominican writes, man worships naturally, in harmony with the rhythm of nature which God is making. A niche in the north wall of the chancel represents the Easter sepulchre in some churches. There the cross and the Bread were laid and guarded from Good Friday to Easter. An Easter egg is a symbol of life appearing in what seems to be dead.

Further Reading: Karl Young, ' The Home of the Easter Play '. *Speculum*, i, 1926, pp. 71–86.; N. C. Brooks, *The Sepulchre of Christ in Art and Liturgy, University of Illinois Studies in Language and Literature*, vol. 7, no. 2, 1921.

(1) *Source*: William of Wadington, Manuel des Pechiez (c. 1300), translated by E. K. Chambers, *English Literature at the Close of the Middle Ages*, Clarendon Press, 1945, p. 13.

Foolish clerks have devised another open folly, which they
call ' miracles '. Their faces are disguised by masks, the madness
which is forbidden by decree. So much the greater is their sin.
They may make a representation, if it is done modestly in the
office of Holy Church, when man renders service to God, of
how Jesus Christ, the Son of God, was laid in the sepulchre,
and of the Resurrection, for the sake of greater devoutness.
But if they make foolish assemblies in city streets or in graveyards after meals, when fools are glad to come, even though they
say that it is done for a good purpose, do not on any account
believe them that it is done for the honour of God, but rather in
truth for that of the devil.

(2) *Source*: Translated from Winchester Trope, 978–80, printed in
Karl Young, *The Drama of the Mediaeval Church*, Oxford 1933, vol. 1,
pp. 254–5.

Angel voice about Christ's Resurrection:

' Whom do ye seek in the sepulchre, O folk of Christ? ' Answer
of the holy women (the three Marys):

' Jesus of Nazareth the crucified, O folk of Heaven. Consolation of the angel voice ':

' He is not here, He has risen as he foretold. Go and tell forth
the news for He is risen.'

Song of the holy women to all the clergy:

'Alleluia, the Lord is risen today, the strong lion is risen, Christ,
the son of God. Thanks be to God, raise the joyful cry! Come
and see the place where the Lord was laid, alleluia, alleluia.'

Again let the angel speak:

' Hasten, hasten and tell the disciples, for the Lord is risen,
alleluia, alleluia.'

The women sing with one voice in gladness:

' The Lord is risen from the sepulchre, He who hung upon
the wood for us, alleluia.

MAY

The picture for the month of May in illuminated manuscripts often shows a scene of pleasure in the woods, such as hawking. On May day branches of trees and flowers were gathered and carried in triumph and a maypole was set up round which there was dancing. A picture of May day dancing, made in the reign of Edward IV, on glass at Betley Hall, Staffs., is reproduced in C. Cox, *Churchwardens' Accounts* as the earliest representation of a maypole.

Further Reading: J. Brand, *Popular Antiquities of Great Britain*, 1905.

Source: Sir Thomas Malory, *Le Morte Arthur*, printed by Caxton (written about 1470).

And thus it past on from Candylmas [2 February, the Purification of the Virgin] untyl after Ester that the moneth of May was come, whan every lusty herte begynneth to blossomme and to brynge forth fruyte. For lyke as herbes and trees bryngen forth fruyte and florysshen in May, in lyke wyse every lusty herte that is in ony maner a lover spryngeth and floryssheth in lusty dedes. For it gyveth unto al lovers courage, that lusty moneth of May, in some thyng to constrayne hym to some maner of thyng more in that moneth than in ony other moneth, for dyverse causes. For thenne alle herbes and trees renewen a man and woman. And lyke wyse lovers callen ageyne to their mynde old gentilnes and old servyse, and many kynde dedes were forgeten by neclygence. For lyke as wynter rasure doth alway arase and deface grene somer, soo fareth it by unstable love in man and woman . . . Therefore lyke as May moneth floreth and floryssheth in many gardyns, soo lyke wyse lete every man of worship florysshe his herte in this world, fyrst unto God, and next unto the ioye of them that he promysed his feythe unto . . . I lyken love now adayes unto somer and wynter. For lyke as the one is hote and the other cold, so fareth love now adayes. Therefore alle ye that be lovers calle unto your remembraunce the moneth of May. . .

MIDSUMMER

The great feast of the Nativity of St. John the Baptist fell in the season when the sun was strongest and St. John as ' a burning shining light '. On its eve it was a general custom to light bonfires, house-holders put lamps outside their houses in London and lights were carried through the streets by a marching Watch. The day is still marked in the calendar as one of the four quarter-days on which pay-ments fall due. The illustration of the Nativity in the Holkham Bible is coloured in bright yellow which contrasts with the sober brown and blue of the picture of John preaching Baptism by Jordan beneath it. The celebrations had pre-christian origins, made holy by the Church. See also pp. 103–4 for Baptism.

Further Reading: J. L. André, ' St. John the Baptist in Art, Legend and Ritual ', *Archaeological Journal*, vol. 50, 1893; F. Bond, *Fonts and Font Covers*, 1908.

Source: Homily on the Feast of St. John the Baptist, cited in a discussion of the customs of Midsummer Eve in J. Brand, *Observations on the Popular Antiquities of Great Britain*, Bohn 1849, pp. 299–300.

In worshyp of Saint Johan the people waked [kept holiday] at home, and made three maner of fyres: one was clene bones, and noo woode, and that is called a Bone Fyre, for people to sit and wake therby; another is clene woode, and no bones, and that is called a Wode Fyre, for people to sit and wake thereby; the thirde is made of wode and bones, and it is callyd Saynt Johannys fyre. The first fyre, as a great clerke Johan Belleth telleth he was in a certeyne countrey, so in the countrey there was soo greate hete the which causid that dragons to go togyther in tokenynge that Johan dyed in brennynge love and charyté to God and man, and they that dye in charyté shall have parte of all good prayers, and they that do not, shall never be saved. Then as these dragons flewe in th'ayre they shed down to that water froth of ther kynde, and so envenymed the waters, and caused moche people for to take theyr deth thereby, and many dyverse sykenesse. Wyse clerkes knoweth well that dragons hate nothyng more than the stenche of brennynge bones, and therefore they gaderyd as many as they mighte fynde, and brent them; and so with the stenche thereof they drove away the dragons, and so they were brought out of greete dysease. The second fyre was made of woode, for that wyl brenne lyght, and wyll be seen farre. For it is the chefe of fyre to be seen farre, and betokenneth that Saynt Johan was a lanterne of lyght to the people. Also the people mad blases of fyre, for that they shulde be seene farre, and specyally in the nyght, in token of St. Johan's having been seen from far in the spirit by Jeremiah. The third fyre of bones betokenneth Johan's martyrdome, for hys bones were brente [burnt by Julian the Apostate].

CHRISTMAS AND BOXING DAY

Among medieval pictures one of the most popular was the Nativity, but the early Church lacked an agreed tradition about the exact date and 25 December is not mentioned before about 180 or even 354. Bede, in discussing chronology, records that ' the ancient Angles kept the new year on December 25 when we celebrate the Nativity. The very night which we now so deeply revere, they called Mothers' Night, presumably because of ceremonies performed during the nightlong vigil '. Christmas was celebrated by fires, of which the yule log is a survival, because it was the point at which the hours of sunlight first began to lengthen; and in ancient Egypt the celebrants would cry ' The Virgin has brought forth! The light is waxing '. Christianity transformed the festival into one in honour of the Sun of Righteousness, St. Augustine said we must celebrate the day on account of Him who made the sun, not on account of the sun itself like the heathen, and Pope Leo the Great fought the pestilent belief that it celebrated the birth of the new sun and not the birth of Christ. This solemn feast was used to celebrate the baptism of Clovis (496), the coronation of Charlemagne as Emperor of the West at Rome (800) and the coronation of William I at Westminster. Thereafter Christmas was a feast which William always marked by wearing his crown.

Further Reading: C. A. Miles, *Christmas in Ritual and Tradition*, 1912. C. C. Polhill, *The Origin of Christmas*, 1925.

(1) Christmas pie (for the salters).

Source: W. Herbert, *History of Twelve Great Livery Companies*, published by the author, 1834-6. II, 563.

Take fesaunt, haare and chykenne or capounne, of eche oone; with ii partuchis, ii pygeonnes and ii conynggys; and smyte hem on peces and pyke clene awaye therefrom alle the boonys that ye maye, and therwith do hem ynto a foyle [crust] of gode paste, made craftely ynne the lyknes of a byrdes' bodye with the lyvours

48. A gentleman's deer-hounds (*cf. p.* 188)

49. Hawking

50. Hare and hound (*cf. p.* 184)

51. Ball.   St. Cuthbert at play—and hurt.   They wear stripes (*cf. p.* 106)

52. Dance   53. Dance (*cf. p.* 280)

and hertys, ii kydneis of shepe, and farcys [forced meat] and eyren [eggs] made ynto balles. Caste thereto poudre of pepyr, salte, spyce, eysell [vinegar], and funges [mushrooms] pykled; and thanne take the boonys and let hem seethe ynne a pot to make brothe therfor, and do yt unto the foyle of past, and close yt uppe faste, and bake yt wel and so serve yt forthe; with the hede of oone of the byrdes stucke at the oon end of the foyle, and a grete tayle at the other, and dyvers of hys longe fedyrs sette ynne connynglye alle about him.

(2) Boxing Day in Bury cemetery, late twelfth century.

Source: *The Chronicle of Jocelin of Brakelond concerning the Acts of Samson Abbot of the Monastery of St. Edmund*, translated by H. E. Butler, Nelson 1951, pp. 92–4. See picture, p. 191.

On the day after Christmas there were gatherings in the cemetery, wrestling bouts and matches between the Abbot's servants and the burgesses of the town; and from words they came to blows, and from buffets to wounds and bloodshed. But the Abbot when he heard of it, after calling to him in private certain persons who had gathered to watch the show, but had stood afar off, ordered the names of the evil-doers to be written down, and caused all of them to be brought before him in the chapel of St. Denys on the day after the feast of St. Thomas; and in the meantime he abstained from inviting a single burgess to his table, as he used formerly to do during the first five days of Christmas. So on the appointed day, having sworn sixteen law-worthy men and heard their testimony, the Abbot said, '. . . because they are laymen and do not understand how great a crime it is to commit such sacrilege, I will, that other may be the more afraid, excommunicate these by name and in public, and that there may be no failure of justice in any respect, I will begin with my own household and servants.' And so it was done, when we had put on stoles and lighted candles. Then all of them went out of the church and, after taking counsel, they stripped themselves and, naked save for their drawers, they prostrated themselves before the door of the church. And when the Abbot's assessors, both monks and clerks, came and told him with tears that more than a hundred men were lying thus naked, the Abbot

N

also wept . . . Therefore after they had all been smartly scourged and then absolved, they all swore that they would stand by the judgment of the Church concerning the commission of sacrilege. And on the morrow they were given penance according to the rule laid down by the canons, and thus the Abbot recalled them all to unity and concord, uttering terrible threats against all those who by word or deed should give cause for dissension. But he publicly forbade all gatherings and shows in the cemetery. So all having been brought back to the blessing of peace, the burgesses feasted with their lord during the days that followed with much rejoicing.

SUNDIALS AND CANDLES FOR CLOCKS, 887

The earliest English sundial is on the Bewcastle Cross, a fine late seventh century relic of Northumbrian sculpture in Cumberland. Twenty-four pre-Conquest examples are known but probably every Saxon church had one, consisting of a vertical semicircular plaque. Sometimes the dials were divided into six, sometimes into eight, and sometimes into twelve compartments, for the same measurements of time were not accepted in areas with populations of different origin. There is a metal portable sun-dial at Canterbury Cathedral. These dials could not work at night like Alfred's candles.

Further Reading: 'Anglo-Saxon Sundials,' *Society of Antiquaries Journal*, vol. 8, 1928, 489. 'A Saxon Pocket Watch,' *Country Life*, vol. 107, June 1950, p. 1890.

Source: Asser's Annals of the Exploits of Alfred, translated, Rev. J. Stevenson, *The Church Historians of England*, vol. 2 pt. 2, Seeleys 1854, p. 477.

. . . . he [Alfred] commanded his chaplains to procure a sufficient quantity of wax; when brought, he ordered them to place it in one scale and to weigh it against some pence placed in the other, and when a quantity had been weighed out which was found equal in weight to seventy-two pence, then he ordered his chaplains to make six candles, all of equal size, and each candle was to have twelve divisions marked by inches lengthways upon it. When this plan was adopted, these six candles were kept constantly burning night and day, without fail, before the sacred reliques of many of God's elect, which always accompanied him wherever he went. But sometimes these candles could not continue alight through a whole day and night, to the same hour on which they were lit on the preceding evening, in consequence of the violent gusts of wind which often blew without intermission day and night, through the doors and windows of the churches, and through the numerous chinks of the buildings, and planks, and walls, and also through the thin canvas of the tents. Thus they were compelled to finish their course before the same hour, by burning quicker than they ought. He reflected how he could prevent this draught of the winds, and by a plan cunningly and wisely invented, he ordered the construction of a beautiful lantern of wood and ox-horn; for white ox-horn, when thinly planed in single layers, becomes as translucent as a glass vessel. This lantern, then, as we said before, was wonderfully made of wood and horn, and the candle placed in it by night shines as clearly without as within, experiencing no hindrance from blasts of wind: for he also ordered a door to be made of horn to close up the opening. When this contrivance was used, the six candles, one after another, for twenty-four hours gave light without intermission, neither more nor less: and when these were burnt out, others were lighted.

CLOCKS

The performance of Divine Service at stated hours, indicated by bells was a routine for all monks. Special services suited stated days.

Time had long been measured by the movement of heavenly bodies and hour-glasses and candles could be used to measure hours. Mechanical clocks driven by falling weights and involving trains of cog wheels and an oscillatory escapement mechanism are mentioned in documents as at London and Canterbury in the late thirteenth century. The earliest surviving example in Europe may be the Cathedral clock at Salisbury or that from Dover castle now in the Science Museum, London, which is probably not as early, 1348, as is sometimes stated. There is an early clock tower at St. Albans. Cog wheels had been long understood and made by millwrights, but they had hitherto been made of wood. The invention of the clock with its metal cogwheels was a significant step towards a world now full of automatic mechanism. Large clocks made by blacksmiths for church towers were familiar by 1350. Suspension of weights drove them, for mainsprings were a late fifteenth century invention.

J. C. Cox examined about sixty sets of late fourteenth and fifteenth century churchwardens' accounts and found that nearly all refer to clocks. The earlier clocks had no dials. Periodically automatic figures called 'jacks' struck bells as at Wells Cathedral.

Further Reading: A. P. Usher, *A History of Mechanical Inventions*, 2nd ed., New York, 1954. Lynn White, 'Technology and Invention in the Middle Ages', *Speculum*, vol. 15, 1940, p. 141–159.

Source: The tank of a water-clock at Bury was big enough to be useful in case of fire. *The Chronicle of Jocelin of Brakelond concerning the Acts of Samson, Abbot of the Monastery of St. Edmund*, translated by H. E. Butler, Nelson, 1951, pp. 106–7. (1198).

There was a wooden platform between the feretory [box for relics] and the High Altar, on which there were two candles, which the guardians of the shrine used to stick and join together in a most unseemly manner by placing one candle on the top of another. And under this platform many things were stored without regard to seemliness, such as flax, thread, wax, and divers utensils; in fact, anything that came into the hands of the guardians was placed there, since the platform had a door and iron walls. So, while the guardians were asleep on the night of the Feast of St. Ethelreda, part of a candle [as is believed] which had been stuck together and had burned down, fell on the aforesaid platform which was covered with cloth, and began to set fire to everything near it both above and below, so that the iron walls were white with the heat. . . In the same hour the clock struck before Matins, and the master of the vestry, when he arose, perceived and saw the fire, and running with all speed beat upon the board as though to announce a death, and cried with a loud voice that the feretory was burned. And we all of us ran together, and found the flames raging beyond belief and embracing the whole feretory and reaching up nearly to the beams of the Church. So the young men among us ran to get water, some to the well, and others to the clock, while yet others with the utmost difficulty succeeded in extinguishing the fire with their cowls and carried off certain small pyxes [containing the Holy Sacrament], before harm could happen to them. And when cold water was poured upon the front of the feretory, the stones fell and were reduced almost to powder. But the nails, by which the plates of silver were fastened to the feretory fell from the wood, which was burnt beneath them to the thickness of my finger, and the plates hung one from another without any nails to support them. But the golden Majesty on the front of the feretory, together with certain stones, remained firm and intact, and seemed fairer after the fire than it was before, because it was all of gold.

HUNTING

Hunting was an important source of meat. It was accompanied by an elaborate ritual and there was a highly specialized vocabulary relating to it. A Saxon royal huntsman explains his work and its rewards in T.S.I.H., i, 27.

(1) *Source*: H. Dryden, *The Art of Hunting or Three Hunting MSS.*, a *revised edition of the Art of Hunting by William Twici, Huntsman of King Edward II*, 1844, revised, Northampton, William Mark, 1908, p. 25. (Early fourteenth century).

When the Hare is taken, and they [the hounds] have chased it, you ought to blow the prize [a blast on the horn], and you ought to give the hounds the halow. What is the halow? The sides, and the shoulders, and the neck, and the head; and the loin shall remain for the kitchen. When the Hart is taken you ought to blow *four moots* [long blasts on the horn], and he shall be undone [cut to pieces] like any other beast. And then if it should happen that his hounds are bold, and if they have taken the Hart by force, the Huntsman shall have the hide, and he that flays the head shall have the shoulder by right [as a perquisite], and the hounds shall be rewarded with the neck, and with the bowels, and with the liver, and it shall be eaten upon the hide. . . . The head shall be carried to the house before the Lord, and the heart, and the tail, and the gullet on a fork. And the menee ought to be blown at the door of the hall, when he is taken to the house. When the buck is taken you ought to blow the prize, and you ought to reward the hounds with the paunch and with the bowels.

(2) The 'Master of Games' is the oldest book on hunting in English. It was written between 1406 and 1413 by Edward, second Duke of York, familiar as the traitor Aumerle in Shakespeare's *Richard II*, but is largely a translation from Gaston de Foix' *Livre de Chasse* or

Gaston Phoebus. Edward dedicated his ' litel symple book ' to his cousin Henry, later Henry V, when he was Master of Game at the court of Henry IV, the prince's father.

Source: The Master of Game by Edward, second Duke of York: the oldest English Book of Hunting, edited by W. A. and F. Baillie-Grohman, Chatto and Windus, 1909, pp. 8–12.

Now shall I prove how hunters live in this world more joyfully than any other men. For when the hunter riseth in the morning, and he sees a sweet and fair morn and clear weather and bright, and he heareth the song of the small birds, the which sing so sweetly with great melody and full of love, each in its own language in the best wise that it can according that it learneth of its own kind. And when the sun is arisen, he shall see fresh dew upon the small twigs and grasses, and the sun by his virtue shall make them shine. And that is great joy and liking to the hunter's heart. After when he shall go to his quest or searching, he shall see or meet anon with the hart without great seeking, and shall harbour [trace to the lair] him well and readily within a little compass. It is great joy and liking to the hunter. [The hunting of the hart is then described with many technical words.] . . . and when he cometh home he cometh joyfully, for his lord hath given him to drink of his good wine at the curée [the rewarding of the hounds], and when he has come home he shall doff his clothes and his shoes and his hose, and he shall wash his thighs and his legs, and peradventure all his body. And in the meanwhile he shall order well his supper, with *wortes* [roots] and of the neck of the hart and of other good meats, and good wine or ale. And when he hath well eaten and drunk he shall be glad and well, and well at his ease. And then shall he take the air in the evening of the night, for the great heat that he hath had. And then he shall go and drink and lie in his bed in fair fresh clothes, and shall sleep well and steadfastly all the night without any evil thoughts of any sins, wherefore I say that hunters go into Paradise when they die, and live in this world more joyfully than any other man. Yet I will prove to you how hunters live longer than any other men . . . They eat and drink less than any other men of this world, for in the morning at the assembly they eat a little, and if they eat well at supper, they will by then have corrected their nature, for then they have eaten but little . . . And since hunters eat little and sweat always, they should live long and in health . . . Wherefore I counsel to all manner of folk of what estate or condition they be, that they love hounds and hunting and the pleasure of hunting beasts of one kind or another, or hawking . . . Phoebus the Earl of Foix . . . never saw a man that loved the work . . . that had not many good qualities in him.

(3) A critic of hunting, 1159.

In the twelfth century John of Salisbury said that the nobles esteemed hunting and hawking so much that they spent more trouble and money on them than on war. This made them as brutal as the beasts they pursued and peasants were evicted for the sake of wild beasts. If a great and merciless hunter passed your home you must bring out, buy or borrow all the refreshment possible or you might be ruined or even accused of treason.

Source: John of Salisbury, *Frivolities of Courtiers and Footprints of Philosophers being a translation of the first, second, and third books and selections from the seventh and eighth books of the Policraticus*, translated by J. B. Pike (1159), University of Minnesota, Minneapolis, 1938, pp. 14–5.

Can you name any man of distinction who has been an enthusiast in the sport of hunting? . . . The founder of the Roman race laid low the seven huge stags not to sate his vanity and pleasure but to keep himself and his followers alive. It is from their purpose and result that deeds are judged. An act is seemly if the cause that preceded it is honorable. Who ever formed an army of hunters and dogs except for the purpose of battling beasts with courage not his own? Why shouldn't he? Perhaps he will bag a tiny beast, a timid hare, with his elaborate equipment. But if the booty be more glorious, a deer maybe or boar, and the hunter's efforts be conspicuous, spontaneous applause bursts out, the huntsmen are wild with joy, and the head of the victim with the usual trophies will be born before the conquering hero. One would think that the capture of the king of the Cappadocians was being celebrated, to judge by the blare of trumpet and squeal of pipe proclaiming the victory. When a female animal is caught, then gloom prevails, or when a noble beast is laid low by the cunning of the trappers rather than by their prowess.

If a wild goat or hare be the victim, it is thought unworthy of the glory of a triumph. . . .

(4) Royal huntsmen.

The monks of Abingdon obtained from Henry I a chapter freeing their manor at Wheatley, Oxon, on the edge of the Royal Forest of Shotover, from the obligation of entertaining such royal officials.

Further Reading: G. H. White, ' The Constitutio Domus Regis and the King's Sport,' *Antiquaries Journal*, vol. 30, 1950, pp. 52–63.

Source: Establishment of the Royal Household, c. 1136, translated in *Dialogus de Scaccario The Course of the Exchequer and Constitutio Domus Regis*, Nelson 1950, p. 135.

Each of four *Hornblowers* 3d. a day. Twenty *Serjeants*: Each 1d. a day. *Fewterers* (Keepers of Greyhounds]: Each 3d. a day, and 2d. for their men; and for each greyhound a halfpenny a day. The *King's Pack of Hounds*: 8d. a day. *Knight-Huntsman*: Each 8d. a day. *Huntsmen*: Each 5d. *Leader of the Lime-Hound* [a leashed hound only loosed to kill a stag at bay] and the lime-hound a halfpenny. *Berner* [feeder of hounds]: 3d. a day. *Huntsmen of the Hounds on the Leash*: Each 3d. a day. Of the great leash four hounds 1d. And of the small leashes six should have 1d. For the great leashes two men, each 1d. a day; and for the small, two men, each 1d. a day. *Brach-Keepers* [small hounds hunting by scent]: Each 3d. a day. *Wolf-Hunters*: 20d. a day for horses, men and hounds: and they should have twenty-four running hounds and eight greyhounds, and £6 a year to buy horses; but they say ' eight '. Each of the *Archers* who carried the King's bow 5d. a day; and the other archers as much. Bernard, Ralf the Rober, and their fellows 3d. a day.

GREYHOUNDS FOR COURSING

Greyhounds were included in the royal packs at least as early as the twelfth century and greyhounds appear as the badges of royal persons and related families long before Tudor times.

Further Reading: H. Stanford London, ' The Greyhound as a royal beast ', *Archaeologia*, vol. 97, 1959, pp. 139–163.

Source: William Clown, Abbot of the Augustinian Abbey of Leicester, described by one of his canons, Henry Knighton, *Chronicon*, ed. J. R. Lumby, Rolls Series 92, vol. 2, 1895, p. 127.

In the coursing of hares he was considered the most celebrated and renowned [Master of Hounds] among all the lords of the kingdom. So much was this so that the King himself [Edward III] and his son Prince Edward [the Black Prince] and several of the magnates of the kingdom used to have an annual engagement of coursing with him. He himself often used to assert in council that he would not have taken delight in the frivolity of such hunting if it had not been solely for displaying civility to the lords of the kingdom and to gain their goodwill and to obtain their favour in the business affairs of the Abbey.

Note. Chaucer's account of the hunting monk who cared little for St. Augustine's rules was written about nine years after the death of this Abbot.

DEER STALKING

Source: The Parlement of the Thre Ages, modernized by H. S. Bennett, *Life on the English Manor*, Cambridge University Press 1937, pp. 271-3.

In May, when there are many things to enjoy, and in the summer season when airs are soft, I went to the wood to take my luck, and in among the shaws to get a shot at hart or hind, as it should happen. And, as the Lord drove the day through the heavens, I stayed on a bank beside a brook where the grass was green and starred with flowers—primroses, periwinkles and the rich pennyroyal. The dew dappled the daisies most beautifully, and also the buds, blossoms and branches, while around me the soft mists began to fall. Both the cuckoo and pigeon were singing loudly, and the throstles in the bank-sides eagerly poured out their songs, and every bird in the wood seemed more delighted than his neighbour that darkness was done and the daylight returned.

Harts and hinds betake themselves to the hills; and the fox and polecat seek their earths; the hare squats by the hedges, hurries and hastens thither to her forme and prepares to lurk there. As I stood in that place the idea of stalking came to me, so I covered both body and bow with leaves, turned in behind a tree and waited there awhile. And as I gazed in the glade near by me I saw a hart with tall antlers: the main stem was unburnished and in the middle very strong. And he was full grown and adorned with horns of six and five tines, and was large, broad and big of body: whoever might catch him, he was a dish for a king. But there followed him a fourth-year buck that most eagerly attended him, and aroused and warned him when the wind failed, so that no one should be sly enough to harm him in his sleep by stealth. He went in front of him when any danger was to be feared.

I let the leash fall to the ground quietly, and settled down my hound by the bole of a birch tree, and took careful note of the wind from the fluttering of the leaves. I stalked on very quietly so as to break no twigs, and crept to a crab-apple tree and hid underneath it.

Then I wound up my bow and prepared to shoot, drew up the tiller and aimed at the hart, but the buck who attended the hart lifted up his nose, looked cautiously around, and eagerly snuffed about.

Then, perforce, I had to stand without moving, and to stir no foot, although gnats grievously troubled me and bit my eyes, for if I had tried to move, or made any sign, all my sport, that I had so long awaited, would have been lost. The hart paused, went on cautiously, staring here and there, but at last he bent down and began on his feed. Then I hauled to the hook [i.e. the trigger of the cross-bow] and smote the hart. It so happened that I hit him behind the left shoulder and the blood streamed out on both sides. He stopped: brayed and then brushed through the thickets, as if everything in the wood had crashed down at the same moment. Soon the attending buck went off to his mates, but they were terrified by his manner and took to the fells. I went to my hound, and quickly grasped him and untied his leash, and let him cast about. The briars and the bracken were smeared with blood, and the hound picked up the scent and pursued the hart to where he was for he had crept into a cave, and, crouched to the earth, had fallen down—dead as a door-nail.

ROAST VENISON

Source: A fifteenth century cookery book from the library of Sir Edward Coke (Holkham MS. 671, fol. 45), printed by Mrs. A. Napier, 1882 (privately), p. 66, and, unknown to her, by the early printer Pynson.

To roste venyson tak feletes of venyson bound and cutt away the skyne and parboile it and let it be throughe stiff. Then lard it with salt and put it on a smale broche [spit] and rost it. And if it be ned leche [slice] it abrod in leskes and lay them in a dische and straw on pouder of ginger and salt. And ye may do with buttes of venyson in the same maner.

HAWKS AND FALCONS

The royal and noble sport of falconry is illustrated on the Bayeux Tapestry, in which Harold rides with hawk on wrist, on various twelfth century seals and in the picture for May in many illuminated Calendars in Books of Hours. In 1005 a falconer describes his life (see *T.S.I.H.*, i, 28–9). Gerfalcons, peregrines, goshawks, and sparrowhawks came from Norway for St. Botolph's Fair, Lincoln, and lanners and sakers came from the Mediterranean. Adelard of Bath wrote a treatise on them, especially on how to vet them, based on books of Harold, in the twelfth century. A. L. Poole says that King John's were fed with doves and pork and chicken once a week. They caught cranes, herons partridges and hares, but not rabbits until their importation in the late thirteenth century. The Guildhall Museum has bells, once fastened to the feet of hawks.

Further Reading: W. Salvin and O. Brodrick, *Falconry in the British Isles*, 1855. H. A. MacPherson, *History of Fowling*, 1898. E. B. Michell *The Art and Practice of Hawking*, 1900.

(1) *Source*: *Gerald the Welshman, Description of Wales*, translated by Sir R. C. Hoare, 1806, 207–8. (1188)

I ought not to omit mentioning the falcons of these parts, which are very large, and of a generous kind, and exercise a most severe tyranny over the river and land birds. King Henry II remained here for some time, making preparations for his voyage to Ireland; and being desirous of taking the diversion of hawking, he accidentally saw a noble falcon perched upon a rock. Going sideways round him, he let loose a fine Norway hawk, which he

Hawk and hounds. 1066. (Bayeux Tapestry).

carried on his left hand. The falcon, though at first slower in its flight, soaring up to a great height, burning with resentment, and in his turn becoming the aggressor, rushed down upon his adversary with the greatest impetuosity, and by a violent blow struck the hawk dead at the feet of the king. From that time the king sent every year, about the breeding season, for the falcons of this country, which are produced on the sea cliffs; nor can better be found in any part of his dominions.

(2) *Source*: Charles Johnson, *Dialogus de Scaccario The Course of the Exchequer* (1176–9), Nelson 1950, p. 122.

Sometimes royal birds are promised to the King for various reasons; that is, hawks or falcons. But if the person promising specifies 'a hawk of this year' [a 'sore' hawk] or 'mewed', or names the place of origin, 'I will give an Irish, Spanish or Norway' hawk, he must make his promise good. But if neither the giver nor the receiver of the promise has settled the point, the giver may please himself whether he is to pay a mewed hawk or

not. But if it is passed by the King's ostringers [keeper of gos-
hawks] as perfect and sound, it will be accepted, wherever hatched.
Again, if the debtor, being summoned, brings an acceptable hawk
to the Exchequer, and there is nobody there to receive it, even
though the Summons be put off for a year or two, he need only
pay which he prefers, a mewed hawk or a ' sore ' one. . . . But
hawks are never summoned for the Easter term, because there
is so little use for them in the summer. For they are then carefully
shut up in mews, that they may moult their old feathers and
recover their beauty. . . . But the hawks owing to the King are
summoned for Michaelmas term, to be fit for the King's service
in the coming winter. . . .

PREPARATION FOR A TOURNAMENT

The Popes tried to stop all tournaments between 1130 and 1316,
but Richard I allowed meetings at five places, at Blyth (Nottingham-
shire), Stamford (near Thetford, Suffolk), near Salisbury, at Brackley,
and between Warwick and Kenilworth. Rough and illegal baronial
gatherings in the reign of Henry III, they became courtly pageants in
the fourteenth and fifteenth centuries. See *T.S.I.H.*, i, 154.

(1) *Source*: Chaucer, *The Knightes Tale.* (late fourteenth century)

But by the cause that they sholde ryse
Erly, for to seen the grete fight,
Unto hir [their] reste wenten they at night.
And on the morwe, whan that day gan springe,
Of hors and harneys, noyse and clateringe
There was in hostelryes al aboute;
And to the paleys rood ther many a route
Of lordes, upon stedes and palfreys.
Ther maystow seen devysing of harneys
So uncouth and so riche, and wroght so weel
Of goldsmithrie, of browding [embroidery], and of steel;
The sheeldes brighte, testers [head-pieces], and trappures;
Gold-hewen helmes, hauberks, cote-armures;
Lordes in paraments [mantles] on hir courseres,
Knightes of retenue, and eek squyeres
Nailinge the speres, and helmes bokelinge,

Gigginge [fixing straps] of sheeldes, with layneres [thongs]
Ther as need is, they weren no-thing ydel;   lacinge;
The fomy stedes on the golden brydel
Gnawinge, and faste the armurers also
With fyle and hamer prikinge to and fro;
Yemen [yeomen] on fote, and communes many oon
With shorte staves, thikke as they may goon;
Pypes, trompes, nakers [drums], clariounes,
That in the bataille blowen blody sounes.

(2) *Source*: 'The Order of Battel in the Court of Chivalry', attributed to Thomas of Woodstock who became Duke of Gloucester in 1385; *The Black Book of the Admiralty*, ed. Sir T. Twiss, vol. 1, Rolls Series, 1871, p. 307.

The kynge shall fynd the feelde for to fight in, and the listes shalbe made and devised by the constable. And it is to be considered, that the listes that shall bee of sixtie paases of length, and fortie paces of brede in goode maner, and the erth be ferme and stabill, and harde, and evyn made, withoute grete stoones, and that the erth be platt, and that the listes be strongly barred rounde aboute, and a gate in the Est, and an oothir in the West, with gode and stronge barris of seven fete of heith or more.

WRESTLING

Wrestling was popular in the medieval as in the ancient world. There were famous matches at Clerkenwell on St. Bartholomew's day and this was a favourite meeting place still in the eighteenth century. The ram was a prize, as below, for both the miller and Sir Thopaz in Chaucer. A thirteenth century contest for a ram at St. Giles's in the Fields between London, and Westminster ended in riot. Dürer illustrated 119 holds and falls.

Source: 'The Tale of Gamelyn,' Edith Rickert, in *Early English Romances done into Modern English, Romances of Friendship*. Chatto and Windus, 1908, pp. 91–5.

[Gamelyn rides off on hearing of a wrestling match, with a ram and ring for prizes. A franklin [freeholder] tells him sadly that his two sons have been killed by the champion.] 'Good friend,' said Gamelyn, 'If thou wilt do me a kindness, hold

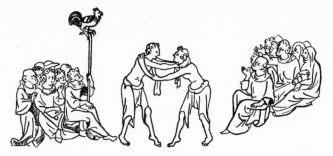

Wrestling match. Early fourteenth century. (Queen Mary's Psalter).

my horse while my servant draws off my shoon [shoes], and help my man to keep watch over my clothes and my steed, and I will go into the place and see how I prosper.'

Barefoot and ungirt, Gamelyn entered; and all the folk in the place marked him and wondered how he durst adventure him to prove his strength against one that was so doughty a champion in fighting and wrestling. [The champion calls Gamelyn a fool.] It was well within the night and the moon shining, when Gamelyn and the champion met together. The champion tried tricks, but Gamelyn was ready, stood firm, and bade him do his best, saying at last: 'Thou art fast about thy business to bring me down. Now that I have proved many of thy tricks, thou shalt prove one or two of mine!'

He turned smartly upon the champion, and showed him but one of all the tricks he knew, throwing him on the left side and breaking three ribs and one arm with a great crack.

'Shall that be counted as a throw or as none?' asked Gamelyn.

'By God,' said the champion, 'whichever it be accounted, he shall never thrive that comes once into thy hand!'

Then said the franklin whose sons were there: 'Blessed be thou, Gamelyn, that ever thou wert born!' And to the champion he said, standing now in no awe of him: 'This is young Gamelyn that taught thee this play.'

The champion, who liked it ill, answered: 'He is master of us all, and his play is right cruel. It is very long ago since I first wrestled, but never in my life have I been handled so sore!'

Gamelyn stood alone in the place, without his sark [shirt], and said: 'If there be any more, let them come on! The champion that so longed for the business, it seemeth now by his countenance that he hath had enough.'

He stood in his place as still as a stone to abide more wrestling; but none came out to him, so wonder sore had he handled the champion.

Then the two gentlemen who had charge of the place drew near to Gamelyn—God save him!—and said: 'Do on your hosen and shoon. For this time, forsooth, the fair is ended.'

'As I hope to thrive,' said Gamelyn, 'I have not yet sold up half my wares!' ... Then the guardians of the wrestling came and brought Gamelyn the ram and the ring, saying: 'Take them, Gamelyn, as the best wrestler that ever came here.'

Thus did he win the prizes, and went home with much joy in the morning.

ACTORS, AND ENTERTAINERS

Praise of plays in Norman London and an account of disorders in 1301 at plays at Clerkenwell, with a note of money spent in 1483 for a play of Noah at Hull are printed in *T.S.I.H.*, i, 96, 139–40 and 226.

Female acrobats are often portrayed in scenes of Salome dancing, or rather standing on her hands, before Herod, for as a medieval sermon explains 'she was a tumbler'. Illustration of the Psalm 'The Fool hath said,' often show a court fool with cock's comb, asses ears, or stick with a bladder. Such a fool's bauble of the fourteenth century with a bronze head in a painted hood is in the British Museum. Such a badge of office did not always save a fool who went too far from whipping or dismissal. The most famous fool or jester was that of Henry I, Rahere, who founded St. Bartholomew's Hospital (see pp. 223-227).

There is a comparison of Easter liturgical drama and ' miracles ' acted in the streets at p. 173.

Bear-baiting.   1066.   (Bayeux Tapestry).

PLATE XVII

SPORTS AND PASTIMES

54. Lady watches mounted swordsmen at a tournament (*cf. p.* 189)

55. Tilting at a tournament

PLATE XVII

SPORTS AND PASTIMES

56. Wrestling, neckcloths and under breeches (*cf. p.* 191)

57. Bear-baiting (*cf. p.* 192)

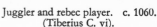

Juggler and rebec player. c. 1060.
(Tiberius C. vi).

A Fool. c. 1325.
(Bromholm Psalter).

Source: Translated from Penitential of Thomas de Chabham (c. 1230), printed by E. K. Chambers, *The Medieval Stage*, vol. 2, pp. 262–3.

There are three kinds of actor. Some change and distort their bodies with shameful leaps and gestures, or expose themselves shamefully or put on hideous masks. All such are damned unless they leave their trade. Some have no occupation but a life of crime and have no fixed abode, but follow the courts of the great. These tell shameful tales behind people's backs to give pleasure. Such are damned, for the Apostle forbids us to eat with such people. Such are wandering buffoons. They serve no purpose save to consume and make scandal. But there is a third type of actor who have musical instruments for the delight of men. Of these there are two varieties. Some haunt public drinkings and low assemblies and there they sing various catches which move men to wantonness and such are damned. But the second class is of those called minstrels. These sing the deeds of princes and the lives of saints. They bring solace to men in sickness and adversity and they do not do the countless shameful deeds of the dancers male and female and the others. . . .

o

CLOTHES OF MONKS

Source: *The Rule of St. Benedict*, a commentary by the Right Rev. Dom Paul Delatte, Abbot of Solesmes and Superior-General of the Congregation of the Benedictines of France, translated by Dom Justin McCann, Monk of Ampleforth, Burns Oates and Washbourne, Ltd., 1921, pp. 346–357.

Let clothing be given to the brethren suitable to the nature and climate of the place where they live; for in cold regions more is required, in warm regions less. It shall be the Abbot's duty, therefore, to consider this.

We think, however, that in temperate climates a cowl and a tunic should suffice for each monk; the cowl to be of thick stuff in winter, but in summer something worn and thin: likewise a scapular [short cloak] for work, and shoes and stockings to cover their feet.

Of all these things and their colour or coarseness let not the monks complain, but let them be such as can be got in the region where they live, or can be bought most cheaply. Let the Abbot be careful about their size, that these garments be not short for those who wear them, but fit well.

When they receive new clothes let them always give back the old ones at once, to be put by in the clothes-room for the poor. For it is sufficient for a monk to have two tunics and two cowls, as well for night wear as for convenience of washing. Anything beyond this is superfluous and ought to be cut off. In the same way let them give up their stockings, and whatever else is worn out, when they receive new ones.

Let those who are sent on a journey receive drawers from the clothes-room, and on their return restore them washed.

Let their cowls and tunics also be a little better than those they usually wear; they must receive these from the clothes-room when setting out on their journey, and restore them on their return.

For their bedding let a mattress, blanket, coverlet, and pillow suffice. These beds must be frequently inspected by the Abbot because of private property, lest it be found therein. And if anyone be found to have what he has not received from the Abbot, let him be subjected to the most severe discipline.

And in order that this vice of private ownership may be cut off by the roots let the Abbot supply all things that are necessary: that is cowl, tunic, stockings, shoes, girdle, knife, style, needle, handkerchief, and tablets; so that all plea of necessity may be taken away.

Yet let the Abbot always be mindful of those words of the Acts of the Apostles: ' Distribution was made to everyone, according as he had need.' Let him, therefore, consider the infirmities of such as are in want, and not the ill-will of the envious. Nevertheless, in all his decisions, let him think of the judgement of God.

CLOTHES OF SERVANTS

Source: Statute concerning diet and apparel, 37 Edward III cap. 8 (translated as in 1577 edition). (1363)

Item for the outragious and excessyve apparaile of dyvers people agaynste theyr estate and degree, to the greate destruction and impoveryshment of all the lande: It is ordeyned that gromes as well servauntes of lordes as they of mysteryes and artyfycers, shall be served to eate and drinke ones a daye of flesshe or of fyshe, and the remenaunte of other vitales, as of mylke, butter, and chese, and other such vitailes, accordying to theyr estate. And that they have clothes for theyr vesture or hosynge, whereof the hole clothe shall not excede two markes, and that they weare no cloth of higher pryce, of theyre dyenge, nor otherwyse, nor nothynge of golde nor of sylver, embrowdered [en]aymeled, nor of sylver, nor nothynge perteinynge to the said thynges. And their wyves, doughters, and children of the same condicion, in their clothyng and apparaile, and they shal weare no vayles passing 12d. a vayle.

CLOTHES OF PEASANTS

Further Reading: G. C. Homans, *English Villagers in the thirteenth century*, 1942.

Source: Statute concerning diet and apparel, 37 Edward III cap. 13 translated as in 1577 edition. (1363)

Item that cariers, ploughmen, dryvers of the ploughe, oxe-herds, koweherdes, shepherdes, deyars [dairyworkers] and all other kepers of beasts, threshers of corne, and all maner of people of the estat of a grome, attendyng to husbandry and al maner of people, that hath not 40s. of goods nor of cattals shal not take nor weare no maner of clothe but blanket and russet wolle of 12d. and shall weare the gyrdels of linnen accordynge to their estate, and that they come to eate and drinke in the maner as perteineth to them, and not excessively. And it is ordeined, that if any weare or do contrary to any of the pointes aforesayd, that he shal forfeit against the kyng al the apparel that he hath so worne against the fourme of this ordinaunce.

KIRTLES

Women's under-tunics had long tight sleeves. These were called kirtles.

Source: ' Launtal Miles ' in *Early English Romances done into Modern English, Romances of Love*, by Edith Rickert, Chatto and Windus 1908, pp. 62–3.

. . . he beheld two gentle maidens coming out of the hoar wood. Their kirtles were of Indian sendal [silk], laced small and pretty and trim—no gayer ladies might be! Their mantles were of green velvet, embroidered featly in gold, and furred with grey *gris* [fur]. Their heads were garlanded, each with a gay coronal of sixty gems and more. Their faces were as white as snow on the downs, and they had brown eyes and rosy cheeks—I never saw their like! The one bare a gold basin, the other a fine milk-white towel of good, rich silk. Their kerchiefs were brightly arrayed with splendid gold thread.

POINTED SHOES

Pointed arches in architecture and pointed script in writing were accompanied throughout the ' Gothic ' thirteenth, fourteenth and fifteenth centuries by a fashion for pointed shoes. Pointed shoes, however, appeared at the court of William Rufus (d. 1100) who liked expensive shoes (see *W.W.I.H.* i). Ordericus Vitalis attributes their invention to Fulk of Anjou, who wanted to hide his ill-formed feet, adding that a fellow called Robert first made shoes with long curved points at the court of Rufus. Men wore the most exaggerated forms of these in the late fourteenth century, but stumpy toes had come in by 1485. Some wore soled hose and about 1450 fashionable pedestrians began to wear boots reaching the thighs such as only travellers and huntsmen had sometimes used.

(1) *Source*: William of Malmesbury, *Chronicle of the Kings of England*, transl. J. A. Giles, Bohn's Antiquarian Library, 1866, p. 337.

All military discipline being relaxed [under Rufus], the courtiers preyed upon the property of the country people, and consumed their substance, taking the very meat from the mouths of these wretched creatures. Then was there flowing hair and extravagant dress; and then was invented the fashion of shoes curved with points; then the model of young men was to rival women in delicacy of person, to mince their gait. . . .

(2) Wooden ' pattens ' kept shoes out of the mud.

Source: London, Letter-Book I, translated by H. T. Riley, *Memorials of London*, 1868, pp. 554–5.

On the 16th day of October, . . . [1400], the reputable men of the trade of *Pouchemakers* presented unto the Mayor and Alder-men a certain petition, as follows.—

' Unto the honourable Lords, the Mayor and Aldermen of the City of London, pray the folks of the trade of *Pouchemakers* in the said city, that it may please your very gracious Lordships to grant unto them and order, that the making of *galoches* [shoes with wooden soles. Chaucer and Piers Plowman use the word] of wood in the said city, of which no one has the governance, and which was formerly by the *Pouchemakers* invented and estab-lished, shall be under their governance and rule, and entered of record, for the common and necessary profit of all the said city;

inasmuch as there is great default in this respect, as well as to false and not durable leather, as to false workmanship, and other secret defaults.

Which petition having been read before the said Mayor and Aldermen, and with no small pains fully understood and estimated, seeing that by such petition it was manifestly shown that the rule and supervision of *galoches*, in the same specified, was clearly required for the benefit and advantage of the public, it was granted by the same Mayor and Aldermen, that the Masters of the said trade of *Pouchemakers* should have the rule and supervision of wooden *galoches* within the liberty of the City; so long as it should seem expedient to the Mayor and Aldermen of the said city, for the time being, and to the commonalty of the said city it should be useful and necessary.

COSTUME: BELTS

Belts were an essential part of old English dress and belt buckles, like brooches, are therefore more common than any other articles of jewellery found in Saxon graves. Famous and beautiful gold buckles found at Faversham and Sutton Hoo show how handsome were the belt buckles worn by Anglo-Saxon princes in the seventh century. Both have patterns of interlaced strapwork and the one from Faversham is set with garnets and gold filigree. In the mid twelfth century ladies wore long girdles, on state occasions. In addition to belts round the waist tranverse belts, called baldrics, were used for carrying a soldier's sword or a huntman's horn. The yeoman in Chaucer's prologue to the Canterbury Tales had a green one for his horn and a fine example is portrayed in the *Holkham Bible* as worn by a highwayman. A Roman on leaving the army was said to take off the belt and the sword-belt was the chief 'ornament of investiture' for knights and 'belted' earls. Handsome baldrics became prominent in the late thirteenth century and remained until about 1420. From the fourteenth century until the end of the middle ages fashionable civil dress included a rich girdle. Joan Evans has pointed out that part of the mitre of William of Wykeham is a lady's girdle set with enamels with monkeys walking on all fours and blowing horns, hares, stags and dogs. Like rings, some girdles in fairy stories are magical, a testimony to the former importance of them and the meaning of signs made on them. In a wall painting at South Leigh, Oxon, the Virgin's girdle outweighs the devil in the scales when a soul is weighed.

Source: *Eulogium*, cited by Camden (on the time of Richard II).

Some [common people] in wide surcoats reaching to the loins, some in a garment reaching to the heels, close before and strutting out on the sides, so that at the back they make men seem like women, and this they call by a ridiculous name, gowne. Their hoods are little, tied under the chin, and buttoned like the women's, but set with gold, silver, and precious stones. Their liripipes, or tippets, pass round the neck, and hanging down before reach to the heels, all jagged. They have another weed of silk, which they call a paltock [short coat]. Their hose are of two colours, or pied with more, which they tie up to their paltocks with white lachets, called herlots, without any breeches. Their girdles are of gold and silver, and some of them worth twenty marks. Their shoes and pattens are snouted and picked more than a finger long, crooking upwards, what they call crackowes, resembling devil's claws, and fastened to knees with chains of gold and silver.

COSTUME: GLOVES

Homer mentions gloves used for gardening and Herodotus describes a glove full of money used as a bribe; but the word gauntlet is of Teutonic origin, for gloves were commoner in northern countries. The nobles and bishops had gloves with embroidery and jewels and gloves strengthened for war were used, though they are not shown in the Bayeux Tapestry and they were less common in England than Germany and Scandinavia until well into the twelfth century. In the early thirteenth century gloves were a forbidden luxury for the anchoresses in the *Ancren Riwle*. In the Holkham Bible shepherds, kings, graduates, soldiers, Pilate the magistrate, Simon of Cyrene the countryman, and a dyer wear them. When a portable valuable possession had to be given in a law court as a pledge a glove was a suitable object to hand. Hence arose the practice of using a glove (as a pledge to appear) in challenges to combat. William of Wykeham's gloves are a famous surviving pair. The York glovers' gild helped produce the *Towneley Mysteries*.

Further Reading. W. M. Smith, *Gloves, Past and Present*, 1918. B. E. Ellis, *Gloves and the Glove Trade*, 1921.

Source: Ordinances of the Glovers, 1349, H. T. Riley, *Memorials of London and London Life*, 1276–1419, 1848, p. 246.

. . . that no one of them shall sell his wares in any house at night, by candle-light; seeing that folks cannot have such good knowledge by candle-light as by day-light, whether the wares are made of good leather or of bad, or whether they are well and lawfully, or falsely, made; on pain of forfeiting to the use of the Chamber [of the City of London] the wares so sold by candle-light. . . .

Also,—whereas some persons who are not of the said trade, do take and entice unto themselves the servants of folks in the same trade, and set them to work in secret in their houses, and make gloves of rotten and bad leather, and do sell them wholesale to strange dealers coming into the City, in deceit of the people, and to the great scandal of the good folks of the said trade; that the Wardens of the said trade may make search in such manner for gloves made of false material, that the same may be found, and brought before the Mayor and Aldermen. . . .

COSTUME: BROOCHES

Brooches, fastened like a safety pin were invented about 1000 B.C., perhaps in central Europe. Until the Norman Conquest they were an essential article of dress, needed to fasten loose cloaks at the shoulder. As cloth was rough and not yet brightly coloured attention was given to the brooch as an object of beauty and fashion. Early Saxon goldsmiths produced work of a quality scarcely rivalled in later centuries. The forms of the brooches varied, some were like saucers, some like rings and some like crosses, according to the tribe of the wearer. Many have been found in graves. The patterns upon them reflect the styles of Rome (classical), Irish (interlace) and the East (birds and beasts). Tight fitting clothes in the thirteenth and fourteenth centuries meant that brooches became unimportant, if costly, luxuries. Edward III and his followers wore as brooches his badges of the fetterlock and the white greyhound and Chaucer's prioress had a gold brooch ' On which ther was first write a crowned A, and after, *Amor vincit omnia.*'

Further Reading: Many articles on early brooches include R. L. S. Bruce-Mitford, ' Late Saxon Disc-Brooches ' (one showing the Five Senses) in D. B. Harden, *Dark-Age Britain*, Methuen, 1956, pp. 171–201. T. D. Kendrick, *Anglo-Saxon Art to* A.D. 900, 1938 and *Late Saxon and Viking Art*, 1919. R. F. Jessup, *Anglo-Saxon Jewellery*, 1950.

Source: Chaucer, *Canterbury Tales*, Prologue, The Monk.

I seigh his sleve purfiled [trimmed] at the hond
With grys [gray squirrel fur], and that the fyneste of a lond;
And, for to festne his hood under his chin,
He hadde of gold y-wroght a curious pin:
A love-knotte in the gretter end ther was. . .
His botes souple, his hors in greet estat.
Now certeinly he was a fair prelat. . .

COSTUME: LIVERY COLLARS, 1478

Liveried retainers in the fifteenth century wore the badges of great lords, the bear and ragged staff of Neville, the portcullis of Beaufort or the rising sun of York.

Source: *Household of Edward IV, the Black Book and the Ordinance of* 1478, ed. A. R. Myers, Manchester University Press 1958, p. 205.

Item, that euery lord and knight within the household weare a collar of the kinges liuery about his necke as to him apperteyneth, and that euery squire, aswell squiers for the bodie as other of the household, likewise weare collers of the kinges liuerie daylie about their neckes as to them apperteyneth, and that none of the said squiers faile, upon paine of loosing a monethes wages.

COSTUME: THE WARDROBE

Source: John Russell's ' Book of Nurture '; *The Babees' Book Medieval Manners for the Young done into modern English from Dr. Furnivall's Texts* by Edith Rickert, Chatto and Windus, 1923, pp. 66–67.

You must attend busily to your lord's wardrobe, to keep the clothes well, and to brush them cleanly. Use a soft brush, and remember that overmuch brushing easily wears out cloth.

Never let woollen clothes or furs go a sevennight without being brushed or shaken, for moths be always ready to alight in them and engender; so always keep an eye on drapery and skinnery.

FUR

The royal charter of the Pellipers or Skinners of London of 1327 laid down exact measurements of furs of minever, hind, squirrel and lambskin, regulations for the secondhand trade, and power to control dealings in fur at the fairs of St. Botolph, Winchester, St. Ives, Stamford, St. Edmund's and elsewhere. Furs were not to be scoured in Cheapside and should be scoured before daybreak so as not to inconvenience the great, unless there was a rush order for a magnate, in which case they might scour by day so long as it was in a cul-de-sac. Detailed rules made in 1365 concentrated their activities to Walbrook, Cornhill and Budge Row, so-called after ' budge ' fur, made from lamb or goat.

In medieval pictures the robe of the Virgin Mary is often lined with vair, a costly fur which indicates her nobility. A law of 1463 forbade the wearing of pure white or grey minniver by those with under £40 p.a. Sable was reserved for lords.

Further Reading: R. T. Wilcox, *Mode in Fur: History of Furred Costume*, 1951 (bibliography). For skins and leather see pp. 52–3.

Source: City Letter Book Regulations about wearing fur, 1281, H. T. Riley, *Memorials of London and London Life*, 1276–1419, p. 20.

. . . no woman of the City shall from henceforth go to market, or in the King's highway, out of her house, with a hood furred with other than lambskin or rabbitskin, on pain of losing her hood to the use of the Sheriffs; save only those ladies who wear furred capes, the hoods of which may have such furs as they may think proper. And this, because that regratresses [retailers], nurses and other servants, and women of loose life, bedizen themselves, and wear hoods furred with gros vair [great vair] and with miniver, in guise of good ladies.

COSTUME: MOTHS, c. 1471-2

A car with six horses belonged to the Royal Wardrobe of Robes. In it, with the robes, were to be carried ' suche bokes as pleseth the king to studye in '. Such books, illuminated in the towns of Flanders for the Burgundian Court, sometimes contain in their illuminated borders some very naturalistically drawn pictures of moths.

Source: *Household of Edward IV*, *the Black Book and the Ordinance of 1478*, ed. A. R. Myers, Manchester University Press 1958, p. 118.

Thes ij wardrobes haue all theyre fumigacions, that the kinges robes, dublettes, shetes and shertes by fumyd be all the yere of the yoman potycary, and that to be truly recordyd to the chambyr-layn.

COSTUME: DRESSING, c. 1460

Source: 'The Office of a Chamberlain' in John Russell's 'Book of Nurture'; *The Babees' Book Medieval Manners for the Young done into modern English from Dr. Furnivall's Texts* by Edith Rickert, Chatto and Windus, 1923, pp. 63–4.

Dressing a lord. Early fourteenth century. (Queen Mary's Psalter).

See that your lord has a clean shirt and hose, a short coat, a doublet, and a long coat, if he wear such, his hose well brushed, his socks at hand, his shoes or slippers as brown as a water-leech.

In the morning, against your lord shall rise, take care that his linen be clean, and warm it at a clear fire, not smoky if the weather be cold or freezing.

When he rises make ready the foot-sheet, and forget not to place a chair or some other seat with a cushion on it before the fire, with another cushion for the feet. Over the cushion and chair spread this sheet so as to cover them; and see that you have a kerchief and a comb to comb your lord's head before he is fully dressed.

Then pray your lord in humble words to come to a good fire
and array him thereby, and there sit or stand pleasantly; and wait
with due manners to assist him. First hold out to him his tunic,
then his doublet while he puts in his arms, and have his stomacher
well aired to keep off harm, as also his vamps [ankle socks] and so
shall he go warm all day.

Thus draw on his socks and his hose by the fire, and lace or
buckle his shoes, draw his hosen on well and truss them up to the
height that suits him, lace his doublet in every hole, and put round
his neck and on his shoulders a kerchief; and then gently comb
his head with an ivory comb, and give him water wherewith to
wash his hands and face.

Then kneel down on your knee and say thus: ' Sir, what robe
or gown doth it please you to wear today? ' Then get him such
as he asks for, and hold it out for him to put on, and do on his
girdle, if he wear one, tight or loose, arrange his robe in the proper
fashion, give him a hood or hat for his head, a cloak or *cappe-de-
buse* [house cap or cape], according as it be fair or foul, or all misty
with rain; and so shall ye please him. Before he goes, brush
busily about him, and whether he wear satin, sendal [silk], velvet,
scarlet [cloth] or grain [crimson cloth], see that all be clean and
nice.

HAIR

Looking-glasses as well as combs were in use before the Roman
Conquest. The Norman Conquest brought a brief fashion for short
hair and clean-shaven faces in England (*W.W.I.H.*, i, p. 48 shows the
contrast between Edward the Confessor and Henry II). Veils hid the
long tresses of women, which often formed long plaits which came, in
the second half of the thirteenth century to be coiled at times round the
head or ears. In the thirteenth century women started to wear linen
bands (barbettes) round the sides of the head over coils of hair. In the
fourteenth century fashionable ladies had their plaits formed into tubes
(crespinettes) each side of the face. At the end of the fourteenth
century ladies' foreheads were made as high as possible by plucking,
like the broad brow of Chaucer's Prioress, and after the beginning of
the fifteenth century the hair is concealed by the headdress. Though
Edward III had a flowing beard (*W.W.I.H.*, i, plate 17) and drooping
moustachios and little pointed beards were quite fashionable in the

second half of the fourteenth and beginning of the fifteenth centuries, men did not wear them for the century and a half before or after. From 1395 to about 1450 men preferred a 'bowl crop' to bobbed hair. For barbers, see p. 227.

Further Reading: A. Gardner, 'Hair and Head-dress 1050–1600,' *Journal of the British Archaeological Association*, 3rd series, vol. 13 (with illustrations from sculpture).

Source: Gerald of Wales, *Description of Wales*, translated by Sir R. C. Hoare, 1806, ii, 294–5. (1188)

The men and women [of Wales] cut their hair close round to the ears and eyes. The women, after the manner of the Parthians, cover their heads with a large white veil, folded together in the form of a crown.

Both sexes exceed any other nation in attention to their teeth, which they render like ivory, by constantly rubbing them with green hazel and wiping with a woollen cloth. For their better preservation they abstain from hot meats, and eat only such as are cold, warm, or temperate. The men shave all their beard except the moustaches (*gernoboda*). This custom is not recent but was observed in ancient and remote ages, as we find in the works of Julius Caesar, who says [*Gallic War*, chap. 13, 14] 'The Britons shave every part of their body except their head and upper lip;' and to render themselves more active, and avoid the fate of Absalom in their excursions through the woods, they are accustomed to cut even the hair from their heads; so that this nation more than any other shaves off all pilosity [hairiness]. Julius also adds, that the Britons, previous to an engagement, anointed their faces with a nitrous ointment, which gave them so ghastly and shining an appearance, that the enemy could scarcely bear to look at them, particularly if the rays of the sun were reflected on them.

HEADDRESSES

Headdresses indicated the ranks of their wearers. In the Holkham Bible alone we find early fourteenth century examples of the tiara of the Pope, the crowns of Emperor and King, the mitre of bishops, the hoods and birettas of doctors and masters, the helmets with visors of the nobility, the simpler helmets with and without nasals to protect the nose and the closely fitting head-coverings of mail of the men at arms, the pointed hat of the county gentleman and of the magistrate, the coif of the rich landowner, the tallith of the rabbi, the yellow pointed hat of the Jew, the turban of the Saracen, the hood of the peasant, the outlaw and the man in the street, the round brimmed hats of the ploughboy and the gardener, various tall hats and a close fitting cap worn by countrymen, the hat on a string of the shepherd, the cover-chiefs and hair nets of ladies, the turban of the sick woman, the wimple of Mary Magdalene and the hood of the mourner. Towards the end of the century women of fashion wore wreaths which were later depressed in the centre and developed into horned headdresses such as that shown on the book-jacket of *W.W.I.H.*, i. The conical headdress worn in the late fifteenth century Flemish picture of Queen Isabel in *W.W.I.H.*, i was only worn for a short period and is Burgundian, not English. It has, however, become the ignorant person's idea of medieval female fashion and is often seen in pageants and inaccurate text book illustrations. For the colours of headwear at a London haberdasher's see pp. 250–1. In 1269 London cappers were ordered to use all wool, to avoid black as it might run in the rain and to do no night work.

Source: City Letter-Book, 1311, H. T. Riley, *Memorials of London and London Life*, 1276–1419, pp. 90–91.

At the request of the hatters, and of the dealers of the City who bought and sold hats, it was ordered that, immediately after the Feast of Easter, diligent scrutiny should be made throughout all the City as to false hats [made of prohibited material], by three or four good men of either calling; and that such good men should at once cause all such false hats as they might find, to be brought here to the Guildhall before the Mayor and Aldermen, to be examined, and to have judgment pronounced as to the same. . . . Afterwards a scrutiny having been made as to such false hats, the examiners aforesaid brought into the Guildhall . . . certain hats, white, black, and grey, which had been found upon divers *haberdasshers* and hatters. And the said hats were examined. . . . And it was found, upon the oath of the said examiners, that 40 grey and white hats, and 15 black hats, belonging to the hatters aforesaid, were of false workmanship, and a mixture of wool and flocks. Therefore it was adjudged that they should be burnt in the street of Chepe.

THE DARK STREETS, 1398

Source: *The first ledger book of High Wycombe*, ed. R. W. Greaves, Bucks. Record Society, vol. 11, for 1947, 1956, p. 42.

Memorandum: that on Maundy Thursday in the twenty-first year of the reign of King Richard II, in the presence of the mayor and community of the town, it was ordered and agreed that no man of whatever condition dwelling within the borough of Wycombe is to go out wandering in the town after ten o'clock at night, unless he has some reasonable cause for his wandering; and if anybody should be found so wandering after the hour aforesaid, he is at once to be taken and imprisoned by the town officers, and kept in prison until he shall be released by the mayor or his deputy and the community.

Item: it was ordained the same day and year that nobody may play at dice in the town under pain of imprisonment; and also he who as host has received him shall pay to the community 40d.

LIGHT AND HEAT, c. 1471-2

A ' nightlight ' was common in medieval bedchambers. Some pictures show a candle of great size, but oil lamps, like those in use in Roman times, were also used. The symbolical significance of good light as opposed to evil darkness gave special point to the description of Christ as the Light of the World. Money for the purchase of candles to burn before particular altars was often left in the wills of the faithful.

Medieval pottery candle sconces for hanging against walls have been found in London with stove tiles such as became popular in Germany.

' Cresset stones ' with between four and sixteen depressions for oil have been found in various monastic ruins. One at Brecon had thirty depressions. The *Rites of Durham* mention one in the church and two in the dormitory.

Source: *The Household of Edward IV, the Black Book and the Ordinance of* 1478; ed. A. R. Myers, Manchester University Press, 1958, p. 90.

Item, for the king and his chambyr also, when the day shortnyth and no prees of grete straungers, iij torches, j tortayis [very large wax candle], and iij prikettes [candles stuck on pricket candlesticks] for the table and cupbourde, if hit be not fasting

day; vj perchers [large wax ' Paris ' candles], x candyls for syzes
of chambre, ij morters [bowls with floating wicks, night-lights]
wax euery nygt; and at the festes or cumyng of lordes or other
straungers worshipfull, hit must be more large by the discression
and recorde of the ussher, by ouersight of the chambyrlayn and
others. Item, for his own person, in the chymney brannyng day
and nygt, xviij shides [billets of firewood], viij fagottes for
wynter season; and if there be mo nedefull chymneys to brenne
for the kinges honour in the grete chambre, then as the chamber-
layn and ussher thinken reasonable; and dayly all thinges to be
recorded by the ussher into the countynghous. . . .

FIRE

A dangerous hearth, 642.

Before the invention of chimneys even large halls had a central
hearth. The smoke went out through a hole in the thatched roof.

Further Reading: C. A. R. Radford, ' The Saxon House: a Review
and some Parallels ', *Medieval Archaeology*, vol. 1, 1957.

Source: Bede, *Ecclesiastical History*, translated by J. A. Giles, 1881,
p. 125.

. . . Another person of the British nation, as is reported,
happened to travel by the same place, where the aforesaid battle
[of Maserfield] was fought, and observing one particular spot
of ground greener and more beautiful than any other part of the
field, he judiciously concluded with himself that there could be
no other cause for that unusual greenness, but that some person
of more holiness than any other in the army had been killed there.
He therefore took along with him some of the earth, tying it up
in a linen cloth, supposing it would some time or other be of use
for curing sick people, and proceeding on his journey, came at
night to a certain village, and entered a house where the neighbours were feasting at supper; and received by the owners of
the house, he sat down with them at the entertainment, hanging
the cloth, in which he had brought the earth, on a post against
the wall. They sat long at supper and drank hard, with a great
fire in the middle of the room; it happened that the sparks flew

58. Soup in the skillet

59. Bacon on the pole

60. Fur wrap and bellows
Three versions of a seated man with shoe off and hat on (*cf. pp.* 170 *and* 208)

61. Medical school

62. Treatment of arm.   Operating table

up and caught the top of the house, which being made of wattles and thatch, was presently in a flame; the guests ran out in a fright, without being able to put a stop to the fire. The house was consequently burnt down, only that post on which the earth hung remained entire and untouched. On observing this, they were all amazed, and inquiring into it diligently, understood that the earth had been taken from the place where the blood of King Oswald had been shed. . . .

CHARCOAL FOR THE SMITH, 1195

Forest laws prevented encroachment on woodland and meant the accumulation of ample supplies of fuel, which however were eventually depleted. One charcoal burner in the New Forest in 1100 is remembered because he found the body of Rufus (see *T.S.I.H.*, i, p. 56). In 1282 there were nearly 900 pits in which to burn wood to make charcoal in one part of the Forest of Dean. The method of working was that described by Theophrastus (d. 287 B.C.) in his *Enquiry into Plants*. There is a good picture of a blacksmith's forge with bellows and anvil (1330) in the Holkham Bible. For Smiths see p. 27.

Further Reading: M. L. Bazeley, ' The Forest of Dean in its Relations with the Crown during the Twelfth and Thirteenth Centuries,' *Transactions of the Bristol and Gloucestershire Archaeological Society*, vol. 33 (1910), pp. 236, 266. J. Walton, ' Charcoal Burners' Huts ', *Gwerin*, vol. 1, no. 2.

Source: Translated from Grant to Fountains Abbey, Bodleian Library, MS. Rawlinson, B. 449, fol. 150v, printed in H. R. Schubert, *History of the British Iron and Steel Industry from c. 450 B.C. to A.D. 1775*, Routledge and Kegan Paul, 1957, p. 341.

William de Stutevill (d. 1203) to the bailiffs and foresters of Knaresborough . . . greeting. Know that I have granted and in this charter confirm to the master smith of Fountains for burning charcoal in my forest of Knaresborough where and how much as he may will of dead wood whether standing or lying and the right to take it where he will within my forest and without. I therefore will and order that he and his may burn in perfect peace and take wherever they will as is laid down free from all hindrance. The rent is 10s. a year and three dacres [score] of horseshoes. The said smith will burn charcoal as long as he will for that rent. The term of this lease runs from Easter 1195.

P

SMELLS

Only castles and monasteries had proper drains. Dungheaps in towns were a continual cause of complaint and Edward III said that York stank worse than any town he knew. Butchers, poulterers, in Winchester and London, fishmongers in Chester, and cooks in Southampton fouled the streets with animal refuse. The water used by seven dyers of Nottingham stank (1395). The fumes of coal caused repeated complaints in London (1307 and 1371) and drove Queen Eleanor from Nottingham Castle in 1257. Town authorities did their best, and at least the countryside was nearer and the crowded acres of town fewer than they were in the first half of the nineteenth century. In the home the smell of onions and garlick would have been more often apparent than now. The first Sanitation act, in 1388, forbade river pollution.

Further Reading: G. R. Salusbury-Jones, *Street Life in Medieval England*, Pen-in-Hand, 1938.

(1) *Source*: *Beverley Town Documents*, Ed. A. F. Leach, Selden Soc., 1900, p. 58. This rule relates to 1467.

. . . wholesomely ordered out, on account of the stink and badness of the air to the destruction of fruit trees, and other disadvantages that may arise therefrom, that no one henceforth dare to build any kiln for burning brick in the aforesaid town of Beverley, or nearer the same town than brick kilns are now built, under the penalty of 100s.

(2) *Source*: *Liber Albus the White Book of the City of London compiled in* A.D. 1419 *by John Carpenter and Richard Whittington*, translated by H. T. Riley, Richard Griffin 1861, p. 503–504.

(A list of official documents too lengthy for inclusion indicates the kind of orders made:)

That the Streets and Lanes shall be cleansed of all impediment from dung and chips, and of all other impediment. . . .

That no Stall shall be more than two feet and a half in breadth, and that it shall be moveable and flexible

That all Streets and Lanes leading towards the Thames from the King's Highways, shall be kept clean

That no one shall throw dung into the King's Highway, or before the house of his neighbour

That each person shall make clean of filth the front of his house, under penalty of half a mark

That chips found in the street shall be at the disposal of the Alderman

That Penthouses which are too low shall be removed

Ordinance that no dung shall lie in the Streets or Lanes of the City. . . .

That Penthouses, Gutters, and Jettees shall be so high that folks can ride beneath them, and at least nine feet in height. . . .

That no Hoards, Palings, or Steps to Cellars, shall be made in the streets, without view of the Mayor and Aldermen

That all who have dung, chips, or other refuse before their doors, shall remove the same

That no Officer shall take [for city purposes] a cart that serves for carrying such refuse. . . .

That the Scavagers shall have power to survey the Pavements, and that all filth in the Streets shall be removed

That all Lanes and Streets shall be cleansed of dung and chips

Item that the Pavements shall be mended, and all refuse removed. . . .

That all Streets and Lanes shall be cleansed of all refuse and obstacles. . . .

Writ for removing dung and other filth at Tourhille [Tower Hill]. . . .

Divers Men elected and sworn, for duly making the Pavements. . . .

Item, that no one shall have his Pavement made higher than that of his neighbours

NUISANCES

Town records are full of complaints of dung heaps in the street, the casting of offal, or dirty water, the slaughter of beasts and the throwing of dead dogs or cats into public places. People were supposed to keep clean the parts of the street in front of their own houses and to have their rubbish carted away. A roadsweeper in the ward of West Cheap, London, is mentioned in 1299 and later, in 1364, there were official inspectors called 'Scavengeours'. Actual removal of rubbish in fourteenth century London was done by 'Rakyers'. An official carter at Coventry was supposed to receive 1d. from each hall and ½d. from each shop (1420). Filth was thrown into rivers and town ditches,

but fish survived in London town ditch until the reign of Henry VIII.
References occur to public lavatories at Leicester, Coventry and
Doncaster as well as London. Attempts were made to keep clean
sources of water used for the victualling trades. For piped water,
baths and washing see pp. 215–220.

Further Reading: Sir J. Simon, *English Sanitary Institutions*, 2nd ed.,
1897. W. H. Godfrey, 'English Cloister Lavatories as Independent
Structures ', *Archaeological Journal*, vol. 106.

Source: *Liber Albus the White Book of the City of London compiled in*
A.D. 1419 *by John Carpenter and Richard Whittington* translated by H. T.
Riley, Richard Griffin 1861, pp. 508–510. (1419)

(A list of official documents too lengthy for inclusion indicates
the kind of orders made:)

If Swine shall be found in the Streets or in the Fosses [moats],
or in the Suburbs, they shall be killed, and he who kills them
shall have them; and he who shall wish to rear them, shall be at
liberty to rear them, out of the King's Highways, in his own
house

That no leper shall be in the City, or shall come there or make
sojourn there. . . .

That such Pigsties as are in the Streets shall be removed; and
if any Swine shall be found in the Streets, they shall be forfeited

Also, Four Men elected and sworn to take and kill such Swine
as shall be found wandering about within the walls of the City,
to whomsoever they may belong. . . .

The Renter of Saint Antony's [Hospital in Threadneedle
Street, privileged to keep swine] sworn that he will not avow any
Swine going about within the City, nor will hang bells about
their necks, but only those which have been given unto them in
pure alms. . . .

The Porters of the Gates of the City sworn that they will not
allow Lepers to enter the City. . . .

Item, that no one who can gain his sustenance shall go about
begging; and that no Lazars shall go about in the City

That the Supervisors of Lepers shall be discharged of Assizes,
Juries, Summonses, Watches, etc.

Writ as to raising 100 shillings upon a tenement of the Lepers,
and delivering the same unto such Lepers for their sustenance. . . .

That Men and Women of ill fame shall be removed by the Alderman. . . . That Women of evil life shall not use hoods that are furred, except with the wool of lambs or the fur of rabbits, etc. . . .

PERSONAL WASHING

As forks were not used the washing of hands was frequent. Etiquette books describe the ceremony at meals, and the picture of Pilate washing his hands in the Holkham Bible shows how it was done by a servant pouring water over the hands. The jugs used for this were called aquamaniles and many of them have been found in the shape of a standing animal. A lion, a ram, a stag and sometimes a knight on horseback are typical of examples in the Victoria and Albert and Ashmolean Museums. Washing of the entire body was less frequent, but it was much commoner than is often suggested.

Source: *Three prose Versions of the Secreta Secretorum*, ed. by Robert Steele, Early English Text Society, Extra Series 74, 1898, pp. 82–3.

Bathes er [are] on of the merueylles of thys werld, ffor yt ys housyd after the ffoure tymes of the yeer, ffor cold accordes to wynter, leuk-warme to Veer [Spring], hoot to somer, drye to heruest. Greet wyt ys it to make ffoure dwellynges by ordre yn bathes, the firste be cold, the seconde leuk-warme, the thyrdde hoot, the ferthe drye; and whenne a man entrys first ynto the bathes, he sholde be a lytyl while yn the firste; and after yn the seconde, and there dwelle a lytil; And after ynto the thridde, and there dwell a lityll; And after in to the ferth entre, & so doo in the selue [same] manere. And whenne he wyl passe out, kepe he the self manere, makynge a litill dwellynge yn ilke chambre so that he passe noght fro ouer greet hete to ouer greet cold, no fro ouer greet cold to ouer greet hete; and be the bathes biggyd [built] in heye stede and wyndy, & haue it ffurnays, gyffand [giving] fflammes, and hote water; And it ys to use thareynne odoures couenables to the tyme thanne beand, that is to wete, to use in Veer and in somer, treble or quatreblee, In heruest and yn wynter to use double. After, him awe to sitte on setys wete with water of Roses, and do wype hym with a fair towaille of lyn, onys and eft [often]; and whenne al thys ys doon, and he deliciously wasshyd, passe he sone to other houses, and use the techinges and oynements folwand [following]. If he be ouercome with hete, kembe his heued [head], and use oynement clensyd, couenable to the tyme; ffor yn Veer and in somer, he sholde use oynement sesaryn [a word unexplained in dictionaries]. . . . In hervest and wynter, he sholde use oynement maad of myrre, and of the iuwys of the herbe that ys clepyd bletes [blite], and to caste upon his heued wroght [artificial] waters attempred [regulated]; And after he sholde wasshe his body, and rubbe it with the self waters, to he be wel wasshyd and clene. After, enoynt his body of oynements couenables to the tyme, And after, passe he thennes by the ordre beyfore taught, and use hit to the tyme he be allegyd. If he haue thrist, drynke he a syrupe of roses, and ete electuary with musk, and after, reche out his armys a lityll. And a litel ouer after take he his mete, that ys dight [prepared] to him, with pees [peace], and drynke good wyn attempred with water, after that he was costomyd to drynke; and take he noght mekyll, but attemperly, and after smoke him with ensens couenable to the tyme, and riste he yn a likyng bedde, and take of slepe a good party, ffor that shall profyte hym Mekyll. After, he shall contenu the remenant of the day in ioye and riste. Thys is the ordre of hele [health] & norsshyng of the body; And he that ys olde, or cold and moyst, dwelle noght longe in the bathe. Notheles he shall sytte thareyn, to his body be moyst of the bathe, and water be cast on hym ofte sithes attemperly, and all so sone as he wille. Hit ys noght couenable for a ffleumatyk men to entre yn Bathes but fastynge, and that he enoynt hym with hote oynements. And he that ys of hote kynde, kepe the techynge byfore taght.

EWERS AND NAPKINS

There was a strict ritual for holding napkins and offering water to wash the hands before a meal. In the thirteenth century a manor in Oxfordshire at Pishill was called Pishill Nap because it had belonged earlier in the century to Robert *Napparius*, a predecessor of the official whose functions are here described. In the Bayeux Tapestry a servant on bended knee, with a napkin draped over his arm, is holding a bowl near the table of William the Conqueror.

Further Reading: F. G. Furnivall, *Manners and Meals in Olden Time* Early English Text Society, Old Series 32, 1868.

Source: *Household of Edward IV, the Black Book and Ordinance of* 1478, ed. A. R. Myers, Manchester University, 1958, pp. 192–3.

Offyce of Ewary and Napry hathe in hym a sergaunt to serue the kynge persone in coueryng of the borde with holsom and clenne untochyd clothis of strangeors and with clene basons and moste pure waters, asseyde [tasted] as oftin as his moste royall person shalbe seruyd. He receyuith the charge of alle naprye be mesure for the kyng and his chambre and halle, and to be renouid if nede be at anny of the iiij festes principalle in the yere. . . . And if he receiue such things of jewelhouse, this sergeant shall do shewe all the newe and olde clothis, towelles, and napkins to be viewid by the countynghouse or comptroller's ouersight, if they be lost and be whome; or if they be perusyd [worn out] clothis, so that with oneste they may no longer serue, then the clothis of the kynges borde, clothis surnape, fote clothe, and such other therto longing ys fee [perquisite] to the sergaunt, except at anny coronacion, by ouersight of comptroller. Alle other clothis so verely perusyd to be assignyd, sume to the awmery [almonry], to the squilery [scullery], to the picherhouse, to wipe and kepe cuppis cleane, to the surgeons and other by the comptrollers' discreccion.

A BATHROOM, AT WESTMINSTER PALACE

The Danes attracted the attention of the Saxons by bathing on Saturdays though one chief was called Wolf the Unwashed, and King John had baths about every three weeks. Knights of the Bath (founded 1399) had ceremonial baths on initiation. Keys and a waste-pipe were supplied at Westminster Palace in 1275 and keys 'for hot and cold water for the king's bath tub' in 1351. References to fourteenth century baths at Eltham Palace, Windsor Castle and elsewhere are also known. See chapter on ' Plumbing, Water-supply, Sanitation ' in L. F. Salzman, *Building in England down to* 1540 *a documentary history*, Clarendon Press, 1952. William Walworth owned public baths called the Stews in Southwark. Public baths acquired a very bad reputation. A number of medieval pictures of baths occur, generally wooden tubs.

Source: Westminster account, translated by L. F. Salzman, p. 276–7. (1325)

William de Wynchelse for 3 boards called righok [timber from Riga] for crests and filetts [flat narrow strips with parallel sides] of the bathing tub, 18d. For oak boards called clouencord for making the covering of the said tub, 6 ft. long and 2½ ft. broad,— 3s. . . . for 100 fagett for heating and drying the *stuwes*—3s. For a small barrell, 2 bokettes and a bowl for carrying water to the stuwes . . . carpenters working on the covering of the bathing tub and the partition in front of the said tub—For 6 pieces of Reigate stone for making a slabbing in front of the partition of the said tub in the King's ground-floor chamber. . . . For 2250 pavingtil for the said chamber . . . for 24 mattis, at 2d. each, to put on the flore and pavement of the King's chamber on account of the cold.

MONASTIC BATH AT CANTERBURY

Further Reading: J. Armitage Robinson, 'Lanfranc's Monastic Constitutions', *Journal of Theological Studies*', vol. 10, 1909, 375–88.

Source: *The Monastic Constitutions of Lanfranc*, translated by D. Knowles, Medieval Classics, T. Nelson and Sons, 1951, pp. 9–10 (between 1070 and 1089).

On the vigil of Thomas the apostle, if it be not a Sunday, the brethren shall be shaved and let those who will take a bath, in such wise that all shall have taken it two days before Christmas Day. If need be, they may take their bath even on the feast of the apostle. Let the bathing be ordered as follows. On the previous day the abbot or superior should appoint a devout and prudent senior and order him to take charge of the matter, to warn the brethren when to bathe, and to see that they conduct themselves there in an orderly way. This senior shall see that all is ready, and that the right attendants are provided—mature men, neither children nor youths. If he see anything unfitting, let him tell the chamberlain, who shall at once remedy it. Then the senior shall return to the cloister and give notice to as many of the brethren as can be accommodated. Let him take care that the youths and novices go not all together, but with their elders. The brethren whom he has notified shall, when shaved, take their change of clothes and go to the place where the baths are prepared

and there, taking off their clothes in due order as they are wont
to do in the dormitory, they shall enter the bathing place as
directed, and letting down the curtain that hangs before them
they shall sit in silence in the bath. If anyone needs anything let
him signal for it quietly, and a servant lifting the veil shall
quickly take him what he wants and return at once. When he
has finished washing himself, he shall not stay longer for pleasure
but shall rise and dress and put on his shoes as he does in the
dormitory, and having washed his hands shall return to the
cloister. The young monks in ward shall go and return with
their masters. The brethren may go to the baths at any hour from
Prime to Compline, but none shall presume to go without the
permission of the brother in charge.

BATHS FOR CONSUMPTIVES

Further Reading: Lawrence Wright, *Clean and Decent*: *the fascinating
history of the bathroom and water closet and of sundry habits, fashions and
accessories of the toilet*, Routledge and Kegan Paul 1960. For another
medicinal bath, of about 1460, see *T.S.I.H.*, i, 210–1.

Source: Sir Percival Horton-Smith Hartley and H. R. Aldridge,
Johannes de Mirfeld of St. Bartholomew's Smithfield, Cambridge University
Press, 1939 (*Breviarium Bartholomei*), p. 87 (late fourteenth century).

Also here is a bath which has proved to be of value. Take
blind puppies, remove the viscera, and cut off the extremities;
then boil in water, and in this water let the patient be bathed:
let him enter the bath for four hours after his food, and whilst
therein keep the head entirely covered, and the chest completely
wrapped around with the skin of a small kid, as a preservation
against exposure to sudden chill.

Another bath of which the patient may avail himself: Take
land-tortoises, and boil them in a cooking-pot. Take the tor-
toises, and boil them in fresh water, and in this water let the
patient bathe; and after the bath anoint the chest with either the
' ointment for consumptives ', or with one of the others mentioned
above (see p. 225).

PIPED WATER, THIRTEENTH CENTURY

A map of the water pipes Christchurch, Canterbury (c. 1167) and of the Charterhouse, just outside Newgate, London, fifteenth century, still survive. Here is an account of the pipes of the Grey Friars, who were established in 1224 just inside Newgate in a place hitherto used by butchers for slaughtering beasts. This unpleasant urban site, typical for a house of Friars, contrasts with the rural sites by rivers favoured by monks in previous centuries.

Source: Register of the London Grey Friars, extract translated in Sir W. Dugdale, *Monasticon Anglicanum, a History of the Abbies and other Monasteries, Hospitals, Friaries and Cathedral and Collegiate Churches*, ed. J. Caley, H. Ellis and Rev. Bulkeley Bandinel, vol. 6, pt. 3, 1830, pp. 1518–9.

Of the Aqueduct of the Friars-Minors at London.

The underwritten built the aqueduct. Imprimis, William, taylor to our lord King Henry III, after the conquest, gave the head of the aqueduct, at the instance of brother William Basinges, who procured all the aqueduct, and fully compleated it; but the cost and expences were administered by our illustrious lord Henry, King of England, of happy memory, abovenamed; Salekyn of Basing, a youth of an excellent disposition, Henry Frowyke, and Henry Basynges, knights. These were the principal co-operators and co-adjutors; and afterwards brother Geoffrey de Camera built the new house at the second head, and improved the former, and searched out all the notable defects, and mended them; and procured and did many other good things for the same. Whose principal assistants were Alan Gille, citizen of London, with his wife; the lord Henry Darcy, who gave 100 shillings for the cistern. John Tryple and others assisting, finished the work. The Friars-Minors had at London, all things computed, £110 17s. 5¼d., to whose souls God be merciful.

For knowing the Course of Passage of the Aqueduct of the Friars-Minors at London.

First, from the threshold of the door of John Sporon, the space of three foot, under the new wall of the friars, the pipe stretches as you go into the street towards Newgate; but still as it lies along the way, it holds the north side of the way, sometimes not coming near the houses, any otherwise than the lying strait requires. Under Newgate it lies 12 foot deep, and extends directly under the wall of St. Sepulchre's church outward, and farther on, it bends with the bending of the street, and stretches along Lekewell; there crossing the two ways, it buts against the window of the house of John Muchtthesh, and there it bends towards Holborn-bridge; between the house of William Irotheges and the bridge, it is laid under the water [of the River Fleet] for the space of three foot, beyond the rivulet of that water, about the space of eight paces, by the wall of the bridge, beyond the breach, by the industry of the friars, where the water of the street runs down in a place that is always muddy. The first cock is hid under ground, but covered for the space of four foot with a marble stone, Thence it extends to Liweone-lane, and there it turns again strait along that lane, or street, towards the north, by the west wall of the lane, the position of it being three foot distant. At the end of that lane, on the left hand, is the second cock, almost seven foot high; and thence it extends, directly crossing the fields and hedges, to the mill of Thomas of B——, which is next to the town, where it sinks down the space of 18 foot. There, on the east side of the mill, towards the north, near the ditch, is the third cock. Thence proceeding almost the space of one furlong to the westward, inclining to the north, there appears a green trench, or furrow, lying east and west, full of briers, and winding westwards, almost eight foot wide, dividing the land of John Derkyne, which lies on the south side, from the land of —— Basyng, which lies on the north side. In that trench, beginning at the east end 16 paces, not leaps, there from the middle part of the breadth of the trench, where the necessary mark for this purpose appears, looking to the north, directly on the land of Thomas ——, for the space of 14 foot it lies hid four foot under ground. The head which is nearest, whence, for the most part, we have our water, is a little remote from the farther head. From that place it extends to the remoter head, towards the west, the little stone house whereof is seen at a distance. The water of this head is brought beyond the ditch of Thomas—on the west, a little inclining to the north, for the space of about 15 paces from the house of the head, by the way which divides the parishes of St.

Giles and St. Andrew. This water, in the house of that head, running down to the trough, overflows, and little of it is received hence by the trough, but it floods the whole house, and is negligently lost along little rivulets, and through the cracks of the wall. The remedy must be applied by the friars, considering the loss and damage of so much expence. Afterwards brother Thomas Feltham brought a washing cistern to the porch, from the pool of the common washing place, and laid out very much in the porch, anno Domini 1300.

Item, in the year of our Lord 1420, the cistern for washing in the cloister was repaired with the money deposited by brother Robert Zengg. The total of the expence was £27 9s. 1½d.

LEPERS

The word leprosy was used in the Middle Ages for a number of different skin diseases, some serious and some as curable as measles. It is wrong to suppose that leprosy was introduced into Europe by the crusaders. A decree of Howel the Good orders (928) the restitution of a woman's goods if she is married to a leper.

Source: Office at the Seclusion of a Leper, translated, R. M. Clay, *Medieval Hospitals in England*, Antiquarian Books, 1909, Appendix A, from *Manuale ad Usum Insignis Ecclesiae Sarum*, printed in *Surtees Society*, vol. 63, p. 105.

First of all the sick man or the leper clad in a cloak or in his usual dress, being in his house, ought to have notice of the coming of the priest who is on his way to the house to lead him to the Church, and must in that guise wait for him. For the priest vested in surplice and stole, with the Cross going before, makes his way to the sick man's house and addresses him with comforting words. . . . Let the priest lead the leper to the Church, when he has sprinkled him with holy water, the Cross going before, the priest following, and last of all the sick man. Within the Church let a black cloth, if it can be had, be set upon two trestles at some distance apart from the altar, and let the sick man take his place on bended knees beneath it between the trestles, after the manner of a dead man, although by the grace of God he yet lives in body and in spirit, and in this posture let him devoutly hear Mass. . . .

Leper. c. 1330. (Holkham Bible).

The priest then with the spade casts earth on each of his feet, saying: ' Be thou dead to the world, but alive again unto God.' . . . When leaving Church after Mass the Priest ought to stand at the door to sprinkle him with holy water. And he ought to commend him to the care of the people. Before Mass the sick man ought to make confession in the Church, and never again . . . when he has come into the open fields . . . he [the priest] ends by imposing prohibitions upon him in the following manner:— ' I forbid you to enter Churches, or to go into a market, or a mill, or a bakehouse, or unto any assemblies of people. Also I forbid you ever to wash your hands or even any of your belongings in spring or stream of water of any kind; and if you are thirsty you must drink water from your cup or from some other vessel. Also I forbid you ever henceforth to go out without your leper's dress, that you may be recognised by others; and you must not go outside your house unshod. Also I forbid you, wherever you may be, to touch anything which you wish to buy, otherwise than with a rod or a staff to show what you want. Also I forbid you ever henceforth to enter taverns or other houses if you wish to buy wine; and take care that even what they give you they put into your cup. . . . Also I command you when you are on a journey not to return an answer to anyone who questions you, till you have gone off the road to leeward, so that he may take no harm from you; and that you never go through a narrow lane lest you should meet some one. Also I charge you if need require you to pass over some toll-way over rough ground or elsewhere, that you touch no posts or things whereby you cross, till you have first put on your gloves. Also I forbid you to touch infants or young folk, whosoever they may be, or to give to them or to others any of your possessions. Also I forbid you henceforth to eat or drink in any company except that of lepers. And know that when you die you will be buried in your own house, unless it be, by favour obtained beforehand, in the Church '.

And note that before he enters his house, he ought to have a coat and shoes of fur, his own plain shoes, and his signal the clappers, a hood and a cloak, two pairs of sheets, a cup, a funnel, a girdle, a small knife and a plate. His house ought to be small, with a well, a couch furnished with coverlets, a pillow, a chest, a table, a seat, a candle stick, a shovel, a pot, and other needful articles. . . . When the priest leaves him he says:—'Worship God and give thanks to God. Have patience and the Lord will be with thee. Amen.'

DOCTORS

In 1381 an illiterate quack wrapped up some inscribed parchment in cloth of gold and told a woman to wear it to cure a fever. He was sentenced to ride bareback through London to the sound of trumpets wearing the parchment and a whetstone round his neck and festooned with his other paraphernalia. (See Riley, *Memorials of London*, p. 464). Chaucer's Doctor of Physick loved gold and cared little for the Bible.

Further Reading: Sir T. C. Allbutt, *The Historical Relations of Medicine and Surgery to the End of the Sixteenth Century*, 1905.

J. J. Walsh, *Medieval Medicine*, 1920.

Source: Sir Percival Horton-Smith Hartley and H. R. Aldridge, *Johannes de Mirfeld of St. Bartholomew's Smithfield*; Cambridge, 1939, (*Florarium Bartholomei*), pp. 123 and 133. (Mirfield, in the first paragraph, is echoing the *Magna Chirugica* of Bruno of Calabria, c. 1252). (Late fourteenth century).

It is necessary moreover that medical men should be well educated, or at least that they should learn their profession from a man of literary attainments; for I consider that an illiterate person is hardly capable of competently performing the functions of a physician.   Nevertheless, at the present time, ignorant amateurs, to say nothing of—what is worse, and is considered by me more horrible—worthless and presumptuous women, usurp this profession to themselves and abuse it; who, possessing neither natural ability nor professional knowledge, make the greatest possible mistakes (thanks to their stupidity) and very often kill their patients; for they work without wisdom and from no certain foundation, but in a casual fashion, nor are they thoroughly acquainted with the causes or even the names of the maladies which they claim that they are competent to cure. . . .

Modern physicians appear to possess three special qualifications, namely, to be able to lie in a subtle manner, to show an outward honesty, and to kill with audacity.   But the physician, if he should happen to be a good Christian (which rarely chances, for by their works they show themselves to be disciples not of Christ, but of Avicenna and of Galen), ought to cure a Christian patient without making even the slightest charge if the man is poor; for the life of such a man ought to be of more value to the physician than his money.

MEDICINE

Further Reading: B. Dawson, *History of Medicine: a Short Synopsis*, 1930.

John Arderne (fl. 1307–70). *De Arte Phisicali et de Cirurgia of Master John Arderne, Surgeon of Newark, dated 1412; translated by Sir D'Arcy Power rom a transcript by Eric Millar, from the replica of the Stockholm MS. in the Wellcome Historical Medical Museum*. London, J. Bale, Sons and Danielsson, Ltd., 1922. Wellcome Historical Medical Museum. Research Studies in Medical History, 1.

Source: Sir Percival Horton-Smith Hartley and H. R. Aldridge, *Johannes de Mirfield of St. Bartholomew's, Smithfield*, Cambridge University Press, 1939. (*Florarium Bartholomei*), pp. 142–3. (Mirfield is here using B. de Gordonio, *Regimen Sanitatis*, chapter 8). (Late fourteenth century)

There are, however, many different kinds of exercise, according to the difference of rank and of persons. For some are strong, and some are weak; some are rich, and some are poor; some are prelates and men of rank, others are members of religious orders and are enclosed within their walls; moreover, the season is sometimes rainy, at other times it is fine. Therefore it is necessary to have several varieties of exercise. The first and most important of these is to walk abroad, choosing the uplands where the air is pure; this is the best of all. Riding is another form of exercise, but this is only for the wealthy. It behoves prelates, however, to have some other method of taking exercise. Let such a man, therefore, have a stout rope, knotted at the end, hanging up in his chamber; and then, grasping the rope with both hands, let him raise himself up, and remain in that position for a long time without touching the ground; then, holding the rope and running with it as far as possible, let him jump into the air, turning himself round and round and strutting fiercely about. Or if this pastime does not please him, let him hold in his hands a stone, weighing thirty pounds, in which a ring has been fixed, and carry it about frequently from one part of his dwelling to another; or let him hold this same stone up in the air for a long time before setting it down, or lift it to his neck, or between his hands: the like also with other methods of exercise, until he begins to tire: or thus: let him hold a staff in his hand, and let another person, pulling straight, try to drag it away from him, if he is able; and let another strive to tear a penny from his closed hand. Another method of taking exercise is to hold the breath and impel it towards the head, or towards the belly, and this is extremely useful. Other forms of exercise are useful for playful youths, such as running, wrestling, jumping, hurling stones, and many other sports in which young men take delight (cf. *T.S.I.H.*, i, p. 96–7).

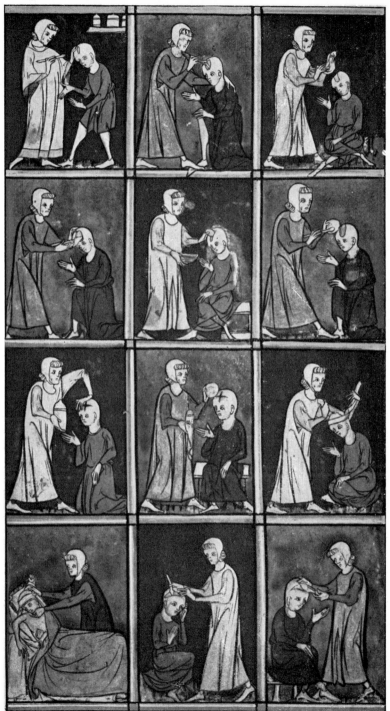

63. Surgery. Doctor treats head injury

64. Orthopaedic patients. Bath. Clothing showing attachment of hose

OINTMENT, LATE FOURTEENTH CENTURY

Pictures of medieval pots of ointment are common, for St. Mary Magdalen is shown with one and pictures of her were popular.

This is a recipe for stone from the *Rosa Anglica* of John of Gaddesden, an authority used by the doctor whom Chaucer describes so vividly. Gaddesden found red cloth helpful for small-pox and cured young Edward III with its help. Jusserand cited this as an example of superstitious absurdity and then discovered that red light was useful and printed his apologies to Gaddesden's memory accordingly.

Further Reading: C. Roth, ' The Qualification of Jewish Physicians in the Middle Ages ', *Speculum*, vol. 28, no. 24

(1) *Source*: J. J. Jusserand, *English Wayfaring Life in the Middle Ages*, translated from the French by Lucy Toulmin Smith, Ernest Benn, fourth ed. (sixteenth impression) 1950, p. 97.

I bethought myself of collecting a good number of those beetles which in summer are found in the dung of oxen, also of the crickets which sing in the fields. I cut off the heads and the wings of the crickets and put them with the beetles and common oil into a pot; I covered it and left it afterwards for a day and night in a bread oven. I drew out the pot and heated it at a moderate fire, I pounded the whole and rubbed the sick parts; in three days the pain had disappeared.

(2) *Source*: Sir Percival Horton-Smith Hartley and H. R. Aldridge, *Johannes de Mirfeld of St. Bartholomew's, Smithfield*, Cambridge 1939, p. 87. (*De Ptisi*). (Mirfeld is here using John of Gaddesden, *Rosa Anglica*, chapter on phthisis.)

Again, an unguent made from the fat of animals is beneficial to phthisical patients, if the chest be anointed therewith. Other useful chest-ointments are those made from fresh butter, oil of sweet almonds, marsh-mallow root, or oil of violets; likewise one made from the fat of pigs, or grease made from ducks or capons. And over these place a lamb's skin. Then on the following day wipe away the ointment with strained bran.

. . . . .

Q

DIET FOR CONSUMPTIVES

Further Reading: Norman Moore, *The History of the Study of Medicine in the British Isles*, Oxford, 1908. J. F. Payne, *English Medicine in the Anglo-Saxon Times*, 1904. ' Herbarium Apuleii ', *Leechdoms, Wortcunning, and Starcraft of Early England, being a Collection of Documents illustrating the History of Science in this country before the Norman Conquest*, collected and ed. by the Rev. O. Cockayne, 1864. Rolls Series 35.

Source: Sir Percival Horton-Smith Hartley and H. R. Aldridge, *Johannes de Mirfeld of St. Bartholomew's Smithfield*, Cambridge University Press, 1939 (*Breviarium Bartholomei*), pp. 81–5.

. . . Milk is of the greatest possible value, especially if it be that of women; asses milk is next to be preferred, and then that of goats. The milk ought to be imbibed direct from the udder; but should this be impossible, then take a salver, which has been washed in hot water, and allow it to stand over another full of hot water; then let the animal be milked into the salver and the milk immediately proferred, for it very quickly turns bad. If it be feared that this has occurred, boil the milk over the fire, add a pinch of salt or honey to it, and let this be absorbed; or drop into the milk either heated stones taken from the river, or a red hot iron. Moreover, wine should not be drunk during the whole period in which the milk remains in the stomach, for the wine causes the milk to coagulate, and this changes it into the nature of a poison. . . .

[Then the virtues of wine, barley-water, honey, river-crab, sugar of roses, and dry figs are discussed.]

The patient can also eat the flesh of all the usual kinds of fowl which fly, except of those which live on the water; likewise the flesh of kids, lambs, and unweaned calves, or of the young rabbit; also the extremities of animals (such as the feet and legs of little pigs), hens and their chickens, and the flesh of a year-old lamb: and of all these only a little should be taken, and but rarely, except in the case of flying fowl, and even this should be taken only in such a small quantity as to be digestible. . . .

SOME SIGNS OF APPROACHING DEATH

Further Reading: Dr. Charles Singer, *From Magic to Science*, 1928.

Source: Sir Percival Horton-Smith Hartley and H. R. Aldridge, *Johannes de Mirfeld of St. Bartholomew's Smithfield*, Cambridge, 1939 (*Breviarium Bartholomei*), p. 71. (late fourteenth century)

Again, take the name of the patient, the name of the messenger sent to summon the physician, and the name of the day upon which the messenger first came to you; join all their letters together, and if an even number result, the patient will not escape; if the number be odd, then he will recover.

The following are the signs of death: Continuous vomitting, a cold sweat, and cold extremities, excessive eructations, convulsions and delirium, together with bowel obstruction of whatever nature.

Again, if a blister, black in colour, appear upon his belly, the patient will die on the following day; similarly if the face be distorted with a pallid swelling, the eyes become greenish, or the legs swollen. Also the patient will die if the veins around the eyes and in the forehead appear black in colour.

Take the herb Cinquefoil, and, whilst collecting it, say a Paternoster on behalf of the patient, and then boil it in a new jar with some of the water which the patient is destined to drink; and if the water be red in colour after this boiling, then the patient will die. . . .

SURGERY

John of Arderne (1306–90?) improved the treatment of gout. clysters and fistula in ano. He obtained his training as a practical army surgeon in the Hundred Years' War, for University Faculties of Medicine did not include the study of surgery. Cupping, leeching and tooth-extraction was left to barbers as all surgery was forbidden to clerics; for both the sight of naked bodies and the shedding of blood was unsuitable for them. On Sundays the Oxford barbers, who counted as members of the University, only shaved those with religious duties to perform.

Further Reading: W. J. Bishop, *The Early History of Surgery*, Robert Hale 1960.

Source: *The Household of Edward IV, the Black Book and the Ordinanc of* 1478, ed. A. R. Myers, Manchester University Press, 1958, pp. 125–6.

Hit is acustumed [c. 1471–2] that a knygt of chambre, or ellez squier for the body, or both, be present euery tym whan the king wull be shaue. This barbour shall haue euery Satyrday at nygt, if hit please the kinge to clensse his hed, legges, or feete, and for his shauing, ij loues, j picher wyne; and the ussher of chambre owith to testyfye, if this is necessaryly dispended or nougt. Also this barbour takith his shauyng clothes, basons, and all his other toolys, and thinges necessary by the chambrelayn is assignement of the jewelhouse.

SCRIBES

Pictures of scribes are common in medieval manuscripts in portraits of their authors; thus St. Jerome is often shown writing in the initial letter of the prologue which precedes the Vulgate, his Latin translation of the Bible. By the second half of the thirteenth century the art of writing was so widespread that voluminous records were written on parchment recording the affairs of quite small and remote manors.

Romanesque, Early English and Decorated architectural forms with rounded and simple pointed forms followed by ones more ornate and horizontal are reflected in the shapes of the letters characteristic of the corresponding centuries; and with the revival of classical learning called the Renaissance a return is made to earlier and simple Roman forms. As literacy spreads there is a tendency for writing to become less careful, and for legal documents to get longer.

Further Reading: N. Denholm-Young, *Handwriting in England and Wales, Cardiff*, 1954.

(1) *Source*: U. T. Holmes, Jr., *Daily Living in the Twelfth Century, based on the Observations of Alexander Neckam*. Madison, The University of Wisconsin Press, 1952, 69–70. For Alexander Neckam see *W.W.I.H.*, i, 112–3.

Let him have a razor or knife for scraping pages of parchment or skin; let him have a ' biting ' pumice for cleaning the sheets, and a little scraper for making equal the surface of the skin. He should have a piece of lead and a ruler with which he may rule the margins on both sides—on the back and on the side from which the flesh has been removed.

Dunstan copying the Rule of St. Benedict, drawn 1150–80. (MS. Royal 10 A xiii.)

There should be a fold of four sheets [a quaternion]. . . . Let these leaves be held together at top and bottom by a strip [of parchment threaded through]. The scribe should have a bookmark cord and a pointed tool. . . . Let him sit in a chair with both arms high, reinforcing the back rest, and with a stool at his feet. Let the writer have a heating basin [of hot charcoal] covered with a cap; he should have a knife with which he can shape a quill pen; let this be prepared for writing with the inside fuzzy scale scraped out, and let there be a boar's or goat's tooth for polishing the parchment, so that the ink of a letter may not run. . . . He should have something with which letters can be canceled. Let him have an indicator or line marker in order that he may not make costly delay from error. There should be hot coals in the heating container so that the ink may dry more quickly on the parchment in foggy or wet weather. Let there be a small window through which light can enter; if perchance the blowing of the north wind attacks the principal window, let this be supplied with a screen of linen or of parchment, distinct in color; green and black offer more comfort to the eyes. Whiteness, when too intense, disturbs the sight and throws it into disorder. There should be red lead for forming red . . . letters or capitals. Let there be dark powder and blue. . . .

(2) The Exchequer with its chequered cloth to aid counting is described in the treatise from which the following extract comes (*T.S.I.H.* i, p. 88). A century later the number of professional scribes available for writing private business documents had become very large. No English ruler before the fourteenth century ever signed his own name (*W.W.I.H.*, i, plate 23 shows Henry III's signature). King John sealed Magna Carta. To say that he signed it is a common ' howler '.

Source: *Dialogus de Scaccario The Course of the Exchequer* (1176–9), ed. C. Johnson. Nelson 1950, p. 29.

The duty of the Scribe who sits next the Treasurer is to prepare the Rolls [which for a certain reason are of sheepskin] for writing. The length of the Rolls [i.e. *the ' pipes ' or sheets of which the Roll is made up*] is that of two membranes, larger than the average and carefully chosen for the purpose, but their width is a little more than a span and a half [*about* 13 *in.*]. They are ruled from the top nearly to the bottom, on both sides, with a reasonable space between the lines. At the head of the Roll, are entered the names of the county and bailiwicks of which the account is

rendered below. A space of three or four finger-breadths is left
blank. Then in the middle of the line is written the name of the
county which is to be dealt with first. Then, at the head of the
next line, the name of the Sheriff is engrossed, and after it the
following formula: ' So-and-so the Sheriff renders account of
such-and-such a county '. Farther on in the same line: ' In the
Treasury ' . . . Then, at the head of the next line is set down how
much has been spent in fixed alms and tithes, and how much
in payments out of the farm of the county. After this at the head
of the line below, as ' lands granted ', are noted the gifts which
royal liberality has made to churches, or to those who served
them, out of the lands which are assigned to the Crown. . . .

A SAXON MANUSCRIPT BIBLE

Some of the most beautiful books ever to be produced were
created in Irish or Saxon monasteries during bright interludes in the
' Dark Ages '. Such are the Lindisfarne Gospels, the Book of Kells
and the tenth century Benedictional of St. Aethelwold. The parchment
pages made of carefully prepared skins were always arranged so that
each of every two facing pages either came from the flesh or the hair
side of the skin. The costlier books often had ornate bindings decorated
with ivory, jewels of precious metal. The quill pen is here called ' the
bird's joy '.

Source: Old English riddle in *The Exeter Book*, pt. ii, poems ix–
xxxii, Early English Text Society, O.S. no. 194, 1934, for 1933, p. 117.

An enemy cut me off from life,
deprived me of mortal strength, wetted me afterwards,
dipped me in water, took me out again,
placed me in the sun, where I quickly lost
the hairs that I had. The hard edge of the knife,
ground free from dross, afterwards cut me;
fingers folded me, and the bird's joy
sprinkled me with useful drops, travelled often
over the brown rim, swallowed the ink,
part of the fluid, stepped again upon me,
left black tracks as it travelled. Afterwards a man
covered me with protecting boards, stretched hide across me.

adorned with gold; I was therefore embellished
with goldsmith's fine handiwork, clasped with wire.
Now let those ornaments, and the red dye,
and the splendid treasures celebrate far and wide
the Protector of nations. . . . My name is famous,
and I myself beneficial to men and holy.

BOOKS

In spite of neglect and deliberate destruction a surprisingly large
number of medieval books survive. All those which are in manuscipt
and which are known to have come from a definite medieval library,
whether a monastery or not, have been recorded by place of origin by
Mr. N. Ker in what is a triumph of modern scholarship. Most medieval
books reflect the religious outlook of the time and Bibles, service
books, sermons, devotional writings and lives of saints are common;
but there are also technical treatises on subjects like medicine for the
doctors, romances for courtiers, secular as well as religious poetry and
music, legal text books for the lawyers, books compiled for administrative purposes, chronicles, guide-books and books of etiquette. The
learned books are in Latin, the courtly books are often in French, and
books in English only become common in the course of the fourteenth
century. One great book collector of the fourteenth century, Richard
de Bury, makes some remarks about the ill-treatment of books which
are reprinted in *T.S.I.H.*, i, p. 151.

Further Reading: The English Library before 1700: Studies in its History,
ed. Francis Wormald and C. E. Wright, Athlone Press, 1958.

Source: Riley, *Memorials of London*, p. 557 (1403).

Be it remembered, that on the 12th day of July, in the 4th
year etc., the reputable men of the craft of Writers of text-letter,
those commonly called ' Limners ' [painters and decorators of
manuscripts], and other good folks of London, who are wont to
bind and to sell books, presented here . . . a certain petition,
in these words, that it may please your sagenesses to grant
unto them, that they may elect yearly two reputable men, the
one a *lymenour* the other a text-writer, to be Wardens of the
said trades; and that the names of the Wardens so elected may
be presented each year before the Mayor, for the time being, and
they be there sworn well and diligently to oversee, that good rule

and governance is had and exercised by all folks of the same trades in all works unto the said trades pertaining, to the praise and good fame of the loyal good men of the said trades, and to the shame and blame of the bad and disloyal men of the same. And that the same Wardens may call together all the men of the said trades honourably and peaceably, when need shall be, as well as for the good rule and governance of the said city, as of the trades aforesaid. And that the same Wardens, in performing their due office, may present from time to time all the defaults of the said bad and disloyal men to the Chamberlain at the Guildhall, for the time being; to the end that the same may there, according to the wise and prudent discretion of the governors of the said city be corrected, punished and duly redressed. And that all who are rebellious against the said Wardens, as to the survey and good rule of the same trades, may be punished, according to the general Ordinance made as to rebellious persons in trades of the said city... And that it may please you to command that this petition, by your sagenesses granted, may be entered of record for time to come; for the love of God, and as a work of charity.'

Which petition having been read before the said Mayor and Aldermen, and fully understood, for the reason especially that it concerned the common weal and profit, that transgressors of the Ordinance aforesaid should be severely punished, as before stated; it was unanimously granted by them that the Ordinance should thereafter be faithfully observed, and that transgressors should be punished in manner as above stated.

PRINTING

In 1475 Caxton helped print with Colard Mansion at Bruges the *Recuyell of the Historyes of Troy*, the first book printed in English. Caxton's first dated book printed in England was the *Dictes or Sayengis of the Philosophers*, 1477. He printed ninety-five more books, at Westminster, before his death in 1491. Provincial presses appeared at Oxford in 1478, run by Theodoric Rood of Cologne, and at St. Albans in 1480. Caxton's books were mostly in English; the first English classical text was Cicero's *Pro Milone*, Oxford, about 1480. No English printed book had a title page before 1486.

Further Reading: E. G. Duff, *The Printers, Stationers, and Bookbinders of Westminster and London*, 1906; The English Provincial Printers, *Stationers, and Bookbinders*, 1912. H. S. Bennett, *English Books and Readers, 1457–1557, Cambridge University Press*, 1952.

Source: William Caxton in *The Recuyell of the Histories of Troye*, 1471.

Thus ende I this book whyche I have translated after my auctor as nyghe as God hath gyven me connyng to whom be gyven the laude and preysyng. And for as moche as in the wrytyng of the same my penne is worn, myn hande wery and not stedfast, myn eyen dimmed with overmoche lokyng on the whit paper, and my corage not so prone and redy to laboure as hit hath ben, and that age crepeth on me dayly and febleth all the bodye, and also because I have promysid to dyverce gentilmen and to my frendes to addresse to hem as hastely as I myght this sayd book. Therefore I have practysed and lerned at my grete charge and dispense to ordeyne this said booke in prynte after the maner and forme as ye may here see. And it is not wreton with penne and ynke as other bokes ben to thende that every man may have them attones. For all the bookes of this storye named the recule of the historyes of Troyes thus emprynted as ye here see were begonne in oon day, and also fynysshed in oon day.

PRIVATE LETTERS FROM AN ETONIAN

Further Reading: C. L. Kingsford, *Prejudice and Promise in 15th century England*, 1925.

Source: modernised from *Paston Letters*, ed. James Gairdner, Constable and Co., 1900, vol. 3, pp. 240–2. [1479]

Right reverend and worshipful brother, after all duties of commendation I recommend me to you, desiring to hear of your prosperity and welfare, which I pray God long to continue to his pleasure and to your heart's desire; letting you weet [know] that I received a letter from you, in the which letter was 8d. with the which I should buy a pair of slippers.

Furthermore certifying you as for the 13s. 4d. which ye sent by a gentleman's man for my board, called Thomas Newton, was delivered to mine hostess, and so to my creancer [creditor], Mr. Thomas Stevenson; and he heartily recommended him to you; also ye sent me word in the letter of 12lb. of figs [for Lent] and 8lb. of raisins; I have them not delivered, but I doubt not I shall have, for Alwedyr told me of them, and he said that they came after in another barge.

And as for the young gentlewoman, I will certify you how I first fell in acquaintance with her; her father is dead, there be two sisters of them, the elder is just wedded; at which wedding I was with mine hostess, and desired [invited] by the gentleman himself, called William Swan, whose dwelling is in Eton. So it fortuned that mine hostess reported on me otherwise than I was worthy, so that her mother commanded her to make me good cheer, and so in good faith she did; she is not abiding where she is now, her dwelling is in London; but her mother and she came to a place of hers five miles from Eton where the wedding was, for because it was nigh to the gentleman which wedded her daughter; and on Monday next coming, that is to say, the first Monday of Clean Lent, her mother and she will go to the pardon at Sheene, and so forth to London, and there to abide in a place of hers in Bow churchyard; and if it please you to inquire of her, her mother's name is Mistress Alborow, the name of the daughter is Margaret Alborow, the age of her is, by likelyhood, eighteen or nineteen years at the farthest; and as for the money and plate, it is ready whensoever she were wedded; but as for the livelihood, I trow not till after her mother's decease, but I cannot tell you for very certain, but you may know by inquiring.

And as for her beauty, judge you that when you see her, if so be that ye take the labour; and specially behold her hands, for and if it be as it is told me, she is disposed to be thick. . . . [Then follows bad Latin verse.]

In haste, with the hand of your brother,
William Paston, junior.

LIBRARIES

Alcuin's library at York (778) was the most important in northern Europe. Many monasteries had libraries and of these Durham had over 300 books and Christ Church, Canterbury over 200, in the twelfth century. Books were kept in boxes or on lecterns and the building of the oldest surviving English library, that of Merton College, Oxford, was not built until 1377 though a catalogue had been made about 1325, and by 1327 Bishop Cobham of Worcester had planned a University library adjoining the Oxford University Church. This building was not actually obtained until 1410. In it the books remained while a new library over the Divinity School was being built (1481–8) which is still called Duke Humfrey's Library in memory of Humfrey Duke of Gloucester (d. 1447) who gave the University many books. Duke Humfrey's library was fitted with lecterns not bookcases until it was restored by Sir Thomas Bodley (after whom the Bodleian Library is called) in 1600–2. The marks left by the lecterns against the walls were discovered in 1960.

Further Reading: J. W. Clark, *The Care of Books*, 2nd ed. 1909.

Source: Summary of Library Statutes of 1412, Strickland Gibson, *Some Oxford Libraries*, 1914, pp. 8–9.

. . . the Librarian, who was to be in holy orders, should once a year hand over to the Chancellor and Proctors the keys of the library: if after visitation he was found to be fit in morals, fidelity, and ability he received them back. Should he desire to resign his office a month's notice was required. His salary was fixed at £5 6s. 8d. a year, for which modest sum he not only took charge of the library, but said masses for the souls of benefactors. He was, however, permitted to claim a robe from every beneficed scholar at graduation. There is a special clause stating that the Proctors should be bound to pay the Librarian's salary half-yearly, for the curious, but very excellent, reason that if his pay were in arrears his care and efficiency might slacken. Lest by too great a number of students the books might receive damage, or study be hindered, admission was restricted to those who had studied in the schools for eight years, an exception being made in the case of the sons of lords who had seats in Parliament. Moreover, every reader had to subscribe to the following oath: ' You shall swear when you enter the Library of the University, to treat in a reasonable and quiet manner all the books contained therein, and to injure no book maliciously, by erasing, or by detaching sections and leaves. The library was to be open from 9 till 11 and from 2 till 4, except on Sundays and the greater Saints' days; and lest too close attention to his duties might affect his health, the Librarian was to be allowed a month's holiday in the Long Vacation. . . . Lastly, a board was to be suspended in the library on which were to be recorded in a fair and elegant hand the titles of the books, with their donors' names; and all books were to be closed at night and the windows fastened.

MUNIMENTS

The number of documents which survive from the medieval period numbers perhaps 50,000 in the estate offices of Oxford Colleges alone. The Government records in the Public Record Office, including Domesday Book among the exchequer records, are vast and most counties have local record offices. All this is additional to the medieval documents collected in the British Museum or the Bodleian Library, Oxford. Much, too, has perished through accident and more probably through neglect.

Source: The History of Ingulf (medieval fiction), translated by Rev. J. Stevenson, *The Church Historians of England*, Seeleys 1854, p. 710.

In our charter-room (to which the stone arch which entirely roofed it in had been no protection, since the flames rushed in through the wooden windows, and which was like a burning furnace or red-hot oven), we found that although the boxes appeared to be safe and uninjured, yet that all the muniments contained in them had been shrivelled up and reduced to ashes by the excessive heat. Our very beautiful writings in the vulgar character, and ornamented with golden crosses and elegant paintings, and highly ornamented letters, and which had been there deposited, were all demolished. The ancient and excellent privileges conferred by the Mercian kings, similarly signed with golden pictures, and written in the Saxon character, were all burnt. The whole of our muniments of this kind, greater and less, were almost four hundred in number, and were all, by a disastrous misfortune, instantaneously lost and destroyed in one black night.

A few years before, however, I had taken from the charter room many duplicates and triplicates of writings in the Saxon character, and kindly given them to our chanter, the lord Fulmar, to be preserved in the cloister, so that the younger amongst us might learn the Saxon character, which had for a length of time, by the Norman influence, been neglected and fallen into disrepute, and at that time was known to none but a few of the elders; for the purpose that, by knowing how to read it, they might, in their old age, be more able to produce these muniments of their monastery in evidence against their adversaries. These writings, deposited in the cloister in an old chest, which was protected by the wall of the church, were alone preserved safe from the conflagration. Thus these documents, formerly of secondary value and laid on one side, and, by reason of the barbarous character in which they were written, held in light esteem and regard, are now our principal and best muniments,—according to the words of the blessed Job, ' The things that my soul refused to touch are as my sorrowful meat.'

TEACHERS

King Alfred persuaded teachers from abroad to come to Wessex, for, as he explains, Danish raids had ruined education (*T.S.I.H.*, i, 21–2). His own biographer, Asser, was one of these teachers, brought in from Wales. In the twelfth century Theobald of Etampes, earliest known lecturer at Oxford, alleged that even in small towns school masters were as common as civil servants. But decay, attributed to the Black Death and the Hundred Years War, led William of Wykeham (d. 1404) to found New College, Oxford, and Winchester College. William Byngham, a London rector, founded a training college called Godshouse (later Clare College, Cambridge) in 1439 as seventy grammar schools had closed in the past half century.

Source: Asser, *Life of Alfred*, translated by J. A. Giles in *Six English Chronicles* (Bohn's Antiquarian Library, 1885).

He [Alfred] sent messengers beyond the sea to Gaul, to procure teachers, and he invited from thence Grimbald, priest and monk, a venerable man, and good singer, adorned with every kind of ecclesiastical discipline and good morals, and most learned in holy scripture. He also obtained from thence John, also priest and monk, a man of most energetic talents, and learned in all kinds of literary science, and skilled in many other arts. By the teaching of these men the king's mind was much enlarged, and he enriched and honoured them with much influence.

In these times, I also came into Saxony [Wessex] out of the furthest coasts of Western Britain; and when I had proposed to go to him through many intervening provinces, I arrived in the country of the Saxons, who live on the right hand, which in Saxon is called Sussex, under the guidance of some of that nation; and there I first saw him in the royal vill, which is called Dene. He received me with kindness, and among other familiar conversation, he asked me eagerly to devote myself to his service and become his friend, to leave everything which I posssesed on the left, or western bank of the Severn, and he promised he would give more than an equivalent for it in his own dominions. I replied that I could not incautiously and rashly promise such things; for it seemed to me unjust, that I should leave those sacred places in which I had been bred, educated, and crowned, and at last ordained, for the sake of any earthly honour and power, unless by compulsion. Upon this, he said, ' If you cannot accede to this, at least, let me have your service in part: spend six months of the year with me here, and the other six in Britain '. To this, I replied, ' I could not even promise that easily or hastily without the advice of my friends '. At length, however, when I perceived that he was anxious for my services, though I knew not why, I promised him that, if my life was spared, I would return to him after six months, with such a reply as should be agreeable to him as well as advantageous to me and mine. With this answer he was satisfied, and when I had given him a pledge to return at the appointed time, on the fourth day we left him and returned on horseback towards our own country.

After our departure, a violent fever seized me in the city of Winchester, where I lay for twelve months and one week, night and day, without hope of recovery. At the appointed time, therefore, I could not fulfil my promise of visiting him, and he sent messengers to hasten my journey, and to inquire the cause of my delay. As I was unable to ride to him, I sent a second messenger to tell him the cause of my delay, and assure him that, if I recovered from my infirmity, I would fulfil what I had promised. My complaint left me, and by the advice and consent of all my friends, for the benefit of that holy place, and of all who dwelt therein [St. Davids] I did as I had promised to the king, and devoted myself to his service, on the condition that I should remain with him six months in every year, either continuously, if I could spend six months with him at once, or alternately, three months in Britain [Wales] and three in Saxony [Wessex]. For my friends hoped that they should sustain less tribulation and harm from King Hemeid, who often plundered that monastery and the parish of St. Deguus, and sometimes expelled the prelates, as they expelled archbishop Novis, my relation, and myself; if in any manner I could secure the notice and friendship of the king.

SCHOOLS

The most striking difference between modern schools and medieval ones is perhaps the disappearance of birch rods. These were the symbol of education and Masters of Arts were given one, which they were expected to use, on taking their degree. Illustrations of King Solomon in illuminated Bibles often show him with one, and pictures of masters using them are frequent. A teacher employed by Alfred was stabbed by the boys; and St. Dunstan's miracles alone saved some Canterbury boys from their ferocious masters. The mother of a famous French scholar, Guibert de Nogent, disapproved of its use and lifted up his shirt to see that it had not been used whenever he came home from school. Guibert hated her interference. The conversation between a Saxon master and his pupils in 1005, the strict rules in the monks' school for novices at Canterbury about 1075 and the sports of the school boys of Norman London are printed in *T.S.I.H.*, i, p. 96. Ideal pictures of individual teaching occur in pictures of the Virgin with her mother, St. Anne.

Further Reading: Educational Charters and Documents, 598 to 1909, by Arthur F. Leach, Cambridge University Press 1911.

(1) *Source*: Council of 994 (?) Book of Ecclesiastical Laws in A. F. Leach *Educational Charters and Documents*, 598 to 1709, p. 37.

xix. Of schools in churches.

If any priest wish to send his nephew or other kinsman to be taught in the churches which are entrusted to our governance, we willingly grant him this.

65. The founder, William of Wykeham, fellows and scholars at Winchester College

66. Rybybe

67. Gittern

68. David with harp and case. Trumpet (*cf. p.* 259)

xx. That priests shall keep schools in the villages and teach small boys freely.

Priests ought always to have schools of schoolmasters in their houses, and if any of the faithful wish to give his little ones to learning they ought willingly to receive them and teach them for nothing. You should think that it has been written (Daniel xii. 3) ' The learned shall shine as the brightness of the firmament ' and that ' those who have educated and taught many to righteousness shall shine as the stars for ever '. But they ought not to expect anything from their relations except what they wish to do of their own accord.

(2) *Source*: J. E. Thorold Rogers, *Oxford City Documents* 1268–1665, Oxford Historical Society, vol. 18, 1891, pp. 161–2. (Inquest on John de Neushom, clerk and teacher of boys found by his wife dead beside the Cherwell). (7 Dec. 1301).

. . . John de Neushom went after dinner to find rods for beating his pupils. He climbed up a willow to cut rods next the mill pond called Temple Mile and fell in by accident and was drowned. The jurors say on oath that nobody was to blame for his death.

LANGUAGE

Every single word in our language has an individual and interesting history which is traced in the *New English Dictionary* with extracts from the earliest writings in which each occurs. Chaucer did much to fuse the native and French elements of our language together. The first royal speech to parliament in English was made in 1362.

Further Reading: V. H. Galbraith, ' Nationality and Language in Mediaeval England ', *Transactions of the Royal Historical Society*, 4th series, vol. 23, 1941, pp. 113–28. Helen Suggett, ' The Use of French in England in the later Middle Ages ', *ib.*, vol. 28, 1946, pp. 61–83.

(1) *Source*: Translated from Higden, *Polychronicon*, (Rolls Series, 1869), ii, 158–9 (c. 1327).

It is plain that there are as many languages as there are races in this island. As the Scottish and Welsh are untainted by other peoples they keep their speech practically in its virgin purity, unless maybe the Scots have assimilated somewhat into their speech by association with the Picts with whom they once mixed

R

as allies. But the Flemings who colonise the Western extremity of Wales have abandoned barbarism and speak in a sufficiently Saxon way. Although the Angles originally inherited a threefold tongue [viz. southern, midland and northern], as originating from three Teutonic tribes, their native language has been corrupted in many particulars by intermixture first with the Danes and then with the Normans and thus they acquire alien accents and rhythms. This corruption of the native tongue now largely proceeds from two factors: contrary to the custom of other peoples boys in schools since the Conquest have been forced to abandon their own language and to form sentences in French, and furthermore the sons of the nobility have been educated in the French idiom from their very cradles. The rustics have wanted to ape them in order that they may thus seem more respectable and so they have striven with might and main to frenchify themselves. So it really seems amazing how the indigenous native language of the Angles, confined as it is in a single island, varies so widely in its pronunciation, while the Norman speech, imported as it is, maintains the same pronunciation among all of the people. The threefold language of the Saxons hardly survives today among a handful of rustics, and those in the East have a dialect which resembles that of the folk in the West (as under the same latitude) more than the peoples of North and South. . . . The whole language of the Northumbrians, especially those of York, rasps in such an uncouth way, that we southerners can hardly understand it. . . .

(2) *Source*: Trevisa's additional note in his translation of the above passage of Higden, (Rolls Series, 1869), ii, 161, 1385.

Iohn Cornwaile, a maister of grammer, chaunged the lore in gramer scole and construccioun of Frensche in to Englische, and Richard Pencriche lerned the menere techynge of hym and othere men of Pencrich; so that now, the year of oure Lorde a thowsand thre hundred and foure score and fyve, and of the secounde kyng Richard after the conquest nyne, in alle the gramere scoles of Engelonde, children leue Frensche and construe and lerne in Englische, and haue therby auauntage in oon side and disauauntage in another side; here auauntage is, that thay lerne her gramer

in lasse tyme than children were i-woned to doo; disauauntage is
that now children of gramer scole conneth na more Frensche
than can hir lift heele, and that is harme for hem and thay schulle
passe the see and travaille in straunge landes and in many other
places. Also gentil men haue now moche i-left for to teche here
children Frensche.

MATHEMATICS

The use of Roman numerals made the use of an abacus desirable
as it was very hard to do sums.

Source: Aldhelm (d. 709), Letter to Bishop Haeddi translated by
A. F. Leach, *Educational Charters and Documents*, 598–1909, p. 9.

As to the principles of arithmetic what shall be said? when
the despair of doing sums oppressed my mind so that all the
previous labours spent on learning, whose most secret chamber
I thought I knew already, seemed nothing, and to use Jerome's
expression I who before thought myself a past master began again
to be a pupil, until the difficulty solved itself, and at last, by God's
grace, I grasped after incessant study the most difficult of all
things, what they call fractions.

INNS OF COURT

John Fortescue became a law student about 1414 and was made a
Sergeant at Michaelmas 1430 when he says ' I very well remember . . .
my bill for gold rings came to fifty pounds ' as customary presents for
each bishop, earl, justice and great man at court. He became a Governor
of Lincoln's Inn in 1425, 1426 and 1429 and was made Chief Justice
on 25 January 1442. The Inns of Court (Lincoln's Inn, Gray's Inn, the
Inner Temple and the Middle Temple) and the Inns of Chancery were
the first professional schools for laymen in England.

Source: Sir John Fortescue, *In Praise of the Laws of England*, written
in exile between 1464 and 1470 for Edward Prince of Wales, son of
his master Henry VI, and translated by Francis Gregor, in 1737.
Chapter 49.

There belong to it [the study of the law] ten lesser inns, and
sometimes more, which are called the Inns of Chancery: in each
of which there are an hundred students at the least; and in some

of them a far greater number, though not constantly residing. The students are, for the most part, young men; here they study the nature of original and judicial writs, which are the very first principles of the law: after they have made some progress here, and are more advanced in years, they are admitted into the Inns of Court, properly so called; of these there are four in number. In that which is the least frequented there are about two hundred students. In these greater inns a student cannot well be maintained under eight and twenty pounds a year; and, if he have servants to wait on him, as for the most part they have, the expense is proportionately more: for this reason, the students are sons to persons of quality; those of an inferior rank not being able to bear the expenses of maintaining and educating their children in this way. As to the merchants, they seldom care to lessen their stock in trade by being at such large yearly expenses. So that there is scarce to be found, throughout the kingdom, an eminent lawyer, who is not a gentleman by birth and fortune; consequently they have a greater regard for their character and honour than those who are bred in another way. There is both in the Inns of Court, and the Inns of Chancery, a sort of academy, or gymnasium, fit for persons of their station; where they learn singing, and all kinds of music, dancing and such other accomplishments and diversions, which are called revels, as are suitable to their quality, and such as are usually practised at court. At other times, out of term, the greater part apply themselves to the study of the law. Upon festival days, and after the offices of the church are over, they employ themselves in the study of sacred and profane history: here everything which is good and virtuous is to be learned: all vice is discouraged and banished. So that knights, barons, and the greatest nobility of their kingdom, often place their children in those Inns of Court; not so much to make the laws their study, much less to live by the profession, having large patrimonies of their own, but to form their manners and to preserve them from the contagion of vice. The discipline is so excellent, that there is scarce ever known to be any piques or differences, any bickerings or disturbances amongst them. The only way they have of punishing delinquents is by expelling them the society: which punishment they dread more than criminals do imprisonment and irons: for he who is expelled out of one society is never taken in by any of the other. Whence it happens that there is a constant harmony amongst them, the greatest friendship and a general freedom of conversation. I need not be particular in describing the manner and method how the laws are studied in those places, since your highness is never like to be a student there. But, I may say in the general, that it is pleasant, excellently well adapted for proficiency, and every way worthy of your esteem and encouragement.

EDUCATION OF NOBLE MINORS

Young nobles were placed as wards until they came of age.

Source: Sir John Fortescue, *On the Laws of England*, translated by Francis Gregor, 1737, chapter 45 (c. 1470).

. . . by this means, our young nobility and gentry cannot so easily degenerate, but will rather, in all likelihood, go beyond their ancestors in probity and courage, and in everything that is virtuous and praiseworthy, being brought up in a superior and more honourable family than that of their parents; nay, though their fathers may have had the good fortune to be educated in the like manner before, yet the father's house, even with this advantage, cannot be compared to that of the superior lord; to whom both, in their turns, have been in ward. Princes of the realm, being under the same regulation, like as other lords, who hold immediately from the king, cannot so soon run into debaucheries, or a downright ignorance: because, during the time of their minority, they are brought up at court. Upon which account I cannot but highly commend the magnificence and state of the king's palace, and I look on it as an academy for the young nobility of the kingdom to inure and employ themselves in robust and manly exercises, probity, and a generous humanity. All which greatly tend to the reputation and prosperity of the kingdom, both at home and abroad; and make a great part of its security against invaders, and render it formidable both to its allies and enemies. This advantage could not accrue to the state if the young nobility and gentry were to be brought up under the care and inspection of their own friends and relations, who are but persons of the same rank and quality with themselves.

OXFORD UNIVERSITY

Important schools for the study of law arose in the twelfth century in connection with the Cathedrals of Canterbury, Exeter and Lincoln, and the convenient central positions of Northampton and Oxford attracted lecturers who had studied at Paris, Bologna or Toledo. At Oxford royal palaces and religious houses of repute helped draw audiences of from 60 to 100 clerks as early as 1117 to lectures by Theobald of Etampes. Robert Pullen, a theologian, and Vacarius, a jurist, followed and in 1184 Gerald of Wales gave a public reading of his book on Ireland to ' all the doctors and their chief students '. Trouble with the townsmen led to a temporary dispersal in 1209, when some scholars settled permanently at Cambridge. Both Oxford and Cambridge won favours from Henry III and Oxford had about 1,500 clerks by 1315. Cambridge remained only a third of the size of Oxford until the early fifteenth century.

Further Reading: The Victoria County History of Oxford, vol. 3. *The University of Oxford*, ed. by Rev. H. E. Salter and Mary D. Lobel, 1954. C. E. Mallet, *History of the University of Oxford*, 3 vols., 1924–7.

Source: The Autobiography of Giraldus Cambrensis, ed. and translated by H. E. Butler, p. 97. (c. 1186).

So having won great name and fame in the island, between Easter and Pentecost Giraldus crossed the seas from Ireland to Wales, where he turned his whole mind to the completion of the *Topography of Ireland*, which he had already begun. And when in process of time the work was finished and corrected, not wishing to place the candle which he had lit under a bushel, but to lift it aloft on a candlestick that it might shine, he determined to read it before a great audience at Oxford, where of all places in England the clergy were most strong and pre-eminent in learning. And since his book was divided into three parts, he gave three consecutive days to the reading, a part being read each day. On the first day he hospitably entertained the poor of the whole town whom he gathered for the purpose; on the morrow he entertained all the doctors of the divers Faculties and those of their scholars who were best known and best spoken of; and on

The Clerk of Oxenford. Fifteenth century.
(Ellesmere Chaucer).

the third day he entertained the remainder of the scholars together with the knights of the town and a number of the citizens.
It was a magnificent and costly achievement, since thereby the
ancient and authentic times of the poets were in some manner
revived, nor has the present age seen nor does any past age bear
record of the like.

ASTRONOMERS

The learning of the ancient world about the heavens was preserved
by the Arabs and their knowledge was studied in Lorraine in the
eleventh century. From Lorraine, Cnut and Harold brought astronomers and mathematicians to England. One Lotharingian, Walcher,
became Abbot of Malvern. In 1091 he made accurate observations of
an eclipse. He predicted another, and in 1120 he adopted for some
lunar tables Arabic degrees, minutes and seconds instead of clumsy
fractions in Roman figures. Adelard of Bath, a layman who taught
that reason was preferable to authority, continued the work, translating the Arabic translation of Euclid and works on trigonometry
and astronomy. The influence of the heavens on crops and on the

Astronomers, Euclid with a sphere observing the sky and Hermannus with an astrolabe. Thirteenth century. (MS. Ashmole 304).

tides is not matched by a detailed influence of the stars on the lives of individuals, and as this was not realised much effort was expended on attempts to forecast the fortunes of individuals by the positions of stars at their birth. Thus the superstition of astrology grew out of the science of astronomy. Astrolabes for observing the heavens were, with balances, the earliest accurate instruments. See also pp. 304–5.

Further Reading: F. R. Johnson, *Astronomical Thought in Renaissance England*, Baltimore, 1937.

Source: Chaucer, *The Astrolabe*.

Litel Lewis my sone, I have perceived wel by certeyne evidences thyn abilite to lerne sciences touchinge noumbres and proporciouns; and as wel considere I thy bisy preyere in special to lerne the Tretis of the Astrolabe . . . ther-for have I geven thee a suffisaunt Astrolabie as for oure orizonte, compowned after the latitude of Oxenford; up-on which, by mediacion of this litel tretis, I purpose to teche thee a certein nombre of conclusions apertening to the same instrument. I seye a certein of conclu-

siouns, for . . . some of hem ben to harde to thy tendre age of
ten yeer to conseyve. This tretis, divided in fyve parties, wole I
shewe thee under ful lighte rewles and naked wordes in English;
for Latin ne canstow yit but smal, my lyte sone. . . .

ALCHEMISTS

The purpose of alchemy was to transmute base metal into gold.
It did not succeed, but alchemists learnt the properties of various
metals and acids and the use of the balance. The word *alchemy* is of
Arabic origin for much of the learning of the ancient world was
preserved by Arab scholars and, only by them and through them, it was
transmitted to medieval Europe. From the word and from the
practice of alchemy is derived modern chemistry. Its hypotheses were
found to be unsatisfactory, but so have the hypotheses of later scientists.

In the *Chanouns Yemannes Tale* Chaucer describes the financial ruin
brought by alchemy and lists many of the chemicals and scientific
instruments used. This story is one of a deliberate cheat who tricks a
priest into paying £40 for a worthless recipe, the first part contains a
convincing description of a laboratory. One can recognise an alchemist
' by smel of brymstoon . . . and threedbare array '.

Further Reading: E. J. Holmyard, *Alchemy*, Penguin Books 1957.

Source: Chaucer: *Chanouns Yemannes Tale*.

. . . Ful ofte it happeth so,
The pot tobreketh, and farewel! al is go!
Thise metals been of so greet violence,
Oure walles mowe nat make hem resistence,
But if they were wroght of lym and stoon;
And percen so, and thurgh the wal they goon,
And somme of hem synken into the ground,
Thus han we lost by tymes many a pound,
And somme are scatered al the floor aboute,
Somme lepe into the roof; withouten doute,
Though that the feend noght in oure sighte hym shewe,
I trowe he with us be, that ilke shrewe!
In helle where that he lord is and sire,
Nis ther moore wo, ne moore rancour ne ire.
Whan that oure pot is broke, as I have sayd,
Every man chit [chides], and halt hym yvele apayd.

Somme seyde, it was long on the fir makyng,
Somme seyde, nay! it was on the blowyng;
Thanne was I fered, for that was myn office;
Straw! quod the thridde, ye been lewed and nyce [foolish],
It was nat tempred as it oghte be.
Nay! quod the fourthe, stynt, and herkne me;
Bycause our fir ne was nat maad of beech,
That is the cause, and oother noon, so theech [may I thrive]!
I kan nat telle wheron it was along,
But wel I woot greet strif is us among.
What! quod my lord, ther is namoore to doone,
Of thise perils I wol be war eftsoone;
I am right siker that the pot was crased [cracked].
Be as be may, be ye nothyng amased;
As usage is, lat swepe the floor as swithe [at once],
Plukke up your hertes, and beeth glad and blithe!
The mullok [refuse] on an heep ysweped was,
And on the floor ycast a canevas,
And al this mullok in a syve ythrowe,
And sifted, and ypiked [picked over] many a throwe.
Pardee! quod oon, somwhat of oure metal
Yet is ther heere, thogh that we han nat al.
Although this thyng myshapped have as now,
Another tyme it may be wel ynow.

COLOUR: HABERDASHERY

The clergy, and their critics the Lollards, wore sombre clothes but manuscript pictures show the popularity of gay colours. A description of the articles in the shop of Thomas Trew, haberdasher of London, indicates the colours of many of his wares (1378). Robert Brunne in *Handlyng Synne* regarded women's saffroned wimples and kerchiefs with the same disapproval as their absurdly long trains.

Source: Translation from City Letter-Book in H. T. Riley, *Memorials of London and London Life*, 1279-1419, 1868, p. 422.

. . . 2 dozens of laces of red leather, value 8d, one gross of *poynts* [tagged laces] of red leather, 18d. . . . one dozen of caps, one half of which are of red colour, and the other half green,

2s. 8d.; one dozen of white caps, called ' nightcappes ', 2s. 3d.; 2 dozens of woollen caps of divers colours, 16s.; 6 caps of black wool, 4s.; 5 caps of blue colour, and one cap of russet, 2s. 6d.; 5 children's caps, red and blue, 2s. 1d.; one dozen of black hures [shaggy fur caps], 4s.; one black hure, 4d.; . . . one red cap, 7d.; one other cap of russet, 7d.; one hat of russet, 6d.; one white hat, 3d.; 2 papers covered with red leather, 12d.; 2 other papers, one of them covered with black leather, and the other with red, 8d.; one purse . . . of sea-green colour, 6d.; . . . one pair of children's boots of white woollen cloth, 2d. . . . 2 pounds of linen thread, green and blue, 2s. . . . 6 purses of red leather, 4d. . . . one black girdle of woollen thread, 2d. . . . one hat of russet, 6d. . . . [Other goods included gaming tables, chains for ferrets, a cage for flies [!], beads, pencases, inkhorns, parchments, boxes, eyeglasses, combs, pepper-mills, whipcord, a wooden block for shaping caps and a whistle.]

COLOUR: RED

Source: Nicholas Upton (on the significance of red, the colour of Mars and of the cross of St. George), *De Studio Militari*, 1654 (written before the death of Humphrey Duke of Gloucester in 1446), pp. 109–110.

This bright red, like light, distracts the sight and does not concentrate as black does. This is why sellers of cloth hang red cloth in front of the light, so that customers looking at other coloured cloths . . . are less able to make an accurate inspection. . . . This is the colour proper for a ruler, and especially for the leader of an army, because it means ferocity. This colour is proper to leaders because they are fierce in their chastisements and against their enemies. . . . This colour is much like that of the carbuncle. . . . So it is of this colour that the arms of England's king were made and he bears Three Lions (' leopards ') passant on a red field. . . .

COLOUR: GREEN

Because of the green of the leaves, 'Vert' and 'Verderers' were technical names in forest administration. The green of springtime is so significant that Dante tells us that Hope, one of the three Christian virtues, is coloured green.

Source: Nicholas Upton, *De Studio Militari*, 1654, pp. 113–4. This book on heraldry was dedicated to Humphrey Duke of Gloucester (d. 1446).

Green is a colour . . . which is a delight to the sight and attracts and soothes the sight. Wherefore deer and other woodland creatures seek green places and throng therein, not just for food but because of the sight. This is why huntsmen clothe themselves in green raiment. For the animals fear the snares of the huntsmen less on account of the sight of the green which it is their nature to love.

COLOUR: PAINTS

The churchwardens accounts of Cowfold, Sussex (1470) mention 'payntyng of the Churche'. This is unusual for church wall paintings, which were very numerous, were often paid for by bequests from parishioners as at Mayfield, Sussex (1471) 'if the parishioners are willing'. Under the pulpit at Boughton, Lincs., were found (1909) little cases of black, white, red and blue.

Here is an exceptionally early reference to painting on canvas. It would not have been a painting on canvas in the modern sense, but a cheap substitute for tapestry or embroidered wall-hangings. A thirteenth century chest at Newport, Essex, is painted inside the lid with oil paintings (predominantly red and green). This may be the earliest English example of oil painting. Painting on panel in England was at its best in the reign of Richard II. Foreign influences were strong and merged in what is called the 'International style'. The London painters had a gild of St. Giles in their church at Cripplegate.

Further Reading: Margaret Rickert, *Painting in Britain in the Middle Ages*, Pelican History of Art, Penguin Books, 1954 (192 plates). W. A. D. Englefield, *The History of the Painter-Stainers Company of London*, 1923. W. R. Lethaby, *London and Westminster Painters of the Middle Ages*, Walpole Soc., 1912.

Source: A Painter's Bond, 17 June, 1284, H. T. Riley, *Memorials of London and London Life*, 1276–1419, p. 23.

. . . Nicholas Bacun, painter, acknowledged that he was bound to Hugh Motun in the sum of 20 shillings, for cinople [sinople, green], vermilion, and canvas, varnish and verdigris; the same to be paid to the same Hugh or his certain attorney, 10 shillings at the Feast of St. Bartholomew [24 August], and 10 shillings at the Feast of St. Michael [29 September], without further delay.

TAPESTRY

Edward III created the office of King's Tapestry Maker. Hitherto most tapestry had been imported from Paris or Arras.

Wall hangings are often shown in medieval pictures of interiors and one of the most important records of peace and war is the long embroidered hanging inaccurately called the Bayeux 'Tapestry'. In 1331 sizes, qualities of wool, and apprenticeships were approved for the Trade of Tapicers. These cover armorial cushions as well as hangings. Finer pictorial work was done abroad and is often referred to by its place of origin, Arras. Weavers from Flanders and Brabant both had gilds in London by 1370. These met in the churchyards of St. Laurence Pountney and St. Mary Somerset. In 1393 and 1394 the Duke of Burgundy gave important pieces to the Duke of Lancaster and Richard II. Henry V had tapestries of Bevis of Hampton and St. Edward the King as well as many pieces with French inscriptions and religious or romantic subjects which can be paralleled in France, and Flanders. The pieces listed below belonged to Sir John Fastolf who built his castle at Caister out of the profits of the Hundred Years' War (see *W.W.I.H.*, i, 237–8).

Despite the fame of English cloth and English embroidery no English medieval tapestry as famous as the Apocalypse tapestry at Angers remains.

Further Reading: A. de Champeaux, *Tapestry*, 1878. W. G. Hunton, *English Decorative Textiles*, 1930.

Source: From wardrobe inventory of Sir John Fastolf (d. 1459), *Archaeologia*, vol. 21, p. 257–259.

Clothis of Arras and of Tapstre warke

Imprimis j. clothe of arras, clyped the Schipherds clothe.

Item, j. of the Assumpsion of Oure Lady.

Item, j. newe banker of arras, with a bere holdyng j. spere in the middys of the clothe.

Item, j. tester of arras with ij. gentlewomen and ij. gentlemen, and one holdyng an hawke in his honde.

Item, j. clothe with iiij. gentle women.

Item, j. testour of arras with a lady crouned and a grete rolle aboughte her hede, the first letter N.

Item, j. clothe of ix. conquerouris.

Item, j. cover for a bedde, of newe arras, and a gentlewoman beyng ther in the corner with a whelp in hir honde and an Agnus Day [Dei] aboughte hir nes. . . .

Item, j. clothe for the nether hall, of arras, with a geyaunt in the myddell, beryng a legge of a bere in his honde.

Item, j. clothe of arras for the dese [dais] in the same halle, with j. wodewose [a savage] and j. chylde in his armys.

Item, j. clothe of the sege of Faleys for the west side of the halle.

Item, j. clothe of arras with iiij. archowryes on schoting [shooting] a doke in the water with a cross bowe.

Item, j. clothe of arras withe a gentlewoman harpyng by j. castell in myddys of the clothe.

Item, j. cover of arras for a bedde, with a mane drawyng water in the myddel of the clothe ought of a welle.

Item, j. lytell tester of arras, whith j. man and a woman in the myddyll.

Item, j. banker of arras with a man schetyng at j. blode hownde.

Item, j. clothe of arras with a lady crounded, and j. rolle abought her hedde with A.N., lynyd with gray canvas.

Item, j. clothe of arras with a condyte in the myddill.

Item, j. clothe of arras, with a gentlewoman holding j. lace of silke, and j. gentlewoman a hauke.

Item, ij. clothis portrayed full of popelers.

Item, j. testyr of blewe tapistry warke with viij. braunchys. . . .

Item, j. banker of rede, with iiij. with white rosys and the armys of Fastolf. . . .

Item, ij. clothis of arras for the chamboure over the nether hall, of huntyng and haukyng.

Item, iiij. clothis of grene and whyte, withe braunchis sutely to the other wreten before.

Item, a coveryng of bedde of aras, withe hontyng of the bore, a man in blewe, with a jagged hoode, white and rede.

MUSIC: SONGS, 1188

Source: *Gerald the Welshman, Description of Wales,* translated by Sir R. C. Hoare, 1806, ii, 319–320.

In their musical concerts they [the Welsh] do not sing in unison like the inhabitants of other countries, but in many different parts; so that in a company of singers, which one very frequently meets with in Wales, you will hear as many different parts and voices as there are performers, who all at length unite, with organic melody, in one consonance and the soft sweetness of B flat. In the northern district of Britain, beyond the Humber, and on the borders of Yorkshire, the inhabitants make use of the same kind of symphonious harmony, but with less variety; singing only in two parts, one murmuring in the base, the other warbling in the acute or treble. Neither of the two nations has acquired this peculiarity by art, but by long habit, which has rendered it natural and familiar; and the practice is now so firmly rooted in them, that it is unusual to hear a simple and single melody well sung; and, what is still more wonderful, the children, even from their infancy, sing in the same manner. As the English in general do not adopt this mode of singing, but only those of the northern countries, I believe that it was from the Danes and Norwegians, by whom these parts of the island were more frequently invaded, and held longer under their dominion, that the natives contracted their mode of singing as well as speaking.

MUSIC: BARDS, 1188

Source: *Gerald the Welshman, Description of Wales,* translated by Sir R. C. Hoare, 1806, ii, 325–6.

There are certain persons in Cambria, whom you will find nowhere else, called Awenddyon [bards], or people inspired; when consulted upon any doubtful event, they roar out violently, are rendered beside themselves, and become, as it were, possessed by a spirit. They do not deliver the answer to what is required in a connected manner; but the person who skilfully observes them, will find, after many preambles, and many nugatory and incoherent, though ornamented speeches, the desired explanation conveyed in some turn of a word: they are then roused from their ecstacy, as from a deep sleep, and, as it were, by violence compelled to return to their proper senses. After having answered the questions, they do not recover till violently shaken by other people; nor can they remember the replies they have given. If consulted a second or third time upon the same point, they will make use of expressions totally different; perhaps they speak by the means of fanatic and ignorant spirits. These gifts are usually conferred upon them in dreams: some seem to have sweet milk or honey poured on their lips; others fancy that a written schedule is applied to their mouths, and on awaking they publicly declare they have received this gift.

MUSIC: AT THE WAYSIDE INN

Source: J. J. Jusserand, *English Wayfaring Life in the Middle Ages*, translated from the French by Lucy Toulmin, Ernest Benn, fourth ed. (sixteenth impression) 1950, p. 108. An extract from a fourteenth century manual, ' How to speak and write good French '.

Then come forward into the lord's presence the trumpeters and horn-blowers with their frestels [pipes] and clarions, and begin to play and blow very loud, and then the lord with his squires begin to move, to say, to dance, to utter and sing fine carols till midnight without ceasing.

MUSIC: A SAXON HORN

The National Museum of Dublin preserves ancient horns found in peat bogs and Polybius recalls the fear inspired in the Romans by the infinite number of the horns of the Celts who raised a terrible clamour (cf. the priests blowing rams' horns at Jericho). In early times horns came to be made of wood or bronze, but the word *bugle* means a wild ox, though the horns of other animals were used and the Horn of Ulphus in York Cathedral is an elephant's tusk. With the finger placed on the mouthpiece horns were used for drinking. Horns are often shown in manuscripts. The most famous was that in the story of Roland. Cf. p. 159.

Further Reading: J. C. Bridge, *Chester Archaeological Society's Journal*, vol. 11 (on old English Horns).

Source: Old English riddle in *The Exeter Book*, pt. ii, poems ix–xxxii, Early English Text Society O.S. no. 194, 1934 for 1933, pp. 103–4.

I was an armed warrior. Now a gallant young bachelor
covers me with gold and silver,
with twisted wires. Sometimes men kiss me.
Sometimes, by means of my sound, I summon
good comrades to battle. Sometimes a horse
carries me over the march. Sometimes the steed of the sea
bears me, bright with ornaments, over the waves.
Sometimes a woman, ring-adorned,
fills my bosom. Sometimes I must lie stripped,
hard and headless, on the boards of a table.
Sometimes, decked with trappings, and beautiful,
I hang on the wall where men are drinking.
Sometimes warriors carry me on horseback,
a noble ornament in an army, when, treasure-adorned,
I must swallow the breath from some one's breast.
Sometimes, by means of my notes, I invite
gallant men to their wine. Sometimes, by my voice,
I must rescue from foes what has been stolen
and put enemies to flight. Discover what I am called.

MUSIC: STRINGS AND WIND

At Christmas 1287 Edward I gave £50 to 125 musicians and when his daughter, Margaret married (1290) he employed 426 minstrels. It is said that in the tenth century St. Dunstan made a bronze organ for Malmesbury Abbey and that St. Alphege made one for Winchester with 400 pipes, blown by 70 men and audible all over the city. Musicians, King David and others, are often seen in manuscript illumination and in such sculpture as that at Beverley and Exeter Cathedral.

Further Reading: G. Reese, *Music in the Middle Ages*, 1941.

(1) *Source*: Chaucer. *The Hous of Fame*.

S

There herde I pleyen on an harpe
That souned bothe wel and sharpe,
Orpheus ful craftely,
And on his syde, faste by,
Sat the harper Orion, . . .
And smale harpers with her gleës [their instruments]
Seten under hem in seës [seats] . . .
Tho saugh I stonden hem behinde,
A-fer fro hem, al by hemselve,
Many thousand tymes twelve,
That maden loude menstralcyes
In cornemuse [bagpipes], and shalmyes,
And many other maner pype,
That craftly begunne pype
Bothe in doucet [dulcet] and in rede,
That ben at festes with the brede;
And many floute and lilting-horne,
And pypes made of grene corne,
As han [have] thise litel herde-gromes,
That kepen bestes in the bromes [scrub] . . .
Tho [then] saugh I in another place
Stonden in a large space,
Of hem that maken blody soun
In trumpe, beme [trumpet], and clarioun;
For in fight and blood-shedinge
Is used gladly clarioninge.

MUSIC: VARIOUS INSTRUMENTS

In addition to the harp, gittern (or guitar), psaltery, rote (crowd
or crot), rybybe (rebec or lyre), clokarde (or chime-bells), bagpipes
(single or double), panpipes, organs, bumbarde (a large shawm,
hautboy or oboe), citol (or cittern), fiddle, recorder (or flute), dulcimer,
trumpet (straight), and clarion (bent or folded trumpet) references to
medieval pictures and carvings of many other musical instruments
occur in F. W. Galpin *Old English Instruments of Music their History and
Character*, 1910. Such are the bandore (a kind of cittern), the curtall
(or bassoon), bells, clappers, clavichord, cornett (curved and straight),
cymballs, drum, flute (vertical or transverse as it is nowadays),

harpsichord (harpsicall or clavicymbal), horns, Jew's harp, kettledrums (or nakers), lute, mandore, organistrum, pipe and tabor, timbrel (or tambourine), triangle and viol (incurved).

Musicians. c. 1325. (Bromholm Psalter).

(1) *The Squyr of Lowe Degre*, an English poem of about 1400, line 1069, lists a number of medieval musical instruments:

> There was myrth and melody
> With harpe, getron and sawtry
> With rote, ribible and clockarde,
> With pypes, organs and bumbarde,
> With other mynstrelles them amonge,
> With sytolphe and with sawtry songe,
> With fydle, recorde, and dowcemere,
> With trumpette and with claryon clere,
> With dulcet pipes of many cordes.

(2) Organs are mentioned in all surviving pre-Reformation church-wardens' accounts. Church services throughout the year presented to the eye and ear Christian doctrine and history. Those used at Salisbury were widely adopted and were known as the Use of Sarum, but as late as 1322 the Bishop noticed that the choir boys had to go round begging from the canons as no endowment hitherto allowed them to devote their time to the services and to their studies. Medieval polyphony, used to distinguish festivals, and largely developed in colleges and private chapels, was historically important as the ancestor of later

techniques of composition, but Dr. Harrison stresses that ' plainsong was the staple fare of the medieval musician, the material of his musical education and the basis of his professional qualification '.

Further Reading: Publications of Plainsong and Medieval Music Society and the Henry Bradshaw Society.

Source: F. L. Harrison, *Music in Medieval Britain*, Routledge and Kegan Paul, 1958, p. 5, quoting Statutes and Customs of Salisbury, for c. 1256 (when there were at least thirteen vicars on each side of the choir).

The church of Salisbury shines as the sun in its orb among the churches of the whole world in its divine service and those who minister in it, and by spreading its rays everywhere makes up for the defects of others. Therefore, lest through our neglect its splendour should be diminished by the unworthiness of its ministers, we ordain that hereafter none shall be presented to the office of vicar in this church unless he has a good and musical voice and skill in plainsong, besides the merits of character required in such ministers.

DANCING

The girls of Norman London used to dance late into the night (*T.S.I.H.*, i, 98). Both the Saxons and the Welsh loved *caroles*, a combination of singing and dancing, and in the fourteenth century Morris dancing is supposed to have been adopted from the Moors of southern Spain. *Caroles* marked the festivities of Christmas and Mayday; and brides were expected to dance with their guests at weddings. Dancing girls also gave acrobatic performances at royal feasts. Of all these dances only those of the Morris men survived, to be performed in the late nineteenth century in the villages round Oxford and there revived without any real break in continuity. Mystical writings of the fourteenth century describe Fifteen Signs preceding the Last Judgement. On the third of these, as illustrated in the Holkham Bible, great sea monsters bray. This idea is derived from *Job* xii, 8, and is a special punishment for those excessively fond of dances, plays and songs. Their future woe was inferred from *Luke* vi, 24–5 long before seventeenth century Puritans spoilt the sports of Merry England. Edward III gave his queen a ' daunsyng chambre ' in Windsor Castle.

Further Reading: M. Dolmetsch, *Dances of England and France*, 1450–1600, 1949 (bibliography).

(1) *Source*: *Arthour and Merlin* (a romance).

> Miri time it is in May,
> Than wexeth along the day,
> Flowers schewen her borioun [burgeon, bud],
> Miri it is in feld and toun,
> Foules miri in wode gredeth [call],
> Damisels carols ledeth.

(Note: Robert Mannyng in *Handlyng Synne* uses *carol* in this sense and calls Stonehenge 'the Karolle of the stones'.

(2) *Source*: 'Launfal Miles.' E. Rickert, *Early English Romances done into Modern English, Romances of Love*, Chatto and Windus, 1908, pp. 71–2.

After meat, Sir Gawayn, Sir Gaheris, and Agravayne went with Sir Launfal to dance on the green beneath the tower where the queen lay, with sixty maidens and more. Launfal, who was loved of all for his largess, was set to lead the dance; and the queen leaned forth and watched them.

'There is Launfal dancing,' she said, 'that man of bounty! I will go down to him. He is the fairest bachelor among all the knights I see. He never had a wife; so, tide me good or ill, I will go about to learn his disposition, for I love him as my life .'

She took with her a company of five and sixty ladies, the fairest she could gather; and in orderly throng they passed down to disport them with the knights.

The queen herself went to the foremost end, between Launfal and Gawayn the courteous; and, following her ensample, her ladies went all to take part in the dance; and indeed it was a fair sight to see them at it, always a lady and a knight together.

When the dance grew slack, the queen took Launfal aside. [She declares her love and is enraged because he will not betray King Arthur.]

GREAT ESTATES

Great estates were managed as if they were kingdoms, though they differed from kingdoms in that their lords were under various obligations to the king to whom fell the whole estates as 'escheats' in case of treason.

In fourteenth century England a group of twenty earls and dukes were outstandingly wealthy. At the top of the scale John of Gaunt had over £12,000 a year. The importance of such magnates compared with both lesser barons and the king was increasing, though royal favour was necessary for survival. The ambitions of great lords and the disorder caused by their retainers culminated in the Wars of the Roses. An example of this occurred in Devon and was thus reported by James Gresham in a letter to John Paston at Norwich.

Further Reading: G. H. White, ' The Great Officers of State ', *Genealogists' Magazine*, vol. 11, no. 15. G. A. Holmes, *The Estates of the Higher Nobility in xiv century England*, Cambridge University Press 1957.

Source: *The Paston Letters 1422–1509*, ed. by James Gairdner, A. Constable, 1900, i, 350. This vast collection of letters is full of personal and legal business with reports of the public events of the time.

... Also there is [28 October 1455] gret varyance bytwene the Erll of Devenshire and the Lord Bonvyle, as hath be many day, and meche debat is like to growe therby; for on Thursday at nyght last passed, the Erll of Denshyres sone and heir come with lx. men of armes to Radford's place in Devenshire, whiche was of counseil with my Lord Bonvyle; and they sette an hous on fyer at Radfords gate, and cryed and mad an noyse as though they had be sory for the fyer; and by that cause Radfords men set opyn the gats and yede owt to se the fyer; and for with th'erl sone forseid entred into the place and intreted Radford to come doun of his chambre to speke with them, promyttyng hym that he shuld no bodyly harm have; up on whiche promysse he come doun, and spak with the seid Erll sone.

In the mene tyme his menye robbe his chambre, and ryfled his huches [chests], and trussed suyche as they coude gete to gydder, and caryed it awey on his own hors. Thanne th'erll sone seid, ' Radford, thou must come to my lord my fadir '. He seid he wold, and bad oon of his men make redy his hors to ride with hem, whiche answered hym that alle his hors wern take awey; thanne he seid to th'erll sone, ' Sir, your men have robbed my chambre, and their have myn hors, that I may not ride with you to my lord your fadir, wherfor, I pray you, lete me ride, for I am old, and may not go.'

It was answerid hym ageyn, that he shuld walke forth with

them on his feete; and so he dede till he as a flyte shote or more from his place . . . forwith come ix. men ageyn up on hym, and smot hym in the hed, and . . . kyt his throte. . . .

HERALDS

A *gentleman* was a person entitled to use a coat of arms and not even a knight was ' gentle ' unless he had either inherited arms or received arms by marriage or by a grant from a prince or herald. Merchants and others had distinctive marks, but these did not count as ' arms '. The description of arms had to avoid all possibility of confusion and so a highly technical language developed for the purpose. Heraldry developed in the thirteenth century and examples of early heraldic glass and seals are illustrated in *W.W.I.H.*, i, pls. 11, 12. By the fifteenth century the study of heraldry had become part of any gentleman's education. Largely illiterate people attached great importance to symbols and their meaning; so, apart from the utility of coats of arms as distinguishing marks for men in armour, some of the objects or ' charges ' used by particular families had inner meanings which would have been more real then then they seem nowadays.

At the Battle of Navarrete (1367) or Najara, Pedro the Cruel defeated his rival, Henry of Trastamara. In the ceremony here described Pedro promoted Sir John Chandos to the rank of Knight-Banneret, symbolically turning his pointed pennon into a square banner. This could only be conferred on a man able to support fifty men-at-arms. For a description of an earlier banner (1138), see *T.S.I.H.*, i, 68.

Further Reading: A. R. Wagner, *Heralds and Heraldry of the Middle Ages*, 2nd ed. Oxford University Press, 1956.
   Coat of Arms.

Source: Sir John Froissart, *The Chronicles of England, France, Spain, etc., etc.* Epitomized edition, Routledge, 1891, pp. 102–3.

It was a beautiful sight to see them approach with their brilliant armour glittering with the sunbeams. . . . Sir John Chandos advanced in front of the battalions with his banner uncased in his hand. He presented it to the [Black] Prince, saying, ' My lord, here is my banner: I present it to you, that I may display it in whatever manner shall be most agreeable to you; for, thanks to God, I have now sufficient lands to enable me to do so, and maintain the rank which it ought to hold '. The prince, Don Pedro being present, took the banner which was blazoned with a sharp stake gules on a field argent, in his hands; and, having cut off the tail to make the square, he displayed it, and returning it to him by the handle, said, ' Sir John, I return you your banner. God give you strength and honour to preserve it '. Upon this, Sir John left the prince, went back to his men with the banner in his hand, and said to them, ' Gentlemen, behold my banner, and yours; you will therefore guard it as it becomes you '. His companions taking the banner, replied with much cheerfulness, that ' if it pleased God and St. George, they would defend it well, and act worthily of it, to the utmost of their abilities '. The banner was put into the hands of a worthy English squire, called William Allestry, who bore it with honour that day, and loyally acquitted himself in the service. The English and Gascons soon after dismounted on the heath, and assembled very orderly together, each lord under his banner or pennon, in the same battle array as when they passed the mountains. It was delightful to see and examine these banners and pennons, with the noble army that was under them.

OATH ON RELICS

People were confident that divine vengeance would soon punish anybody who broke a solemn oath.

Source: Laws of King Cnut (1017–1035); B. Thorpe, *Ancient Laws and Institutes of England*, 1840, p. 171.

And if any one swear false oath on a relic, and he be convicted, let him forfeit his hands, or half his ' wēr ' [what he is valued at in money]; and let that be common to lord and bishop. And let him not be thenceforth oath-worthy; unless he the more thoroughly before God make ' bot ' [amends], and find him ' borh ' [surety] that he will ever after abstain from the like.

TRIAL BY COMBAT, c. 1290

People believed that God would bless a just cause by victory.

Source: Britton, *the French Text carefully revised with an English translation introduction and notes by Francis Morgan Nichols*, vol. 1, Clarendon Press 1865, pp. 106–8.

Then let them both be brought to a place appointed for that purpose, where they must swear thus. ' Hear this, ye Justices, that I John (or I Peter) have neither eaten nor drunk anything, nor done or caused to be done any other thing, whereby the law of God may be abased, and the law of the devil advanced or exalted.' And thus let it be done in all battles in appeals of felony. And let proclamation be immediately made, that no one, except the combatants, whatever thing he see or hear, be so bold as to stir, or cry aloud, whereby the battle may be disturbed; and whosoever disobeys the proclamation shall be imprisoned a year and a day.

Next, let them go to combat, armed without iron and without the slightest armour, their heads uncovered, their hands and feet bare, with two staves tipped with horn of equal length, and each of them a target of four corners, without any other arms, whereby either of them may annoy the other; and if either of them have any other arms concealed about him, and therewith annoy or offer to annoy his adversary, let it be done as shall be mentioned in treating of battle in a plea of land.

If the defendant can defend himself until the stars can be seen in the firmament, and demands judgment whether he ought to combat any longer, our will is, that judgment pass for the defendant, and so in all battles between champions; and in the case of felony the appellor shall be committed to prison. . . .

And if the defendant be vanquished, let the judgment be this, that he be drawn and hanged, or put to such other painful death as we shall direct, and that all his movable goods be ours, and his heirs disinherited; and his children shall be incapable of ever holding land in our realm. And let not any, unless they would be suspected themselves of the felony, presume to intercede for him; and let the accuser, who without delay shall prosecute such felony with good effect, receive from us a notable reward. Appeals may likewise be sued for us in the same manner for counterfeiting our seal and our coin, and also for violating our consort, or our daughters, or the nurses of our children; and in such cases, the judgment is, to be drawn and hanged. . . .

ORDEAL BY WATER

Trial by ordeal by water was abolished in the third year of the reign of Henry III. The accused person was undressed, and cast, with his thumbs and his toes tied together into water. If he sank he was 'not guilty'. In the twelfth year of the reign of Henry II the sheriff of Norfolk and Suffolk accounted for the property of Richard Haiward and others who thus perished. For the parallel ordeal by fire see *T.S.I.H.*, i, 24, where the relevant law of King Athelstan is translated.

Source: Translation in W. Dugdale, *Origines Juridiciales*, 1680, pp. 86–7.

The three days fast and other holy Duties performed (as in the Tryal by Fire Ordale) Holy water is given unto the party accused, which he is to drink with the following Execration; Let this water be to thee now a Tryal. Whereupon this following Conjuration is to be used to the cold water wherein the person supposed guilty is to be put; viz.

I adjure thee, O thou Water, in the name of the Father Almighty, who created thee in the beginning, commanding thy use for humane necessities, and that thou shouldest be separated from the Waters above. I adjure thee, by the unspeakable name of the Lord Jesus Christ, Son of the living God, under whose feet, the Sea and Element being severed, was trode upon; and who was pleased to be baptized in the watery Element. I also adjure thee by the Holy Ghost, which descended upon the Lord when he was baptized. I adjure thee likewise by the name of the holy and individual Trinity, by whose will the Element of waters was divided, and the people of Israel forthwith passed thorough dry foot; At whose invocation the Prophet Helisaeas caused the Axe which fell out of the Helve, to swim upon the water, that thou do not in any manner receive this man N. if he be guilty of what he is accused, by his act, consent, or knowledge, or any other device; but make him swim upon thee; to the end there may be no counterfeiting with thee, or any exploit of the Enemy, that may disguise it. And by the name of Christ, we command thee, that for his sake thou obey us, unto whom every creature doth service; whom Cherubim and Seraphim do praise; saying, Holy, Holy, Holy, Lord God of Hosts, who ruleth and reigneth world without end.

PRAYERS BEFORE UNDERGOING THE ORDEAL

Source: William of Malmesbury, *Chronicle of the Kings of England*, transl. J. A. Giles, Bohn's Antiquarian Library, 1866, pp. 22–23 (describing Glastonbury, early twelfth century.)

The antiquity [of Glastonbury Abbey], and multitude of its saints, have endued the place with so much sanctity, that, at night, scarcely any one presumes to keep vigil there, or, during the day, to spit upon its floor; he who is conscious of pollution shudders throughout his whole frame: no one ever brought hawk or horses within the confines of the neighbouring cemetery, who did not depart injured either in them or in himself. Within the memory of man, all persons who, before undergoing the ordeal of fire [handling hot iron] or water, there put up their petitions, exulted in their escape, one only excepted: if any person erected a building in the vicinity, which by its shade obstructed the light of the church, it forthwith became a ruin. And it is sufficiently evident, that, the men of that province had no oath more frequent, or more sacred, than to swear by the Old Church, fearing the swiftest vengeance on their perjury in this respect.

JUSTICES IN EYRE, 1176-9

Itinerant Justices travelling round the counties from time to time became a useful means whereby the King could check the power of the sheriffs and could keep the counties in touch with the central government.

Source: Charles Johnson, *Dialogus de Scaccario The Course of the Exchequer* (1176–9), Nelson 1950, p. 77.

. . . making choice of prudent men, he [Henry II] divided the kingdom into six parts, so that the justices chosen, whom we call ' Justices in Eyre ' might go on circuit through them and restore the rights which had lapsed. They, giving audience in each county, and doing justice to those who considered themselves wronged, saved the poor both money and labour [of going to the royal court at Westminster]. But, as it happens, in these proceedings different offences are punished in different ways, according to their nature, some by corporal and others by pecuniary penalties. These latter are carefully set down in the Eyre Rolls and, when the Exchequer sits, are handed to the Treasurer in full court. But let the justices see to it that they hand over their rolls to the Treasurer correct and in order! For, once they have been handed over, not even the justices themselves may alter one jot, though all should agree to it.

JUDGES, 1464-70

Source: Sir John Fortescue, *On the Laws of England*, translated by Francis Gregor, 1737, chapter 51.

... from thenceforth [after appointment], he changes his habit in some few particulars, but not in all: for when only a Serjeant-at-Law, he is clothed in a long robe, not unlike the sacerdotal habit, with a furred cape about his shoulders, and an hood over it with two labels or tippets; such as the Doctors of Law use in some universities, with a coif, ... But after he is made a Judge, instead of the hood he shall be habited with a cloak, fastened upon his right shoulder; he still retains the other ornaments of a Serjeant, with this exception, that a Judge should not use a party-coloured habit, as the Serjeants do, and his cape is furred with minever, whereas the Serjeant's cape is always furred with white lamb; which sort of habit, when you [Prince Edward, son of Henry VI] come in power, I could wish your highness would make a little more ornamental, in honour of the laws, and also of your Government. You are to know further, that the Judges of England do not sit in the King's Courts above three hours in the day, that is, from eight in the morning till eleven. The courts are not open in the afternoon. The suiters of the court betake themselves to the pervise, and other places, to advise with the Serjeants-at-Law, and other their counsel, about their affairs. The Judges, when they have taken their refreshments, spend the rest of the day in the study of the laws, reading of the Holy Scriptures, and other innocent amusements, at their pleasure; it seems rather a life of contemplation than of much action: their time is spent in this manner, free from care and worldly avocations.

Nor was it ever found that any of them has been corrupted with gifts or bribes. And it has been observed, as an especial dispensation of Providence, that they have been happy in leaving behind them immediate descendants in a right line. . . . And I think it is no less a peculiar blessing, that from amongst the Judges and their offspring, more Peers and great men of the realm have risen, than from any other profession or estate of men whatsoever who have rendered themselves wealthy, illustrious, and noble by their own applications, parts, and industry. Although the merchants are more in number by some thousands and some of them excel in riches all the Judges put together. . . .

TOWN GOVERNMENT

Customs and constitutions varied from town to town and in each the exact wording and the date of the charter which it obtained from its lord was important as well as the circumstances of its origin and growth. Each had its own laws. The word ' by-laws ' is derived from *by*, a word meaning a town in Danish and the last syllable of the names of many towns, like Rugby and Selby, in the part of England controlled by the Danes.

Further Reading: J. Tait, *Story of Early Municipal History*, 1922.

(1) Judgments of Pillory for Lies, Slanders, Falsehoods and Deceits.

Source: *Liber Albus the White Book of the City of London compiled in* A.D. 1419 *by John Carpenter and Richard Whittington*, translated by H. T. Riley, Richard Griffin, 1861, pp. 517–526.

(A list of judgments too lengthy for detailed inclusion).

A certain man adjudged to the Pillory for pretending that he was a Sheriff's Serjeant, meeting the Bakers of Stratforde, and placing them under arrest until they had paid a fine. . . .

Judgment of Pillory for putrid meat. . . .

Judgment of Pillory for forestalment [buying up improperly for a profit] of poultry. . . .

Judgment of Pillory for selling two stinking capons. . . .

Judgment of Pillory for a stinking rabbit sold. . . .

Judgment of Pillory for selling a putrid pigeon

Judgment of Imprisonment upon a person for a year and a day, and of Pillory each quarter for three hours, with a whetstone tied round his neck, for lies which were disproved [cf. the old phrase ' lying for the whetstone ']

Judgment of Pillory upon a person for pretending to be a Summoner of the Archbishop, and summoning the Prioress of Clerkenwelle; as also for pretending to be a Purveyor for the King

Judgment of Pillory for selling a peck of stinking eels

Judgment of Pillory for enhancing the price of corn

Judgment of Pillory for selling oats, good on the outside and the rest bad

Judgment of Pillory for making false deeds. . . .

Judgment of Pillory for deficiency of coal in sacks. . . .

Judgment of Pillory for rings and buckles made of latten [brass] plated with gold and silver, and sold for gold and silver

Judgment of Pillory upon certain Bakers, who had holes in their tables, called ' *moldyngbordes* ', by means whereof they stole their neighbours' dough. . . .

Judgment of Pillory for cutting a certain purse. . .

Judgment of Pillory upon a person for taking away a child, to go begging with him. . . .

Judgment of Pillory upon a person for false dice, with which he played and deceived people. . . .

Judgment of Pillory for a false obligation [forged bond]. . . .

Judgment of Pillory for a certain false and counterfeit letter

Judgment of Pillory for a deception committed, namely, counters [jettons or Nuremberg tokens made of brass] passed as gold. . . .

Judgment of Pillory for lies uttered against the Mayor and Aldermen. . . .

Judgment of Pillory for selling a stinking partridge. . . .

Judgment of Pillory for lies uttered against William Walworthe [the slayer of Wat Tyler]

Judgment of Pillory upon Two Men for begging under false pretences. . . .

Judgment of Pillory for Soothsaying as to a mazer that had been stolen. . . .

Judgment of Pillory for enhancing the market

Judgment of Pillory for practising the Art Magic. . . .

Judgment of Pillory for placing a certain piece of iron in a loaf of bread

Judgment of the Pillory for cutting off a baselard [short sword]; and Abjuration of the City. . . .

Judgment of Pillory upon John Hasilwode, for a false seizure of ale. . . .

Judgment of Pillory for false bow-strings. . . .

Judgment of Pillory upon one who feigned himself a holy Hermit

Judgment of Pillory upon three men, counterfeiters of the Seal of his lordship the Pope, and of others, Lords of England

Judgment of Pillory upon Laurence Neuport, who exposed divers counterfeit Bulls [from the Pope]

(2) The Recorder of the City of London, 1419.

Source: *Liber Albus, the White Book of the City of London compiled in* A.D. 1419 *by John Carpenter and Richard Whittington*, translated by H. T. Riley, Richard Griffin 1861, p. 38.

The Recorder of the City of London should be, and of usage has been, one of the most skilful and most virtuous apprentices-at-law [barristers of less than 16 years' standing] in the whole kingdom. His duty is, always to be seated at the Mayor's right hand when recording pleas and delivering judgments; and by his lips records and processes holden before the Mayor and Aldermen at Saint Martin's le Grand, in presence of the Justiciars assigned for the correcting there of errors, ought orally to be recorded. And further, the Mayor and Aldermen have been accustomed commonly to set forth all other matters touching the City in presence of his lordship the King and his Council, as also in all the royal Courts, by the mouth of such Recorder, as being a man more especially imbued with knowledge, and conspicuous for the brilliancy of his eloquence.

The Recorder's fee was in former times greater or smaller, according as the occasion and his own deserts demanded. . . But at the present day, and indeed for many years past, his fee has stood at a fixed sum of one hundred marks. The Recorder has also from the Chamber by way of fee, the like vestments, whether lined or edged with fur, as often as the Mayor and Alderman in each year receive the same; his clerk also is provided therewith, like the sergeants of the Chamber. The Recorder is also wont, and his clerk, to sit at table with the Mayor, etc.

SANCTUARY

(1) At Durham is a great bronze chiselled knocker placed in Norman times on the door of the sanctuary and a register records 283 persons admitted there between 1464 and 1524 for crimes which included 195 murders and homicides. At Beverley is a famous stone chair in which a criminal was safer than anywhere in England. At Hexham sanctuary extended for a mile or more around the outside of the church and there is a similar chair there and another at Sprotborough, Yorks. In *W.W.I.H.*, vol. 1 there is a drawing by Matthew Paris of Hubert de Burgh seeking sanctuary. The artist explains that Hubert took sanctuary more than once and that the illustration will serve for both occasions. This extract shows the punishment of Nicholas le Porter who took some escapers from the Carmelite church at Newcastle. He might have been killed.

Further Reading: Rev. J. C. Cox, *The Sanctuaries and Sanctuary Seekers of Medieval England*, 1911.

Source: J. J. Jusserand, *English Wayfaring Life in the Middle Ages*, translated from the French by Lucy Toulmin Smith, Ernest Benn, fourth ed. (sixteenth impression), 1950, p. 81 (Order from the Bishop to the parson of St. Nicholas, Durham, 1313).

We order that on Monday, Tuesday, and Wednesday of the Whitsun-week just coming, he shall receive the whip from your hands publicly, before the chief door of your church, in his shirt, bare-headed, and barefoot. He shall there proclaim in English the reason for his penance and shall admit his fault; and when he has thus been whipped the said Nicholas will go to the cathedral church of Durham, bareheaded, bare-foot, and dressed as above, he will walk in front, you will follow him; and you will whip him in the same manner before the door of the cathedral these three days, and he will repeat there the confession of his sin.

(2) *Source*: Gerald the Welshman, *Description of Wales*, translated by Sir R. C. Hoare, 1806, ii, 335 (1188).

PLATE XXV

PUBLIC LIFE

70. Fortune's wheel. A new king rises and an old king, Edward II, falls.

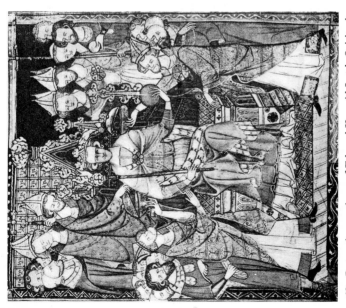

69. Coronation, perhaps of Edward II, amid Lords Spiritual and Temporal.

71. Peasants with spade, pitchfork and scythe.

Barons in chain-mail and pointed helmets (kite shaped shields wi early heraldic devices.)

72. Bishops and Abbo with mitr and croziers.

Nightmares of Henry I. Three classes threatening him, 1130–4. Secular pictures are very rare so early.

We observe that they [the Welsh] show a greater respect than other nations to churches and ecclesiastical persons, to the relics of saints, bells, holy books, and the cross, which they devoutly revere; and hence their churches enjoy more than common tranquillity. For peace is not only preserved towards all animals feeding in churchyards, but at a great distance beyond them, where certain boundaries and ditches have been appointed by the bishops, in order to maintain the security of the sanctuary. But the principal churches to which antiquity has annexed the greater reverence extend their protection to the herds as far as they can go to feed in the morning and return at night. If, therefore, any person has incurred the enmity of his prince, on applying to the church for protection, he and his family will continue to live unmolested; but many persons abuse this indemnity, far exceeding the indulgence of the canon, which in such cases grants only personal safety; and from the places of refuge even make hostile irruptions, and more severely harass the country than the prince himself.

(3) *Source*: *Calendar of the Coroners Rolls of the City of London*, 1300–1378, ed. R. R. Sharpe, London Corporation Library Committee, printed by R. Clay and Sons, 1913, pp. 84–5. 24 May, 1324.

John de Whetely of Chester and . . . John le Belringere sat playing and drinking . . . strife arose between them, so that . . . John de Wheteley drew his knife . . . and fatally struck . . . John le Belringere therewith on the throat inflicting a mortal wound an inch and a half long and two inches deep, and when the said John le Belringere at length left the house he fell down outside the door of the house and forthwith died. Being asked who were present when this happened, the jurors say no one except . . . John de Wheteley. Being asked what became of the said John, they say that he immediately fled to the church of All Hallows at the Hay, where the said Coroner and Sheriffs immediately came to him; that the said John confessed himself guilty of the felony and refused to surrender himself to the King's peace but asked to abjure the realm and did abjure it on Sunday the Feast of Pentecost following. He chose the port of Bristol to cross the sea in five days, viz.: the first day to Wicombe, the second to Oxford, the

T

third to Hegheworth (Highworth, Wilts.), the fourth to Malmes-
buri, and the fifth to Bristol, thence to cross the sea at the first
tide. . . .

ANARCHY, 1143

The cruel lawlessness of the barons during the feeble reign of
Stephen is described in the Anglo-Saxon Chronicle entry for 1137
(*T.S.I.H.*, i, p. 64). William Cumin seized the bishopric of Durham.
A monk thus describes his conduct (1143).

Further Reading: K. C. Newton, 'A Feudal Landowner and Lawlessness in the 14th century ', *Essex Review*, vol. 64, no. 256.

Source: Simeon of Durham, translated by Rev. J. Stevenson in
The Church Historians of England, vol. 3, pt. 2, Seeleys 1855.

His soldiers were incessantly making forages; they ranged
through every spot in the whole district; whatever they could
lay their hands on they plundered; their inroads ceased neither
day nor night; all that came in their way was destroyed—some
of it they burnt, some they destroyed; all the produce of the
fields they ruined either by treading it down or by depasturing
cattle upon it; and thus the land which had been cultivated
became barren and devastated by being trodden under foot.
Just as effectually as locusts give proof of presence by nipping
off the leaves and flowers from a tree, so wherever these men
passed it became a wilderness. They associated with themselves
such as were the most depraved and the most notorious for their
excesses; one struggled against the other for mastery in evil; the
greater the cruelty the greater the admiration. Even to hear of
their doings was terrible; but to see them was something yet
worse. Their insolence was not confined to ravages and plunder-
ings only, but was extended to the cruel bodily torments, inflicted
not in secret, and in the darkness of the night, and upon only a
few individuals, but perpetrated openly; and in the sight of day,
and upon men of the nobler rank. Their torments were of many
and various kinds, difficult to describe and incredible to believe.
Men were hung from the walls of their own houses; cords being
tightly twisted round their middle, and heavy armour or large
stones tied to the neck and feet, so that the extremities of the

body were bent towards the ground, which, however, they did not touch. Upon one occasion more than twelve persons were discovered together suspended in this manner; others of them they plunged into the bed of the river in the depth of winter, after having broken the ice with which it was covered; and having tied ropes round them, they alternately dragged them out of it and thrust them back again, feeding their cruelty with such a spectacle of misery. The feet of some they thrust through holes made in the wall, and thus exposed their naked bodies to the extremity of the cold, leaving them in this misery all the night long. In addition to all these, they employed a most refined piece of cruelty, by which the limbs were wedged together and thrust within a very narrow chest, a novel device in the mystery of tormenting which eclipsed all former efforts. It was in direct antagonism to the older punishment of the rack, which stretched the limbs to an undue length; whereas, by this present device, they were crushed and cramped up into a narrow space, by which process they were sometimes fractured. Who is able to give an account of the immensity of the chains, or the stench of the prison-house, or the sharpness of the hunger to which they were exposed? But let me not be tedious; everywhere throughout the town there were groans and various kinds of deaths. In consequence of such horrible proceedings the place, which had hitherto been so highly honoured, now became a terror to all, and was surnamed the place of the tortures of hell.

BEGGARS

The Church taught the importance of acts of mercy and the charity of kings and magnates could be so great that on Good Friday 1203 King John paid £80 to feed a thousand poor people and the following May he provided bread and gruel daily to three hundred in London and eighteen hundred elsewhere. Edward I supplied 666 with food every Sunday. In the Holkham Bible Picture Book Christ is shown with a crowd of unfortunates, a blind man with a stick, a spotted leper with defective nose and two of the halt and maimed. Such crowds of cripples and blindmen flocked for healing in 1327 to a memorial which Thomas of Lancaster had placed in St. Paul's. Two hundred beds were provided for such paupers at St. Leonard's Hospital, York, and there were many others.

Further Reading: Brian Tierney, *Medieval Poor Law*: a *sketch of Canonical Theory and its application in England*, California University Press, 1959.

Professor Hilda Johnstone, ' Poor Relief in the Royal Households of Thirteenth Century England ', *Speculum*, iv, (1929), p. 149.

(1) *Source*: Statute of Labourers, 23 Edward III cap 7 (translated as in edition of 1577). (1350)

Item because that many valiaunt beggers, so long as they may live of begging, do refuse to labour, geving themselves to Idlenesse and vice, and sometime to theft, and other abhominations: None upon the said payne of imprisonment, shal under the colour of pitie or almes geve any thing to such, which may labour, or presume to favour them towardes their desires, so that thereby they may be compelled to labour for their necessarie living. Wherefore our said soveraigne lord the king, the 14 day of June the 23 yeare of his raigne, hath commaunded to al the sheriffes of England by diverse writts, that they shal do openly to be proclaimed and holden, al and singuler the premisses in the counties, boroughs, marchaunt townes, sea portes and other places in their bayliweekes, where to them shal seeme expedient. And that they doe thereof due execution, as afore is said.

(2) *Source*: *Calendar of Coroners' 1913 Rolls of the City of London*, A.D. 1300–1378, ed. R. R. Sharpe printed for the Corporation by R. Clay and Sons, 1913, p. 61 (3 July 1322).

. . . many poor people lay dead . . . within Ludgate around the gate of the Preaching Friars in the Ward of Farndone. On hearing this . . . the Coroner and Sheriffs proceeded thither, and . . . diligently enquired how it happened. The jurors say that when at daybreak of that day a great multitude of poor people were assembled at the gate of the Friars Preachers seeking alms, Robert Fynel, Simon, Robert and William his sons and 22 other male persons, names unknown, Matilda, daughter of Robert le Carpenter, Beatriz Cole, Johanna, ' le Peyntures ', Alice la Norice [the nurse] and 22 other women, names unknown, whilst entering the gate were fatally crushed owing to the numbers, and immediately died thereof and of no other felony.

CRUSADES

From an English point of view the most important episode in the conflict between the Christian and Mohammedan worlds was the Third Crusade in which Richard I played a distinguished part (see *W.W.I.H.*, i, p. 102 and *T.S.I.H.*, i, pp. 101–2) at the siege of Acre and in which Ranulf Glanville shared the sufferings of the starving army (*W.W.I.H.*, i, p. 100). Robert Curthose and Richard Earl of Cornwall, the brothers of William II and Henry III, and Edward I, as prince, were also crusaders. The most devoted crusaders were members of the fighting orders of monks, the Templars and the Hospitallers.

Further Reading: F. C. Woodhouse, *Military Religious Orders of the Middle Ages*, 1879.

Sir C. Oman, *History of the Art of War in the Middle Ages*, 2nd ed., 2 vols. 1924. R. C. Smail, *Crusading Warfare* (1097–1193). *A Contribution to Medieval Military History*. (Cambridge Studies in Medieval Life and Thought, N.S. vol. 3). Cambridge University Press, 1956.

Source: *Gerald the Welshman, Itinerary through Wales*, translated by Sir R. C. Hoare, 1806, ii, 38–9.

. . . the word of the Lord was persuasively preached [on the Pembrokeshire side of the River Teivi] both by the archbishop and the archdeacon, and many were induced to take the cross; one of whom was an only son, and the sole comfort of his mother, far advanced in years, who, steadfastly gazing on him, as if inspired by the Deity, uttered these words:—' O, most beloved Lord Jesus Christ, I return thee hearty thanks for having conferred on me the blessing of bringing forth a son, whom thou mayest think worthy of thy service.' Another woman at Aberteivi, of a very different way of thinking held her husband fast by his cloak and girdle, and publicly and audaciously prevented him from going to the archbishop to take the cross; but, three nights afterwards, she heard a terrible voice, saying ' Thou hast taken away my servant from me, therefore what thou most lovest shall be taken away from thee '. On her relating this vision to her husband, they were struck with mutual terror and amazement; and on falling asleep again, she unhappily overlaid her little boy, whom, with more affection than prudence, she had taken to bed with her. The husband, relating to the bishop of the diocese both the vision and its fatal prediction, took the cross, which his wife spontaneously sewed on her husband's arm.

WAR IN THE MARCHES, 1188

Further Reading: J. E. Morris, *The Welsh Wars of Edward I*, Oxford, 1901.

Source: *Gerald the Welshman*, *Description of Wales*, translated by Sir R. C. Hoare, 1806, ii, 354–5.

In this, as well as in every other military expedition, either in Ireland or in Wales, the natives of the marches, from the constant state of warfare in which they are engaged, and whose manners are formed from the habits of war, are bold and active, skilful on horseback, quick on foot, not nice as to their diet, and ever prepared when necessity required to abstain both from corn and wine. By such men were the first hostile attacks made upon Wales as well as Ireland, and by such men alone can their final conquest be accomplished . . . but the Gallic soldiery is known to differ much from the Welsh and Irish. In their country [Normandy, Flanders etc.] the battle is on level, here on rough ground; there in an open field, here in forests; there they consider their armour as honour, here as a burden; there soldiers are taken prisoners, here they are beheaded; there they are ransomed here they are put to death. Where, therefore, the armies engage in a flat country, a heavy and complex armour, made of cloth and iron, both protects and decorates the soldier; but when the engagement is in narrow defiles, in woods and marshes, where infantry have the advantage over cavalry, a light armour is preferable. For light arms afford sufficient protection against unarmed men, by whom victory is either lost or won at the first onset; where it is necessary that an active and retreating enemy should be overcome by a certain proportional quantity of moderate armour; whereas with a more complex sort, and with high and curved saddles, it is difficult to dismount, more so to mount, and with the greatest difficulty can such troops march, if required, with the infantry. . . .

THE BAGGAGE TRAIN, 1360

Edward III marched with a great army from Rheims to Paris, shortly before the conclusion of peace. The presence of hounds was later paralleled in the Peninsular War when the Duke of Wellington kept his pack. For a similar, but peaceful, progress towards Paris, made in 1158 by Thomas Becket, see *T.S.I.H.*, i, 78–80.

Further Reading: G. H. Fowler, ' Munitions in 1224,' *Transactions of the Bedfordshire Historical Records Soc.*, vol. 5, 1920.

Source: Froissart, *Chronique*, vol. 1, chapter, 210, translated extract.

You ought to know that the King of England and the rich brought with them on their carts tents, pavilions, mills, cooking ovens, horse smithies and everything needful. And to furnish this they brought along quite six thousand carts, each with four good strong carthorses brought out of England. And on the carts they had many boats, so cleverly made of boiled leather that it was surprising to see them. They could carry three men so as to float on even the biggest lake or fishpond and fish at will. Thus they were quite comfortable in Lent—that is to say the Lords and people of standing. But the common folk had to make do with what they could get. Furthermore the king personally had thirty mounted falconers with birds and sixty couples of strong hounds and the same number of greyhounds. With these he went hunting or fishing every day according to his fancy. Many of the noble and wealthy also had their dogs and birds like the king. They were arranged in three columns.

EVACUATION AND SCORCHED EARTH

Source: Matthew Paris, *English History*, Bohn's Antiquarian Library, 1854, p. 238. (1257)

About the same time the King [Henry III] issued his warrants throughout all England, calling on each and every one who owed knightly service to their lord and king to be ready and prepared, provided with horses and arms, to follow him into Wales, on the feast of St. Mary Magdalen, whither he was about to proceed on an expedition to check their violence; as they were roving about at will, seizing the castles of the frontier nobles, and even those of the English, with impunity, putting the garrisons to death, and spreading fire, slaughter, and incendiarism in all directions. The Welsh, thereon, learning that the king intended to take the field against them with his army, prudently sent away their wives, children, and flocks into the interior of the country, about Snowdon and other mountainous places inaccessible to the English, ploughed up their fields, destroyed the mills in the road which the English would take, carried away all kinds of provisions, broke down the bridges, and rendered the fords impassable by digging holes, in order that, if the enemy attempted to cross, they might be drowned. Fortune favoured them in this war; for their cause appeared, even to their enemies, to be just; and what chiefly supported and encouraged them was the thought that, like the Trojans, from whom they were descended, they were struggling, with a firmness worthy of their descent, for their ancestral laws and liberty.

MASSACRE

After a month or more of mining and countermining the miners caused part of the wall of Limoges to fall and fill the ditch so that Edward the Black Prince, the Duke of Lancaster and the other English could enter. There followed a massacre which shows how merciless the days of chivalry could be (1370).

Source: Froissart, *Chronicle*, translated by Sir John Bourchier, Lord Berners, 1523-5, ii, 355.

Than the Prince, the Duke of Lancastre, the Erle of Cambridge, the Erle of Penbroke, Sir Guyssharde Dangle, and all the other, with their companyes, entred into the cyte, and all other fote men redy aparelled to do yvell, and to pyll and robbe the cytie, and to sle men, women, and chyldren, for so it was commaunded them to do. It was great pytie to se the men, women, and chyldren, that kneled downe on their knees before the Prince for mercy; but he was so enflamed with yre that he toke no hede to theym, so that none was herde, but all putte to dethe as they were mette withal, and suche as were nothyng culpable: there was no pyte taken of the poore people who wrought never no maner of treason, yet they bought it derrer than the great per-

sonages, suche as had done the yvell and trespace. There was
nat so harde a hert within the cytie of Lymoges, and yf he had any
remembraunce of God, but that wepte pyteously for the great
mischefe that they sawe before their eyen: for mo than thre
thousande men, women, and chyldren were slayne and beheeded
that day: God have mercy on their soules, for I trowe they were
martyrs.

SAXON COAT OF MAIL

An early form of armour was a leather garment strengthened with
rings of iron. Later mail was made entirely of iron rings and later
still breastplates and carefully fitted joints of steel were made. Fourteenth and fifteenth century armour can be studied in the exactly dated
and carefully engraved representations found on funeral brasses. In the
account of the Battle of Agincourt in *T.S.I.H.*, i, p. 194 there is
mention of caps of boiled leather. This refers to *cuir bouilli*, a kind of
armour made of leather which was moulded to shape and then hard-
ened by heat.

Source: Old English Riddle translated by W. S. Mackie in *The
Exeter Book*, pt. ii, poems ix–xxxii, Early English Text Society, O.S. no
194, 1934 for 1933, pp. 125–6.

First of all the wet plain, extremely cold,
brought me forth from its interior.
I know in my thoughts that I am not made, by excellent skill,
from fleeces of wool or from hairs.
Woofs are not wound for me, nor have I a warp,
nor for me does a thread resound from the force of many strokes,
nor does the whirring shuttle glide over me,
nor shall weavers' rods strike me from anywhere.
The worms that deck the fine yellow cloth with embroidery
did not weave me by the skill that the fates have given them.
Nevertheless before men far and wide over the earth
I shall be called a pleasing garment.
Say truly, man skilled in clever thoughts
and wise in words, what this garment is.

ARMS AND THE MAN

Source: Statute of Winchester, 13 Edward I, cap. 6 (translated as in 1577 edition). (1285)

And further it is commaunded that every man have in his house harneis for to kepe the peace after the auncient assise that is for to saye every man betwixt fiftene yeres of age and 40 yeres shall be assessed and sworne to armour accordinge to the quantitie of their lands and goods, that is to wit from £15 lands and goodes 40 markes, that is to witte an hawberke, a brest plate of yron, a sworde, a knife, and an horse. And from £10 of landes and 20 markes goods, a hawberke, a brest plate of yron, sworde and a knyfe, and from £5 landes, a doublet, a brest plate or yron, a sworde, and knyfe, and from 40s. lande and more unto 100s. of lande, a sworde, a bowe and arrowes and a knyfe. And he that hath lesse than 40s. yerely, shall bee sworne to kepe gisarmes [halberds with hooks], knives and other lesse weapons. And he that hath lesse than 20 markes in goodes shall have swordes, knives, and other lesse weapons, and all other that maye shal have bowes and arrowes out of the foreste, and in the foreste bowes and boltes. And that viewe of armour be made every yere two times. And in al hundredes and fraunchises two constables shal be chosen to make the view of armour, and the constables aforesaide shal present before Justices assigned: such defautes as they doe see in the countrey aboute armour. . . .

ARMOURERS

Little is known about the craftsmen who made chain mail and fragments cannot be so easily dated as can fragments of the plate armour which superseded it.

Further Reading: J. P. C. Kent, ' Monumental Brasses—a New Classification of Military Effigies ', *Journal British Archaeological Association*, 3rd series, vol. 12.

T. Morley, *Some Account of the Worshipful Company of Armourers and Braziers*, 1878.

Source: Chaucer, *The Knightes Tale*.

. . Ther maystow seen devysing of herneys
So uncouth and so riche, and wroght so weel
Of goldsmithrie, of browding, and of steel;
The sheeldes brighte, testers [headpieces], and trappures [horse
    trappings],
Gold-hewen helmes, hauberks, cote-armures;
Lordes in paraments [mantles] on hir courseres,
Knightes of retenue, and eek squyeres
Nailinge the speres, and helmes bokelinge,
Gigginge [fitting with straps] of sheeldes, with layneres [thongs]
    lacinge;
Ther as need is, they weren no-thing ydel;
The fomy stedes on the golden brydel
Gnawinge, and faste the armurers also
With fyle and hamer prikinge [riding] to and fro;
Yemen on fote, and communes many oon
With short staves, thikke as they may goon;
Pypes, trompes, nakers [drums], clariounes,
That in the bataille blowen blody sounes.

ARMOUR

Illustrations of armour from the Bayeux Tapestry, from Matthew
Paris, from seals and elsewhere show the changes of successive generations from the Norman Conquest to the reign of Richard III in
W.W.I.H., vol. 1. A drawing from the Holkham Bible Picture Book of
Armageddon is reproduced on the front end-paper of *T.S.I.H.*, vol. 1
because it shows the different kinds of armour and weapon, new-fangled
and old-fashioned together, and divided according to the income-
group of the wearers, as observed by an artist in the first half of
fourteenth century England. Here is a late fourteenth century description of a knight such as is often portrayed on funeral brasses, but it is
better than a brass in that the poet is able to describe what is invisible
because it is worn underneath the armour. Little medieval armour
survives, but Mill Stephenson's catalogue of brasses makes it easy to
see what military (or other) brasses survive from this and other periods
in every parish church, according to county. Froissart gives the best
insight into the thoughts and deeds of the knights who wore such
armour. For the work of the charcoal burners who smelted the iron
and of the medieval iron and steel business see pp. 209, 24–8.

Further Reading: C. J. Ffoulkes, *European Arms and Armour* (Historical Association Leaflet no. 85), 1932. C. Blair, *European Armour, circa* 1066 *to circa* 1700, Batsford 1958.

Source: Chaucer, *Canterbury Tales* (Sir Thopas).

He dide next his whyte lere [skin]
Of clooth of lake [linen] fyn and clere
    A breech and eek a sherte;
And next his sherte an aketoun [quilted tunic],
And over that an habergoun [breastplate]
    For percinge of his herte;
And over that a fyn hauberk,
Was al y-wroght of Jewes werk,
    Ful strong it was of plate;
And over that his cote-armour [surcoat]
As whyt as is a lily-flour,
    In which he wol debate.

His sheeld was al of gold so reed,
And ther-in was a bores heed,
    A charbocle [carbuncle] bisyde;
And there he swoor, on ale and breed,
How that ' the geaunt shal be deed,
    Bityde what bityde! '
His jambeux [leg armour] were of quirboilly [boiled leather]
His swerdes shethe of yvory,
    His helm of laton bright;
His sadel was of rewel-boon [perhaps whale tooth]
His brydel as the sonne shoon,
    Or as the mone light.

His spere was of fyn cipress,
That brodeth werre, and no-thing pees,
    The heed ful sharpe y-grounde;
His stede was al dappel gray,
It gooth an ambel in the way
    Ful softely and rounde . . .
Men speke of romances of prys,
Of Horn child and of Ypotys,
    Of Bevis and sir Gy,
Of sir Libeux and Pleyn-damour;

But sir Thomas, he bereth the flour
  Of royal chivalry.
His gode stede al he bistrood,
And forth upon his wey he glood [went]
  As sparkle out of the bronde [torch];
Upon his crest he bar a tour,
And therin striked a lily-flour,
  God shilde his cors from shonde [shame]!
And for he was a knight auntrous [adventurous],
He nolde [would not] slepen in non hous,
  But liggen in his hode;
His brighte helm was his wonger [pillow]
And by him baitheth [feeds] his dextrer [horse]
  Of herbes fyne and gode.

BOWS

Archers were well paid. They had contributed to the Norman victory at Hastings but the importance of English archers increased greatly between the thirteenth and fifteenth centuries after the success of long bows at Falkirk (1298). They wore no more armour than an open helmet and a mail shirt with short sleeves and ' bracers ' of horn or leather to protect the left wrist from the bow string. A large shield propped in front of them on stakes driven into the ground gave some shelter. Fourteenth century archers had horses for transport.

In 1365 the sheriffs had to forbid able-bodied men playing ball games as, instead, they were to practise archery on Sundays and holidays. A fletcher ' fledged ' arrows, generally with goose feathers.

Crossbows were first seen in Europe about 1100. A papal attempt to limit their use to fighting infidels failed, but in England crossbows did not replace the more rapidly discharged longbows.

The best arrowheads were Sheffield steel. The Holkham Bible shows, the difference between barbed hunting arrows and the heavier warheads. The Guildhall Museum has arrows with flat sections on their shafts to which burning tow could be fastened.

The British Museum has a yew bow from Berkhamstead Castle. It is plain, but bow-tips in the London Museum are carved. The London Museum has a leather ' bracer ' to protect the archer's arm, with the motto ' Well shot '.

Archery Practice.   c. 1340.   (Luttrell Psalter).

Further Reading: Sir R. W. F. P. Gallwey, *The Crossbow*, 2 parts, 1903–7. J. E. Morris, ' The Archers at Crecy ', *English Historical Review*, vol. 12, 1897, pp. 427–36.

(1) *Source*: *Gerald the Welshman, Description of Wales*, translated by Sir R. C. Hoare, 1806, i, 92. (Twelfth century)

It seems worthy of remark, that the people of what is called Venta [Gwent or Monmouthshire] are more accustomed to war, more famous for valour, and more expert in archery, than those of any other part of Wales. The following examples prove the truth of this assertion. In the last capture of the aforesaid castle, which happened in our days, two soldiers passing over a bridge to take refuge in a tower built on a mound of earth, the Welsh, taking them in the rear, penetrated with their arrows the oaken portal of the tower, which was four fingers thick; in memory of which circumstance, the arrows were preserved in the gate. William de Braose also testifies that one of his soldiers, in a conflict with the Welsh, was wounded by an arrow, which passed through his thigh and the armour with which it was cased on both sides, and through that part of the saddle which is called the *alva*, mortally wounded the horse. Another soldier had his hip, equally sheathed in armour, penetrated by an arrow quite to the saddle, and on turning his horse round, received a similar wound on the opposite hip, which fixed him on both sides of his seat. What more could be expected from a balista? Yet the bows used by this people are not made of horn, ivory, or yew, but of wild elm; unpolished, rude, and uncouth, but stout; not calculated to shoot an arrow to a great distance, but to inflict very severe wounds in close fight.

(2) *Source*: *Statutes of Ireland*, 1572, 5 Edward IV cap. 4. (1465)

. . . Every Englyshe man and Irishe man, that dwell wyth Englysh men and speake Englyshe, that be betwixt 60 and 16 in age shal have an Englyshe bowe of his owne length and one fistmele [breadth of a fist] at the least betwixt the nyckes, with twelve shaftes of the length of three quarters of the Standarde, the Bowes of Yew, wyche hassell, Ashe, Awburne [alder], or any other reasonable tree accordynge there power and the Shaftes in the same maner wythin twoe Monethes next after the publicacion of this estatute on payne of two pence a man from Moneth to other, till that he shall have and continue the Bowe and shaftes, and in lewe of the Bowe and shaftes broken and lost to have newe under payne of two pence every Moneth till it be done. And yet not prohibitynge gentlemen on horsebacke to ryde accordynge their best disposition to ryde wyth Speare, so that they have Bowes with theire men for tyme of necessitie.

CASTLES

The Bayeux Tapestry shows the construction of the first castle by William I at Hastings. Labourers are piling up earth. It also shows an attack on a castle with fire. Stone made castles were costly and by 1200 there were fewer than in 1150. Yet documents mention 350.

(1) *Source*: *Gerald the Welshman, Itinerary through Wales*, translated by R. C. Hoare, 1806, i, 201-2. (Here a castle is seen as the home of a baronial family rather than a centre of warfare, late twelfth century.)

Manorbier near Pembroke is excellently well defended by turrets and bulwarks, and is situated on the summit of a hill extending on the western side towards the sea-port, having on the northern and southern sides a fine fish-pond under its walls, as conspicuous for its grand appearance, as for the depth of its waters, and a beautiful orchard on the same side, inclosed on one part by a vineyard, and on the other by a wood, remarkable for the projection of its rocks, and the height of its hazel trees. On the right hand of the promontory, between the castle and the church, near the site of a very large lake and mill, a rivulet of never-failing water flows through a valley, rendered sandy by the violence of the winds. Towards the west, the Severn sea, bending its course to Ireland, enters a hollow bay at some distance from the castle; and the southern rocks, if extended a little further towards the north, would render it a most excellent harbour for shipping. From this point of sight, you will see almost all the ships from Great Britain, which the east wind drives upon the Irish coast, daringly brave the inconstant waves and raging sea. This country is well supplied with corn, sea-fish, and imported wines; and what is preferable to every other advantage, from its vicinity to Ireland, it is tempered by a salubrious air. . . . It is evident, therefore, that Maenor Pirr is the pleasantest spot in Wales; and the author may be pardoned for having thus extolled his native soil, his genial territory, with a profusion of praise and admiration.

(2) On the accession of Henry II (1154) unlicensed castles had to be demolished. They had been built in Stephen's disorderly reign (see *T.S.I.H.*, i).

Source: William of Malmesbury, *Chronicle of the Kings of England*, ed. J. A. Giles, Bohn's Antiquarian Library, 1847, pp. 509–510. (1140).

There were many castles throughout England, each defending their neighbourhood, but, more properly speaking, laying it waste. The garrisons drove off from the fields, both sheep and cattle, nor did they abstain either from churches or church-yards. Seizing such of the country vavassours [yeomen] as were reputed to be possessed of money, they compelled them, by extreme torture, to promise whatever they thought fit. Plundering the houses of the wretched husbandmen, even to their very beds, they cast them into prison; nor did they liberate them, but on their giving every thing they possessed or could by any means scrape together, for their release. Many calmly expired in the midst of torments inflicted to compel them to ransom themselves, bewailing, which was all they could do, their miseries to God. And, indeed, at the instance of the Earl [of Gloucester], the legate, with the bishops, repeatedly excommunicated all violators of churchyards and plunderers of churches, and those who laid violent hands on men in holy or monastic orders, or their servants: but this his attention profited but little. It was distressing, therefore, to see England, once the fondest cherisher of peace and the

PLATE XXVII

WAR

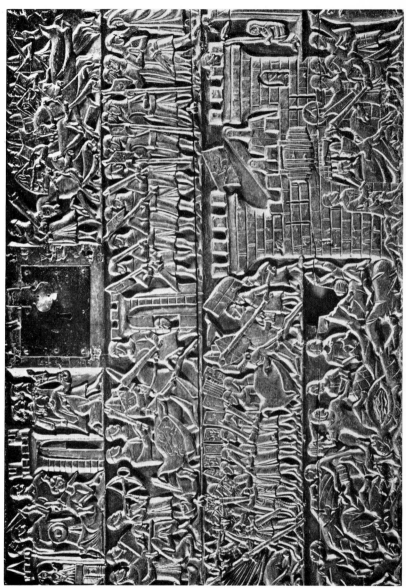

73. Battle of Courtrai, 1302. An early defeat of mounted knights by infantry. (*cf. p.* 115)

74. Crossbowman

75. Castle (*cf. pp.* 285–294)

Gaoler and prisoners. c. 1330. (Holkham Bible).

single receptacle of tranquillity, reduced to such a pitch of misery that, not even the bishops, nor monks, could pass in safety from one town to another.

(3) Edwardian Welsh Castles.

Most of the royal castles built to keep the Welsh down were erected between 1277 and 1289. In 1277 Builth, Aberystwyth, Flint and Rhuddlan were under construction and in 1283 Conway, Caernarvon and Harlech. Four thousand men, some brought from as far

U

away as Northumberland, were at work on the last three in 1283–4. Work at Caernarvon and Beaumaris began in 1283 and 1295 respectively and continued until 1323. The cost, in medieval money, was about £80,000. Meanwhile improvements were made at Montgomery, Carmarthen, Dynevor, Dryslwyn, Carreg Cennen, Kidwelly, Llanstephan and Laugharne; and lords were building castles at Ruthin, Denbigh, Chirk, Hawarden and Hope. These castles were built on improved plans with long curtain walls and great gatehouses.

Further Reading: J. Goronwy Edwards, *Edward I's Castle-Building in Wales*. The Sir John Rhys Memorial Lecture, British Academy, 1944. From *Proceedings of the British Academy*, vol. 32, 1951.

Source: *Ministers' Accounts for West Wales* 1277 *to* 1306, translated by Myvanwy Rhys, Cymmrodorion Record Series, no. xiii, 1936, p. 9 and foll. Account of Ralph de Broucton, clerk, my Lord the King's Receiver in West Wales, (1277–1280).

Item he counts for wages of knights and sergeants at arms, and for making provision for Llanbadarn castle, and for fellers of trees in divers passes, and for the upkeep of Dinevor and Carreg Cennen castles, from the said day, the octave of Holy Trinity [May 30], until Sunday, the octave of St. Peter's Chains [August 8], by the view and testimony of John de Handon, Sir Payn de Cadurciis' chaplain, appointed thereto by order of the same— £105 3s. 5d. Item he counts on wages of barons, knights, sergeants at arms crossbowmen on foot and the others necessary for war, from the feast of St. Peter's Chains in the fifth year of the same King's reign until Christmas in the sixth year of the same King's reign, as appears more fully from the attestation rolls of Sir Payn's said chaplain appointed thereto—£1,255 4s. 7d. Item he counts on the works of the castle and vill of Llanbadarn, viz. for masons, hodmen, quarrymen and other workmen, throughout the above-mentioned period, by the view and testimony of the aforesaid chaplain—£440 10s. 8d. Item he counts for ships hired for those bringing stones and chalk, and for many other outlays, and the divers other things to do with the said works, for the above-mentioned period, as appears from the rolls of the said John as above—£146 9s. 4d. And he counts on escort of my Lord the King's treasure throughout the aforesaid period— £8 11s. 4d., viz. for its carriage on 4 occasions. And the same Ralph counts for his wages, for the entire year—£10 5s. and no more, that year, because he received four pounds at Worcester . . . 40s. at Carmarthen . . . and 40s. at Kidwelly. . . .

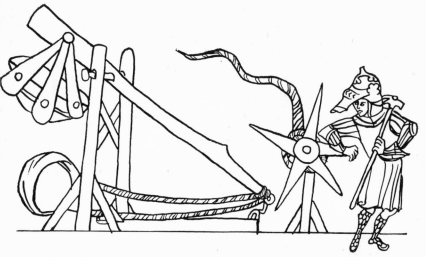

Catch of catapult released. 1326–7. Christ Church, Walter de Milemete).

(4) Exeter Castle shows that even as early as the eleventh century attention was paid to strengthening the entrance to the bailey of a castle. Strong gatehouses became important features of the great castles built by Edward I. This successful achievement by a member of the heroic Douglas family against the English in the fourteenth century wars between England and Scotland gives an incidental side-light on victualling.

Further Reading: W. D. Simpson, *Scottish Castles*, Edinburgh, H.M. Stationery Office, 1959.

Source: J. Froissart, *Chronique*, vol. 1 chapter 56, translated extract. (1340)

Sir William Douglas and his companions took two hundred wild Highland lances and put to sea. They obtained a supply of oats, meal, coal and straw and quietly landed at a harbour near Edinburgh, a place which was an especial nuisance to them. When armed, they sallied out under cover of darkness taking ten or twelve of the trustiest whom they clad in tattered coats and hats to look like poor merchants. They loaded twelve ponies with twelve sacks, some full of oats, others with meal or coal. Then they set their comrades in ambush in a derelict old abbey which lay uninhabited near the foot of the castle rock. At day-

A gun, rather earlier than one in a Christ Church manuscript which is generally
described as the earliest picture of one. British Museum, Walter de Milemete
once at Holkham.

break the merchants (who were secretly armed) set out towards
the castle with all their horses as heavily laden as possible. When
they were on the slope Sir William Douglas and Sir Simon
Fraser went in front and told the porter at the gatehouse that
they had taken the great risk of bringing grain and meal. If
there was any demand they would gladly sell it at reasonable
prices. The porter said that the goods were needed, but it was
too early for him to dare to wake up the castellan or his steward;
so he made them advance and opened the gate for them. They
just went right in with their loads through the gate of the bailey
which was opened for them. Sir William Douglas had noticed
that the porter had all the other keys of the great castle gate—
and he had cunningly asked the porter which key opened the
big gate and which key opened the wicket. When the first gate
was opened, as related, they set their ponies inside and unloaded
two with bags of coal right on the threshold so that the door
would not shut. Then they seized the porter and killed him so
quietly that not a word was heard. They took the keys and un-
locked the castle gate. Then Sir William blew on his horn and
his comrades threw off their tattered coats and upset the other
bags across the entrance so that the gate could not be shut. When
the others hidden in ambush heard the horn they rushed out
towards the castle. The horn woke the castle guard [but too
late].

(5) Even before guns became important castles had lost much of their military importance for the large armies of the Hundred Year's War fought pitched battles.

In the fifteenth century 'overmighty subjects', interested. in comfort and show as well as in defence, built great fortified palaces of varying designs. These were in form and purpose half way between the fortresses of earlier centuries and the great Tudor houses of sixteenth century England. These late castles generally had a tower house for the lord and a quadrangle round which lived the retainers who wore his livery and whom he maintained as a private army until the Tudors suppressed 'Livery and Maintenance'. Michael de la Pole's manor at Wingfield, Suffolk, Sir John Fastolf's lofty tower at Caister, Norfolk, Lord Lovel's castle at Wardour, Wilts, are examples of the period. Many were built of brick, like Kirby Muxloe, Leics.

Bodiam, Sussex (1386), was built as a defence against French marauders. It is an early example, copied from France, of a quadrangular plan.

The chatelaine of Wark Castle, Northumberland (1341), was one of many ladies who found plenty to do and organize in the castle of an absent husband. While her husband, William de Montacute, was imprisoned in France, Catherine, Countess of Salisbury, held Wark Castle against Scottish, invaders until Edward III raised the siege. The story of Edward's love for her is repeated in a legend, which is certainly untrue, about her dropping a garter at Court. This Edward is supposed to have picked up with the remark ' Honi soit qui mal y pense ', which became the motto of the Order of the Garter which he then founded. In both tales mistakes are made over the christian name of the Countess. See Beltz, *Memorials of the Order of the Garter*, pp. xliii–xlvi.

Further Reading: W. Douglas Simpson, ' The Moated Homestead, Church and Castle of Bodiam ', *Sussex Archaeological Collections*, vol. 72, 1931, pp. 69–99, and his articles on Warkworth, Hurstmonceaux, Buckden Palace, ' Castles of Livery and Maintenance ' and ' Bastard Feudalism ', listed by A. J. Taylor in A. L. Poole, *Medieval England*, Clarendon Press, 1958, pp. 126–7. B. H. St. J. O'Neil, *Castles*, H.M.S.O., 1953, traces the history of castles as illustrated by the scores of examples now under the Ministry of Works, for all of which separate guides with dated plans are available.

Source: Froissart, *Chronique*, vol. 1, chapter 78, translated extract.

In the morning the Scots left. King Edward arrived the same day at midday. . . . He said that all should lodge there as he wanted to see the castle and the noble lady in command, for he had not seen her since her marriage. As soon as King Edward

was disarmed, he took ten or twelve knights to study the nature
of the Scottish assaults and the counter-measures. As soon as
Lady Salisbury knew of his arrival she had the gates opened and
came out dressed with amazing richness. No one could refrain
from gazing at her with admiration for her great nobility and
beauty and her gracious speech and bearing. When she reached
the king she bowed to the ground before him thanking him for
his aid, and led him to the castle to feast and honour him, as she
very well knew how to do. Everyone was amazed at her, and the
king himself could not stop gazing at her. He thought he had
never seen a lady so noble, gay and handsome. A lasting fire of
love was kindled in his heart for it seemed no one in the world
was so adorable as her. They went into the castle hand in hand
and the lady led him first into the hall and then into her chamber,
which was fully worthy of such a lady. The king kept looking
at her so continuously that she became abashed. After gazing
long at her he went away to a window. There he leant in deep
thought. The lady went to feast the other knights and squires,
ordered the preparation of the dinner and the laying of the tables
and preparation of the hall. When all her arrangements were
made and her orders given she came back cheerfully to the king.
He was as pensive as ever. [So she asked what was the cause and
he declared his love. She answered that she was sure he would
never dishonour her and her husband. He left the castle sadly
and pursued the Scots.]

DISASTERS: FIRE

There had been great fires in London in 1132, 1135 and 1161, the
first starting in the house of Becket's father. In 1161 there were
terrible fires in Canterbury, Winchester; and Exeter, as well as London
and Winchester, suffered again in 1180. Glastonbury was burnt in
1184 and Chichester in 1187. Timber and thatch were bad fire risks
and water was only available from buckets. The fire of Hell was a
continual threat to the wicked and fire in this world was a menace
which it seemed almost impossible to resist.

Source: The History of Ingulf, translated, Rev. J. Stevenson, *The
Church Historians of England*, vol. 2, pt. 2, pp. 708–9. (This is actually
medieval fiction and not written by an eye-witness).

Our plumber, who had been employed on the tower of the church [at Croyland, 1091] in repairing the roofs, neglected to extinguish his fire in the evening, but with fatal madness covered it over with some dead cinders, in order that he might be more prepared to begin his work in the morning; and so he descended to supper. After supper, when all our servants had gone to bed, and were buried in deep slumber, a strong north wind arose and accelerated the coming of this truly unparalleled misfortune upon us. For this wind, entering into the tower through the numerous open lattices, blew the dead cinders into a blaze, and drove the living flame upon the nearest pieces of wood, where, finding a material dry and congenial, it fastened upon it more firmly, and began also to seize upon the thicker beams. The inhabitants of the town, although they had for a long time seen a great light in the belfry, thought that either the clerks of the church or the plumber were performing some of their duties, till at length, perceiving the flames belching forth, they began to shout and batter at the gates of the monastery—for it was that still time of the night when we were all reposing in our beds, enjoying our first and deepest sleep. At last, the loud clamour of the populace aroused me, and hurrying to the nearest window, I distinguished as clearly as if it were noonday all the servants of the monastery in the direction of the church, shouting and wailing and rushing hither and thither in disorder. Clad in my night-dress, and awaking our companions, I hastily descended into the cloister, and there the whole place shone as though illumined by a thousand lights. Thence running to the door of the church, and attempting to enter, I was almost cut off by a stream of molten brass from the bells, and by dropping of boiling lead. However, withdrawing and beholding that the flames within were everywhere triumphant, I directed my steps towards the dormitory, when I was severely burnt on the shoulder by the lead, which was running down and rapidly penetrating into the cloister; indeed, I should have been well nigh burnt to ashes, had I not sprung back with great speed into the court of the cloister, where observing that the fire-vomiting flames were still rolling their smoke from the church tower, and that they had reached the nave, and were throwing a continuous train of sparks in the direction of the dormitory of the brethren (who were yet plunged in the sleep, it might be, of death), I called to them, and had difficulty in awaking them, even with my loud shouts. On recognising my voice, they leaped from their beds in excessive terror, in their night-dresses and half-naked; and on hearing that the cloister was on fire, they rushed through all the windows of the dormitory in pitiable confusion. Many were wounded; many were bruised; and, sad to relate, many had their limbs broken by the fall. . . . I attempted to regain my chamber, in order to get the clothes which I had there and distribute them wherever there appeared to be peculiar necessity. So great, however, was the heat at the entrance to the hall, and so dangerous the stream of molten lead which kept pouring down on all sides, that even the boldest of the young men dared not attempt to enter. . . . Then the tower of the church fell upon its southern side, and I, terrified at the crash, dropped upon the ground half dead, in a swoon.

DISASTERS: PLAGUE

The Black Death was only the worst of many outbreaks. This account was written by a monk of Malmesbury before it had reached Bristol and spread over the whole country. Henry Knighton's account of the plague at Leicester is in *T.S.I.H.*, i, p. 135. Melcombe Regis (Weymouth) had recently supplied 20 ships, compared with Bristol's 22 and London's 25, for Edward III's successful siege of Calais.

(1) *Source*: *Eulogium Historiarum* (Rolls Series), vol. 3, p. 213, translated by F. A. Gasquet, whose book on the *Great Pestilence* contains many other extracts from contemporary writers (1893 ed. p. 72, and p. 92).

The cruel pestilence, terrible to all future ages, came [in July 1348] from parts over the sea to the south coast of England into a port called Melcolme, in Dorsetshire. This plague sweeping over the southern districts, destroyed numberless people in Dorset, Devon, and Somerset. . . . On account of this scarcity [of labourers], women and even small children, were to be seen with the plough. . . .

(2) *Source*: Robert of Avesbury (Registrar of the Court of Canterbury), *De Gestis Edwardi III* (Rolls Series), p. 406 (Gasquet, p. 74).

It passed most rapidly from place to place, swiftly killing ere mid-day many who in the morning had been well, and without respect of person (some few rich people excepted), not permitting those destined to die to live more than three, or at most four, days.

(3) *Source*: instruction from the Bishop of Bath and Wells to his clergy, 17 Jan. 1349, Wilkins, *Concilia*, vol. 2, pp. 735–6, (Gasquet, pp. 81–2).

. . . at once and publicly instruct and induce, yourselves or by some other, all who are sick of the present malady, or who shall happen to be taken ill, that *in articulo mortis*, if they are not able to obtain any priest, they should make confession of their sins (according to the teaching of the apostle) even to a layman, and, if a man is not at hand, then to a woman.

(4) *Source*: *Chronicon Galfridi Le Baker de Swynebroke*, ed. E. M. Thompson, pp. 98–9.

The following year it devastated Wales as well as England, and then passing over to Ireland it killed the English inhabitants there in great numbers, but the pure-blooded Irish, living in the mountains and high lands, it hardly touched till A.D. 1357, when unexpectedly it destroyed them everywhere.

DISASTERS: WAR

(1) *Source*: Simeon of Durham, translated by Rev. J. Stevenson in *The Church Historians of England*, vol. 3, pt. 2, Seeleys 1855, p. 551.

In consequence of the Normans having plundered England— in the preceding year [1068] Northumbria and some other provinces, but in the present and following year [1069–70] almost the whole realm, yet principally Northumbria and the adjacent provinces—so great a famine prevailed that men, compelled by hunger, devoured human flesh, that of horses, dogs and cats, and whatever custom abhors; others sold themselves to perpetual slavery, so that they might in any way preserve their wretched existence; others, while about to go into exile from their country, fell down in the middle of the journey and gave up the ghost.

It was horrific to behold human corpses decaying in the houses, the streets, and the roads, swarming with worms, while they were consuming in corruption with an abominable stench. For no one was left to bury them in the earth, all being cut off either by the sword or by famine, or having left the country on account of the famine. Meanwhile, the land being thus deprived of any one to cultivate it for nine years, an extensive solitude prevailed all around. There was no village inhabited between York and Durham; they became lurking places to wild beasts and robbers, and were a great dread to travellers. [Those who describe the atrocities of enemies sometimes exaggerate.]

(2) Here is an account from a Northern monastery of the revenge taken by Malcolm, King of the Scots, for a plundering attack made on Cumberland, then part of his dominions (1070).

Further Reading: R. L. Storey, ' The Wardens of the Marches, 1377–1489', *English Historical Review*, vol. 72, no. 285.

Source: Simeon of Durham, translated by Rev. J. Stevenson in *The Church Historians of England*, vol. 3, pt. 2, Seeleys, 1855, p. 553.

. . . scarcely able to contain himself for fury, he ordered his troops no longer to spare any of the English nation, but either to smite all to the earth, or to carry them off captives under the yoke of perpetual slavery. Having received this licence, it was misery even to witness their deeds against the English. Some aged men and women were beheaded with the sword; others were thrust through with pikes, like swine destined for food; infants snatched from their mother's breasts were thrown high into the air, and in their fall were received on the points of lances and pikes thickly placed in the ground. The Scots, more savage than wild beasts, delighted in this cruelty, as an amusing spectacle. These children of the age of innocence, suspended between heaven and earth, gave up their souls to heaven. Young men also and maidens, and whoever seemed fit to toil and labour, were bound and driven before the face of their enemies, to be reduced in perpetual exile to slaves and bondmaids. Some of these females, worn out by running in front of their drivers further than their strength would bear, falling to the earth, perished even where they fell.

Seeing these things, Malcolm was not yet moved to pity by

tears, nor groans of the unhappy wretches; but, on the contrary, gave orders that they should be still further pressed onward in the march. Scotland was, therefore, filled with slaves and handmaids of the English race; so that even to this day, I do not say no little village, but even no cottage, can be found without one of them.

Note: by his Saxon wife, St. Margaret, Malcolm was father of Matilda, Queen of Henry I, the only English forebear of the later king of England, Edward I.

DISASTERS: FAMINE

In periods and places where many people live with their families mainly on the produce of their own work on the land food tends to be short at the end of the winter and fasting in Lent is unavoidable by the poor. A period of bad weather can lead to real shortage. The intercession of certain Saints with God came to be regarded as a good way of making the weather favourable. The effect of weather on the people's life was so clear and direct that medieval chronicles often refer to exceptional droughts or periods of wet or unusual cold.

Source: account of St. Wilfrid and the famine in Sussex, 681. Bede, *Ecclesiastical History of England*, translated by J. A. Giles, G. Bell, 1881, p. 194.

But Bishop Wilfrid, by preaching to them, not only delivered them from the misery of perpetual damnation, but also from an inexpressible calamity of temporal death, for no rain had fallen in that province in three years before his arrival, whereupon a dreadful famine ensued, which cruelly destroyed the people. In short, it is reported, that very often forty or fifty men, being spent with want, would go together to some precipice, or to the sea-shore, and there, hand in hand, perish by the fall, or be swallowed up by the waves. But on the very day on which the nation received the baptism of faith, there fell a soft but plentiful rain . . . [Wilfrid], when he came into the province, and found so great misery from famine, taught them to get food by fishing; for their sea and rivers abounded in fish, but the people had no skill to take them, except eels alone. The bishop's men having gathered eel nets everywhere, cast them into the sea, and by the blessing of God took three hundred fishes of several sorts. . . .

DISASTERS: FLOODS

(1) The floods of 1467 were exceptionally bad but floods are recorded from time to time.

Source: Ingulph, Continuator, pp. 443–4, translated in H. C. Darby, *The Medieval Fenland*, Cambridge, 1940, p. 56.

Throughout the whole of this county, and in Hoyland especially, there was scarcely a house or building, but what the streams of water made their way and flowed through it. Nor must you suppose that this happened hurriedly and in a cursory manner only: but continuously, during a whole month, the waters either stood there without flowing off, or else, being agitated by strong gusts of wind, swelled and increased still more and more day after day. Nor on this occasion did the embankments offer any effectual resistance, but on the contrary, though materials had been brought from other quarters for the purpose of strengthening them, they proved of very little service for that purpose; and however diligently the work might have been attended to in the day time, as the waters swelled and rose, the spot under repair was completely laid bare during the night. Then was there grief and lamentation among all, and outcries and tumult among the Hoylanders.

(2) H. G. Richardson regards this as the first appearance of the Commission of Sewers when the central government began to organise local efforts centrally.

Source: Patent Rolls, 42 Henry III, m. 14d., translation in H. C. Darby, *The Medieval Fenland*, Cambridge, 1940, p. 155. (1258)

Whereas the king has learned that a recent inundation of the sea and marsh in the parts of Holland has caused great cost and danger and at another time he has commanded the sheriff of Lincoln to distrain all persons having lands and tenements in those parts who ought to repair and keep up the dikes, bridges and walls of the sea and marsh there, the king has appointed him [Henry de Bathe] to provide and ordain with the said sheriff, for making the said repairs and distraint; and therefore he commands him at his next passing through those parts to attend to this.

PAGANISM

Witchcraft and Paganism did not wholly vanish with the Conversion of Christianity. Indeed the days of the week still are named after heathen gods.

Further Reading: Richard Bernheimer, *Wild Men in the Middle Ages* Harvard University Press, 1952. R. W. V. Elliott, ' Runes, Yews, and Magic ', *Speculum*, vol. 32, no. 2.

Source: B. Thorpe *Ancient Laws and Institutes of England*, 1840, p. 292. (before 690)

1. The Apostle says: ' No one who serves idols will possess the kingdom of God.' If anyone makes minor sacrifices to demons he will do penance for 1 year; and 10 years for major sacrifices.

2. If any one eats or drinks in ignorance by a heathen shrine he is to promise never to do so again and to do 40 days penance on bread and water. If he does it deliberately, that is to say after a priest has declared that it is sacrilege and the table of demons he shall do penance on bread and water for thrice 40 days. But if he did it in honour of the demons and to glorify the idol, he is to do penance for 3 years.

3. If anyone sacrifices to demons for a second or a third time he incurs 3 years penance; then 2 years without any offering of communion. In the third five years, at the end of a five year period, he is capable of perfection.

4. If anyone eat what has been sacrificed to idols and was under no compulsion, he is to fast 12 weeks on bread and water; if it was done of necessity he is to fast 6 weeks.

5. If any keep feasts in the abominable places of the heathen, taking and eating their food there, they should be subject to penance for 2 years, and be offered on probation for full two years, and after that be accepted to perfection; when offered test the spirit and discuss the life of each individual.

6. If any do sacrilege, that is summon diviners who practice divination by birds, or does any divination with evil intent, let him to penance for 3 years, and for one of these on bread and water.

7. Christians may not leave the Church of God and go to divination, or name angels or make covins which are known to be forbidden. If any be found serving this occult idolatry, in that he abandons our Lord Jesus Christ, the son of God, and gave himself to idolatry. . . .

8. It is unlawful for clerks or laymen, to be sorcerers or inchanters, or to make amulets which are proved to be fetters for their souls; those who act thus we command to be driven from the Church.

9. If anyone destroy a person by black magic he is to do penance for 7 years, 3 of these on bread and water.

10. If any use love potions and hurt nobody, if he is a layman he is to do penance for half a year; if he is a clerk, 1 year on bread and water; if he is a subdeacon, he is to do penance for 2 years, 1 year on bread and water; if he is a deacon, 4, 2 on bread and water; if he is priest, 5 years, 3 on bread and water. But if thereby any one deceive a woman of her bringing forth, then he is to do further 3 years penance on bread and water, lest he be accused of homicide.

11. If anyone seeks diviners whom they call prophets, or does any divinations, in that this too is diabolical, let him do penance 5 years, 3 of these on bread and water.

12. If anyone take lots, which they call contrary to the principles of the Saints, or have any lots whatsoever, or take lots with evil intent, or make divination, let him do penance 3 years, 1 on bread and water.

13. If any woman do divinations or diabolical incantations, let her do penance 1 year, or thrice 40 days or 40 days, according to the enormity of the crime of the penitent.

14. If any woman place her son or daughter on the roof for the sake of a cure or in an oven, let her do penance 7 years.

15. If any burn grain where a man has died for the sake of the living or of the house, let him do penance 5 years on bread and water.

16. If any for the health of his little son should pass through a fissure in the ground and should close it after himself with thorns, let him do penance 40 days on bread and water.

17. If any seek out divinations and pursue them in the manner of the heathen, or introduce such men into their houses, for the sake of finding something out by evil arts or to make an expiation, let them be cast out if they be of the clergy; but if they are secular let them after confession be subjected to 5 years of penance, according to the rules ordained of old.

18. If any make or perform a vow at trees, or springs, or stones, or boundaries, or anywhere at all except in the house of God, let him do penance for 3 years on bread and water. This is sacrilege or diabolical. If any eat or drink there let him do penance for 1 year on bread and water.

19. If any go at the New Year as a young stag or cow, that is, if he share the habit of wild beasts and is clad in the skins of cattle and puts on the heads of beasts, any such who thus transform themselves into the likenesses of beasts are to do 3 years penance.

20. If any one is an astrologer [*mathematicus*], that is one who changes the mind of a man by the invocation of devils, he is to do 5 years penance, 1 on bread and water.

21. If anyone is a sender of storm, that is to say a sorcerer, he is to do penance 7 years, 3 on bread and water.

22. If anyone makes amulets, which is detestable, he should do 3 years penance, 1 on bread and water.

23. Anyone who makes a habit of auguries and divinations is to do penance 5 years.

24. Any who observe soothsayers, or inchanters, and devilish amulets and dreams and herbs, or who keep holy the fifth day in honour of Jove [Jeudi; or of Thor: Thursday], or New Year's Day, as do the heathen, is to do penance 5 years if a clerk and 3 years if a layman.

25. Those who take care when the moon is eclipsed to practise as they trust by their cries and witchcrafts to defend her in sacriligious fashion are to do penance 5 years.

26. Those who fast in honour of the moon to bring about healing are to do penance 1 year.

WITCHCRAFT

For the witch of Berkeley (1065), see *T.S.I.H.*, i, 37–9. For fashionable fifteenth century witches, *id.*, 213–5.

Source: Penitential of Archbishop Ecgbert (735–766). B. Thorpe, *Ancient Laws and Institutes of England*, 1840, p. 379–380.

If any stick a needle in any man let him fast 3 years, 1 year with bread and water, and for 2 years with bread and water on 3 days in the week. And if a man die of the prick then let him fast 7 years, as is above written.

And if any make use of potions, for the sake of the love of anyone, and give anything in the food or the drink or by inchantments of any sort that their love may be thereby increased; if a layman do this, let him fast for half a year on Wednesdays and Fridays on bread and water and let him eat his food on other days, excepting only meat. If he is a clerk let him fast 1 year, on bread and water on 2 days in the week, and on the other days let him abstain from meat. If he is a deacon, let him fast 3 years, on bread and water on two days each week and let him abstain from meat on the other days. If he is a priest let him fast 5 years, 1 on bread and water and for 4 with bread and water on Fridays, and on the other days let him abstain from meat.

If any exercise divinations and soothsayings or keep vigils at any spring or at any other creature, except at the church of God, let him fast for 3 years, 1 on bread and water and 2 on bread and water on Wednesdays and Fridays, and on the other days let him have his food except meat only.

A woman deserves the same if she cure her child by any sorcery or if she draw it over the ground to the cross roads.

ASTROLOGY

Many passages in literature can only be understood by an acquaintance with astrology, without which words like ' ill-starred ' are meaningless. From Babylonian times it was believed that human character and life was under the influence of the seven planets. The moon was regarded as a planet, the one nearest the earth and the most earthly. The sun was also thought to be a planet. The coldest and most remote was thought to be Saturn. Men's dispositions were saturnine, jovial, martial or mercurial if they were born under the influence of Saturn, Jupiter, Mars or Mercury. Each had their peculiar virtues and corresponding vices. In Dante's *Paradiso* the Heaven of Saturn is that of the great mystics who exemplified the contemplative virtues, aloof from the world. See also pp. 147–8

Further Reading: T. O. Wedel, *Medieval Attitude towards Astrology*, Yale, 1920.

Source: Translated from Bartholomew the Englishman, *On the Properties of Things*, Book 8, chapter 23. (Thirteenth century)

... the planet Saturn is malevolent, cold and dry, of the shades of night and heavy. Thus it is represented in legend as an old man. Its orbit is the most distant from the Earth yet it has the most baleful influence on it. It takes 30 years to run its course because of its distance from the Earth. It does more harm when going than coming, so in legend it is thought to have a curved sickle (which cuts when withdrawing not when advancing). In temperature it is pale and livid like lead, for it has harsh and fatal qualities like coldness and dryness. Thus a child born under its rule or conceived under it, either dies or has the worst characteristics.... The subjects of Saturn ... are of pale and grey complexion, both in hair and flesh, harsh and savage. They do not shrink from vile things and dirty clothes and they like unclean beasts and everything sour; for a melancholy humour prevails within them. ... Its colour is black and leaden ... [other planets were associated with other colours and metals, and each with a day of the week.]

SUPERSTITION

Reports of miracles were frequent and it did not seem improbable that they had been wrought by Simon de Montfort, Thomas of Lancaster and Edward II: the visible appearance of the Devil seems to have been fairly common and well attested. Some had faith in unchristian supernatural phenomena as well.

Source: Chaucer, *The Persones Tale* (1387–1400).

What seye we of hem that bileven in divynailes, as by flight or by noyes of briddes, or of bestes, or by sort [lots], by geomancie, by dremes, by chirkinge of dores, or crakkinge of houses, by gnawinge of rattes, and swich manere wreccednesse? Certes, al this thing is deffended [forbidden] by god and by holy chirche.

x

CATHEDRALS

A Cathedral is a church dignified by the seat of a Bishop. Of 33 medieval churches which became eventually cathedrals only 16 were originally designed as such. Of these Old St. Paul's was destroyed in the Great Fire of London. There were fifteen (later seventeen) medieval English bishoprics. Of these, as befits the tradition of Rome, ten had cathedrals on the sites of Roman towns. Most are in important old towns, for Lanfranc and William I moved them from country sites to growing towns so that the Bishops of Dorchester (Oxon), Ramsbury, Elmham and Selsey became Bishops of Lincoln, Salisbury, Thetford (later Norwich) and Chichester. Henry I created Ely and Carlisle. A Cathedral was ruled by a Dean and Chapter not by a Bishop. The forms of service followed at Salisbury became generally adopted, under the name of the Use of Sarum.

Drawings of all English medieval Cathedrals are on the endpapers of *W.W.I.H.*, vol. 1. Its index indicates historical events connected with particular ones. Monks managed the Cathedrals of Canterbury, Durham, Norwich, Rochester, Ely, Bath and Coventry.

Further Reading: John Harvey, *English Cathedrals*, 2nd ed., Batsford 1956. Monographs and guidebooks on separate Cathedrals. G. H. Cook, *The English Cathedral through the Centuries*, Phoenix House, 1957.

Source: Eadmer, *De reliquiis S. Audoeni*, translated in Willis, *Architectural History of Canterbury Cathedral*, 1845, pp. 9–12.

When Augustine came to Kent he set up his throne in a fourth century Roman church at Canterbury. This Roman-Saxon cathedral was burnt in 1067 and was rebuilt by Lanfranc. Lanfranc's biographer, Eadmer, described the ancient cathedral.

This was that very church which had been built by Romans, as Bede witnesses in his history, and which was duly arranged in some parts in imitation of the Church of the blessed Prince of the Apostles, Peter, in which his holy relics are exalted by the veneration of the whole world. The venerable Odo had translated the body of the blessed Wilfrid, Archbishop of York, from Ripon to Canterbury, and had worthily placed it in a more lofty receptable, to use his own words—that is to say, in the great altar which was constructed of rough stones and mortar, close to the wall at the eastern part of the presbytery. Afterwards another altar was placed at a convenient distance before the aforesaid altar, and dedicated in honour of our Lord Jesus Christ, at which altar the divine mysteries were daily celebrated. In this altar the blessed Elphege had solemnly deposited the head of St. Swithun, which he had brought with him when he was translated from Winchester to Canterbury, and also many relics of other saints. To reach these altars, a certain crypt which the Romans call a confessionary had to be ascended by means of several steps from the choir of singers. This crypt was fabricated beneath in the likeness of the Confessionary of St. Peter, the vault of which was raised so high that the part above could only be reached by many steps. Within this crypt had at the east an altar, in which was enclosed the head of the blessed Furseus, as of old it was asserted. Moreover, the single passage [of entrance], which ran westward from the curved part of the crypt, reached from thence up to the resting-place of the blessed Dunstan, which was separated from the crypt itself by a strong wall; for that holy father was interred before the aforesaid steps at a great depth in the ground, and at the head of the saint stood the matutinal [morning] altar. Thence the choir of singers was extended westward into the body of the church, and shut out from the multitude by a decent enclosure.

In the next place, beyond the middle of the length of the body, there were two towers which projected beyond the aisles of the church. The south tower had an altar in the midst of it, which was dedicated to the blessed Pope Gregory. At the side was the principal door of the church, which of old by the English and even now is called the Suthdore, and is often mentioned by this name in the law-books of the ancient kings. For all disputes from the whole kingdom, which cannot legally be referred to the King's Court or to the hundreds or counties, do in this place receive judgment. Opposite to this tower and on the north, there was another tower in honour of the blessed Martin, and had about it cloisters for the use of the monks. And as the first tower was devoted to legal contentions and judgments of this world, so in the second the younger brethren were instructed in the knowledge of the offices of the church, for the different seasons and hours of the day and night.

The extremity of the church was adorned by the oratory of Mary, the blessed Mother of God, which was so constructed that access could only be had to it by steps. At its eastern part there was an altar consecrated to the worship of that Lady, which had within it the head of the blessed virgin Austroberta. When the priest performed the divine mysteries at this altar he had his face turned to the east, towards the people who stood below. Behind him to the west was the pontifical chair, constructed with handsome workmanship and of large stones and cement, and far removed from the Lord's table, being contiguous to the wall of the church which embraced the entire area of the building. And this was the plan of the church of Canterbury.

FASTING

(1) *Source*: Penitential of Archbishop Ecgbert (735–766), B. Thorpe, *Ancient Laws and Institutes of England*, 1840, p. 385.

If anyone from illness or softness cannot undergo fasting and austerity, it is lawful for him to buy off his fast by piety and his worldly possessions. If accordingly he is rich let him give 30s. for 12 months fast. If he is not so wealthy let him give 20s. If he is less wealthy still let him give 10s. Finally if he be a poor man who cannot give 10s. let him give 3s. For a rich man can more easily give 30s., than a poor man can give 3s. A lawful shilling is always 12 pennies. Alms of this kind can be paid in three ways. One is that they be laid upon the altar of God; another is that a man can be bought from slavery and then set free; a third is, that they be distributed to God's poor.

(2) *Source*: Chaucer: *The Persones Tale* (1387–1400).

And thou shalt understanden eek that god ordeyned fastinge; and to fastinge appertenen foure thinges. Largenesse to povre folk, gladnesse of herte espirituel, nat to be angry ne anoyed, ne grucche for he fasteth; and also resonable houre for to ete by mesure; that is to seyn, a man shal nat ete in untyme, ne sitte the longer at this table to ete for he fasteth.

A POWERFUL PENITENT

Source: Canons enacted under King Edgar (956–975). B. Thorpe, *Ancient Laws and Institutes of England*, 1840, pp. 414–5.

Thus may a powerful man, and rich in friends, with the support of his friends, greatly lighten his penance. . . . Let him then lay aside his weapons, and vain ornaments, and take a staff in his hand, and go barefoot zealously, and put on his body woollen or haircloth, and not come into a bed, but lie on a pallet, and so do, that in three days the series of 7 years be dispensed with thus: let him proceed with aid; and first let him take to him 12 men, and let them fast 3 days on bread, and on green herbs, and on water; and get, in addition thereto, in whatever manner he can, seven times 120 men, who shall also fast for him 3 days; then will be fasted as many fasts as there are days in 7 years.

When a man fasts, then let the dishes that would have been eaten be all distributed to God's poor; and the three days that a man fasts, let him abandon every worldly occupation, and by day and by night, the oftenest that he can, let him remain in church, and with almslight earnestly watch there, and cry to God, and implore forgiveness, with groaning spirit, and kneel frequently on the sign of the cross; sometimes up, sometimes down, extend himself; and let the powerful man try earnestly to shed tears from his eyes, and bewail his sins; and let a man then feed those three days as many of God's poor as he possibly can; and on the fourth day, bathe them all, and shelter them, and distribute money; and let the penitent himself employ himself in washing their feet, and let as many masses be said for him on that day as can possibly be obtained, and at the last, let absolution be given. . . .

EXCOMMUNICATION

Further Reading: R. Hill, ' The Theory and Practice of Excommunication in Medieval England ', *History*, vol. 42, no. 144.

Source: *The Autobiography of Giraldus Cambrensis*, ed. and translated by H. E. Williams, Jonathan Cape, 1937, p. 54 (the climax of a quarrel about the dedication of a church which Giraldus, as Archdeacon, regarded as an encroachment by the Bishop of St. Asaph, because the diocese was different).

And when the Bishop, that he might not seem to have done nothing at all, began in a loud voice to excommunicate in general terms all enemies and adversaries of St. Asaph, the Archdeacon in a still louder voice, together with his folk in the churchyard, excommunicated all those who presumed to appropriate or disturb the rights of St. David; and looking back at the bells, which hung above their heads hard by, he ordered that they should all be rung at triple intervals for the shaming of their adversaries and for confirmation of his sentence. And when this was done, since the Welsh greatly dread such ringing of bells when they are rung against themselves, the Bishop and his men straightway broke off their sentence of excommunication and mounting their horses made off as fast as they could. But the people who had gathered from every side to behold this spectacle, raised a great shout behind them, after their fashion, and pursued them as they fled with clods and sticks and stones.

RELICS

The Blood of Hayles and other famous relics attracted the devout and many relics are listed in the inventories of monastic possessions. Relics were zealously acquired by gift, purchase or even theft. Some became objects of superstition. On her way from Bristol Margery Kempe impressed the Cistercian monks at Hayles Abbey by her demonstrative devotion. She had recently sailed on pilgrimage to St. James, having had in answer to her prayer fair wind and weather, unlike the passengers described on p. 83. The relic of the Holy Blood was brought to Hayles from Germany by Edmund Earl of Cornwall.

Further Reading: C. F. Battiscombe, ' The Relics of St. Cuthbert ', *Transactions of the Architectural and Archaeological Society of Durham and Northumberland*, vol. 8, 1937, p. 48. P. Norland, 'An Early Group of Enamelled Reliquaries ', *Acta Archaeologica*, Vol. 4, 1933, p. 1.

(1) *Source*: W. Butler-Bowdon, *The Book of Margery Kempe*, Jonathan Cape, 1936, p. 163. (Early fifteenth century).

She abode not long there [Bristol], but went forth to the Blood of Hayles, and there she was shriven and had loud cries and boisterous weepings.

Then the religious men had her in amongst them, and made her good cheer, save they swore many great oaths and horrible. And she rebuked them therefor, after the Gospel, and thereof had they great wonder.

Nevertheless some were right well pleased, thanked be God for His goodness.

(2) *Source*: Chaucer, *Prologue of the Pardoner's Tale.*

' Good men,' seye I, ' tak of my wordes kepe;
If that this boon [a shoulder bone] be wasshe in any welle,
If cow, or calf, or sheep, or oxe swelle
That any worm hath ete, or worm ystonge,
Tak water of that welle, and wash his tonge,
And it is hool [whole] anon; and furthermore,
Of pokkes and of scabbe, and every sore
Shal every sheep be hool, that of this welle
Drinkethe a draughte; tak kepe eek what I telle . . .
Heer is a miteyn [mitten] eek, that ye may see.
He that his hond wol putte in this miteyn,
He shal have multiplying of his greyn,
When he hath sowen, be it whete or otes,
So that he offre pens, or elles grotes. . . . '

THE BIBLE

There were Old English biblical translations but most early Bibles
were in Latin. This was readily understood by those who could read,
of whom all, in the early Middle Ages, were clergy. Great illuminated
Bibles were produced in the twelfth century and in the thirteenth
century many small portable Bibles were produced. Pictures on walls
and in glass were ' the Bible of the Poor '. Most attention was given
to the scenes connected with the great occasions of the Christian
year. Incidents in the Old Testament were illustrated in so far as they
were foreshadowings of events in the New Testament, and were
therefore relevant to the story of Paradise Lost through the disobedi-
ence of the old Adam and Eve and Paradise Regained through the
Virgin and the New Adam. The Bible associated with Wycliffe's
name survived in whole or in part in no fewer than 150 copies, despite
efforts to suppress it. It was not the only translation, and Wycliff's
enemies, the Friars, themselves did much to spread the story of Christ
though with apocryphal additions.

Further Reading: Beryl Smalley, *Study of the Bible in the Middle Ages*,
1941. Margaret Deanesley, *Lollard Bible and other Medieval Biblical
Versions*, 1920. *Selden Infancy*. MicroMethods Filmstrip.

Source: Translation of captions to illustrations to Apocryphal
Infancy stories in the Holkham Bible Picture Book. (These were made
for a Friar. Lollards objected to such additions to the Bible as lies.
The Friars defended them.) *Holkham Bible*, E.P. Filmstrip.

. . . How Jesus led the children of Egypt to the water and climbed upon it. They could not do so and were drowned, and he raised them from the dead.

How Jesus climbed on the sunbeams. The others could not do so and tumbled down to the ground and broke their limbs, and Jesus healed them.

How Jesus went to find some water at the well and broke the pots of his playmates, and then he made them whole again.

How Jesus came to seek the children of the Jews with whom he used to play. And their fathers had hidden them in an oven. And Jesus asked what was in the oven and they said that it was pigs. And Jesus said let it be pigs.

How the Jews went to draw their children out of the oven and found pigs instead of their children. This was indeed what Jesus had said. And they were wrath and sad. And this is why they are said to eat no pork. . . .

LOLLARDS

A vivid hostile account of the Lollards at Leicester, the misadventures of Margery Kempe, suspected of being a Lollard at Leicester in 1417, and the recantation of Bishop Peacock in 1457 have been related in *T.S.I.H.*, vol. 1 and the lives of Wycliffe and Oldcastle in *W.W.I.H.*, vol. 1. Lollards attacked not only unworthy priests or popes but the priesthood and the papacy as institutions. They did not spare either the dogmas or the financial basis of the oldest and richest institution in Christendom, and regarded as superstitious what all had regarded hitherto as holy. They attacked pilgrimages and images, even the sacrament of the Mass.

Further Reading: England in the time of Wycliffe, ed. E. P. Cheyney. Philadelphia, Department of History of the University of Pennsylvania, 1895. Translations and reprints from the original sources of European History, 2, no. 5.

K. B. McFarlane, *John Wycliffe and the Beginnings of English Nonconformity*, 1952. H. B. Workman, *John Wyclif*, 1926.

Source: death of Sir John Oldcastle (the last important Lollard), 1417, *The Brut, or the Chronicles of England*, ed. F. W. D. Brie, Early English Text Soc., 1908, p. 386.

Convycte be [by] the clergy of Lollardye, and dampned before the Iustice unto deth for treson . . . he was hadde unto the Tour agen, and ther he was laide on a hurdil, and drawn through the cite to Saint Gyles Felde, and there was made a new paire of galows, and a stonge chayne, and a coler of yron for hym, and there he was hanged and brent on the galous, and alle for his lewdeness and fals opynyons.

CONTENTS OF THE PARISH CHURCH, 1305

Archbishop Winchelsey required the provision for the Church of more than Archbishop Peckham, who, in 1280, ordered the provision of vestments, chalice, missal (Book for Mass), processional cross and paschal candles. Here is a list of what Winchelsey required. The vestments can be studied in funeral brasses. See p. 346.

Further Reading: A. H. Thompson, *Parish History and Records* (Historical Association. Leaflet no. 66, revised ed.) 1926.

(1) *Source*: Translation and notes by P. H. Ditchfield, *Old Village Life*, Methuen 1920, pp. 104–5. See also Lyndwode, *Provinciale*, pp. 251–2; *Vetus Liber Archidiaconi Eliensis*, ed. Feltoe and Minns, Cambridge 1917, p. 150; *English Historical Review*, vol. 50, pp. 411–3.

Legend [book of scripture readings], Antiphonal [service-book used by cantors at the antiphon-lectern in the choir], Grayle [a ' gradual ', book with musical parts of the Mass], Tropary [book of tropes or sequences, verses sung before the Gospel at Mass], Ordinale, Missal, Manual [portable service-book], Chalice, the best Vestment with Chasuble [vestment for Eucharist], Dalmatic [robe with long sleeves] and Tunicle [plainer and shorter robe than Dalmatic], and a Cope for the choir with all their belongings, that is amice [ornamented linen collar worn over surplice], girdle, maniple [originally a strip of fine linen worn over left wrist of celebrant to wipe the chalice, later an ornament] and stole, etc., the frontal for the High Altar, with three cloths; three surplices, a rochet [a frock of white lawn with tight sleeves], the processional cross, a cross to carry to the sick, a thurible [metal vessel for incense], a lantern, a bell to ring when the Body of Christ is carried to the sick; a pyx of ivory or silver for the Body of Christ, the Lenten veil [to hang before the high altar];

the Rogation Day banners (for ' Gang Week ' when the parish bounds were beaten); the bells with their cords; a bier to carry the dead upon; the Holy Water vat (from which the clerk might sprinkle parishioners); the osculatorium for the Pax (a ' pax-brede,' an ornament by which the kiss of peace was given), the Paschal candlestick (for holding the candle lit at Easter services); a font with its lock and key (to prevent the removal of water for witchcraft); the images in the church; the image of the patron Saint in the chancel; the enclosure wall of the cemetery; and all repairs of every sort, except those of the chancel which pertain to the Rectors or Vicars.

(2) Moveables in Holkham Church, 1368.

A record of the furnishings of 358 Norfolk churches survives from 1368. One hundred of these had fallen into ruin when the list was printed in 1948. They mention 4000 books and many vestments. None can be traced. For many English parishes the earliest inventory of church property to survive is from 1552. The list of church goods is in each case preceded by various regular payments due from the church concerned. The book was made for the archdeacon when visiting the parishes as a checklist.

Source: Translated from *Archdeaconry of Norwich Inventory of Church Goods temp. Edward III*, transcribed by Dom Aelred Watkin, Monk of Downside, Norfolk Record Society, vol. xix (2 parts, 1947–8), part 1, p. 93.

. . . 1 ordinale [or directory] with a martyrology. 2 antiphonals. 1 lectionary by itself. 2 psalters. a canon of penance with statutes of synods in a martyrology. 3 manuals of which 1 is with a psalter. 1 missal. 2 graduals of which 1 is with a troper [book of sequences or proses sung at Mass]. 1 troper by itself. 4 pairs of vestments. 4 linen sheets. 2 towels. 3 corporal cloths. 1 altar frontal. 1 silk cope for the ministers at Evensong etc. a Lenten veil. 8 surplices. 1 rochet. 2 silver-gilt chalices and 1 of tin. 4 cruets. 1 chest. a lamp. a lantern. a censer. a carpet. 2 portable crosses. a bell. 2 superaltars [portable altars]. 1 altar frontal *in ambone* [a high place]. 2 handbells. a pix for the Eucharist. a chrismatory [vessel for consecrated oil] and font with locks. 2 tin candlesticks. a gold cloth given by Sir Walter Helveton. another breviary, given by Sir William de Heverynglond, rector of the church. a vestment with tunic and dalmatic [deacon's

vestment] given to the altar of St. Mary by William de Methel-
wolde, rector of the church. a new psalter given by Sir Stephen
de Wadton, once perpetual vicar. a breviary given by Sir Richard
Dallyn. 2 procession-books. 1 Epistle-book. Also 1 vestment of
cloth of gold of red colour given by Sir John Porte vicar of the
church of Holkham.

THE SACRAMENTS

By the reign of Edward I fonts were generally made with eight
sides. On one of these the Rood was sometimes carved and on the
others the seven sacraments. Of thirty-two examples there are nineteen
in Norfolk, eleven in Suffolk, one in Kent and one in Somerset. Freda
Derrick, *Tales told in Church Stones*, 1935, reproduces examples—the
sacrament of Orders with a candidate receiving a ' suitable tonsure '
from Nettlecombe, Somerset, Baptism from Gresham, Norfolk, and
Great Glemham, Suffolk, Confirmation from Sloley, Norfolk, the
Holy Eucharist from Gresham, Norfolk, Penance from Westhall,
Suffolk, Marriage from Nettlecombe, Somerset, and Extreme Unction
from the same church. Excellent fifteenth century specimens at
Walsoken, Norfolk, and Laxfield, Suffolk, are reproduced in J. C. Cox,
English Church Fittings, Furniture and Accessories (1923). For Baptism
and Marriage, see pp. 103 and 99.

' Houseling cloth ' to prevent accidental fall of consecrated wafer
at Communion. Early fourteenth century. (Queen Mary's Psalter).

Further Reading: G. McN. Rushforth, ' Seven Sacraments Composi-
tions in English Medieval Art ', *Antiquaries Journal*, vol. 9, 1929.

Source: Chronicle at Melrose, translated by Rev. J. Stevenson, *The Church Historians of England*, vol. 4, pt. 1, pp. 224–5. (1268)

It happened that immediately after he [Simon de Montfort] had been killed, and stripped of the arms in which he had been clad, some of the sons of Belial came up and cut the hands and feet off the corpse; and it is respecting one of the hands that the following narrative is told: There was a certain man belonging to the frontier lands [of Wales], an inhabitant of the county of Chester, who had been in the battle of Evesham, along with Edward [later Edward I], and who, after the battle, became possessed of this hand of Simon's, about which I have been speaking. He sent it to his wife by a companion as wicked as himself, thinking that she would be rejoiced at the death of their enemy, of which this hand was a conclusive proof. The attendant, on his arrival at his master's farm, did not find the lady of the farm at home, but he hastened on to the parish church, where she was, which was situated at no great distance from his lord's dwelling-house. When he arrived there, carrying in his bosom the said hand, wrapped up in a cloth, he went up to the lady, and, whispering in her ear, he told her of the death of Simon, and added, ' See, here is a token that he is killed', intending to show her the hand which had been cut off. But the woman, not liking to be put to the blush, or perhaps fearing God, refused at that time either to look at the hand or to touch it, although the retainer of her husband earnestly urged her to take what he had brought, and keep it in her own possession. As he was entreating her to act thus wickedly, the lady said, ' Keep it covered up until divine service is finished '. Obeying his lady's command, he withdrew, and took his place among the crowd, that he might hear the mass; and it happened that at the elevation of the blessed host, as the people were lifting up their hands, this attendant also lifted up his hand to adore the Lord, whom the priest had just elevated. Behold! the hand of the holy man, whom this servant of a bond-slave of the devil was carrying, was, without any assistance whatever on his part, raised up above his head by God's power, in order that thus the supremacy of his exaltation might be perceived all the more clearly, towering above every head, even that of the tallest man of the multitude there assembled. And having thus adored the Lord of Majesty at his elevation, as I have stated, when the priest bowed himself before the altar to adore the Lord, quicker than language can express, it again stooped to the same place whence it had gone out, not without the power of God, for the cloth into which it had been sewn was found to be as firmly stitched together as it had been at the first, nor could the bearer discover any alteration in it. [She tells the messenger to take the hand back to her husband. Many of the congregation saw this miracle].

THE FONT

Further Reading: G. C. Druce, ' Lead Fonts in England ', *British Archaeological Journal*, 2nd series vol. 39, 1934; G. C. Dunning, ' The Distribution of Black Tournai Fonts ', *Antiquaries Journal*, vol. 24, 1944. See also p. 103.

Source: Provincial Constitutions of St. Edmund, Archbishop of Canterbury (1236); D. Wilkins, *Concilia Magnae Britanniae et Hiberniae*, 1737, vol. 1, p. 636.

Fonts are to be kept closed by locks, because of witchcraft.

Likewise chrism [holy unguent] and holy oil are to be kept under key.

If anyone responsible for their custody is negligent in this he is to be suspended from his ministry for three months; and if anything evil results from his lack of caution he is to be liable to a more serious punishment.

THE PULPIT

Preachers were important in Saxon and Gothic England as they were under the Puritan Commonwealth, the Friars gave increased emphasis to preaching in and after the thirteenth century and a good idea of a preacher's approach is given by the treatment of sacred themes in the Holkham Bible. Extracts from medieval sermons occur on pp. 133 and 348. There are some sixty medieval stone pulpits, dating from the end of the fourteenth century, in English parish churches. Of these the oldest is at Long Coombe, Oxfordshire. There are also some hundred pulpits carved of oak, mostly fifteenth century. Norfolk and Devon have most of these. Those at Burlingham St. Edmund and Burnham Norton, Norfolk, Southwold, Suffolk, and Burford, Oxfordshire, retain their original paint. Bromyard and others wrote practical manuals on the technique of preaching with collections of suitable anecdotes with morals.

Further Reading: F. T. Dollman, *Examples of Ancient Pulpits*, 1849. J. C. Cox, *Pulpits and Lecterns in English Churches*, 1915. G. R. Owst, *Preaching in Medieval England*, Cambridge, 1926.

Source: Constitutions of Archbishop Peckham (d. 1292), translated from William Lyndwood, *Provinciale*, Oxford 1679, pp. 54–5.

. . . We ordain that every priest having cure of souls should four times a year, that is to say once in each quarter of the year, on a solemn day or on several, personally or by deputy, explain to the people in their own language, without any fantastic weaving of any subtleties the fourteen articles of the faith, the ten commandments, the two commands of the Gospel, namely the twofold love [of God and neighbour], the seven works of mercy, the seven deadly sins with what follows them, the seven chief virtues and the seven sacraments of grace.

CHURCH DUES

Source: Laws of King Ethelred (978–1016), v. 11–12. B. Thorpe, *Ancient Laws and Institutes of England*, 1840, p. 131.

And let God's dues be willingly paid every year: that is, plough-alms, 15 days after Easter, and a tithe of young by Pentecost [Whitsun], and of earth-fruits by Allhallows' mass, and Rome-'feoh' [payment] by St. Peter's mass, and light-scot [tax] thrice in the year.

And it is most proper that soul-scot [tax] be always paid at the open grave: and if any corpse be laid out of its proper shrift-district else-where, let soul-scot be, nevertheless, paid to the minster to which it belonged; and let all God's dues be diligently furthered, as is needful, and let festivals and fasts be rightly held.

TITHES

The Church had a right to one tenth of the harvest.

Further Reading: G. S. Hewins, *Notes on Ancient Tithe Barns*, 1938.

(1) *Source*: Laws of King Edgar (956–975), I, B. Thorpe, *Ancient Laws and Institutes of England*, 1840, p. 111.

And let a tithe of every young be paid by Pentecost [Whitsun]; and of the fruits of the earth by the equinox; and every church-scot [tax] by Martinmas, on peril of the full ' wite ' [fine] which the doom-book [the law] specifies: and if any one will not then pay the tithe, as we have ordained, let the king's reeve go thereto, and the bishop's, and the mass-priest of the minster to which it is due; and assign to him the ninth part; and let the eight parts be divided into two, and let the land-lord take possession of half, half the bishop; be it a king's man, be it a thane's.

(2) *Source*: *The Autobiography of Giraldus Cambrensis*, ed. and trans-lated by H. E. Williams, Jonathan Cape, 1937, p. 40.

Now about the same time [late twelfth century] there came to pass a thing, which I have also thought worthy of note, namely that a certain man of these parts, one Roger, surnamed Bechet, owed ten stone of wool to his creditor at the time of shearing. Having no more than this amount, he sent the tenth stone, despite the protest of his wife, to his baptismal church of Caereu, and the remaining nine to his creditor at Pembroke, begging him to have patience, for he would soon make good the deficiency. Now his creditor, on receiving the wool, weighed it and found the weight to be ten stone; and though he weighed it again and again, he always found the full tale of ten stone; and, so he made answer to his debtor that he had received satisfaction in full. Wherefore by his example, the wool having been miraculously multiplied like the oil of Elisha [2 Kings iv. 2], many persons in those parts are either converted to the payment of those tithes or confirmed in their readiness to pay.

CHURCHWARDENS' DISBURSEMENTS, 1349

Further Reading: Charles Drew, *Early Parochial organisation in England*, St. Anthony's Press, 1954.

Source: *Churchwardens' Accounts of Croscombe, Pilton, Yatton, Tintin-hull, Morebath, and St. Michael's, Bath, ranging from* 1349 *to* 1560, edited by Rt. Rev. Bishop Hobhouse, Somerset Record Society, vol. 4, 1890, pp. 225–228. These are the oldest churchwardens' account known to survive. They cover 226 years in 77 rolls. An allowance was paid to churchwardens at Bath sometimes for their duties, an item absent in the accounts of other parishes. There was a feast at audit-time. The parish owned a small flock of sheep and considerable house-property given for the endowment of obituary services. These endow-ments were enough to make it generally unnecessary for Bath to raise money by ' ales ' in the Church-house.

[A list of rents is followed by these miscellaneous incomings.]

Also they received 2s. left in the will of William de Wyke for a missal.

And 9½d. from collections against Christmas.

And 11d. from collections against Easter.

And 20s. from the bequest of John Michel for holding annual anniversaries of himself and others.

And 6s. received of J. Annatt.

And 10d. for the sale of silk covering.

And 5d. for the sale of another silk covering.

And 12d. for the sale of old cloths left to the said church.

And 12d. for the sale of one old brazen jar and for 1 flagon.

And for 2s. 3d. for the sale of one brazen jar.

And 2s. 6d. for the sale of old timber from Robert Golde's holding.

And 6s. for the sale of old timber from Adam Storche's holding.

And 6s. 8d. for the sale of wool by the bequest of the wife of Thomas Stote.

And 12d. for produce from Adam Storche's garden.

And 3d. for the produce of the garden of the neighbours, etc.

And 1d. for candles sold to Robert le Doyere.

Total 52s. 8½d.

Total income £4. 12s. 11d.

The outgoings begin with nineteen payments of rent-charges payable to the clergy for obituary offices and totalling 38s. 8d.

Then come miscellaneous outgoings.

Wax bought against Christmas	3s. 2d.
Making the same	6d.
Lichil [?=wick]	1d.
4 lbs. wax bought against Easter	4s.
Making the same	1½d.
½ lb. wax for torches	6d.
Making same	3d.

PLATE XXIX

THE CHURCH

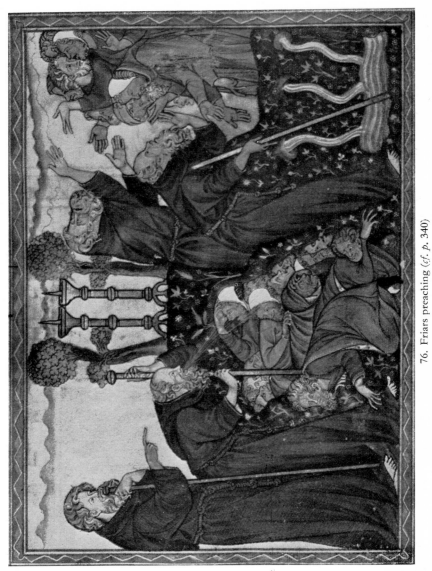

76. Friars preaching (cf. p. 340)

77. Mass. Priest with Host, acolyte with Candle

78. Dedication of Church. Holy water stoop and ladle (*cf. development of height of mitre from Plate XXVI*)

1 lb. wax for the candle of Adam Storche at the feet of St. Kather-
    ine   12d.

Making same $\frac{1}{2}$d.

Oil bought for a lamp   10$\frac{1}{2}$d.

2 candles newly made at the feet of St. Michael   1d.

Withies for wattling   20d.

Straw   4d.

Fee for clerk lighting lamp per annum   1d.

Fee of laundress for washing clothes and other ornaments   2d.

Proctor's annual fee   3d.

Parchment for making up account   1d.

Purchase of one missal   46s. 2d.

                               Total 60s. 3$\frac{1}{2}$d.

Fee

Fee of clerk for making up account   4d.

Bread and ale for proctor's expenses   3d.

                  Grand Total   £4. 19. 6$\frac{1}{2}$d.

PARISH CLERGY

The nature of government and church records alike is to record crime not virtue. Accordingly it is in literature that there is preserved the best account of a good and simple parish priest, in Chaucer. The particular emblem of the priestly office was the chalice which he used in celebrating Mass. Forty-seven medieval chalices survive, often a hemispherical bowl separated from a round, or later from a lobed base by a stem, in the centre of which projects a knob or ' knop '. Pewter chalices were sometimes buried with priests and chalices are carved on the monumental brasses with which some are commemorated. In the later middle ages bishops' registers, and literature are full of references to good and bad priests from Piers Plowman's ' Sloth ' (who was better at finding a hare than explaining Psalm I) to the poor and good parson in Chaucer.

Further Reading: R. A. R. Hartridge, *Vicarages in the Middle Ages*, 1930. E. L. Cutts, *Parish Priests and their People in the Middle Ages*, 1891. G. W. O. Addleshaw, *Rectors, vicars and patrons in twelfth-and early thirteenth-century canon law*, St. Anthony's Hall, Publications no. 9, 1956.

(1) *Source*: Canons Enacted under King Edgar (956–975). B. Thorpe, *Ancient Laws and Institutes of England*, 1840, pp. 395–6.

Y

. . . And we enjoin, that they, at every synod, have, every year, books and garments for divine ministry, and ink and vellum for their ordinances; and provision for three days.

And we enjoin, that every priest at the synod have his clerk, and an orderly man for servant, and no ignorant person who loves folly; but let all go with decorum, and with fear of God Almighty. . . .

And we enjoin, that no priest receive another's scholar, without leave of him whom he previously followed.

And we enjoin, that every priest, in addition to lore, diligently learn a handicraft.

And we enjoin, that no learned priest put to shame the half learned, but improve him, if he know better.

And we enjoin, that no high born priest despise the lower born; because if it be rightly considered, then are all men of one birth.

And we enjoin, that every priest provide for himself lawfully, and let no one be a monger unlawfully, nor a covetous merchant.

And we enjoin, that every priest grant baptism as soon as it is demanded; and everywhere, in his shrift-district, command, that every child be baptized within 37 days; and that no one be too long unconfirmed.

And we enjoin, that every priest zealously promote Christianity, and totally extinguish every heathenism; and forbid well-worshipings, and necromancies, and divinations, and enchantments, and man-worshipings, and the vain practices which are carried on with various spells, and with ' frith-splots ' [sacred spots], and with elders, and also with various trees, and with stones, and with many various delusions, with which men do much of what they should not.

(2) Bad priests.

Source: Law of the Northumbrian Priests, B. Thorpe, *Ancient Laws and Institutes of England*, 1840, p. 418 (probably 1020–3).

Let him make ' bot ' [amends] for it:
If a priest despise or insult another with word or deed;
If a priest fight with another;
If a priest be aiding to another in wrong;

If a priest refuse another lawful succour;

If a priest leave another unwarned of that which he knows will harm him;

if a priest neglect the shaving of beard or of locks;

if a priest, at the appointed time, do not ring the hours, or sing the hours;

if a priest come with weapons into a church;

if a priest misorder the annual services of the church, by day or by night;

if a priest misconduct an ordeal;

if a priest enwrap his tonsure;

if a priest love drunkenness, or become a gleeman or an ' ale-scop ' . . .

If a priest forsake a woman [cf. p. 101] and take another, let him be excommunicated. . . .

THE PARISH CLERK

Parish clerks made the responses in church and sprinkled holy water on all the houses in the parish. The clerks of London used to perform plays at Clerkenwell, a spring just outside the city called the well of the clerks as early as the first half of the twelfth century (for these plays see *T.S.I.H.*, i, 140). It was not until the post-medieval period that parish clerks were given various administrative functions making them more like the clerk of a modern civil parish. Chaucer has made an imaginary parish clerk at Oxford, an Oxford student's rival for the love of a carpenter's wife, more vivid than any real clerk.

Further Reading: W. E. Tate, *The Parish Chest: a Study of the Records of Parochial Administration*, latest edition.

Source: Chaucer, *The Millere his Tale*.

Now was ther of that chirche a parissh clerk,
The which that was ycleped Absolon;
Crul [curled] was his heer and as the gold it shoon,
And strouted [projected] as a fanne, large and brode,
Ful streight and evene lay his joly shode [parting].
His rode [complexion] was reed, his eyen greye as goos;
With Powles wyndow corven on his shoos,
In hosen rede he wente fetisly.

Yclad he was ful smal and proprely,
Al in a kirtel of a lyght waget [blue]
Ful faire and thikke been the poyntes set;
And there upon he hadde a gay surplys,
As whit as is the blosme upon the rys [bough].
A myrie child he was, so God me save,
Wel koude he laten blood and clippe and shave,
And maken a chartre of lond or acquitaunce.
In twenty manere koude he trippe and daunce,
After the scole of Oxenforde tho,
And with his legges casten to and fro,
And pleyen songes on a small rubible [rebeck];
Therto he song som tyme a loud quynyble [treble],
And as wel koude he pleye on his giterne [guittar].
In al the toun nas brewhous ne taverne
That he ne visited with his solas,
Ther any gaylard tappestere was . . .
This Absolon, that jolif was and gay,
Gooth with a sencer [of incense] on the haliday,
Sensynge the wyves of the parisshe faste,
And many a lovely look on hem he caste; . . .
[He serenades the carpenter's wife, combs his hair, sends her spiced wine, meed and spiced ale and wafers piping hot]
Somtyme to shewe his lightnesse and maistrye
He pleyeth Herodes upon a scaffold hye . . . [He hopes to kiss her]
But first he cheweth greyn and lycorys,
To smellen sweete, er he hadde kemd his heer.
Under his tonge a trewe-love [special leaf] he beer. . . .

BISHOPS

Bishops organized the parish priests in wide areas called dioceses and to do this they needed the help of well educated clerks. These formed a household and an office or ' chancery ' which grew in importance and had to be well read in the special laws of the church, or ' canon law '. Certain monasteries and parishes were exempt from the rule of any bishop. The greatest authority on this was William Lyndwood, Bishop of St. David's (d. 1446). Some bishops were saintly men, but the Bishops of Durham were soldiers and princes as well as churchmen, as Odo of Bayeux who fought the English at Hastings had been. After the mid fourteenth century most bishops were graduates. The first headmaster to be a bishop was Wainflete. The lives of the most important Bishops and the arms of their dioceses are included in *W.W.I.H.*, i.

As shepherd of the people a Bishop's emblem was a hooked staff or crozier. The finely wrought crozier of William of Wykeham is preserved at New College. He also wore on his head a mitre. Mitres were originally low as shown in the drawings of Matthew Paris in the thirteenth century, but by the end of the fourteenth century they had become lofty (see pictures in *W.W.I.H.*, i, p. 127 and pl. 21).

Further Reading: C. J. Offer, *Bishop's Register*, 1929. (This shows the ordinary work of a bishop as an administrator).

Source: [Saxon] Institutes of Polity, Civil and Ecclesiastical. B. Thorpe, *Ancient Laws and Institutes of England*, 1840, p. 427.

A bishop's daily work. That is rightly, his prayers first, and then his book-work, reading or writing, teaching or learning; and his church hours at the right time, always according to the things thereto befitting; and washing the feet of the poor; and his alms-dealing; and the direction of work, where it may be needful. Good handycrafts are also befitting him, that crafts may be cultivated in his family [household], at least that no one too idle may dwell there. And it also well befits him, that at the ' gemōt ' [assembly] he oft and frequently promulgate divine lore among the people with whom he then is.

ARCHDEACONS

Bishops delegated much of their administrative work to archdeacons who had to visit and inspect churches and inquire into and punish crimes against the laws and moral ideas of the Church. This led to much unpopularity and the doubt whether it was possible for an archdeacon to go to Heaven. Friars were exempt from the archdeacon's jurisdiction and had no fear of the summoner, the archdeacon's agent. Accordingly in the *Canterbury Tales* Chaucer puts hard words about the summoner into the friar's mouth, and the summoner, in return, gives an unkind account of a friar.

Further Reading: A. H. Thompson, *Diocesan Organisation in the Middle Ages: Archdeacons and Rural Deans*, 1944.

Source: Chaucer, *The Freres Tale*.

Whilom ther was dwellinge in my contree
An erchedeken, a man of heigh degree,
That boldely dide execucioun
In punisshinge of fornicacioun,
Of wicchecraft, and eek of bauderye,
Of diffamacioun, and avoutrye [adultery],
Of chirche-reves [churchwardens], and of testaments,
Of contractes, and of lakke of sacraments,
And eek of many another maner cryme
Which nedeth nat rehercen at this tyme;
Of usure, and of symonye also.
But certes, lechours dide he gretest wo; . . .
For smale tythes and for smal offringe
He made the peple pitously to singe.
For er the bisshop caughte hem with his hook,
They weren in the erchedeknes book.
Thanne hadde he, thrugh his jurisdiccioun,
Power to doon on hem correccioun.
He had a Somnour [Summoner] redy to his hond,
A slyer boy was noon in Engelond.

HEARTH-PENNY

Source: Laws of King Edgar (950–975), I, 4. B. Thorpe, *Ancient Laws and Institutes of England*, 1840, p. 112.

And let every hearth-penny be rendered by St. Peter's mass-day: and he who shall not have paid it by that term, let him be led to Rome, and in addition thereto pay 30 pence, and bring then a certificate thence, that he has there rendered so much; and when he comes home, pay to the king a hundred and twenty shillings. And if again he will not pay it, let him be led again to Rome, and with another such ' bot ' [indemnification]; and when he comes home, pay to the king two hundred shillings. At the third time, if he then yet will not, let him forfeit all that he owns.

BENEDICTINE MONKS

There were some sixty abbeys and priories following the rule of St. Benedict, and founded in Saxon or early Norman times in the province of Canterbury, but in the province of York the only ones were Durham, St. Mary's, York (and its priory St. Bees), Whitby and Selby.

Further Reading: Biographies of individual Abbots of the Benedictine monasteries of St. Albans, Westminster, etc., and of Abbot Clown of the Augustianian house of Leicester in David Knowles, *The Religious*

Receiving the tonsure at Repton.   Twelfth century.   (Guthlac Roll).

Orders in England, vol. 2, The End of the Middle Ages, Cambridge University Press, 1955.

(1) *Source*: The ideal Abbot, *The Rule of St. Benedict,* a commentary by the Right Rev. Dom Paul Delatte, Abbot of Solesmes and Superior-General of the Congregation of the Benedictines of France, translated by Dom Justin McCann, Monk of Ampleforth, Burns Oates and Washbourne, Ltd., 1921, pp. 35–55.

An Abbot who is worthy to rule over the monastery ought always to remember what he is called, and correspond to his name by his works. For he is believed to hold the place of Christ in the monastery, since he is called by His name, as the Apostle says: ' Ye have received the spirit of the adoption of sons, in which we cry: Abba, Father.'

And therefore the Abbot ought not [God forbid] to teach, or ordain, or command anything contrary to the law of the lord; but let his bidding and his doctrine be infused into the minds of his disciples like the leaven of divine justice.

Let the Abbot be ever mindful that at the dreadful judgment of God, an account will have to be given both of his own teaching and of the obedience of his disciples. And let him know that lack of profit which the father of the household may find in his sheep, shall be imputed to the fault of the shepherd. Only then shall he be acquitted, if he shall have bestowed all pastoral diligence on his unquiet and disobedient flock, and employed all his care to amend their corrupt manner of life: then shall he be absolved in the judgement of the Lord, and may say to the Lord with the prophet: ' I have not hidden thy justice in my heart, I have declared thy truth and thy salvation, but they contemned and despised me.' So at the last to those disobedient sheep may their punishment come, overmastering death.

Therefore when anyone takes the name of Abbot, he ought to govern his disciples by a two-fold doctrine: that is, he should show forth all that is good and holy by his deeds, rather than his words: declaring to the intelligent among his disciples the commandments of the Lord by words: but to the hard-hearted and the simple-minded setting forth the divine precepts by the example of his deeds. And let him show by his own actions that those things ought not to be done which he has taught his disciples to be against the law of God; lest, while preaching to others, he should himself become a castaway, and God should say to him in his sin: 'Why doest thou declare my justice, and take my covenant in thy mouth? Thou hast hated discipline, and hast cast my words behind thee.' And again, ' Thou sawest the mote in thy brother's eye, didst thou not see the beam in thine own? '

Let him make no distinction of persons in the monastery. Let not one be loved more than another, unless he be found to excel in good works or in obedience. Let not one of noble birth be put before him that was formerly a slave, unless some other reasonable cause exist for it. If upon just consideration it should so seem good to the Abbot, let him advance one of any rank whatever; but otherwise let them keep their own places; because whether bond or free, we are all one in Christ, and bear an equal burden in the army of one Lord: for ' with God there is no respecting of persons '. Only for one reason are we to be preferred in His sight, if we be found to surpass others in good works and in humility. Let the Abbot, then show equal love to all, and let the same discipline be imposed upon all according to their deserts.

For the Abbot in his doctrine ought always to observe the rule of the Apostle, wherein he says: ' reprove, entreat, rebuke ': suiting his action to circumstances, mingling gentleness with severity; showing now the rigour of a master, now the loving affection of a father, so as sternly to rebuke the undisciplined and restless, and to exhort the obedient, mild, and patient to advance in virtue. And such as are negligent and haughty we charge him to reprove and correct. Let him not shut his eyes to the faults of offenders; but as soon as they appear, let him strive, as he has the authority for that, to root them out, remembering the fate of Heli, the priest of Silo.

Those of good disposition and understanding let him correct, for the first or second time, with words only; but such as are froward and hard of heart, and proud, or disobedient, let him chastise with bodily stripes at the very first offence, knowing that it is written: ' The fool is not corrected with words '. And again: ' Strike thy son with the rod, and thou shalt deliver his soul from death.'

The Abbot ought always to remember what he is, and what he is called, and to know that to whom more is committed, from him more is required; and he must consider how difficult and arduous a task he has undertaken, of ruling souls and adapting himself to many dispositions. Let him so accommodate and suit himself to the character and intelligence of each, winning some by kindness, others by reproof, others by persuasion, that he may not only suffer no loss in the flock committed to him, but may even rejoice in their virtuous increase.

Above all let him not, overlooking or undervaluing the salvation of the souls entrusted to him, be more solicitous for fleeting, earthly, and perishable things; but let him ever bear in mind that he has undertaken the government of souls, of which he shall have to give an account. And that he may not complain for want of worldly substance, let him remember what is written: ' Seek first the kingdom of God and his justice, and all these things shall be added unto you.' And again: ' Nothing is wanting to them that fear him.'

And let him know that he who has undertaken the government of souls, must prepare himself to render an account of them. And whatever may be the number of the brethren under his care, let him be certainly assured that on the Day of Judgement he will have to give an account to the Lord of all these souls, as well as of his own. And thus, being ever fearful of the coming judgement of the shepherd concerning the state of the flock committed to him, while he is careful on other men's accounts, he will be solicitous also on his own. And so, while correcting others by his admonitions, he will be himself cured of his own defects.

(2) Election of an Abbot of Bury, 1182.

Samson, the successful candidate, is described by Jocelin in *T.S.I.H.*, i, 104–6. See also pp. 39, 45, 51.

Source: *The Chronicle of Jocelin of Brakelond concerning the Acts of Samson Abbot of the Monastery of St. Edmund*, translated by H. E. Butler, Nelson and Sons, 1949, pp. 11–15.

And one said of another, ' That brother is a good monk, a person worthy of approval: he knows much concerning the Rule and the customs of the Church; though he be not so perfect a philosopher as certain others he might well fill the office of Abbot.

Abbot Ording was an illiterate man, and yet he was a good Abbot and ruled this house wisely; moreover, we read in the fables that it proved better for the frogs to choose a log for their king, in whom they could trust, than a serpent . . .' To this another made answer, ' How may that be? How can he, a man who has no knowledge of letters, preach a sermon in Chapter, or on feast days to the people? . . . God forbid that a dumb image should be set up in the Church of St. Edmund, where it is known that there are many men of learning and of industry.' Again another said of yet another, ' That brother is literate, eloquent and prudent, strict in his observance of the Rule; he has greatly loved the Convent, and has endured many ills for the possessions of the Church; he is worthy to be Abbot.' And another replied, ' From all good clerks, O Lord deliver us; that it may please Thee to preserve us from all Norfolk barrators [sharp lawyers], we beseech Thee to hear us '. Again one said of a certain brother, ' That brother is a good manager, as is proved by the performance of his tasks and by the offices that he has filled so well, and the buildings and repairs that he has made. He knows how to work hard and to defend our house, and he is something of a clerk, though ' much learning maketh him not mad '. He is worthy to be Abbot.' The other made answer, ' God forbid that a man who cannot read or sing or celebrate the holy offices, a wicked man and unjust, a flayer of the poor—God forbid that such an one should be made Abbot! ' Again a certain brother said of someone, ' that brother is a kindly man, affable and amiable, peaceful and composed, bountiful and generous, a literate man and eloquent, a very proper man in aspect and bearing, who is loved by many both within and without. And such a man, God willing, might be made Abbot to the great honour of the Church '. The other made answer, ' Nay; it would be an onus rather than an honour to have such a man; for he is over nice about his food and drink, thinks it a virtue to sleep long, knows how to spend much and gain little, snores when others keep vigil, would always be in the midst of abundance and gives no thought to the debts that grow from day to day, nor to the expenditure, how it may be met; hating all toil and anxiety and caring for naught, provided that one day go and another come—a man that loves and cherishes flatterers and liars, and himself says one thing and does another. From such a ruler may the Lord defend us! ' Again one said of his comrade, ' That man is wiser almost than any of us, both in the things of the world and the things of the Church. . . ' Another replied, ' . . . yet, if he chances to hold any office, he is apt to be disdainful, scorning monks and loving men of the world more than he should.' [One is condemned for having an impediment in his speech, one because he was a novice and others for being old and decrepit.] I once saw Samson the sub-sacrist sitting by at gatherings of this kind at the time of blood-letting, when the cloister monks are wont to reveal the secrets of their hearts, each to each . . . I saw him sitting by and smiling, without a word, and noting the words of each; and I heard him repeat some of the aforesaid opinions after twenty years had passed. [Jocelin loses a benefactor and friend by describing him as unworthy to be Abbot.]

(3) Chapter at Canterbury, late twelfth century.

The Constitutions made by Lanfranc for Canterbury were ' applied, at least in great part, at a dozen or so of the principal cathedrals and abbeys of England.' Biblical initials at the beginning of *Proverbs* often show Solomon with a bundle of rods and a man sitting with a bare back as here described.

Further Reading: R. A. L. Smith, *Canterbury Cathedral Priory*, Cambridge, 1943. R. Willis, *History of the Conventual Buildings of Christ Church*, Canterbury, 1869. C. E. Woodruff and W. Danks, *Memorials of Canterbury Cathedral*, 1912.

Source: *The Monastic Constitutions of Lanfranc*, translated by D. Knowles, Nelson 1951, pp. 111–2. (c. 1075)

When each day the smallest bell begins to ring for chapter, all the brethren sitting in choir shall at once rise and stand facing the east and waiting, while the brethren elsewhere in the monastery shall enter the choir. No one at that time shall hold a book, nor read nor look at a book; no one shall for any reason whatever remain seated in the cloister; but when the bell ceases to ring all in order shall follow their leader out of church.

When the brethren are seated in chapter the superior gives a sign, and the reader, after asking a blessing, reads and gives out the customary lesson and notices. Then, after the sermon, the superior says, 'Let us now speak of matters of discipline.' If anyone is accused who bears a name common to one or more others, and the accuser does not make it absolutely definite beyond doubt, then all of that name shall at once arise and humbly offer themselves for penance, until the accuser says clearly whom he means to accuse. This he shall do by specifying, if possible, the dignity in order or office, as follows: 'Dom Edward the priest,' or 'deacon,' or 'subdeacon,' or 'sacristan,' or 'master of the children or juniors,' or something of that sort. . . .

The accuser shall not, during the chapter in question, inflict punishment on him he accuses. The brother who is lying prostrate shall, when questioned in the usual way, answer *mea culpa*. . .

He who is to undergo punishment shall be scourged either with a single stout rod while he lies in his shift on the ground, or with a bundle of finer rods while he sits with his back bare. In each case he is punished at the discretion of the superior, who should consider the degree and the magnitude of the fault. While he is being scourged all the brethren should bow down with a kindly and brotherly compassion for him. No-one should speak, and no-one look at him save for the seniors who may make intercession for him. No-one who is accused may in the same chapter accuse his previous accuser. The abbot or prior shall appoint him who is to administer punishment, taking care that neither child, nor junior, nor novice is bidden.

CLUNIACS, 1077-8

About 912 Odo, Abbot of Cluny, made reforms but continued to live under the rule of St. Benedict. The founders of the first Cluniac house in England here speak for themselves.

Source: Lewes cartulary, extract in Sir W. Dugdale, *Monasticon Anglicanum, A History of the Abbies and other Monasteries, Hospitals, Frieries and Cathedral and Collegiate Churches*, ed. J. Caley, H. Ellis and Rev. Bulkeley Bandinel, vol. 5, 1825, pp. 1-2 and 12.

. . . I William de Warren and Gundreda my wife were going on a pilgrimage to St. Peter's at Rome, and in passing through France and we visited various monasteries to pray. We learnt in Burgundy that we could not go forward safely because of the war between the Pope and the Emperor so we stopped at the great and holy monastery of St. Peter at Cluny and there prayed to St. Peter. We found the holiness, piety and devotion there very great as also the respect which the good prior paid to us with the whole convent, and they received us into their fraternity. We thus began to have more love and devotion towards that house and that order than towards any of the other houses which we had seen. But Hugh, the holy abbot, was not then at home. It had long been our wish and intention, as advised by Archbishop Lanfranc to found some religious house for our sins and the safety of our souls; and we then thought that we should not get any greater happiness than by making one of any order than that of Cluny. So we sent and asked Hugh the abbot and all his holy congregation that they would let us have two, or three, or four monks out of their holy flock and we would give them a church which we had built of stone in place of a wooden church under the castle of Lewes. This had of old been dedicated to St. Pancras and this we would give them with, at the first, as much land and beasts and goods as would keep twelve monks there. But the holy abbot at first was stern towards us in hearing our request because of the distance of a foreign land and especially because of the sea. But after we had obtained licence from our lord, King William, to bring monks from Cluny to English land, and after the abbot on his part had sought the king's wish, at last he granted and sent to us four of his monks, Lanzo and three companions. To them we gave at first all that we had promised them and confirmed this by a writing which we sent to the abbot and convent of Cluny, for they refused to send us monks before they had confirmation from us and from the king . . . [Later in the troubled time of King William Rufus Lanzo obtained a charter too.]

CLUNIAC AND CISTERCIAN MONKS

Source: *Gerald the Welshman*, *Itinerary through Wales*, translated by Sir R. C. Hoare, 1806 (and corrected), i, 67. (Twelfth century)

With respect to the two Orders, the Cistercian and the Cluniac, this may be relied upon; although the latter are possessed of fine buildings, with ample revenues and estates, they will soon be reduced to poverty and destruction. To the former, on the contrary, you would allot a barren desert and a solitary wood; yet in a few years you will find them in possession of sumptuous churches and houses, and encircled with an extensive property. The difference of manners (as it appears to me) causes this contrast. For as without meaning offence to either party, I shall speak the truth, the one feels the benefits of sobriety, parsimony, and prudence, whilst the other suffers from the bad effects of gluttony and intemperance: the one, like bees, collect their stores into a heap, and unanimously agree in the disposal of one well-regulated purse; the others pillage and divert to improper uses the largesses which have been collected by divine assistance, and by the bounties of the faithful; and whilst each individual consults solely his own interest, the welfare of the community suffers; since, as Sallust observes, ' Small things increase by concord, and the greatest are wasted by discord.' Besides, sooner than lessen the number of one of the thirteen or fourteen dishes which they claim by right of custom, or even in a time of scarcity or famine recede in the smallest degree from their accustomed good fare, they would suffer the richest lands and the best buildings of the monastery to become a prey to usury, and the numerous poor to perish before their gates.

The first of these Orders, at a time when there was a deficiency in grain, with a laudable charity, not only gave away their flocks and herds, but resigned to the poor one of the two dishes with which they were always contented. But in these our days, in order to remove this stain, it is ordained by the Cistercians, ' That in future neither farms nor pastures shall be purchased; and that they shall be satisfied with those alone which have been freely and unconditionally bestowed upon them.' This Order, therefore, being satisfied more than any other with humble mediocrity, and, if not wholly, yet in a great degree checking their ambition; and, though placed in a worldly situation, yet avoiding, as much as possible, its contagion; neither notorious for gluttony or drunkenness, for luxury or lust; is fearful and ashamed of incurring public scandal, as will be more fully explained in the book we mean (by the grace of God) to write concerning the ecclesiastical Orders.

CISTERCIANS

The ' White Monks ' was a name given to the Cistercians because they wore habits of undyed wool, produced by the sheep which was a basis for their wealth. Strict in observing the Rule of St. Benedict, they cultivated undeveloped areas, especially in the north where William I had caused deliberate devastation. The story of their foundation is told in *T.S.I.H.*, i, 59–61. They were the only monastic order with an English founder, and after Waverley, Surrey, was founded in 1118 they spread rapidly for a century in England, and rather later in Wales. Their success in business and a puritanical attitude (reflected in the architectural ruins of their abbeys) caused some twelfth century writers to make bitter remarks about them. Their leader, St. Bernard, hated ' immoderate length, superfluous breadth, costly polishing, and strange designs ' in churches and fantastic sculptured figures whereby ' we are more tempted to read in the marble than in our service books '.

Further Reading: J. Bilson, 'Architecture of the Cistercians ', *Archaeological Journal*, vol. 66, 1909.

Source: Byland Cartulary, translated from W. Dugdale, *Monasticon Anglicanum, A History of the Abbies and other Monasteries, Hospitals, Frieries and Cathedral and Collegiate Churches*, vol. 5, 1825, pp. 349–354. Cistercian settlement at Byland, 1138–1177.

. . . While Abbot Gerold and his monks were travelling from Furness to the Archbishop of York with nothing except the books and gear which they could take on a wain drawn by eight oxen they were getting near Thirsk when they happened to meet the steward of the lady Gundrea, widow of Nigel de Albini and mother of Roger de Mowbray then a minor and a ward of King Stephen, but soon due to come into his estate. The steward wondered at the movement of such men and asked Abbot Gerold about his troubles. When informed about them, the steward humbly begged the abbot to dine with his lady, then at Thirsk Castle in the vicinity. The Abbot agreed, trusting to God's will. The steward went on ahead to the castle and told his lady about the visit of those whom piety had impelled him to ask to dinner in his lady's name. The Abbot and monks drew near with the wain behind them, and the lady took a private look at their distress from a window in an upstair room. The sight reduced her to tears. She was very glad that they came and was impressed

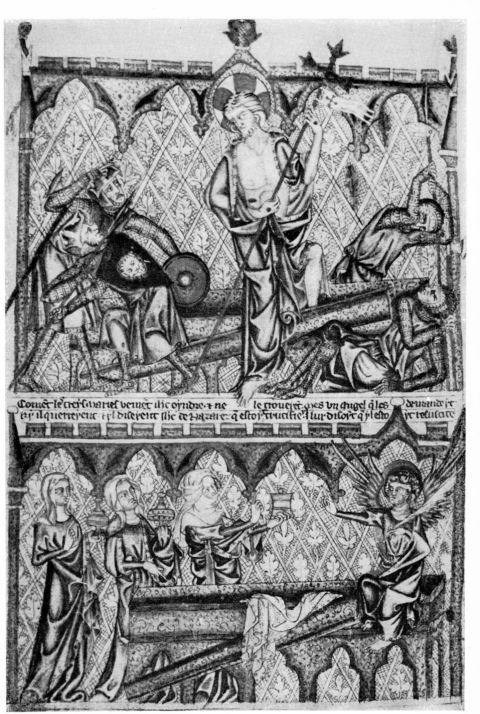

79. Resurrection and empty Easter sepulchre, with three Marys (*cf. p.* 172)

80. Heaven and hell. The blessed accepted and rewarded. The wicked led away by a
devil with a chain. Note the scales and tankard, the wheelbarrow and Hell's mouth heating
the cauldron and steamer.

by their humble demeanour, so she kept them all, supplying their wants. She would not let them leave her and promised to help their board and lodging. The Abbot and convent could not possibly or decently follow the lady round from manor to manor in different counties, so she sent them to her kinsman, Robert de Alneto, a Norman, once a monk at Whitby and then a hermit at Hode, and there she kept them supplied until her son Roger de Mowbray came into estate. [In practice the despatch of food through a lay brother was inconvenient so the steward persuaded Roger, when they were in council together, to give some land instead. After four years this proved too little and Gundrea persuaded Roger in 1143 to give them the vill of Byland.]

. . . The monks migrated from Hode to a place by the River Rye in Byland and built a little cell where their tilery now is, not far from the abbey which the noble lord Walter le Spek of Helmslet had founded 12 years before, called Rievaulx. And thus Abbot Roger [successor of Gerold] and his monks remained by the Rye for five years.

It had been the intention of Roger de Mowbray that if practicable the abbey should have been built on the south bank of the Rye with all the advantages which Rievaulx enjoyed on the north bank. But the lie of the land made this impossible and the convents were too close together for each could hear the bells of the other at each hour of the day and night and this was improper and altogether intolerable.

On getting possession of the vill of Byland Abbot Roger and his monks decided to reduce it to a grange [outlying farm]. With this in view they allotted some land to the inhabitants at Stute-kelde where they could build a new vill . . . Roger de Mowbray gave more land out of waste at Cukewald under Blakhow-hill . . . and there they industriously built a little stone church, a cloister, buildings and workshops as can be clearly seen on the ground and there they remained for 30 years. [Mowbray had to go to look after some property in Normandy and while he was away the monks found it hard to keep their land.] While Abbot Roger and his monks dwelt in the western part of Cukewald they began an energetic clearance of the wood and drew the water out of the bogs by means of long wide dykes. When the land was

z

drained they prepared a broad, suitable and worthy site in the eastern part of Cukewald between Whitaker and Cambe-hill near Burtoft and Bersclive and there they built a beautiful great church as may still be seen which may God preserve and fulfil for ever. Thither they moved from Stockyng on the eve of All Saints, 1177.

GREY FRIARS

Henry III founded Franciscan houses at Canterbury, Southampton, Oxford, Nottingham and Winchester and Edward I founded one at Cambridge. All Franciscan houses were in towns, and groups of between seven and nine houses were divided between seven custodies or wardenships, those of London, York, Cambridge, Bristol, Oxford, Newcastle and Worcester. In the thirteenth and fourteenth centuries the Friars, whether Franciscan or Dominican, dominated theological thought and both universities. There are remains of thirteen out of sixty-one English houses, all except Winchelsea having flat east ends. They had large aisles for the public separated from choirs for the friars. The London one was 300 ft. long.

Further Reading: A. G. Little, *Franciscan History and Legend in English Mediaeval Art*, 1937 (British Society of Franciscan Studies, vol. 19). A. R. Martin, *Franciscan Architecture in England*, Manchester 1937.

(1) *Source*: Rule of St. Francis, 1209, translated in Sir W. Dugdale, *Monasticon Anglicanum*, a *History of the Abbies and other Monasteries, Hospitals, Frieries and Cathedral and Collegiate Churches*, ed. J. Caley, H. Ellis and Rev. Bulkeley Bandinel, vol. 6, pt. 3, 1830, p. 1505.

. . . I firmly enjoin all the brothers, that they, upon no account, receive any money, either by themselves or by a third person. However, to supply the necessities of the sick, and for clothing of the other brothers, special care shall be taken by means of the minister's particular friends, and the guardians, according to times, and places, and cold countries, as they shall find necessity requires; saving always, as has been said, that they receive no money. . . . The brothers shall not make any thing their own, neither house nor place, nor any other thing; and they shall go confidently to beg alms, like pilgrims and strangers in this world, serving our Lord in poverty and humility. Nor are they to be ashamed, because our Lord, for our sake became poor in this world. This is that height of most extreme poverty which has

constituted you, my most dear brethren, heirs and kings of the
kingdom of Heaven, has made you poor in goods, and exalted
you in virtues; let this be your portion. . . . And wheresoever the
brothers are and happen to meet, let them show that they are of
the same family, and confidently make known to one another
their wants; for if a mother nourishes and loves her carnal son,
how much more diligently is every one obliged to nourish his
spiritual brother? And if any one of them falls sick, the other
brothers are to serve him as they would be served themselves.

(2) The first Franciscans, Friars Minor, or Grey Friars sometimes
received an unfriendly reception. In the *Liber Conformitatum* of Bartholomew of Pisa there is a story about the Friars first coming to Oxford.
They were lost in Baldon wood and took shelter in a grange belonging
to the Benedictine monks of Abingdon (presumably at Cuddesdon or
Wheatley). They were mistaken for mummers and were driven away,
though one monk sheltered, and later joined them. The *Chronicle of
Lanercost* says that when they first landed at Dover a nobleman, from
whom they sought shelter, took them for vagabonds and idiots and
locked them up. It was decided that they were spies and robbers. One
of them jokingly offered a rope to hang themselves and they were
allowed to proceed to Canterbury.

Source: Father Cuthbert, *The Friars and How they came to England
being a translation of Thomas of Eccleston's ' De Adventu F. F. Minorum in
Angliam*, Sands and Co., 1903, pp. 132-9. (1224).

[Eccleston begins by giving brief notes on each of the four
clerics and five lay-brothers who arrived at Dover in 1224. He
ignores such misadventures as those related above.] . . . These
nine having then been charitably conveyed across to England
by the monks of Fécamp and cordially provided for in their
necessities, on arriving at Canterbury sojourned for two days at
the priory of the Holy Trinity. Then four of them at once set off
for London, namely Brother Richard of Ingworth, Brother
Richard of Devon, Brother Henry (the Lombard), and Brother
Melioratus. The other five went to the Priests' Hospice, where
they remained until they found themselves a dwelling.

And this happened shortly afterwards, when they were given
a small chamber at the back of a school-house, where from day to
day they remained shut up. But when the scholars had gone
home in the evening the brethren went into the schoolhouse, and

Z.I

there made a fire and sat near it. And sometimes at the evening conference they would put on the fire a small pot in which were the dregs of beer, and they would dip a cup into the pot and drink in turn, each speaking meanwhile some word of edification. . . . At times the beer was so thick that when the pot was to be put on the fire they had to put in water, and so drank rejoicing.

In like manner, at Salisbury, it frequently happened that the brethren had but the dregs of beer to drink, and this they drank with much merriment and joy at the hour of conference around the kitchen fire, and he esteemed himself fortunate who could in a friendly way seize the cup from another.

At Shrewsbury it was the same at the first coming of the brethren thither, as Brother Martin, an old man who began the house there, would tell with glee. . . . In the convent of London itself. . . I have seen the brethren drink beer of such sourness that some preferred to drink water . . . for want of bread I have often eaten spelt, even in company with . . . guests in the hospice. . . . They rented a house in Cornhill, and made for themselves little cells, filling in the walls with dried grass.

BLACK FRIARS

A Black Cloak, covering a white tunic, gave to the Friars founded by St. Dominic the name of Black Friars at least as early as 1342. They were sometimes called the ' Shod Friars ' to distinguish them from the Grey Friars or followers of St. Francis because they wore shoes not sandals. Like the Franciscans they settled in large towns. In London the site of their convent is perpetuated in the name 'Black Friars'. Piers Plowman satirised the splendour of their London convent ' with crochetes at corners ', as contrasting with their supposed poverty. The Black Friars were great preachers and were accordingly often called ' Preaching Friars '. The importance they attached to sermons led to the construction of churches with wider aisles than hitherto, a tendency helped by the type of ' decorated ' arch of the fourteenth century which displaced the narrow pointed arches of the thirteenth.

Further Reading: R. F. Bennett, *Early Dominicans*, 1937. William A. Hinnebusch, O.P., *The Early English Friars Preachers*, Instituto Storico Domenicano, Santa Sabina, Rome 1951.

Source: Piers Plowman.

With arches on everiche half and belliche [beautifully] y-corven,
With crochetes on corners with knottes of golde,
Wyde wyndowes y-wrogt y-written full thikke
Schynen with schapen scheldes to schewen aboute,
With merkes of marchauntes y-medled between . . .

MONASTIC GUESTS

Source: First Statute of Westminster, 3 Edward I cap. 1 (translated as in 1577 edition). (1275)

. . . And because that abbots and the religious of the land have ben overcharged and sore greved by the resort of great men and other, so that their goods have not bene sufficient for themselves, wherby they have ben greatly hindered and empoverished that they can not mainteine themselves nor such charitye as they have bene accustomed to do: It is provided that none shal come to eate or lodge in any house of religion of any others foundation then of his owne at the costs of the house, onles he be required by the governour of the house before his comming thither. And that non, of his own costs, shal entre and come to lye there against the wil of them that be of the house. And by this statute the king entendeth not that the grace of hospitalitie should be withdrawen from such as nede, nor that the foundours of such monasteries should overcharge, or greve them by their often commyng. It is provyded also, that none high nor low, by coulour of kindred, affinitie of alyance or by any other occasion shall course in any parke, nor fysh in any pond, nor come to eate or to lodge in the house or manour of a prelat, or any other religious personne, againste the wil of the lorde or the bailiffe, neyther at the coste of the lord nor at his owne. And if he come in, or entre withe the good wil or against the will of the lord or his bailiffe, he shal cause no doore locke, nor windowe, nor nothinge that is shutte, to be opened or broken by himself nor any other, nor no maner of vittaile nor other thing shal take by coloure of buinge nor otherwise. And that none shal threshe corne, nor take corne, nor any maner of vyttaile, nor other goodes of prelate, man of religion, or any other clerke, or laie person by colour of biyng nor otherwise against the wil and licence of him, to whom the thing belongeth, or of the keper, be it within market town or without. And that none shal take horses, oxen, ploughes, cartes, shippes, nor barges, to make cariage without the asent of him to whom such things belong. . . . And that none shal send to the house or manour of a man of religion or of any other person, his men horse or dogges to sojourne, nor none shal them receive, and he that doth (seyng the kyng hath commaunded the contrarie) shal be grevously punished. . . .

DEATH

Source: *Regularis Concordia Anglicae Nationis Monachorum Sanctimonialium*, translated by Dom Thomas Symons, Medieval Classics, T. Nelson and Sons, 1953, pp. 65–6. (c. 970)

When the brother has departed this life, his body shall be washed by those appointed to do so: when washed it is clothed in clean garments namely, in shirt, cowl, stockings and shoes, no matter what his rank. But if he is a priest a stole may be placed about him over his cowl, if such be the rule. The body shall then be borne into the church with the chanting of psalms and the tolling of bells. And if the brother died before dawn, in the night or after the dark hours, in the early morning, let him be buried before the brethren have their meal, when the Masses have been celebrated, provided that those things necessary for a burial can be prepared: otherwise let the brethren be appointed by turns to chant psalms unceasingly by the body throughout the day and the following night until early morning when it shall be committed to the earth.

When all things proper to the Burial Office have been completed, let the brethren straightway begin the seven Penitential psalms and, returning to the church let them prostrate before the holy altar, finish those psalms for the dead brother. Thenceforward for seven successive days the Office of the Dead shall be said in full, and all shall make the offering at the Morrow Mass; moreover, after each of the regular hours they shall sing, prostrate, one of the Penitential psalms followed by a prayer. Thence-

Funeral Procession. The child comes to life. c. 1330. (Holkham Bible).

forth until the thirtieth day the Office of the Dead shall be said daily with three lessons as usual, one choir at a time making the offering at Mass. But on the thirtieth day the Office of the Dead shall again be said in full. During these thirty days each priest shall say a special Mass daily for the dead brother, in the secret places of the oratory; and with all devotion each deacon shall chant the entire Psalter and each subdeacon fifty psalms; and if on account of his work he cannot do this on one day he shall do so on another. . . .

RESPECT FOR GRAVEYARDS, 1223 AND 1240

Archery practice on Sundays and Holy days was common in churchyards in the fourteenth century and later; and suitable stones in church walls are often grooved where arrows have been sharpened upon them. The North walls of churches in Wales, as at Lansilin near Oswestry, are sometimes marked with a line some two feet from the ground, used in a ball game.

Source: Constitutions of Richard Poore, Bishop of Salisbury, 1223; D. Wilkins, *Concilia Magnae Britanniae et Hiberniae*, 1737, vol. 1, p. 600.

We prohibit dances and vile and dishonourable games which lead to indecency from being performed in churchyards. The lawsuits of laymen are not to be conducted there because it has been an ancient custom there, and this especially applies to cases which are concerned with trials involving bloodshed. We also forbid laymen from announcing scotales [public drinkings to raise money] in church, nor may priests or clerics make such announcements either inside or outside churches.

Source: Constitutions of Walter de Cantilupe, Bishop of Worcester, 1240. D. Wilkins, *Concilia Magnae Britanniae et Hiberniae*, 1737, vol. 1, p. 666.

We believe that graveyards, containing those who are to be saved of whom many are purged and await the robe of glory, are befouled by brute beasts. We therefore enjoin that they be decently enclosed with a hedge or wall. Those responsible are to be compelled thereto by the law of the church.

Also we forbid rectors and priests of churches to feed beasts at the church gates or to let them enter under pain of heavy punishment.

For the respect of both graveyard and church we forbid the holding of markets, the hearing of lawcases concerning blood, and the performance of dishonourable games in graveyards or other holy places, or indeed anyway else on Sundays. This especially applies to the eves of saints days and church feasts, for it redounds rather to the dishonour than the honour of saints. . . . Nor are any buildings to be raised in churchyards save perhaps in time of war; and if such are made they are to be demolished.

'DEATH DUTIES'

A lord had a right to take the best beast of a dead tenant, a due called a mortuary was also due to the priest.

Source: The Rector of Harwell complains about a fraud by the agent of the Honour of St. Valery to which Harwell manor belonged. Rosalind M. T. Hill, 'A Berkshire Letter-Book', *Berkshire Archaeological Journal*, vol. 41, 1937, pp. 28–29. The addressee is not named but was probably the Earl or Countess of Cornwall.

Greeting. I thank you as warmly as possible for the comfort and instinctive kindness which you have often shown to me and still continue, by holy inspiration, to show, although I regret that it is far beyond my deserts. I entreat you, however, to continue to show such kindness towards me. Since, as I think, you have already heard of the quarrel which took place between your beadle and myself last Sunday, although the report which reached you was not a true one, if I may I will tell you the truth of the matter as follows. On the said Sunday morning your beadle and I arrived separately at the house of the widow of R... C... de B..., to choose your heriot and the mortuary due of the church and we found there one horse, one cow and two scraggy calves. The said widow had, as I heard, hidden a mare of the value of at least half a mark, with the consent and connivance of your said beadle. From among the said animals the beadle chose as heriot in your name a cow, which he had taken away before I came, and I chose a horse in the name of the rector of the church as the mortuary due. When we had made our choice, the kinsmen of the dead man bore his body to the church, and the horse which was chosen as the mortuary due was led before the body into the churchyard, according to the custom. At this point your beadle came suddenly and seized the said horse, not because it was the widow's property but because it was the due of the church. He did so without any reason or any wrong having been done to himself, to the prejudice of the church and the dishonour and loss of the rector. Therefore I urge you as strongly as possible to allow the church to enjoy its rights and customary dues and to cease, if you will, from all such interference. Please ask me any questions you like about the matter. Farewell.

MONUMENTAL BRASSES

In 1208 the first recorded English monumental brass was made, though the earliest surviving examples are of the latter decades of the century. The fashion spread, especially among bishops and abbots. Perhaps 100,000 were made in fourteenth century England, for all the wealthier classes except princes. Of these some 4,000 remain and provide a wonderful record of the costume of ladies, priests and merchants and the armour of knights showing development decade by decade. Brasses remained popular in the fifteenth and sixteenth centuries but only 5 out of 500 examples from the first half of the fifteenth century show aristocrats. They are commoner in eastern England than elsewhere and more survive in England than anywhere on the Continent. Perhaps the best ecclesiastical brass is that of the Abbot of St. Albans reproduced in *W.W.I.H.*, vol. 1, plate 19.

Further Reading: H. W. Macklin, *The Brasses of England*, 1907, is but one of numerous useful works. The Victoria and Albert Museum has a vast collection of rubbings. Mill Stephenson lists all known examples by parish and county in *List of Monumental Brasses in British Isles*, 1926.

Source: Brass of John Spicer at Burford, d. 1431.

> I pray yow all for charite
> hertely that ye pray for me
> to oure lord that sytteth on hye
> fful of grace and of mercye.
> The wiche rode-soler [rood loft] in this chirche
> Upon my cost y dede do wirche
> Wt. a laumpe brenyng bright . . .
> to worschip God both day and nyght . . .
> Now Jese that dydyst on a tre
> On us have mercye and pite. Amen.

CHANTRY CHAPELS

The finest chantry chapel built is that of Richard Beauchamp, Earl of Warwick, a good example of ' perpendicular ' work.

A desire for masses and services after death led to the foundation of many chantries in the fourteenth century. The encroachment on space in parish churches by chantries devoted to the spiritual welfare of particular individuals can still often be observed though the endowments of the chantry priests were swept away by the Reformation. These endowments testify to widespread piety. At the Reformation exact records of existing chantries were made. These have been printed for some counties and are an interesting source of local history. There were then over two thousand of them, to many of which were attached schools. Henry V built the first great royal chantry.

Further Reading: Annual Chantries' Accounts, 1475–1545, edited by Edith E. Williams, *The Chantries of William Canynges in St. Mary Redcliffe, Bristol*, William George's and Sons, 1950.

Lost accounts for building of Beauchamp Chantry, Warwick: J. G. Nichols, *Description of the Church of Saint Mary, Warwick, and of the Beauchamp Chapel* (1838).

Source: Will of Richard Beauchamp, Earl of Warwick, 1435, N. H. Nicolas, *Testamenta Vetusta*, 1826, i, 23.

I will that when it liketh to God that my soul depart out of this world, my body be buried within the collegiate church of Our Lady of Warwick, where I will that in such place as I have desired, which is well known, there be made a chapel of Our Lady built in fair and goodly fashion; within the middle of which chapel I will that my tomb be made. . . . Also I will that there be said every day, so long as the world lasts, in the aforesaid chapel . . . three masses.

THE DOOM

The Holkham Bible ends with a picture of Christ showing his wounds and accompanied by two angels with the instruments of the Passion. With His right hand He bids the good ' Come unto me,' and with His left he spurns the rich men who must weep and howl (*James*, v, 1–7). The gang of damned on a chain recalls the words of the First Demon in the Chester *Judgment*: ' I have tyed them on a row; they shall neuer passe that place '; and a wall painting at Pickering. Below are Heaven and Hell. Among the damned are a baker and an ale-wife. This scene is represented on the walls of perhaps 150 different churches, and is placed, in nine cases out of ten over the chancel arch—a symbolic gateway between this world and the next. (The damage to the left hand side of the page is caused by handling the book, which was evidently unbound in the Middle Ages.) The devils on a chain and the treatment of Heaven as a battlemented gallery are both paralleled in alabasters.

Further Reading: W. L. Hildburgh, ' English Alabaster Carvings as Records of the Medieval Religious Drama ', *Archaeologia*, vol. 93.

(1) *Source*: Covenant for decorating Beauchamp Chantry Chapel, Warwick, 1449 (see p. 53).

John Brentwood, citizen and steyner of London, 12 Feby. 20 Henry VI, doth covenant to paint fine and curiously to make at Warwick, on the west wall of the new Chapell there, the dome of our Lord God Jesus, and all manner of devices and imagery thereto belonging of fair and sightly proportion, as the place shall serve for, with the finest colours and the finest gold: and the said Brentwood shall find all manner of stuffs thereto at his charge; the said executors paying therefore xiii li. vi s. viii. d.

(2) *Source*: *Towneley Mysteries*, p. 367 (expressing the feelings of one who contemplates the Doom).

> Alas! that I was borne!
> I se now me beforne,
> That Lord with Woundys fyfe;
> How may I on hym loke,
> That falsly hym forsoke,
> When I led synfull lyfe?

HELL

Source: Old English Sermon on Sunday attributed to Bede. Rev. J. M. Neale, *Mediaeval Preachers and Mediaeval Preaching*, Mozley, 1856, p. 362.

. . . it was the Lord's will that Paul should see the punishments of that place. He beheld trees all on fire, and sinners tormented on those trees; and some were hung by their feet, some by their hands, some by their hair, some by the neck, some by the tongue, and some by the arm. And again, he saw a furnace of fire burning with seven flames, and many were punished in it; and there were seven plagues round about this furnace: the first, snow; the second, ice; the third, fire; the fourth, blood; the fifth, serpents; the sixth, lightning; the seventh, stench; and in that furnace itself were the souls of the sinners who repented not in this life. There they are tormented, and every one receiveth according to his works: some weep, some howl, some groan; some burn and desire to have rest, but find it not, because souls can never die. Truly we ought to fear that place in which is everlasting dolour, in which is groaning, in which is sadness without joy, in which are abundance of tears on account of the tortures of souls; in which a fiery wheel is turned a thousand times every day by an evil angel, and at each turn a thousand souls are burnt upon it. After this he beheld a horrible river, in which were many diabolic beasts, like fishes in the midst of the sea, which devour the souls of sinners; and over that river there is a bridge, across which righteous souls pass without dread, while the souls of sinners suffer each according to its merits. . . .

HEAVEN

Source: *Vision of Adam of Eynsham*, translation printed by William de Machlines, 1482.

Of the swete pele and melodye of bellys that he herde in paradyse. . . .

. . . sodenly y herde ther a solenne pele and a rynggyng of a mervelus swetenes, and as al the bellys yn the worlde, or whatsumever ys of sownyng, had be rongen togedyr at onys. Trewly yn thys pele and rynging brake owte also a mervelus swetenes, and a variant medelyng [mingling] of melody sownyd wyth alle. . . . Ful delectable hyt was to hym, as he seyde, from that tyme forthe, as ofte as he herde any solenne pele of ryngyng of bellys, bycause hyt wolde then cum to hys mynde ageyne, the ful swete pele and melody the whyche he herde when he was amonge the blessyd sowlys yn paradyse. . . .

INDEX